*The publisher and the University of California Press
Foundation gratefully acknowledge the generous
support of the Constance and William Withey
Endowment Fund in History and Music.*

Turkey

Turkey

A PAST AGAINST HISTORY

Christine M. Philliou

UNIVERSITY OF CALIFORNIA PRESS

University of California Press
Oakland, California

© 2021 by Christine M. Philliou

Library of Congress Cataloging-in-Publication Data

Names: Philliou, Christine May, author.
Title: Turkey : a past against history / Christine M. Philliou.
Description: Oakland, California : University of California Press, [2021] |
    Includes bibliographical references and index.
Identifiers: LCCN 2020030582 (print) | LCCN 2020030583 (ebook) |
    ISBN 9780520276383 (hardback) | ISBN 9780520276390 (paperback) |
    ISBN 9780520382398(ebook)
Subjects: LCSH: Karay, Refik Halit, 1888–1965—Criticism and interpretation. |
    Political culture—Turkey—History—20th century. | Turkey—Politics and
    government—20th century.
Classification: LCC DR576 .P47 2021 (print) | LCC DR576 (ebook) |
    DDC 956.1/02—dc23
LC record available at https://lccn.loc.gov/2020030582
LC ebook record available at https://lccn.loc.gov/2020030583

Manufactured in the United States of America

25 24 23 22 21
10 9 8 7 6 5 4 3 2 1

For my children, Daphne Narenj and Erfan Elias,

and for all the journalists and writers, in Turkey and all over the world, who risk their lives to make all voices heard.

CONTENTS

NOTE ON TRANSLITERATION

Throughout this book I have used standard modern Turkish spelling for Turkish and Ottoman names and terms. This is complicated by the fact that the time frame of the study straddles the 1928 Alphabet Reform, which changed the alphabet from a modified Arabic script, used for Ottoman Turkish since the fourteenth century, to an adapted Latin one. Each letter of the modern Turkish alphabet represents a single sound. Most consonants are pronounced more or less the same as in English. Following are the exceptions:

c is pronounced as *j* in John (*Cumhuriyet*).

ç is pronounced *ch* as in chair (*çay*).

ş is pronounced *sh* as in shiver (*şive*)

j is pronounced as in French or as s in measure (*jandarma*).

ğ is most often silent, lengthening the previous vowel (*oğlu*).

Modern Turkish has eight vowels:

a is pronounced as the *a* in father (*Ankara*).

e is pronounced as *e* in jet (*muhalefet*).

ı is pronounced similarly to the *u* in "uh" or the *oo* in "good" (*hırka*).

i is pronounced roughly like "ee" in "feed" (*Bilecik*). (The letter carries a dot even when capitalized, to differentiate it from the "undotted" *ı* above.)

o is pronounced as *o* in open (*Çorum*).

ö is pronounced is pronounced like the French eu (*Erenköy*).

u is pronounced is as oo in room (*İstanbul*).

ü is pronounced like the French u (*Atatürk*).

The study also spans the periods before and after the 1934 Surname Law, which required all Turkish citizens to adopt a patronymic. I use the standard convention of the field, which is to place the post-1934 patronymic in parentheses when referring to a given person before 1934. So, until 1934 Yakup Kadri (Karaosmanoğlu) had yet to adopt his surname. The same was true for Mustafa Kemal (Atatürk), Refii Cevat (Ulunay), Rıza Tevfik (Bölükbaşı), and many others mentioned in the following pages. Refik Halid (Karay) is the main exception; since he is the main figure in the book and appears so often, I refer to him simply as Refik.

Within modern Turkish, there is a fluctuation between transliterating the final consonants d/t and b/p, with the former (d and b) representing a more archaic style and the latter a more contemporary one. This is why Refik Halid is sometimes spelled Refik Halit in works in modern Turkish; Halide Edib is alternatively spelled Halide Edip, etc. I have chosen, somewhat arbitrarily, to use the more archaic d/b style, so with the exception of citing published works that refer to him as Refik Halit, I have used Refik Halid (and Mehmed Halid rather than Mehmet Halit for his father, etc.).

And finally, although the proper modern Turkish spelling of Istanbul would be İstanbul, I refer to that Ottoman capital city, and subsequently the largest city in the Republic of Turkey, as Istanbul.

Key dates in the Ottoman Empire/Republic of Turkey

Key dates in Refik Halid Karay's life:

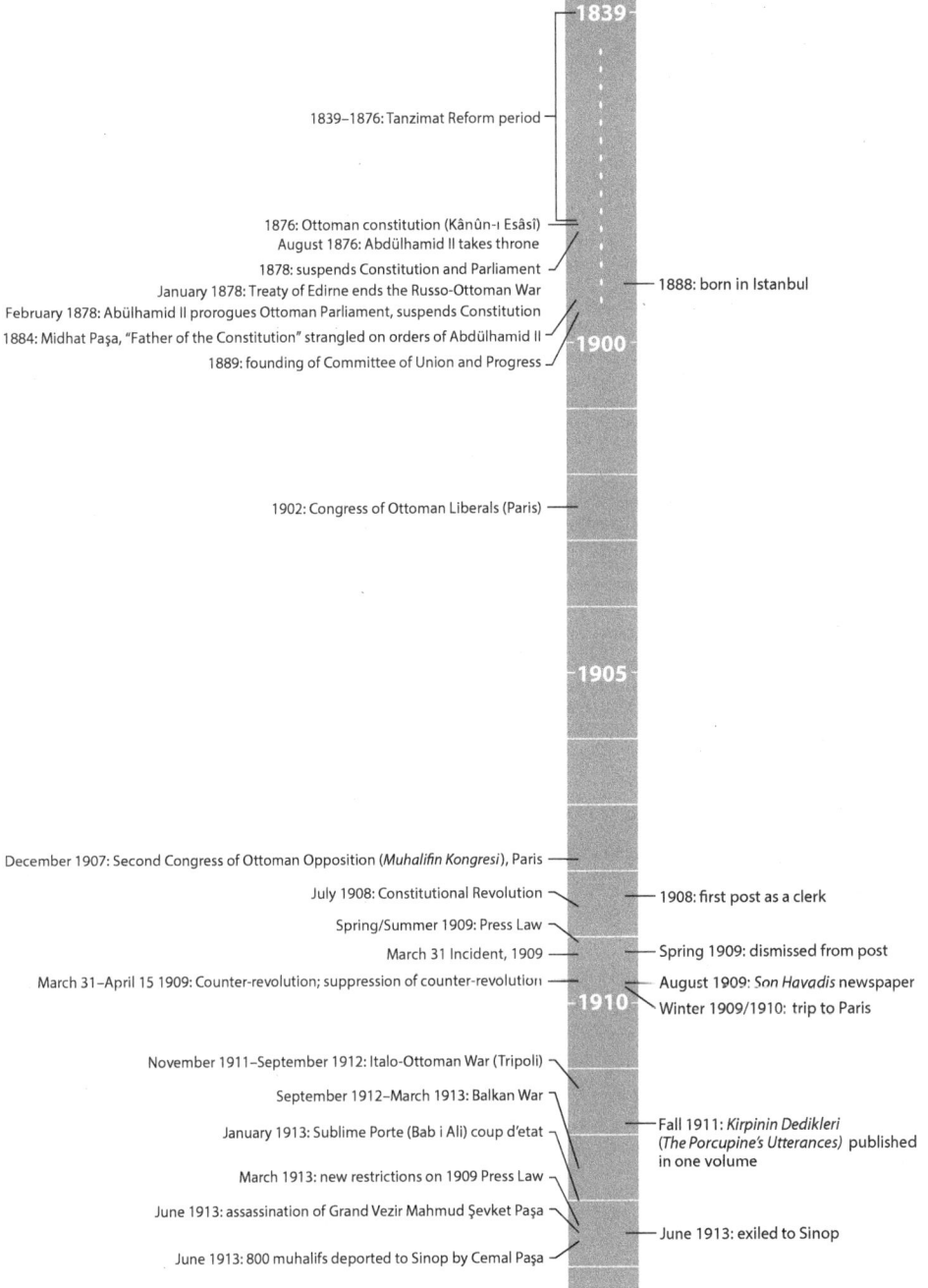

1839

1839–1876: Tanzimat Reform period

1876: Ottoman constitution (Kânûn-ı Esâsî)
August 1876: Abdülhamid II takes throne
1878: suspends Constitution and Parliament
January 1878: Treaty of Edirne ends the Russo-Ottoman War
February 1878: Abülhamid II prorogues Ottoman Parliament, suspends Constitution
1884: Midhat Paşa, "Father of the Constitution" strangled on orders of Abdülhamid II
1889: founding of Committee of Union and Progress

1888: born in Istanbul

1900

1902: Congress of Ottoman Liberals (Paris)

1905

December 1907: Second Congress of Ottoman Opposition (*Muhalifin Kongresi*), Paris

July 1908: Constitutional Revolution

1908: first post as a clerk

Spring/Summer 1909: Press Law

March 31 Incident, 1909

Spring 1909: dismissed from post

March 31–April 15 1909: Counter-revolution; suppression of counter-revolution

August 1909: *Son Havadis* newspaper

1910

Winter 1909/1910: trip to Paris

November 1911–September 1912: Italo-Ottoman War (Tripoli)

September 1912–March 1913: Balkan War

January 1913: Sublime Porte (Bab i Ali) coup d'etat

Fall 1911: *Kirpinin Dedikleri* (*The Porcupine's Utterances)* published in one volume

March 1913: new restrictions on 1909 Press Law

June 1913: assassination of Grand Vezir Mahmud Şevket Paşa

June 1913: exiled to Sinop

June 1913: 800 muhalifs deported to Sinop by Cemal Paşa

Key dates in the Ottoman Empire/Republic of Turkey	Key dates in Refik Halid Karay's life:
August 1914: Ottoman Empire enters period of "Active Neutrality"	1914: Marries Nâzime in Sinop while in exile
November 1914: Ottoman Empire enters World War One in earnest	July 1915: transferred to Çorum
Spring 1915–1916: Armenian Genocide	August 1916: transferred to Ankara
	October 1916: transferred to Bilecik
October 30, 1918: Ottoman defeat in World War One; Armistice of Mudros	January 1918: returns to Istanbul
January 1919: Paris Peace Conference convenes	Fall 1918: first novel: *The True Face of Istanbul* (İstanbul'un İç Yüzü)
May 1919: Greek invasion of Izmir	
June–September 1919: mobilization of resistance forces under leadership of Mustafa Kemal [Atatürk]	April–October 1919: Post Telegraph and Telephone General Directorate, first tenure
1920: Last Ottoman Parliament passes National Pact [Misak-ı Millî]	March–April 1920: PTT General Directorate, second tenure
March 16, 1920: British occupation of Istanbul becomes official	
July 1920: Treaty of Sèvres	1920: Second, expanded edition of *Kirpinin Dedikleri* (The Porcupine's Utterances) published
August/September 1921: Battle of Sakarya	
September 1922: Final push westward of Turkish national forces against Greek occupation forces; fire of Izmir	
October 1922: Nationalists claim victory, sweep into Istanbul	January–November 1922: publishes *Aydede* satirical newspaper
1 November 1922: Abolishment of Ottoman Sultanate	
11 November 1922: Turkish Grand National Assembly recognized by Treaty of Lausanne, negotiations for which were in progress	9 November 1922: flees Istanbul for Beirut
July 1923: Treaty of Lausanne ratified	
September 1923: Republican People's Party established	
October 1923: Republic of Turkey is established	
March 1924: Abolishment of Caliphate	1924–5: *Minelbab İlelmihrab* (From the Door to the Pulpit) controversy
April 1924: Constitution for the Republic of Turkey ratified	
1924–5: Progressive Republican Party established; disbanded	
1925: Şeyh Sait Rebellion	1923–1938: second exile (Beirut, Jounieh, Aleppo)
25: Law on the Maintenance of Order (*Takrir-i Sükûn Kanunu*) passed	
1925–1927: Independence Tribunals (*İstiklal Mahkemeleri*)	
October 1927: Mustafa Kemal delivers Great Speech (*Nutuk*) to Second Party Congress of Republican People's Party	1927: marries Nihal
1928: Alphabet Reform	
1930: Liberal Party founded; disbanded	
1934: Surname Law (Mustafa Kemal becomes Atatürk)	
10 November 1938: death of Atatürk	June 1938: return to Istanbul
December 1945: *Tan* Incident	
1946: Democratic Party established; start of the multi-party period	1948: Resurrected *Aydede* satirical newspaper from 1922, this time in order to publish *Minelbab İlelmihrab* (From the Door to the Pulpit) in its entirety for the first time
1950: electoral victory of Democratic Party, the first opposition party of RPP to come to power	
1960: Coup d'état removes Adnan Menderes and DP from power	
1961: New Constitution promulgated	1965: dies in Istanbul

1915

1920

1925

1930

1965

Introduction

HOW HAPPY *IS* HE WHO
CALLS HIMSELF A TURK?

TURKEY HAS LONG BEEN BRANDED as a country unique in the history of the modern Middle East. This uniqueness is in large part due to the very moment of Turkey's inception. As a member of the Central Powers, the Ottoman Empire suffered defeat in World War I. But even as the state lay in ruins, supine before the victorious Entente powers, Turkish nationalists refused to accept the terms dictated to them in Europe. Acceptance of defeat would have involved the negation of a Turkish sovereign entity. Breaking from the position of the Ottoman government in occupied Istanbul, the nationalists instead demanded self-determination and independence—and successfully escaped the colonial mandate status that the victorious allies were fitting it for, a fate that would come to define much of the Arab Middle East. This remarkable achievement was sealed when Mustafa Kemal (Atatürk), having led the Turkish national movement to victory, established an independent single-party republic in 1923 in Anatolia, abolishing the Ottoman Sultanate (1922) and the Caliphate (1924) in the process. He forged a path of autonomy and national self-determination that was the envy of the defeated Germans and Hungarians, not to mention Syrians, Iraqis, and others under colonial mandate and direct colonial rule, thereby earning the respect of his anti-imperialist neighbors to the north, the Soviets. Under the new republic, the Turks would be the master of their own ship—but what course would they chart?

Once the republic was established, Turkey had to confront the same challenge that so many other formally independent, presumptive democracies faced in the twentieth century: the challenge of reconciling aspirations for liberal democracy with the political exigencies of authoritarianism. In Turkey's case, what was presented to the world as a new and unique path—between democracy and authoritarianism—was also the continuation of

I

a longer Ottoman struggle over constitutionalism. The remnants of these conflicts survived just below the surface of the new, independent republic and shaped political authority therein in important ways.

This book is a historical exploration of the unique form of political authority that evolved between Ottoman constitutionalism and Turkish authoritarian democracy. It does not explore the singular nature of political authority in the republic by focusing directly on the looming presence of the founder and first president of the republic, Mustafa Kemal Atatürk. Neither does it take at face value the official history he forged of the War of Independence. Instead, it seeks to provide a new perspective on political authority and historical experience in Turkey by looking at politics and culture of the twentieth century through the prism of internal opposition and dissent: before, during, and after the establishment of the Turkish Republic, and surrounding the official telling of its history.

This book explores the meanings of the Turkish word *muhalefet*, denoting both opposition and dissent, as an analytical concept and, I argue, a cipher for understanding the nature of political authority in the late Ottoman Empire and Republican Turkey, as well as the politics of memory and history that are still in play today in Turkey.[1] Related to the word *hilaf*, contrary, and *ihtilaf*, or disagreement, *muhalefet*'s first meaning is opposition, as in that of an opposition party, common to the political vocabulary of many languages. But it also denotes a more subtle kind of internal defiance or disagreement—dissent—and indeed in contemporary Turkish culture, the word *muhalefet* is often associated with the dissent voiced by journalists and public intellectuals. Today the word carries a charged valence, of the principled heroism—often doomed to tragedy—of someone from a position of privilege, that is, within the Turkish elite, who speaks truth to power. It is principled because contestation, even from a position of privilege, carries an expectation of justice, as well as a cost; it is tragic because it rarely brings about change in that power. The range of meanings and connotations that the term *muhalefet* has today in Turkey has grown out of this fraught and often overlooked history—running against and alongside political power—that spans the twentieth century.

Since the concept of *muhalefet* is diffuse and is defined against power, there is no single political program that typifies it over time. In the early years covered in this study, it was often associated with a liberal agenda for a pluralist, parliamentary democracy, but later those with more radical visions could lay claim to the concept. Since it was a heterogeneous category, held together by dint of a common stance of opposition among *muhalifs*, we

[margin annotations:] I shd just truth how no leverage our power

Much overused - truth

cannot say there was a single typical or quintessential *muhalif* who could serve as a synecdoche for it. The socialist poet Nâzım Hikmet, the "Turkish Joan of Arc" Halide Edib, and the general who broke with Mustafa Kemal, Kâzım Karabekir, could all be termed *muhalifs* (opponents/dissidents), yet their agendas diverged in significant ways beyond that common label. They all belonged within the category of Turk, however, and enjoyed the privileges of membership in the Ottoman-Turkish elite, broadly defined. Rather than try to treat the entirety of *muhalefet*, or all *muhalifs* across several political eras, then, I have chosen to track closely the life and writings of one figure who, through his actions and claims, enjoyed a unique relationship to the concept in the late Ottoman and Republican periods.

REFIK HALID KARAY

I employ the biography and oeuvre of the writer and self-proclaimed *muhalif* Refik Halid Karay (1888–1965) as a case study in *muhalefet*. He lived and wrote across the divide between the Ottoman constitutional era and the Republic of Turkey, providing us with a line of continuity from which to trace the many orders of change between the two state formations and historical eras. His relationship to the term *muhalefet* was certainly complicated; in his words and actions he embodied so many of the conflicting meanings and shifting paradoxes of the concept over time. He proclaimed himself a *muhalif* at key points, suppressed his dissent at others, and even invested the concept with a historical and literary narrative at still others, elevating it almost to an ideology before eschewing it altogether and finally embracing it anew at the end of his life. Of equal importance is that he straddled the worlds of literature and politics. Because he combined politics and literature and continually cast and recast the recent past before, during, and after the forging of official history, his work allows us to see the ways that *muhalefet* was both a product of an imaginary and a feature of politics. Viewing his posthumous legacy as an iconic *muhalif*, furthermore, allows us to connect the genealogy of *muhalefet* across the twentieth century with the current associations that the term carries in Turkey today.

Refik Halid Karay is invoked today as an iconic *muhalif* by those on both the right and the left, and by Islamists and secularists—he is still very much part of the arena of the contested politics of memory and history in Turkey. His works and his image—as "the Porcupine" (*Kirpi*), his most famous nom de plume—are embedded in the current culture of *muhalefet*. Despite the claims he often made in his writings, Refik was anything but a stalwart and principled opponent in his actions, as these pages make painfully clear. That contradiction, I contend, was built into the paradoxical concept of *muhalefet* itself. He was a typical child of privilege, born to a family in the Ottoman bureaucratic establishment during the reign of Sultan Abülhamid II, a period during which the Ottoman Constitution of 1876 was suspended. He wrote prolifically, beginning shortly after the Ottoman Constitutional Revolution of 1908 (which restored the 1876 Constitution) and continuing until his death in 1965, through two stints of exile and several regime changes—a lifespan that brings us well into the Turkish Republic's post–World War II multiparty era.

Karay's changing fortunes—as an outsider and yet one who, at the end of the day, always retained his elite privilege—reflect in turn the distinct incarnations that the concept of *muhalefet* underwent, as the Ottoman regime went through a larger metamorphosis. It began the period as a constitutional monarchy that came to be driven by the Committee of Union and Progress (CUP or Unionists), a secret society-turned-organization-turned-political party. The empire itself was reduced after World War I to a defeated country under Allied occupation. Out of the ashes of that empire, a Turkish national movement established a new basis of sovereignty and a new base of power— shifting from Istanbul to Ankara—becoming a single-party republic under Mustafa Kemal in the process. Finally, from the late 1940s, that single-party system was expanded to accommodate a sustained opposition party, leading to a multiparty system by the 1950s.

But Refik Halid had a more personal connection to the official history of the republic. At a crucial point in the formation of the Turkish national resistance-cum-independence movement—the summer of 1919—he directly opposed Mustafa Kemal (Atatürk) in his bid to proclaim and organize that national resistance movement against the foreign occupation of the Ottoman Empire. In what became known as the Telegraph Episode, Refik Halid, from his post in the General Directorate of Post, Telegraph, and Telephone, forbade the telegrams sent by Mustafa Kemal in Samsun from being circulated and helped call for the latter's recall and arrest as a renegade, refusing to recognize the legitimacy of Mustafa Kemal or the national resistance movement. In the context of Mustafa Kemal's official history, Refik Halid was a traitor and collaborator with the British occupation forces, working against the Turkish nation that was attempting to assert its independence.[2] I deal with this episode in greater depth in chapter 4, but for now what matters is that this was a specific point of convergence—and conflict—between the narrative of official history in the Turkish Republic and Refik's alternative, dissident account of history. And in this book it is also a turning point in the larger history of *muhalefet*, as the moment when the internal conflict of the Ottoman establishment shifted into a conflict over the legitimacy of a new, presumptive national political authority.

MUHALEFET AS CIPHER

Beyond its potential significance against the backdrop of contemporary Turkish politics and culture, the following history—of Refik Halid Karay's life, works, and changing relationship to the concept of *muhalefet*—unlocks three major problems in scholarship on the late Ottoman Empire and modern Turkey: first, the relationship between Ottoman liberalism and the constitutionalism of the Young Turk movement and particularly the Committee of Union and Progress (CUP); second, the problem of continuity and rupture in the transition from the Ottoman Empire to the Republic of Turkey; and third, the politics of memory regarding the Ottoman past, particularly the late Ottoman past, in the Turkish Republic. As the story of *muhalefet* and of Refik Halid Karay takes us through the late nineteenth and twentieth centuries, it engages with these three problems in turn.

The first problem is the relationship between Ottoman liberalism and the unfolding of Ottoman constitutionalism.[3] Ottoman liberalism was articulated by the Young Ottomans in the 1860s and 1870s, leading to the promulgation of the Ottoman Constitution in 1876. Young Ottomans went to great lengths to envision a liberal order for the empire, debating the role of consensus, consultation, and opposition and dissent. When its beloved constitution was abrogated by Sultan Abdülhamid II soon after its institution, liberalism and its interlocutors went underground. The Young Turk movement took up the mantle of constitutionalism a generation later, in exile and in hidden recesses of the Ottoman military itself. That movement was made up of countless factions and tendencies, but it would ultimately be driven by the Committee of Union and Progress, which formed in 1889 and rose to power in and after the Constitutional Revolution of 1908.

The precise relationship between the two movements—Young Ottomans and Young Turks—is often passed over, or explained away by generational differences. And it is easy to see how the two could be elided, because both movements claimed the banner of constitutionalism and liberal democracy. The Young Turks' major demand, after all, was the restoration of the 1876 Ottoman Constitution, a document that had been designed and authored by Midhat Paşa and his fellow Young Ottomans. It would be natural to assume that adherents of both movements would have shared the same political vision. And yet there were serious social and political fissures between the two movements, and thus fissures within the broader Ottoman establishment. Since there were plenty of Ottoman liberals in subsequent generations after the original Young Ottomans, the rift between Ottoman liberals and the emergent CUP faction of the Young Turk movement persisted into the Second Constitutional Era of 1908 and evolved long after. And this, I argue, was the birth of *muhalefet* in the twentieth century.

Young Ottomans, as well as later generations of Ottoman liberals, were often elite-born Francophiles and members of the Istanbul Ottoman bureaucracy. Many who spearheaded the CUP, in contrast, were of more modest origins, either Balkan born or immigrants from Russia, often educated in the Ottoman military academies under German training in the late nineteenth and early twentieth centuries.[4] *Muhalefet*, I argue, would shift in meaning as the Young Turk constitutionalist coalition fragmented into Unionists (CUP) and their internal opposition. The concept of *muhalefet* went from being a theoretical ideal in a hypothetical constitutional order, to being the term associated with Ottoman liberals and other groups, including religious figures and other traditional elements, against the emergent CUP after 1908.

Chapter 1 takes a close-up look at this prehistory of *muhalefet* through a consideration of Refik Halid's origins, upbringing, and early sensibilities as a child of the Ottoman bureaucracy. In his values and prejudices he represented a continuation of Young Ottoman sensibilities two generations after the fact, in a Young Turk world. This rift, I argue, was emblematic of the emergent conflict within the Ottoman establishment that led to a new set of meanings for *muhalefet*. Chapter 2 explores the unfolding of Ottoman constitutionalism between 1908 and 1913, when many and diverse understandings, and many parties and factions of constitutionalism, underwent a polarization into "Unionists" and "liberals," with the liberals taking on the identity of *muhalefet*, or opposition. I show how the social and institutional differences between Young Ottomans and Young Turks then evolved into partisan political rifts, highlighting Refik's early satirical writings as Kirpi, or the Porcupine.

If the first problem in scholarship had to do with the relationship between Ottoman liberalism and the Young Turk/Unionist movement at the turn of the twentieth century, the second one has to do with the historical and political relationship between the Ottoman Empire, occupied in defeat in 1919 and abolished in 1922, and the Republic of Turkey, established in 1923.[5] This problem—of continuity and/or rupture—grows out of the claims of total rupture from the Ottoman past and total unity of the Turkish nation in its struggle for independence as laid out in the official history of the Turkish Republic. Mustafa Kemal (Atatürk) set the parameters of this official history in his epic four-day "Great Speech" (Nutuk) in 1927, marking the consolidation of his authority within the single-party state, serving as both head of the party and first president of the Turkish Republic. In this version of events, Mustafa Kemal's personal story is conflated with that of the Turkish nation, and the singular nature of his political authority made it virtually impossible to discuss any other version of events until the 1950s.[6] This claim of absolute rupture sidesteps the many and complicated relationships between the modern republic and the late Ottoman past, and its force was so strong that one anthropologist claimed that even as late as the 1980s there was a forced "amnesia" and "prohibition" surrounding the period of transition, meaning the Turkish War of Independence.[7]

The middle chapters examine the transitional period through the lens of *muhalefet*, as well as Refik's life and works, offering an alternative narrative to that espoused in official history. Through it we gain a vista on the political conflict within the Ottoman/Turkish establishment that led to the abolishment of the Sultanate and Caliphate and the establishment of the Turkish Republic, from the point of view of Ottoman liberals in Istanbul. Having originally opposed the Unionists during their time in power, the liberals persisted by opposing the nationalist resistance movement in Anatolia. From Refik's perspective and that of other members of the *muhalefet*, the core problem throughout the World War (1914–1918) and the Armistice/War of Independence (1918–1922) eras was the Committee of Union and Progress—both the CUP's actions and policies and the Unionist legacy in postwar and national politics. And indeed, while there was a rupture in the formal structure of the state between the Ottoman and Republican eras, the continuity between the two eras was reflected in the personnel, social networks, and political culture of Unionism. Erik Zürcher and others have long since pointed out this continuity; the middle chapters expose a different dimension of it by looking at the continuing meaning of *muhalefet* through the transformation of Unionism from an Ottoman into a Republican framework. Unionists were renouncing their ties to the CUP after the empire's defeat and remaking themselves into a Turkish nationalist resistance to fight foreign occupation, and then into a national independence movement. Those who identified as *muhalifs* against the CUP remained in opposition to the nationalist movement. The basis for their opposition was the contention that the nationalist movement was none other than the CUP in a new guise. The revelation that came in historical scholarship in the 1980s, then, of continuity of Unionism between the Ottoman and Republican states, was known, and objected to, by those in this internal opposition as the transition was taking place.

The third problem that this history of *muhalefet* addresses also grows out of the republic's official history, mentioned previously. Namely, because of the conflicted relationship to the Ottoman past in the Turkish Republic—the continuities were both known and deliberately suppressed in order to match the official history of rupture and national unity—the politics of memory and history were themselves a highly contested arena in the republic. The overwhelming hegemony of Kemalist official history suppressed alternative narratives and experiences for decades, and that hegemony has still not been entirely overturned. When we look closely through Refik's experience and writings, we see three distinct phases in these politics of memory and history: the early republic (1923–1927; see chapter 5); the single-party Kemalist period (1927–1945; see chapter 6); and the multiparty period (1945–1965 and beyond; see chapter 7 and the epilogue). In chapter 5 we see Refik continuing to enact *muhalefet* from exile, challenging a still-shaky Kemalist hegemony by attempting to publish his memoir of the recent Armistice/War of Independence period. Chapter 6 discusses how he had a "change of convictions," deciding from his Syrian exile that he would leave *muhalefet* behind and prove his loyalty and patriotism to the new republic. This change of convictions had a palpaple effect on his writings, as he redacted his old *muhalefet* writings, and recast his role in the past in line with his new image as a Kemalist. And in chapter 7 he witnessed the reinvention of Turkey as a multiparty democracy in the new global context of the Cold War, after 1945. This final change ushered in a new relevance for *muhalefet* and for the past history of *muhalefet* dating back to 1908, leading to a new profusion of literary writings regarding the Ottoman past. The politics of memory and history shifted along with the shift to a single-party republic, and again to a multiparty democracy, and Refik's writings and their reception are a vivid illustration of these changes.

Muhalefet as an analytical concept does much to address the three major problems in historiography. But the word also did important work for political and historical actors going through these shifts in political authority. Those familiar with existing scholarship will recognize that this study focuses on what Erik Zürcher has dubbed the "Unionist period" between the Constitutional Revolution of 1908 and the establishment of the multiparty regime by 1950. And the ongoing relevance of *muhalefet* in this Unionist period had to do with the problem of Unionism in the past as much as the Unionist legacy in the present, as we will see. Between these years, institutionalized opposition in the form of an opposition party—first to the Unionists, and then to Mustafa Kemal's Republican People's Party, which carried important vestiges of the Unionist project forward—was an elusive dream, experiencing a series of episodic failures (in 1909–12, 1920, 1924–25, and 1930). In this period it was the *imaginary* of *muhalefet* that held the greatest significance. That imaginary was invoked at crucial junctures, since the *reality* of a viable partisan opposition party was not attainable. It was also during this period that the word *muhalefet* shifted from its earlier meanings and became synonymous with opposition to the Unionists. As the Unionist regime collapsed after World War I, *muhalefet* then became tied to the question of continuity from the Unionist to the national, Republican regime. This is why Karay as both a literary and political figure has much to teach us about power and *muhalefet*, for it was during those times that the idea and history of *muhalefet* were invoked as a symbol for what was missing in a system that was to be a pluralist democracy. *Muhalefet* as a word and an idea was a surrogate, a placeholder, and a marker of absence and failure. It was also invoked as a vehicle to condemn the failures and shortcomings of those in authority, who were often Unionists and former Unionists. Examining the genealogy of *muhalefet*, then, helps us understand some of the core contradictions of power in twentieth-century Turkey.

Exploration into the history and nature of political authority is the central project of this book. It may seem counterintuitive that I elaborate many of my arguments in the following chapters with literary texts rather than conventional political or government sources. I do not spend much time situating Refik within the history of Turkish literature either; those familiar with Turkish literature will be able to see the ways he was typical of his day as well as the ways in which his writing was extraordinary. Rather, I use his writings as an instrument to explore the relationship between politics and imagination; I thus interpret Refik's literary texts as a historian more than as a literature scholar.[8] Refik voiced his opposition and dissent in several genres: polemical essays, short stories, serialized novels, and even plays. And it is not a coincidence that many of Refik Halid Karay's best-known and most popular writings were works of satire. In that, he was not unique; satire has been and remains a uniquely important form of political dissent and social critique, both in the late Ottoman Empire and in Turkish society to this day.[9] As a genre it is an important link between politics and imagination, and we might even call it the genre with the most unique relationship to the culture of *muhalefet.*

But in a different sense, satire is also significant to this story because the notion of *muhalefet* as principled opposition, when held up to historical scrutiny, is a joke. It is a joke because the principled *muhalif*s are ultimately, by definition, already part of the privileged establishment; the lines they cross appear to be dangerous but almost always involve eventual acceptance back into the fold of elite society and privilege. When they truly cross a red line, and there are some instances of that in this story, they cease to be *muhalif*s and become traitors to the nation (*vatan haini*), which means banishment or even death. The joke of *muhalefet*, or opposition from within, sheds light on the unique stakes of privilege, power, and dissent, not to mention on the meaning of belonging—to an Ottoman, and then Turkish, elite.

. . .

Readers may be taken aback by the relative absence of discussion regarding Islam, and even of the question of secularism, a principle that was at the heart of the single-party republic under Mustafa Kemal Atatürk.[10] This is particularly surprising, one might think, given that the political appropriation of Islam is a defining characteristic of the party that was elected in 2003 and currently remains in power in Turkey—the Justice and Development Party (AKP, for Adalet ve Kalkınma Partisi). This absence reflects what I found when I followed the sources—literary and political—by and about Refik Halid Karay and his relationship to the concept of *muhalefet*. It also reflects the contours of the argument I put forth here: that it was not ideology (Islam, as deployed in the twentieth century, acts as an ideology, as does secularism) that was driving the conflict within the Ottoman, and then Turkish, establishment. Instead, ideology emerged as the language through which to express contestation and preexisting fissures regarding the understanding of constitutionalism and democracy.[11] Islam as a belief system embedded in the

Ottoman state and society is of course part of the political landscape. Many from the ulema class were affiliated with the opposition circles that Refik Halid Karay was also connected to, and those figures used the iconography and language of Islam to express their opposition in the Second Constitutional Era and beyond, as we will see.[12] But for the purposes of this study, it was not until the 1950s, with the advent of the multiparty system, that mass politics became consequential to the conflicts within the Turkish elite and to the constitution of political authority in the republic. And it was at that time that the language of Islam was appropriated by mainstream political parties and movements.

Finally, while discussions regarding Islam are relatively absent, another matter, which is usually invisible in conventional histories of the Ottoman and Turkish twentieth century, is an important subplot woven through this book: the Armenian Genocide. Denial of the 1915 genocide is a defining feature of a modern Turkish national identity. The issue of culpability for the genocide and other war crimes was also a key catalyst for the very transition at the heart of this book, and a key reason that the CUP officially disbanded, leaving such a complicated and ambivalent legacy in its wake in modern Turkey. What I found when I followed the sources generated by and about Refik Halid Karay is that more nuanced stances regarding the genocide, beyond the complete denial of nationalists, existed—for a time—for those who claimed to be part of *muhalefet*. I have tried to thread this theme through chapters 3, 4, and 6, by examining Refik's stance toward and writings about the genocide and Armenians in three distinct eras: as the genocide was happening in the midst of World War I; during the Armistice period, when Unionist war crimes were being discussed in relation to the emergent national movement; and in the single-party republic, when memory of the genocide, and of *muhalefet*, needed to be redacted in order to satisfy the criteria of loyalty to the Kemalist state and Turkish nation. My hope is first, to show that the category of *muhalefet/muhalif* operated and continues to operate as a fascinating liminal category—for those excluded from power but included in the larger national category of Turk, as against the truly excluded non-Muslim, non-Turk Armenians; second, to examine where the red lines were between *muhalefet* and treason when it came to discussion of the genocide—stances toward the genocide could be a litmus test to locate these red lines; and third, to open future avenues for the integration of the history of the genocide into the dominant narrative of Turkish state formation.[13]

The seven chapters proceed chronologically, tracing seven different phases in the relationship between Refik Halid Karay and *muhalefet* against the backdrop of the often dizzying macrochanges in politics and society. Each chapter is a portrait of an era, with discussion of Karay's itinerary, political actions, and writings, which were if nothing else a running commentary on the politics of the day. I argue that each era brought forth a new valence for *muhalefet*, but that the relevance of the term remained constant as an indicator of unresolved political pluralism that persisted throughout all the changes. The evidentiary basis for the study is often the literary and political works of Karay himself, which I use to highlight the changing dynamics and preoccupations of *muhalefet*. Each chapter contains verbatim translations of works by Refik Halid Karay, sometimes in their entirety. This is because I take seriously the form as well as content of his literary imagination and of his engagement with political critique, and my intention in doing this is to share that expression directly with the reader. His writing stands out as powerful and evocative of the moments in which he was writing. He was associated with literary and journalistic circles from one era to another, which I point out in the relevant chapters, but there is also something distinctive about his ability to put literature and politics in dialogue that makes him exceptional. His work points to the fact that the literary dimension—as part of the imaginary of *muhalefet*, and as part of the imagination of someone who proclaimed himself a *muhalif*—is an inextricable part of the political history of the term. And in the first chapter, this means providing discussion and examples of Refik Halid's work before he identified as a *muhalif*, in order to get a sense of his literary proclivities.

As the chapters progress into the Armistice (1918–22) and single-party Republican (1922–45) periods, his efforts to cast and recast the recent past, and to craft a historical narrative for *muhalefet*, constitute a fascinating and unfinished counternarrative to official history. I do not elaborate on the details of that official history, but use it as a foil against which to present the counternarrative by and about Refik. This official history was forged in 1927; it was a narrative about the War of Independence and formation of the republic, and the hegemony of the narrative was bound up with the authority of Mustafa Kemal (Atatürk). Refik was directly involved in the events that were being narrated; he appeared as a villain in the 1927 narrative of Nutuk itself, and he continued to express his dissent through his counternarratives from exile in the early republic. His ultimate acceptance back into the republic in 1938 was due to his reorientation away from *muhalefet*, his submission to Kemalism, and his acceptance of the official history.

And this, I argue, is another defining dimension of *muhalefet*: in the political sphere there is an unfinished project for pluralism, and in the narrative/literary sphere there is an unfinished project for multivocality. As the political authority, specifically Mustafa Kemal, generated an orthodox, official history, focused on political unity and historical rupture, engaging in *muhalefet* took on yet another dimension: that of challenging and sometimes even disregarding that master narrative with a counterimagination. Refik Halid Karay supplies us with both the political opposition and dissent and the unfinished attempts to construct a narrative imagination that would accompany that opposition and dissent. He engaged in a direct confrontation with Mustafa Kemal at a crucial juncture in the latter's bid to organize a national resistance movement, in June 1919. He opposed the national movement from its inception, through its victory in 1922, and for the first several years of the republic. His tale of *muhalefet*, coupled with his counternarrative, which was itself a form of *muhalefet*, is uniquely important to the larger history of *muhalefet*.

Chapter 1, "Against Power?," describes Refik Halid's early years as a child of a longtime Istanbul family, ensconced in the Hamidian establishment, particularly the French-educated bureaucracy. The chapter also narrates the separate story of the emergence of *muhalefet* as a political concept among the liberal Young Ottomans in the nineteenth century and its repurposing on the eve of the 1908 Constitutional Revolution. The term came back into currency in late 1907. It was used to signify the coalition of opposition parties, all of which were constitutionalist and opposed to the "despotism" (*istibdad*) of Sultan Abdülhamid II (r. 1876–1909), who prorogued parliament and the Ottoman Constitution in 1878. I trace Refik Halid's first published writings from 1909, providing verbatim translation of one, "Ayşe's Destiny," and extensive discussion of another, "Against Power," to show his interests and preoccupations before his personal story met the larger story of *muhalefet*.

In chapter 2, "The Contradictions of Ottoman Constitutionalism and the Remaking of *Muhalefet*," Refik Halid's story meets that of *muhalefet*. The background is the fragmentation of the constitutionalist coalition after July 1908, a process that caused the meanings of *muhalefet* to shift and proliferate. In the course of the five years between 1908 and 1913, *muhalefet* came to mean parliamentary opposition as well as dissent that was espoused by journalists and writers working outside the confines of political parties. I argue that by the end of the period it also became synonymous with a particular group of individuals whom we can call the liberal opposition to the CUP. In the midst of these changes, a formative moment in the making of *muhalefet*, Refik Halid became a satirist and an associate of the Liberal Entente coalition party. The outcome of his meeting with *muhalefet* was his Porcupine persona, under which he published numerous satirical stories in 1910–12. I track examples of his Porcupine stories and provide a full translation, "How Do They Collect Taxes?," to demonstrate the changing meanings and uses of *muhalefet*. This was happening in a political landscape which came to be dominated by the CUP, before 1908 a constituent part of the *muhalefet* and now the power against which *muhalefet* was becoming defined. The chapter ends with the deportation from Istanbul in June 1913 of the "muhalefet"—now a specific group of approximately eight hundred individuals, including Refik Halid, who were opposed to the CUP—to the Black Sea port town of Sinop.

Chapter 3, "The Joke," turns to World War I, which Refik Halid experienced in Anatolian exile. This was a period of interruption for *muhalefet*, since the space for contestation was closed off due to extreme wartime censorship. Refik Halid wrote very little during this period and did not produce any political satire. And yet it was also a period of incubation for those who had been involved in *muhalefet*, as serious grievances in response to the Unionist takeover of the Ottoman state and the wartime regime accrued. Refik Halid was exiled ostensibly for a joke he had written as the Porcupine in 1912, which was also the name of one of the few stories he penned during his wartime exile. Turning on a discussion of "The Joke," I reconstruct his wartime experience in Anatolia and argue that the bigger joke was the extent to which he seems to have collaborated with members of the Unionist regime and enjoyed protection from the dangers and privations of the war despite having been exiled for his opposition. What I seek to show here are the ways he, as a *muhalif*, was both included—in the larger privilege enjoyed by the ruling establishment—and excluded, by dint of having contested aspects of the Unionist regime before the war.

Chapter 4, "*The True Face of Istanbul*," refers to the first novel Refik Halid wrote, *İstanbul'un İç Yüzü*, throughout the summer and autumn of 1918. This chapter covers the pivotal period between the Ottoman defeat in the Great War and the victory of the Turkish nationalist movement under Mustafa Kemal Paşa (Atatürk) (1918–22), when "Istanbul" would begin to refer to the Ottoman government in Istanbul, in contradistinction to the presumptive Turkish national government in Ankara. During this Armistice period, contestation was the order of the day as the future of the empire hung in the balance. *Muhalefet* reemerged from its wartime slumber and, for a brief moment, took center stage, both in politics and in the imagination. Refik Halid, fresh from his Anatolian exile, played an instrumental role in this remaking and elevation of the idea of *muhalefet*, opposing the remnants of the CUP and with that the nationalist movement, which he and other *muhalifs* saw as a reconstituted CUP. This chapter details Refik Halid's personal opposition to Mustafa Kemal in the summer of 1919 from the former's post as director of the Post, Telegraph, and Telephone service, and then, after Refik Halid's defeat in that confrontation, his personal project to bring *muhalefet* to life in the imagination. I argue that Refik Halid leveraged the concept of *muhalefet* in this moment, partly in earnest and partly as a way of justifying his otherwise indefensible position, collaborating with the British colonial occupiers against the Turkish national movement. To demonstrate this I offer several of the stories and essays he penned between 1919 and 1922 and provide a verbatim translation of one, "The Ankara Fire." Many of these stories were later excised from Republican-era editions of his work, signaling the potency and continued relevance of his criticisms in the republic.

Chapter 5, "*Muhalefet* from Abroad," shows how Refik Halid continued his efforts to keep opposition alive in the imagination as in politics, from his second exile, this time in Beirut, where he fled upon the nationalist victory in late 1922 (he remained in Syria until summer 1938). A member of the List of 150 (*Yüzellilikler*)—individuals who were stripped of their Turkish citzenship and banned from the republic—he was now considered not a *muhalif* but a *vatan haini*, or traitor to the nation, at the very moment of political inception for the nation. This was a demonstration that the nationalists had won and were now defining the terms of patriotism and belonging. His major act of opposition to the fledgling Turkish Republic was his attempt to publish his memoirs of the preceding Armistice period in a newspaper in Istanbul, generating a flurry of controversy in 1924 in the Istanbul press at a vulnerable moment for the Kemalist Republic. This controversy was part and parcel of the larger contestation underway between Ankara, as the new capital, and Istanbul, politically marginalized but still the largest and culturally the most important city, over the precise form that the new republic and its constitution should take. The chapter considers his engagement in opposition from abroad and his predicament and experience of exile in French Mandate Syria/Lebanon, where he wrote about his sentiments toward the new regime in Turkey and his experiences as a foreigner in a place that had been, only a few years before, part of the empire to which he had belonged.

Chapter 6, "*There Is a World Underground*," also the title of a novel he wrote in the 1940s, turns to Refik Halid's project to reinvent himself—not as a *muhalif*, but as a loyal Kemalist and patriotic Turk. The project dated from the "change of convictions" he experienced in 1928, while still in his Syrian exile; he would make peace with the regime and with Mustafa Kemal and convince them to accept him back into the fold. His reinvention was aimed at being pardoned and allowed to return to Istanbul, which he did in summer 1938, shortly before the death of Atatürk. This chapter explores his reinvention in two stages: before (1928–38) and after (1938–45) his return. Before his return, we see evidence of his new designs in his literary writings, his covert and overt activities in support of Turkish ambitions for the contested Hatay province, and his personal correspondence. After his return to Istanbul we see how he embarked on a public relations project to reframe his past activities of *muhalefet* and to redact his past writings to effectively delete the imagination of *muhalefet* he had contributed to building in the Armistice period. In his new life as a Kemalist, Refik Halid turned away from contestation of anything and proclaimed himself to be "*toleran*" of everyone—except his past self as a *muhalif*, of course, which he roundly attempted to delete from the record. I provide close readings and translations of some examples of his work between 1938 and 1945—particularly the new rendition of his 1921 "The Ankara Fire" into an ode to Ankara—and examine how and why he whitewashed his past by deleting and redacting his past political writings. I also explore some of the subtle ways that he persisted as a critic of the Unionist project and its formative role in the republic. In the larger arena of Turkish politics between 1928, when Mustafa Kemal's power had been consolidated and the new elite consensus was achieved, and 1945, the space for *muhalefet* was also underground, with fissures and factions operating within the Republican People's Party, not in opposition to it.

Finally, chapter 7, "*Muhalefet* in the Free World," turns to Refik Halid and *muhalefet* in the transformations of the Cold War. After 1945, when Turkey entered the so-called free world as a bulwark against communism, the space for contestation and opposition received unprecedented international sanction, leading to Turkey's shift to a multiparty system. With the 1950 electoral victory of an opposition party for the first time in the republic's history, discussions of *muhalefet* past and present, as well as hagiographical accounts of liberal *muhalifs* from the recent past, suddenly began to proliferate. Karay was now a kind of elder statesman of *muhalefet* who enjoyed associations to the Demokrat Parti. He settled into the role of advocate for journalists and freedom of expression and became a prolific writer of pulp novels. At the end of his life he once again claimed the banner of *muhalefet*. After his death in 1965 he became a kind of icon of *muhalefet*, although a *muhalefet* that carried the baggage of decades of unresolved political conflict.

The advent of the multiparty system in 1945–50 was in one sense the "real" beginning of *muhalefet*, as it was the first time that there was a sanctioned, institutional space for an opposition party within the Republican system. The elusive dream of *muhalefet* had been achieved: dissent could finally come out into the open and be channeled into political parties or expressed relatively freely in the press. And yet both parties were cleaved out of the same centrist establishment, allowing for a different kind of limitation on expression of dissent. In another sense, the era of multiparty democracy is the denouement for this story of *muhalefet*, which chronicles a time when the word bridged political imagination and political realities and compensated for the absence of institutionalized political opposition. *Muhalefet/muhalif* took on in the 1950s the range of meanings and connotations that it has in twenty-first-century Turkey. When it did, it already contained within it the fraught history that is the heart of this book and of Refik Halid Karay's life.

. . .

The present study is a genealogy—although not necessarily *the* genealogy— of *muhalefet*. It is both an examination of the contradictions of authoritarian democracy in twentieth-century Turkey and a prehistory of the current concept of *muhalefet* as it is deployed by political actors across the spectrum today. Taken together, the following chapters detail the ways *muhalefet* was ever changing and yet remained at the intersection of politics, literature, and history. The motto of the Turkish Republic from its inception was, "How happy is he who calls himself a Turk!" I offer this "past against history" as an antidote to that story of unity and rupture. How did Turks emerge from Ottomans? What were the fissures within the category of "Turk," and what was the basis for those fissures? What was the experience of those Turks in a position of privilege who were not entirely happy with the power of the day? How did they express their discontent? And how was the sphere of disagreement, dissent, and opposition imagined? How, finally, did that imagination—in both its absence and presence—shape the country?

TARABYA

Mosque of
Eyüp

EYÜP

GOLDEN HORN

KASIM
PAŞA

*Area of
Inset Map
Below*

Esentepe
(Şişli)

Yıldız Palace

Dolmabahçe
Palace

Beşiktaş

BOSPHORUS

Çırağan
Palace

Beylerbeyi
Palace

BEYOĞLU/
PERA

Tophane

GALATA

ÜSKÜDAR

Mısır Çarsısı
(Spice Market)

Galata Bridge

Şehzadebaşı
Mosque

PTT headquarters

Süleymaniye
Mosque

Aghia Sophia

Top Kapı
Palace

OLD CITY

Samatya

Bâb-ı Âli Avenue

British Embassy

Grand Rue de Péra/
İstiklal Caddesi

Tokatlıyan Hotel

Galatasaray
Lyceum

Tünel Meydanı/
Tramway Plaza

Galata Tower

GALATA

Karaköy

Galata Bridge

KADIKÖY

Erenköy

SEA OF
MARMARA

Princes
Islands

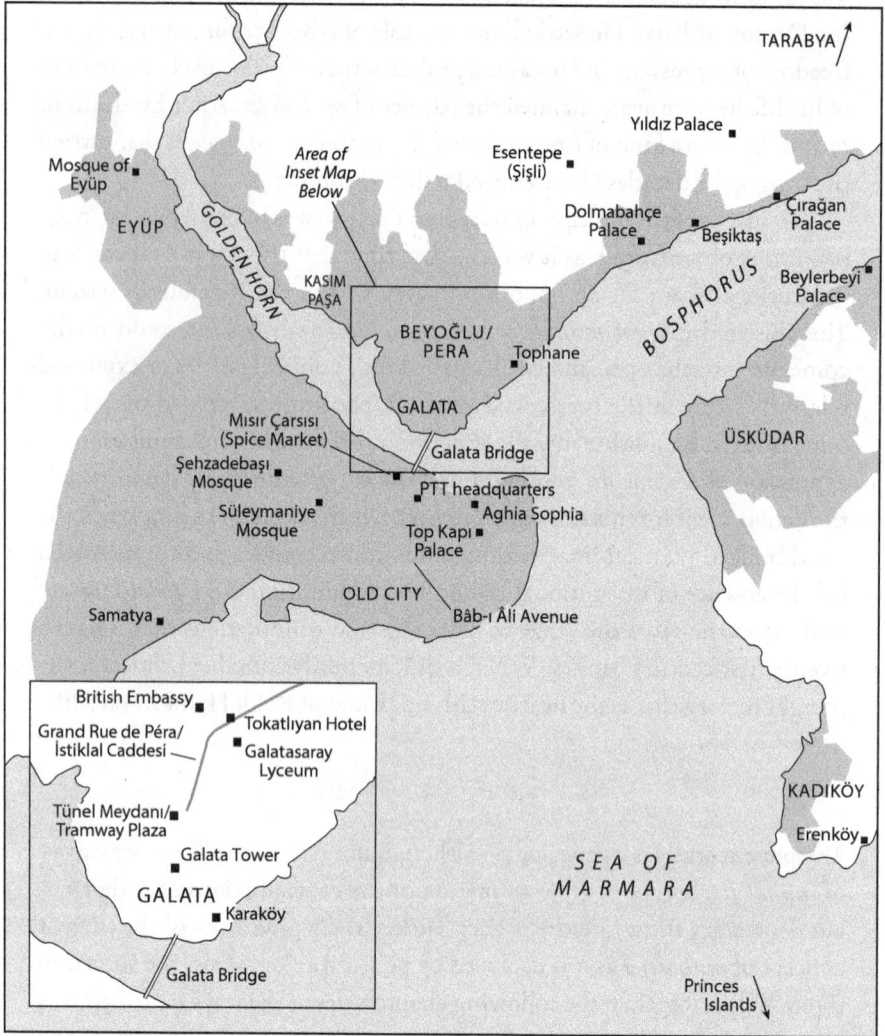

MAP 1. Istanbul at the turn of the twentieth century, with Beyoğlu/Pera quarter inset

ONE

Against Power?
(1888–1909)

REFIK HALID WAS BORN IN 1888 into a comfortable family that was part of the Istanbul bureaucratic establishment. He came of age during an era when political opposition was being driven underground by Sultan Abdülhamid II (r. 1876–1909). In his early years, he had no direct connection to political opposition, or to the concept of *muhalefet*. *Muhalefet* as an ideal—meaning space for disagreement, dissent, and multivocality—had been a preoccupation of the Young Ottoman movement in its struggle to envision a just and liberal constitutional order in the 1860s and early 1870s. Abdülhamid's suspension of the constitution in 1878 interrupted that conversation for nearly three decades. As opposition to Hamidian absolutism gained momentum in the 1890s, it was formulated within a language of liberalism and Ottoman patriotism, not expressly as *muhalefet*. Only in late 1907 did *muhalefet* return to currency, used to indicate the coalition of constitutionalist parties united against the tyranny of Abdülhamid. And it was only after 1908, when the Young Turk revolution ushered in the Second Constitutional Era, that Refik Halid and *muhalefet* met in earnest. After this encounter, the course of Refik Halid's life and that of *muhalefet* became inextricable.

This chapter traces the period prior to this convergence and reconstructs the formation of Refik Halid as a product of the Ottoman establishment and as a writer. It begins with a consideration of his early life and background, which owing to a dearth of contemporary firsthand sources is often largely filtered through the lens of his post-1909 career and reputation. In retelling the story of Refik Halid's development, the chapter examines two short stories that he wrote just before he stepped into the worlds of *muhalefet* and satire. It then examines the broader class tensions that helped bring *muhalefet* to the fore in 1907 and, ultimately, to restore the constitution in 1908.

In the absence of contemporary sources about Refik Halid prior to 1909, his biographers are careful to emphasize two aspects of his early life: his privilege and pedigree on the one hand, and his spirited, rebellious character on the other. Following Refik Halid's own lead, they are conspicuously silent about aspects of his life that detract from this reputation, such as his vested interest in the old regime for the first year after the Constitutional Revolution of 1908. The choice of what to include—and what to omit—from his story reflects the view of *muhalefet* that would take shape in later decades; namely, the image of the *muhalif* as a consistently principled opponent. Upon closer inspection, however, we see that even the most principled *muhalif* had partisan and class interests.

The story of Refik Halid's privilege and pedigree begins with his birth on March 14, 1888, to Mehmed Halid and Nefise Ruhsar, both from families that were part of the distinguished class of Muslims associated with the Ottoman state. As a child, Refik lived in a village on the Asian shore of the Bosphorus near Beylerbeyi, a seaside village named for the Ottoman palace rebuilt under Sultan Abdülaziz (r. 1861–76) and home to many Ottoman grandees of the Tanzimat and Hamidian eras. From 1890 onward, the family spent summers in a villa purchased from relatives that was located in the Erenköy district, just inland from the quay of Kadıköy on the Asian bank of the Bosphorus. The family wintered in a mansion in the Emin Nurettin neighborhood of Şehzâdebaşı, on the southern side of the Golden Horn near the historic Şehzâde and Süleymaniye mosques and much of the Ottoman administration.[1] This quarter was inhabited by many Muslim state officials and their families. Like their villa in Erenköy, it was a place where the family enjoyed the company of those of a similar social station. As Refik Halid frequently mentions in his fiction and memoirs, his was a childhood populated by midlevel bureaucrats.[2]

Indeed, the Halid family, having lived for several generations in Istanbul, was ensconced in Istanbul society and the continually expanding—some might say moribund—Ottoman bureaucracy.[3] Refik's father, Mehmed (1849–?), was chief treasurer or cashier (*serveznedar*) of the Ministry of Finance. He was also the superintendent (*nazır*) of the Ottoman Bank, which was founded in the wake of the Crimean War (1853–56) as a joint venture between the Ottoman government and British and French interests.[4] While the top positions at the bank were reserved for Europeans, and jobs immediately below those were kept for non-Muslim Ottoman subjects, Mehmed Halid apparently held a position that involved some authority. A biographer of Refik, writing in the 1940s, pointed out defensively that as *serveznedar*, Mehmed had bureaucrats under his watch who were in charge of both Anatolia and the Danube province and that his job "was not just about counting money."[5]

But considering the ever-growing public debt that had accumulated since the Crimean War and increased with the Ottoman defeat in the Russo-Ottoman War (1877–78), it was not an ideal moment for Mehmed Halid to work in imperial financial administration. Both the Finance Ministry and the Ottoman Bank were linked to the Ottoman Public Debt Administration (OPDA), which was formed in 1881 after the Ottoman central government defaulted on loans to foreign creditors. The OPDA controlled a third of the empire's revenues and became an important symbol of the compromised status of the state vis-à-vis Europe. Alongside the oppressive capitulatory regime, European oversight of Ottoman finances through these institutions was an important target of criticism and animus for the Young Turk movement. As such, the topic of Mehmed Halid's position and the family's socioeconomic status would prove to be a problem for Refik Halid—and for sympathetic biographers, who had to walk a fine line between emphasizing his father's position of responsibility and downplaying the role he played in propping up the semicolonial position of the Hamidian financial bureaucracy.

When famed poet and writer Yahya Kemal (Beyatlı; 1884–1958) reflected on a meeting with Mehmed Halid in 1912, he offered a view that pierced through subsequent constructions of the family's pedigree. "Halid Bey," Yahya Kemal wrote, "clad in his robe (*entari*) and furs, with his pronunciation, his way of eating and enjoying himself, and his way of dealing with people, made it clear that he was a commoner, and that he was deeply resentful of the Unionists, and more generally of the whole 'revolutionary' generation [of which Yahya Kemal, and for that matter Refik Halid, were members]. As for Niyazi Bey [Refik's brother], had he not been sitting with us at the table, he would have been thought by any guest to have been the butler."[6] In describing this scene, Yahya Kemal called into question the family's status in a changing world and pointed to cleavages within the Ottoman establishment that were beginning to appear, only to deepen in time. The Erenköy villa, Yahya Kemal reflected in the 1950s, had an ostentatious portrait of Refik's parents "in the style of a *tuğra* [i.e., old-fashioned and tasteless], painted by hand by a house painter-artist (*boyacı bir sanatkar*) on the wall."[7]

Yahya Kemal's open disdain for Mehmed Halid's status was laden with a deep ambivalence toward the recent Ottoman past that was shared by many in Turkey in the 1950s. It reflected the animosity that many Unionists harbored toward people like Mehmed Halid, who worked in the French-run OPDA and were considered to have collaborated with the capitulatory regime. As the locus of the empire's loss of sovereignty, institutions such as the OPDA had fueled the Unionist movement. Even as early as 1912, the ways of the aging Hamidian "bureau-aristocracy" of Istanbul would have elicited the hostility of someone like Yahya Kemal, who not only came from provincial origins in the Balkans but had lived for many years in Paris and later forged strong connections with the Committee of Union and Progress (CUP).

Refik Halid's extended family, according to his biographers, included a number of prominent statesmen and artists, some of whom would be sources of pride and others targets of opprobrium in the national era. For example, his paternal uncle, Rıza Paşa, was a graduate of the War Academy. Wounded at the Siege of Plevna during the Russo-Ottoman War, he is said to have died later while commanding the Ottoman forces in Mecca. Another of Refik's uncles, Behlül Efendi, was a prominent Mevlevi flutist. Behlül Efendi was apparently also a maternal relative of Mehmet Akif (Ersoy) (1873–1936), the composer of the Turkish national anthem. The family, particularly Refik Halid's father, was also affiliated with the Mevlevi Sufi order. This was yet another marker of some social status—or aspirations to it—since this order was associated with the upper echelons of society. In contrast to the more popular Bektashi order (in which were found craftsmen and Janissaries until the order was banned in 1826), Mevlevis included many followers from the upper ranks of the Ottoman ulema and bureaucracy.[8] On his mother's side, Refik was said to be descended from the Crimean Tatar Khanate. Although it is not clear when Nefise Ruhsar's ancestors joined the thousands of Muslims who migrated to the Ottoman territories after imperial Russia's annexation of the Crimea in 1783, according to one of Refik's biographers, at the turn of the twentieth century some members of the family, including Refik, were still receiving a small pension from the office of the Şeyhülislam (Chief Müfti) because of their descent from the Crimean khans.[9]

Most likely the fashioning of this pedigree—laid out repeatedly and in rote fashion by Refik Halid's biographers and originating, no doubt, from Refik himself—was in part an attempt to claim an Ottoman pedigree despite the family's status as commoners and Mehmed Halid's position as only a midlevel bureaucrat. It was sufficient to claim a class status in contrast, and in opposition, to the modest backgrounds of the up-and-coming members of the Young Turk elite. And it would have given Refik Haild a solid, if not unassailable, status in the old imperial hierarchy of Hamidian Istanbul. His was certainly not the only family that had achieved a position in the Tanzimat-era bureaucracy and that was eager to construct a longer, aristocratic history. On the basis of his confessional, ethnic, and linguistic identity, the family history would later make Refik Halid ripe for inclusion, one would think, in the elite of a future Turkish nation-state. Neither he nor his biographers mention, for instance, that his maternal grandfather was a Greek convert from the island of Chios, a claim that may have undermined his construction of a pure Turkish, imperial pedigree.[10] Instead they emphasize his paternal roots in Anatolia and maternal links to the Turco-Mongol Crimean dynasty, which put him ahead of—and in tension with—many Muslims from the Balkans and Russian territories who could not make similar claims. While the latter would vehemently espouse Turkist ideas, they would do so as outsiders who had to assimilate into Turcophone Istanbul.

EDUCATING AN OTTOMAN

For children of affluent families in the Hamidian era, education began in the home and then continued in elite institutions that trained Ottoman statesmen and intellectuals. Refik Halid was no exception. At the age of four he had a tutor (lala) named Veli Ağa, who hailed from Anatolia and wore a Reading coat, denoting the tight-fitting cutaway or tuxedo jacket worn by Hamidian bureaucrats; it tended to symbolize elitism and a slavish submission to the regime. Veli Ağa took the young Refik to mosques and other neighborhood sites.[11] The boy received his initial instruction in literature from his maternal uncle, İhsan, an accounting clerk at the Finance Ministry and member of the Tatar Aid Society, who later got Refik Halid his first post as a clerk at the same ministry. Refik later recalled starting school at the age of eight; in summer he attended a coed "stone school" (taş mektebi), Mekteb-i Latif, near his family's Erenköy villa, and in winter he went to the primary school later named "Şemsülmaarif mektebi" (Light of Knowledge School), near the Şehzâdebaşı mansion.[12]

Information about the instruction Refik received between ages eight and twelve is sparse. We know that his school seems to have moved several times in the few years he was attending and that this occurred against the backdrop of Hamidian efforts to alter the course of education reforms that dated to the Tanzimat era (1839–76). The Education Regulation, which remained the framework for educational reform for the next half century, called for the establishment of a French-style centralized education system at the secondary level. But between the promulgation of that reform and Sultan Abdülhamid's accession to the throne, little had been done to make the plans a reality across the empire. By the 1880s, when the new sultan turned his attention to education, he had different goals than statesmen such as Ali and Fuat Paşa, who had played a major role in fashioning the Tanzimat "reordering" of state and society. Instead of a wholesale imitation of French education, Abdülhamid espoused a kind of reactive or defensive modernization that entailed a selective adaptation of French schooling infused with Islamic and Ottoman content. These changes caused significant flux in the formal structure of schooling. While the 1869 plan had had three levels of schooling—*sıbyani* (elementary), *rüşdiye* (middle), and *sultani/Darülfünun* (university)—problems with funding and training personnel meant that the lower two levels were "unable to produce students sufficiently qualified for the higher levels."[13] The *rüşdiye* schools were thus downgraded to the primary level, and a new class of schools, the *idadi*, was established to fill the gap between *rüşdiye* and *sultani* schools. By the 1890s, an estimated ten thousand *idadi* schools had been built around the empire.

For Refik Halid and his cohort, gone were the *medreses* of the past. In their place were schools like the Galatasaray Lyceum, where Refik enrolled in 1901, at the age of twelve or thirteen. Also known as Mekteb-i Sultani, or the Imperial School, Galatasaray was founded in 1868 in Beyoğlu, the European, largely non-Muslim quarter of Istanbul.[14] It became the showcase of the Tanzimat-era Ottoman education system and was open to students of all confessional backgrounds—a first in the history of the Ottoman Empire. It served as the training ground for the Hamidian diplomatic corps, and the language of instruction was French. Despite the ecumenical spirit of a multiconfessional student body consistent with Ottomanism—a form of supranational identity politics dating to the 1860s and 1870s, which sought to create a cohesive imperial identity and stave off ethnic nationalisms—there seemed to be little space left for Ottoman influence. Under the direction of Louis de Salve, the school "[imported] teachers, administrators, textbooks, and even bed-frames" and provided a space for the French "to cultivate hundreds of Francophones and Francophiles."[15]

The school's initial success was tempered by a series of setbacks: the first was the French defeat in the Franco-Prussian War of 1870–71; the second was the deaths of Ali and Fuad Paşas (1869 and 1871, respectively), the controversial, Francophile architects of the later Tanzimat reforms.[16] Suddenly the whole endeavor began to look suspect, and the school was seen by many within the government as a vehicle for French influence. After 1870 it was retooled and a series of less high-profile Ottoman directors followed de Salve. In 1877 Abdülhamid appointed the prominent Islamic reformer Ali Suavi Efendi as director, and during his brief stint the school became a showcase for Hamidian-style modernization.[17] As the Ottomans entered into a war with Russia that same year, Ali Suavi waged a war within the school: he increased Muslim enrollment; reduced scholarships for non-Muslim students; expelled all Russian students and any Bulgarian students deemed dangerous; and fired a series of teachers, presumably for siding with Russia.[18] At the same time, he bolstered "European" subjects such as physical sciences, biology, and statistics, while also introducing the study of Muslim jurisprudence, philosophy, literature, and argumentation and incorporating Arabic, Ottoman Turkish, and Persian language instruction. This was consonant with the findings of an 1887 curriculum review commission that was chaired by the Şeyhülislam himself. The Şeyhülislam was assisted by Mehmed Recai, an official from the civil bureaucracy, who recommended: "1. Abolishing Latin and philosophy courses and allowing nothing to be read of the biographies of European philosophers and writers; 2. The serious instruction twice a week of lessons in Islamic principles (*akaid*), which will be entrusted to qualified *ulema*; and 3. Transferring Arabic, Persian, and Turkish classes, which are called Oriental studies at the *Mekteb-i Sultani* [Galatasaray Lyceum], to the supervision of a Muslim official."[19]

The battles over the Galatasaray curriculum—which must have constituted a jarring experience for the twelve-year-olds enrolled at the dawn of the twentieth century—signified deeper issues about the political and cultural identity of the Ottoman establishment. Ottoman elites had internalized different strains of European culture and politics, as well as distinct cultural sensibilities and political interests that did not always align in a shared vision for educational reform. For example, those seeking to embark on careers in the Ottoman bureaucracy had to synthesize French and Ottoman/Islamic structures of knowledge.[20] While they were coming to identify with French-universalist notions of culture and politics, the messages they were receiving from teachers and elders about how to achieve the ideal synthesis was inconsistent and confusing, likely producing new anxieties among the vanguard that institutions such as Galatasaray were designed to educate. Indeed, these anxieties were felt on many fronts, including growing concern for the morality and behavior of the students, signified by a request in 1893 from the minister of education that inspectors be hired to monitor the behavior of students in schools like Galatasaray, seen as particularly dicey because of its location in the European quarter, which was known to be more tolerant of sinful nightlife involving music, dancing, and alcohol.[21] Thus, by the time Refik Halid enrolled, surveillance—the solution of choice for perceived problems ranging from moral licentiousness to provincial political challenges—added to the tensions that characterized his years as a boarding student.

These years, from roughly 1901 through 1906, were formative to Refik Halid's intellectual and artistic development, as well as his future social and political horizons. And yet, as one classmate recalls, Refik Halid was more of a daydreamer than a highly diligent student or a hotblooded youth in need of surveillance:[22] "He was truly bored within the four walls of the school. The lessons that were really the most important to him were the writing lessons. He found himself in a circle at school that, like him, valued contemplation and imagination. During breaks they would not play, but would read, talk, and discuss. In the end he quit school before graduating, and was thrown into the school of life (nature; *tabiat*)."[23] In a story written during the Armistice period (1918–22), Refik Halid echoed his classmates' recollections: "When I was little one of my bad habits was skipping school. From the age of eight until the age of 18, that is, the 10 years during which I was obliged to attend school, I never missed an opportunity to play hooky."[24] At the same time, he downplayed his formal education, stating that he was "by nature a writer." He continued, "I write things without even knowing anything about them. I am a career writer [*alaylı muharrir*, as opposed to someone with formal instruction], like a police officer risen through the ranks, that's me."[25] Whereas the term "alaylı" was usually applied to the career officers in the military—particularly in the context of the Unionist ascendancy in Ottoman governance after 1908—he used it to invoke his role on the front lines of another kind of battle, one against, and yet within the Ottoman literary establishment. This was one of myriad stories that contributed to the construction of the privileged yet rebellious, educated yet free-thinking, and cultured yet rough-and-tumble *muhalif*.

In 1906, age eighteen and in his third year at Galatasaray, Refik Halid and two of his friends refused to get up and leave when his French teacher, Monsieur Dubois, whom he later described as "half-senile," rang the bell and dismissed the class. Everyone else left, but "[he], with some silly egotism, stayed in [his] place." The teacher "grabbed [him] by his collar" and took him to the assistant director, one Monsieur Feuillet. When Feuillet opened Refik Halid's file, he saw that "a year before [he] had been caught sneaking out the back door of the school and had been punished." Feuillet then called Refik Halid "malhonnête" and threatened him with a week's suspension and a prison sentence. When Refik Halid said that it was not fair to punish him in this way—and not others who had done the same thing—Monsieur Feuillet demanded he reveal the names of the others. To this he responded, "you go investigate and find them yourself." When he tried to enter the school the following Saturday, Refik was blocked by guards and had to return home. After he tearfully recounted the ordeal to his father, Mehmed Halid "sent someone to go work it out," and the Ottoman director, Abdurrahman Şeref Efendi, overruled both the French assistant director and the teacher. The director also pardoned Refik Halid and revoked his suspension and prison sentence, reducing his punishment to copying several columns. As Refik Halid would later recall, "the matter was resolved and I was victorious."[26] One might even wonder if Refik Halid, looking back from the 1940s, framed the incident as a foreshadowing of the larger act of defiance that he would perpetrate against Mustafa Kemal in the Telegraph Episode of summer 1919, the watershed moment detailed in chapter 4.

But Refik had soured on school and was ready to embark on a new path, aided in large part by his father. Mehmed Halid agreed to let him terminate his studies at Galatasaray if he could gain admission to law school and arranged for him to take the entrance exam for the law school that had been opened by the Ministry of Justice in 1880 and had become a faculty of the university (Darülfünun-ı Şahane) in 1900. After intense study, Refik passed the entrance exam and began law school in 1907. Perhaps not surprisingly, he soon realized that law school was not for him, and he would later write that "the classes in law school seemed so insipid and vacuous (*laftan güzaftan*) that I could barely get through the second year."[27] Indeed, studying the law must have seemed particularly vacuous in 1907, since the constitution of 1876 was still suspended. While pressure was mounting in many quarters to have it reinstated, students in the law faculty would memorize laws that had been promulgated by an increasingly illegitimate political authority. Refik Halid chafed against this state of affairs and, according to his later recollections, realized that he did not want to become a lawyer. Instead of an *avukat* (lawyer or barrister), he claims that he would have wanted to be something that did not exist in the Istanbul of his day, invoking again the image of a *muhalif* as romantic rebel: a "'European-style prosecutor' . . . a prosecutor who challenges the judge and the lawyers."[28]

In his second year in the faculty, as was common for law students at the time, Refik Halid took a job as a secretary in the central offices of the Finance Ministry (*devair-i merkeziye kalemi*), a stint that lasted about two months— although one biographer later maintained that it lasted closer to fourteen months, which is an important discrepancy, examined later in the chapter. According to an essay he wrote four or five years later, his paternal uncle set him up with the job because the uncle "couldn't stand [his] rebelliousness" anymore.

Refik Halid was reluctant, to say the least, to work in an office; as he greeted his new colleagues and sat down, he recalled, "I wouldn't be this ashamed in front of my fellow inmates were I to go to prison." He already felt a culture shock when they asked him if he had a reed-pen, and he told them, to their dismay, that he wrote with a European-style pen. This, they said, would ruin his calligraphy (*hüsn-ı hatt*), which made him blush because "[Ottoman] calligraphy was as foreign to me as brain surgery," since he had attended "French school." The "torture" continued, as they made him practice his handwriting, showing more concern for the form of the letters than for what he was writing. In a decidedly nontraditional, even cheeky, choice for Ottoman calligraphy, he chose to practice the phrase "Bomonti bira," or "Beaumonti beer." When he returned home after the first day he had a series of comic nightmares in which when he returned to work, his colleagues greeted him with the traditional and antiquated Ottoman greeting, "*Sabah şerifler hayırlı olsun,*" to which he responded, "*Bonjur efendim.*" The dreams, he concluded, signified that he really didn't belong, and that he was not "one of the local birds."

Despite having been swiftly promoted to the third rank (*rütbe-i sâlise*), when he realized that all he could buy with his monthly net salary was an undershirt (out of 52 kuruş, he took home 24 after taxes), he left the job. But Refik Halid neglected to mention that his "decision" to do so coincided with the July 1908 Constitutional Revolution, and that his departure was not the result of a dream or a sudden financial epiphany, but a direct result of the staff purges launched by the CUP, the secret revolutionary society that had plotted the revolt. He had recounted his first encounter with Ottoman bureaucracy whimsically. But it was actually bound up with the very serious political and social conflict that was unleashed along with the restoration of the Ottoman Constitution in 1908–9. His tenure and departure had everything to do with the first contradictions of Ottoman constitutionalism and *muhalefet* therein.[29]

BIRTH OF A WRITER

Before the restoration of the constitution in July 1908, censorship had been notoriously severe, and newspapers with any relation to political issues were either shut down or published outside of Ottoman realms, whether in Egypt or beyond the empire in France and Switzerland.[30] Thus, when Refik Halid was a student, literature—divorced as yet from journalism or politics—was one of very few outlets for anyone interested in writing. Even though Refik began writing after his departure from the civil service in the summer of 1909, he would later portray himself as a born writer who got his start at the age of twelve, while in the middle grade at Galatasaray. It was there that he joined the ranks of poets, or "şair," a term used then for anyone interested in literature. In fact, there were two groups of "poets" at the school, all of whom would become prominent writers and intellectuals. One group, slightly older than he, included Ahmed Haşim (1884–1933; born in Baghdad to provincial officials), Emin Bülent (Serdaroğlu, 1886–1942; poet and eventual founder of the Galatasaray football club), and İzzet Melih (Devrim, 1886–1966). The other group, slightly younger, included Müfit Ratip (1887–1920; credited with becoming the first theater critic in Istanbul), Refik Halid himself, and one "İzzet who died a faculty professor." A figure who was friendly with both circles was the "most enthusiastic writer Abdülhak Şinasi (1887–1963), a prominent figure whose father, Mahmut Celalettin Bey, had started some of the first literary periodicals, including *Hazine-i Evrak* (Treasury of Documents)."[31]

Like the earlier generation of Ottomans educated in the 1870s and 1880s— years when Galatasaray was even more Francophone and Francophile—Refik Halid and his friends were influenced almost exclusively by French literary forms. But eventually, as he noted, many would depart from wholesale imitation and attempt to express local experience in local idioms. This is what we find in Refik Halid's early work, when he became an active writer but was not yet overtly political—even in the wake of the Constitutional Revolution. His writing changed in 1910–11 and more so in 1912. Between 1908 and 1912 he was on at least two different but related writing trajectories: literature, including social realism and then satire, and the more practical field of journalism. Both took him, after 1909, into the new literary and publishing world made possible after the revolution.

The Road to The Light of Dawn *(*Fecr-i Âti*)*

The literary changes that occurred in the nineteenth-century Ottoman Empire reflected political changes. On the heels of translations of major European literary works like *Robinson Crusoe* and *The Count of Monte Cristo* in the 1860s and 1870s, throughout the Tanzimat and early Hamidian era, traditional forms of poetry were superseded by novels and other literary forms imported directly from Europe, particularly France.[32] But to Refik Halid's chagrin, the still small group of novelists and other prose writers were overwhelmingly from extremely privileged backgrounds that allowed them to write about topics with little connection to the social realities of most Ottoman subjects' lives. As Refik Halid recalled later in life, he had always felt a "profound indifference" toward these earlier periods of Ottoman literature.[33]

By the early 1890s, a larger and slightly less elite cohort—many the children of state officials and graduates of Galatasaray and other Francophone schools—had come of age and were integral to shaping the terms of literary debate and expression. Members of this generation, including Halid Ziya (Uşaklıgil) (1865–1945), Tevfik Fikret (1867–1915), and Ahmet Rasim (1867–1932), became involved with a literary journal called *Servet-i Fünun* (Wealth of knowledge). The journal was founded in 1891 by Ahmet İhsan (Tokgöz) (1868–1942) and Recaizade Ekrem (1847–1914), among others, and its stated purpose was to inform readers about new cultural and literary forms in Europe, particularly France. *Servet-i Fünun* became eponymous, not just because of the journal of that name but also the circle of writers that produced it, as part of the Edebiyat-ı Cedide (New Literature) movement.[34]

In November 1901 *Servet-i Fünun* was shut down because it had published an article translated from French by Hüseyin Cahit (Yalçın), with the seemingly innocuous title "Literature and Law" (*Edebiyat ve Hukuk*).[35] For Refik Halid, the journal's suspension meant that the circulation of new texts occurred informally during the years that he would have been exposed to their discussion and transmission while at Galatasaray. While he was likely engaged in intellectual exchanges with the classmates and elders with whom he remained in contact after leaving for the law faculty, like others of his generation, he was shaped by frustration at the journal's being silenced by the Hamidian government.

The publishing world came alive again in 1908, when *Servet-i Fünun*, like so many other journals and gazettes, resumed publication a few days after the constitution was restored on July 26, 1908. To distinguish themselves and their literary and intellectual concerns from those of the "Servet-i Fününists," whom they saw as speaking for an older generation, Refik Halid and his friends explored new forms and styles. Frustrated with the romanticism and lack of interest in social and political ills in the "Western" literature produced by their Ottoman elders, they wanted to explore new forms from Europe, especially the short story and the accompanying realism and naturalism, even if these genres were already considered by many Europeans to be passé.

The move toward new forms of expression went hand in hand with mounting frustrations with business-as-usual politics. A new group began gathering at the Hilal publishing house, located near the Bâb-ı Âli (Sublime Porte) neighborhood, which is still a center for publishing and bookselling. Faik Ali (Ozansoy) (1876–1950), who hailed from Diyarbakir and was from a long line of poets and the brother of the well-known writer Süleyman Nazif, bridged *Servet-i Fünun* and its spinoff. He gave the new journal the name *Fecr-i Âti*, or *Light of Dawn*.[36]

As Refik Halid would later write, the journal's title signaled "the red light at sunrise and sunset . . . the shade of red that promises a future."[37] In attendance at the first meeting were Refik Halid and several friends from Galatasaray, including some of the major intellectual and cultural, if not political, figures of the next generation: Hamdullah Suphi (Tanrıöver), Yakup Kadri (Karaosmanoğlu), Fazıl Ahmet (Aykaç), Mehmed Fuad (Köprülü), İsmail Suphi (Soysallıoğlu), Şahabettin Süleyman, Emin Bülent (Serdaroğlu), İsmail (Hakkı), Müştak (Mayakon), Celâl Sahir, Müfit Ragıp, and Ahmet Samim.[38] "Drunk" with excitement and enthusiasm about the future, the men published a manifesto for their new movement that appeared in *Servet-i Fünun* on 13 Şubat 1325 (February 25, 1910).[39] Published under the title "Manifesto of the Fecr-i Âti Literary Circle," the statement emphasized that "art is personal [*şahsi*] and esteemed [*muhterem*]," and that it should not rely on any ideology, but express the experience of the moment.

The group broke up before they could produce anything beyond the manifesto, but the effort remained an important moment in Refik Halid's literary and intellectual life. As one of the signatories, ten years later Refik Halid would reflect on this experience and hint at the growing tensions in both the literary and political scenes:

> At the time we entered the literary world there was only one school. *Servet-i Fünun* had defeated all opposition [a witty parallel between *Servet-i Fünun* in the literary realm and the CUP in the political realm]. In the new age, *Servet-i Fünun* literature started to come alive with our pens. We swirled poetry and prose together. There were many among us who wrote columns and columns of prose with "oh"s and "ah"s. On the one hand it was an innovation that opened the way to spoken narrative, and on the other to free verse.... [I]t was always a problem of form, it was a time that was all about form [*şekil*]. We were still playing with words.[40]

After his experiences at *Servet-i Fünun* and *Fecr-i Âti*, Refik Halid continued to work with Yakup Kadri and other members of the movement. He recalled that after the latter fell apart, "some among us turned to the country [*memleket*] and took, with our novice, but homegrown stories, a useful step in our literature.... The imitations stopped and some people started using their brains."[41] "Using their brains," for Refik Halid, translated into a new engagement with politics and a concomitant discovery of satire, which needs to be understood within the context of how he entered journalism and publishing—fields that would constitute his home for the rest of his life.

While both he and his hagiographer-biographers play down his family and political ties to the establishment—instead emphasizing his literary activities during the Second Constitutional Era and how he tried his hand at new genres—journalism and satire would become his primary occupations. Journalism had come first, accidentally, during the days after he first joined *Servet-i Fünun*. Refik Halid recalls that he wanted to engage in a "free profession" and considered a career in business. As he and his older brother were about to set up a commission with a British merchant, they learned that their would-be partner had to leave for England. Concerned that Refik would be idle for several months, his brother took him to the offices of *Servet-i Fünun* and, with the help of his brother's old friend and the journal's founder, Ahmet İhsan (Tokgöz, 1868–1947), he was accepted as an unpaid intern.[42]

He describes the first day as another struggle: after the director and Refik Halid's brother left him at his desk, he looked around and saw one Suphi, whom he didn't know, an Armenian translator, and a police officer-security guard. "They put a French news agency telegram in front of me and said, "Translate this. I wrote, I scribbled, I strung the sentence together again, I crossed it out again, I got embarrassed, with blood, sweat, and tears I tried, but it didn't look like I had much talent."[43] Within a week he had settled in, translating telegrams and collecting, writing up, and editing the news—albeit without a byline.

Two months in, he signed his first article, "Guano Fertilizers" (*Guano gübreleri*), as "RH." His recent biographer Ali Birinci, who as the head of the Turkish History Foundation had extraordinary access to Turkish archives and libraries, has not been able to find the article. Refik Halid said in 1918 that it would be an exaggeration to call it an article anyway and asked, "What are Guano fertilizers? I won't tell, and don't ask." But he points out that in writing this story, he "got to know [him]self," realizing that writing was his vocation; like fertilizer, it helped him grow, bear fruit, and mature.[44] In line with his humor, it is entirely possible that "Guano fertilizers" never existed and was merely an amusing commentary on the trials and tribulations involved in becoming a published writer.

The internship led to a position as a translator and writer at *Tercüman-ı Hakikat* (Translator of the truth) that paid 400 kuruş per month. Within months he was writing lead articles under his own byline for both the journal and *Servet-i Fünun* and had started writing shorter pieces for *Resimli Kitap* (Illustrated book), a monthly journal published between 1908 and 1913 and edited by Ubeydullah Esat and Faik Duran.

By August 1909 Refik Halid had come into his own, and for a brief period he was a newspaper owner. After receiving permission from the Ottoman Ministry of the Interior and Security Directorate, along with a 200 kuruş loan from his father, he opened a new "Turkish political and literary [daily] newspaper" called *Son Havadis: Müstakil ve Meşrutiyetperver Akşam Gaze-tesidir* (Latest news: An independent and constitutionally-minded evening newspaper).[45] As opposed to more pointed newspapers like *Tanin* (the CUP party organ), *Son Havadis* did not advance a partisan platform. Instead, it seemed to be an effort to create a nonpartisan and independent daily—as the paper's subtitle claimed—for Istanbul. Devoid of explicit or polemical political discussions, the content offered a broad sampling of political and social issues and advanced a vision of a liberal, constitutionalist public sphere.

At the age of twenty-one, together with Yakup Kadri, his translator friend from *Fecr-i Âti*, Refik Halid published the first issue on September 1, 1909. They published fifteen issues before closing the paper down because it was too difficult to manage.[46] The effort involved in publishing the daily paper is clear from the first, and only extant, issue. *Son Havadis* consisted of four large pages, each with five columns split into two sections. Articles included news items about the empire's internal affairs, including military and bureaucratic appointments, and about its foreign affairs, including ambassadorial appointments, as well as news from non-Muslim communities, such as matters involving the Armenian community and Patriarchate. One front-page feature was called "Forty-Five Years Ago Today" and included stories from within the empire and beyond. There was also a police log; an obituary section; a translation of a French murder mystery written by Claude Ferrer (a French writer and Turcophile then popular in Istanbul), titled "Tarihi tefrikamız: Öldüren kim?" (Our historical serial: Who is the killer?), and a reminiscence about childhood by a man who was turning forty-six. The first issue also included a large section of translated telegrams from foreign and domestic news agencies, with news from as far afield as Panama and as close as Athens and Fez. On the back page, in addition to classified ads, including "mansion for sale—urgent," and the only large commercial advertisement of the issue, for "Kâni Silk Shop" in Eminönü, was a feature called "Vilayetler postası," or Provincial post[card], signed by "C," a travelogue about the town of Edirne. In its range of features, the paper helps us understand the horizons and values that made up an elite and middle-class Ottoman liberal vision, distinct from the partisan polemics that were also underway in the press at the same time.

Social Conflict and Literary Imagination: Two Stories

As he honed his skills translating, writing, and editing news, Refik Halid began to publish short stories that provided a contrast to the optimism and empowerment that came with the 1908 Constitutional Revolution. In two such stories, he depicts instead characters who are morally compromised, powerless, and socially pessimistic, complicating our understanding of the Second Constitutional Era.[47]

The first, "Ayşe's Destiny" ("Ayşe'nin talihi"), was published in 1909 in Faik Sabri (Duran)'s *Muhit* magazine and tells a shockingly bold story.[48] Writing from the perspective of a lower-class young woman who is nearly raped by an upper-class man, the story gives readers a sense of Refik Halid's early style and concerns. Since it is one of the few direct sources we have from Refik Halid's early life, I provide a full translation of the text here:[49]

Ayşe lives in a dilapidated mansion on the outskirts of the city. She and her mother (who cleans the "antique-sellers' house" (*Antikacıların evi*) some distance from theirs), live like sentries keeping watch amid the cobwebs (*bekçi gibi*) in the ruins of a house, which forty years ago must have hosted the most entertaining of parties. Now, long abandoned, it yells out to anyone passing by, "You, and yes, everyone, will one day become like me, with broken walls and crooked rocks, and one or two dogs running around on you!" Ayşe looked out through the iron grid window at the sky, and the flies and bees circling the hole next to the barn's windows, closed up with corrugated tin. As she collected the laundry, her dress soaked and clinging to her body, she lit the stove and waited for the rain. As the sky darkened, making everything as dark as the inside of the wood stove, Ayşe heard a noise.

She saw a man, wearing a *kalpak* on his head and a woolen coat (*aba*) on his back. Holding a rifle, he was petting the ears of his dog. Ayşe realized it must have been the antique-seller's son, caught in the rain on the way back from hunting. Not thinking anything, she asked "Who is it? What do you want?" The man was startled to hear the young, high voice, and asked, "Isn't Fatma Hanım [the girl's mother] here?" Ayşe replied, "she went to your house, to clean wood, what are you going to do?" The man told her to open the door so he wouldn't get soaked in the rain. She did, and ran into the kitchen. As he caught a glimpse of her beauty and brown eyes, he asked, "Girl, aren't you scared here all by yourself?" He was testing to see if she was alone. Ayşe felt a terrible shame and ran inside, but Ali Bey flew after her.

She covered her face with her hands, and stood leaning on the pot against the stove, with her soaking wet dress. Feeling afraid, she screamed when she felt the hot touch of a stranger's hand on her body, and ran to the other corner. Ali Bey, because of the pleasure he got from the rain, the darkness, her naked, wild, burning hot body, followed her and opened his arms to pounce on her. But his feet slipped on the foul water that had been slowly seeping from one corner of the kitchen and he fell, hitting his head on the sharp rocks of the stove, and toppled over like a scarecrow. The other flew outside, for a while not hearing anything but the pitter patter of the rain on the house. She peeked inside and saw Ali Bey, with his cloak on his back and his boots on his feet, lying down in the foul water. The girl, whose heart felt suffocated under a monster's paw, ran inside to see if it was a trick and he was just pretending to be dead. She saw a pink road running through the foul water. You could see the liquid running on the foul water, from Ali Bey's brain, burst open. He was dead.

Ayşe's eyes clouded up, as if something in her heart had broken. She couldn't believe it, didn't want to believe it. She was afraid in the full sense of the word; before her eyes she saw crowds of people and soldiers, their rifles glinting and their bayonets out. She woke up, and realized she had to move this dead body, but how? She looked around, and somehow her not even nineteen-year-old body found the strength to carry this wet, swollen corpse; with revulsion she turned him over. The dead body's eyes, still open, closed by themselves at that moment.

At this moment she heard something swing the door open, and then start to crawl into the house. She ran to the window like a crazy person: the dead man's dog was there, looking frantically for his owner. The girl froze, suddenly losing her courage. What to do with him? Would he allow her to drag his owner's corpse in the mud, through the garden to get to the barn? She felt a constant pain in her temples, like the vessels in her neck would burst. Her heart was pounding as if it were going to go to pieces, little things were flying around like flies in front of her eyes.

She longed to die. . . . But she had decided, she would clean up everything before her mother returned. She took the copper pot from the kitchen, and opened the door a crack, the dog stuck its nose in, sniffing; she opened it a bit more, and then a bit more; she hit that head as if it were in a vise, with all the strength she could; the pot fell to one side, the dog toppled over the other way, after struggling for a while he turned to stone.

After the rain let up, she went to the barn with a shovel, dug a hole, and dragged the two bodies there. The dead man's pocket-watch was still ticking. She thought about whether to take it, but in the end left it. She buried them in manure, she got wet up to her buttonholes. She cleaned the kitchen, hung the pan back on the stove. After the water boiled she made some bean stew (*fasulye*). Her work was done. She waited for her mother.

The next day, she spent from morning until night in the barn, digging a bigger hole, hiding Ali Bey and his dog there and taking the manure off them. That night she slept, dead to the world, in the shelter of her body's fatigue from the day's work. Those who were still alive occupied themselves for a while about Ali Bey and his dog's strange disappearance, and then slowly their concern abated, and went away.

A month later, a young villager saw Ayşe's mother on the way to work; at that moment he thought of her daughter left alone in the house; he ran there immediately, jumping over an old hole in front of the ruined house. Ayşe was in the house, lighting the stove and chopping wood. She turned her head at the rattle of the door, and standing up, she saw the villager looking at her and grinning; she covered her eyes with her hands. So as not to have to feel the shame and guilt, not to have to knock him down and kill him again, she left herself defenseless.

The feeling of despair is palpable in this story, which closes with the message that Ayşe would sooner be raped than have to feel the guilt and shame that would come with killing again, even though she did *not* actually kill her assailant the first time, just his dog. With no authority—legal or social—to appeal to, her only options were to commit murder—as in her mind she had done before—or allow herself to be raped, which would likewise, one would think, have brought her tremendous shame. This was no doubt also a commentary on the despair surrounding political authority at the time. With all the supposed freedoms of constitutionalism, only confusion reigned as to who was in charge to dispense justice.

In another early story, "Against Power" ("Kuvvete karşı"), Refik Halid writes about a midlevel Muslim bureaucrat, Suphi Bey, who accompanies his Rum (Christian) mistress İzmaro to the theater in Beyoğlu, the European quarter where Refik Halid had enjoyed the nightlife during and after his years at Galatasaray Lyceum.[50] He decribes İzmaro in the most respectable of terms and sensitively portrays the intimate emotional bond between the couple, while also revealing that she lives as a kept woman in a boardinghouse near Beyoğlu's main strip. The couple's respectable, bourgeois evening is ruined by drunk and rowdy American sailors, who disrupt the performance and then assault Suphi Bey by stealing his fez, mocking him, and making eyes at İzmaro in a restaurant after the play. The story is told as an inner monologue, with Suphi's feelings of humiliation and resentment building throughout the evening, until he decides, after he and İzmaro return home, to go back out and stand up to the sailors. He waits for them on a dark corner, holding a knife, and lunges at the nine sailors in what can only be termed a suicidal move. The story ends with him getting beaten and stabbed to death by the Americans, in his futile bid "against power."

The story can be read as a commentary on the impunity with which American (and European) soldiers could act in Ottoman lands—and a shockingly prescient one, given that it was written in 1909 and not 1919, when Allied occupation forces did in fact sweep through the city. The foreigners' denigration of Suphi's evening, his neighborhood, his culture, and finally his woman is too much to bear. In fact, the dishonor is so painful that he would prefer to die fighting than go home in peace. Yet one wonders if the protagonist (and Refik Halid) is also furious at the society in which he lives—not only because, as he notes to himself, his fellow theatergoers and restaurant customers are too cowardly to defend their compatriots, but also because he lives in a society in which his relationship with İzmaro is illicit. Suphi's social-psychological perception of his situation, like Ayşe's in the earlier story, creates a prison from which the only way out is suicide. To oppose power— whether American sailors, a rapist, or the strictures of one's own traditional society—is futile at best, deadly at worst. These stories were an exercise in the craft of writing; while somewhat derivative of already passé French writers like Guy de Maupassant in their form, they laid bare the psychology and emotions of shame, humiliation, and powerlessness—emotions that, one can imagine, were very common at that moment—with a stark frankness about social, moral, and gender norms that is not characteristic of contemporary Ottoman literature.[51]

The stories raise the question of whether Refik Halid was trying to convey the ambivalence that took hold after the March/April 1909 counterrevolution, or if he was sending a message to readers that both encompassed and transcended politics and sought to take the moral pulse of the society. They also suggest that he was trying to express the kinds of contestation that existed within society over the shedding of political tradition and the embracing of political liberty. By all accounts, the Constitutional Revolution was not aimed at social revolution or emancipation, but only the narrowest kind of political freedom and economic modernization. And these freedoms and openings were only vehicles for the goal of "saving the empire." For twenty-one-year-old Refik Halid, these were very conservative goals. His stories convey the social and emotional underside of the revolution and hint at the complexities of power and its opposition in the changing political order.

EUROPEAN TOUR
(CA. OCTOBER 1909–CA. JANUARY 1910)

Late 1909 was a good moment to leave Istanbul. The honeymoon period of the Second Constitutional Era lasted less than a year, and on March 31, 1909, the euphoria generated by the constitution was broken by violence, when a so-called counterrevolution in Istanbul was crushed by the Action Army (*Hareket Ordusu*), a military force led by members of the CUP that swept in from Rumeli.[52] Sultan Abdülhamid II was forced to abdicate and placed under house arrest in Salonica, the site of the CUP's organizational headquarters. In his place, the CUP appointed a weak new sultan, Mehmed V (Reşat), and quickly moved to impose martial law.[53]

Six months later, Refik Halid headed to Paris, along with his older brother, Hakkı Halid, and their friend Agah Efendi.[54] As in the Hamidian era, Paris was an important destination for Ottoman dissidents—even if Refik Halid and his companions were not among them—this time for those who opposed the CUP rather than Sultan Abdülhamid.[55] By the summer of 1909, the main leaders of the 31 March Incident, including Ali Kemal (editor of *İkdam*), Ahmed Cevdet Bey (proprietor of *İkdam*), and Mevlanzâde Rıfat (proprietor of *Serbesti*)—had all fled the country and continued their work.[56]

Refik Halid wrote surprisingly little about his Paris experience, discussing it only around 1940, a few years after returning to Istanbul from his second round of exile. In a story titled "First Journey" ("İlk Sefer") he mentions no political motive for the trip and shifts between a first- and third-person account, in which the third person is a "half-educated youth" journeying to a legendary city.[57] The story provided Refik Halid with an opportunity to show how he was part of European culture and society as well as the ways in which he was a foreigner in Europe. For contemporary readers conversant in the writings of a wider Ottoman milieu, there were clear echoes of Tahtawi's classic early nineteenth-century work about his voyage to Paris.[58]

Refik Halid begins the story with a long, formulaic paragraph peppered with flowery Ottoman descriptions of Istanbul at sunset. He then asks,

> What, are you bored? You should be; the five or six lines above are copied from Cenab Şahabettin's *Hac Yolunda* (On the pilgrimage road); one of the most important examples of travel narrative! When I decided to write the story of my trip to Europe at age 21 I said, "Let me do my readers a favor. . . . Let me start my piece with an example of a past masterpiece, give them a taste of boredom, and then return to the narrative and let them breathe a sigh of relief!"

After this critique of Ottoman literary tropes, he proceeds to compare the trip to Paris with Cenab Şahabettin's story of the hajj, implying that his journey to the French capital was a pilgrimage of sorts. Indeed, he alludes to questions of faith when he recalls that at age twenty-one, he was still amazed at the wisdom of everything the Europeans did. "I was one of the faithful," he writes, "who believed in European civilization."[59] The story, however, is ultimately one of disillusionment—whether as he experienced it in 1909 or in the thirty years that transpired between the journey and his writing about it.[60]

The loss of a kind of faith in European civilization begins during his first stop in Athens, where he is unimpressed by the Acropolis and writes:

The Acropolis, probably because of years of neglect, made less of an impression on me than even Anadoluhisarı [the fifteenth-century fortress on the Bosphorus]. I found it completely at odds with the shining history I half-knew about it. So much so that I supposed I was looking at an imitation and not the real thing, and left feeling cheated. I could neither imagine those great figures in my mind there, nor could I square the grandeur of ancient Greek history with the small town of Athens and its coarse light.[61]

Rather than ruins, Refik Halid was interested in prosperity and cultivation (*mamure*). He "was running to see all the things we didn't have: parks, boulevards, electricity, telephones, statues, freedom for women," airplanes, underground trains, and cars.[62] His first contact with these things came in Naples, where he began to describe his experiences through food and French literature. Beginning in this southern Italian city, he eats pasta and recalls Lamartine's *Graziella*—itself a reminiscence of pleasant childhood memories—and longs for a return of romanticism. As he moves to Marseilles, he tries bouillabaisse and thinks about the "French" fairy tale "Little Red Riding Hood." On the train to Paris, he sits across from an attractive young woman and recalls the stories of Maupassant.[63] And when the train stops in Dijon, he remembers a mystery he read at age thirteen that took place on a train in that station. Upon his arrival in Paris, he summons a novel that he had just read by Paul Bourget—an author who, like Refik Halid, made a name for himself in literary journalism.[64]

His knowledge of Paris came from serialized novels like those by Xavier de Montepin that were translated into Ottoman Turkish from French. Notre Dame, St. Michel, Place de l'Ètoile, the Champs-Élysées, and the Seine all occupied important places in his imagination. But like his view of Athens, his first impression of Paris was disappointing. The taxi resembled those in Istanbul, and there were only a few boulevards. "Compared to the boulevards I had imagined," he writes, "they are small, uninspired, and not much different from those in Naples and Marseilles." And what's more, Paris's distance from the sea made it feel dull.[65]

Writing at age fifty, Refik Halid's pilgrimage to Paris was important precisely because it was so disappointing. He would never again travel to Europe. Dispirited and lonely, Refik was in Europe but missed his *Fecr-i Âti* friends. And by February 1910 he was back in Istanbul, where he signed the *Fecr-i Âti* manifesto and shifted to writing political satire. Until that point in his life—even as he looked back from middle age—political opposition and dissent seemed rather irrelevant for this ostensible *muhalif*.

CLASS STRUGGLE AND THE REAWAKENING
OF *MUHALEFET*

Refik Halid's world was inhabited by privileged, French-educated Ottoman bureaucratic families. In the 1860s and 1870s, men of a similar ilk had drafted the first Ottoman constitution and begun to grapple with the concept of *muhalefet* as an abstract ideal. In fact, Young Ottoman intellectuals such as Namık Kemal, Ziya, and Reşad Bey had been debating it since the publication of the first issue of *Hürriyet* in 1868.[66] For them *muhalefet* signified dissent, disagreement, multivocality, and the act of debating its place in a hypothetical constitutional order. These were the same men who integrated French political ideas and French literature into their very identity as Ottoman gentlemen, as Refik Halid learned to do a few generations later. These heirs to the Young Ottomans of Refik Halid's father's and then his own generation seemed willing to accept the extensive control over Ottoman financial and political affairs that the French and British had established during the Hamidian period, perhaps because they benefited in various ways from Hamidian despotism. Rather than seeing, for instance, French control over the Public Debt Administration as a humiliating, semicolonial relationship that compromised the empire's dignity, they saw it as a fact of life. And they benefited from the privilege that accompanied this complicity.

But alongside an Ottoman establishment suspended between constitutionalism and despotism, a new elite was taking shape. This was within the ranks of the CUP, a secret society formed in 1889. An important wing of the CUP, the wing that grew within the empire as opposed to in exile in France or Egypt, emerged out of the German-trained Ottoman military. In a broad coalition that included bureaucrats and intellectuals, many of whom had been forced into exile for their constitutionalist activities, and men who rose through the military ranks, some Unionists were very distinct from these Ottoman gentlemen. Not least of all, they hailed from more modest backgrounds and often came from the Balkans and Russia, making them outsiders to high society in the imperial capital.[67] They were hungry for change, desperate for solutions to the ineffective modernization tactics of the Hamidian regime, and fed up with the gradualist Tanzimat bureaucracy, of which Refik Halid had been a product. And they were much more concerned with expedience than with gradual change. For our story this means two things: first, that Refik Halid had inherited the liberal, elitist sensibilities of his elders, even as their ideas about constitutionalism and democracy were suspended, literally and figuratively, by Abdülhamid's absolutism, and second, that because of this state of suspension, several different visions for change were developing among the ranks of the Ottoman state and those abroad and in exile.

Yet the political landscape on the eve of the 1908 Constitutional Revolution was more variegated than the conventional view of a split between modernizers working for secular progress and reactionaries clinging to Islam and tradition.[68] Ottoman politics and culture, even through the small lens of Refik Halid's early life and work, point to important interrelationships between politics and literature; between individuals and families associated with the bureaucracy and those connected to the military; and between those hailing from Istanbul and those from outside the capital, especially the Balkans and Russia. There were also rifts between adherents of French thinkers and literature and those influenced by German political and military strategists, perhaps best captured by the very emergence of the CUP leadership and the role they would play after 1908. As new groups with new expectations emerged and obtained influence, they could all mobilize around the goal of restoring the Ottoman Constitution. *Muhalefet*, then, was not only born as an academic concept alongside *meşrutiyet*, or constitutionalism but reborn in the contingent relationships and shared goals of groups—indeed, emergent political parties—opposed to Abdülhamid.

We can track this shift in the usage of *muhalefet* from abstract ideal in the 1860s to political reality in the months and years leading up to July 1908. Two congresses were held in Paris for the movement aimed at restoring the Ottoman constitution: one in 1902 and one in December 1907. These congresses were attended by representatives from several groups that agreed on the larger goal of restoring the constitution, for their own reasons and from their own positions. The 1902 congress, led by Prince Sabahaddin, employed a language of liberalism (*Hürriyetperverlik*) and patriotism (*hamiyet*) to appeal to and unite Ottoman constitutionalists.[69] A search of the major constitutionalist newspaper, *Şura-yı Ümmet*, published in Cairo, brings up only one headline that included the word *muhalefet* (in reference to its narrow meaning of an opposition party) before 1908. The term *muhalefet*, rather than being ubiquitous as it was before 1876, seems to still have been in a state of relative suspension.

The second congress of the constitutionalists, also held in Paris, in December 1907, showed a marked change on at least two fronts. First, it was termed the Congress of Ottoman Opposition (*Osmanlı Muhalifin Kongresi*), explicitly resurrecting a form of the term *muhalefet* and positioning the coalition of groups advocating for the restoration of the constitution as a united opposition to the despotism of Abdülhamid II. Second, it was attended by three specific opposition parties that together represented the opposition coalition—opposed, that is, to the tyranny of Abdülhamid and in favor of restoring the constitution. Those three parties were the Decentralization and Individual Initiative Party of Prince Sabahaddin (the so-called liberals); the Committee of Union and Progress, represented by Ahmed Rıza; and the Armenian Revolutionary Federation, represented by Khachatur Malumian. Within this constitutionalist coalition, which was now explicitly claiming a banner of *muhalefet*, were bureaucrats, intellectuals, military men, and Jacobins, both Muslim and Armenian Socialist.

As we see when we turn next to Refik Halid's development into the Porcupine, a more "prickly" opposition figure, the divisions in Ottoman society were never as simple as those postulated by Niyazi Berkes, Bernard Lewis, and others as a divide between modernizer-secularizers and religious reactionaries.[70] This has become the dominant framework by which to understand late Ottoman and modern Turkish politics, more so today than ever before. The articulation of this framework for understanding politics, I argue, was actually driven first by the CUP and then by the ways that nationalists privileged difference in their recounting of history. Both the CUP and Turkish Republican nationalists strategically obfuscated the more subtle fissure *within* the constitutionalist elite that Refik Halid and many of his contemporaries were a part of. We have seen that many future *muhalifs* were elite, and elitist Ottoman liberals, not categorically opposed to constitutionalism but with an entrenched class identity and political vision. Unlike some of the Young Turks in exile or most CUP military figures, they were among those whom Nader Sohrabi terms children of the patrimonial establishment—a group that by far outnumbered their Jacobin contemporaries.[71] In order to see how politics unfolded among those in the establishment and for the newcomers to power, I now turn to the making and unmaking of Ottoman constitutionalism between 1908 and 1913—where Refik Halid met *muhalefet* and turned into the Porcupine.

TWO

The Contradictions
of Ottoman Constitutionalism
and the Remaking of *Muhalefet*
(1908–1913)

THE PORCUPINE SPEAKS

THE OTTOMAN CONSTITUTION was restored in July 1908 after more than 30 years. The euphoria expressed across the empire marked the end of one struggle: for the formal restoration of constitutionalism. But that euphoria soon faded as a much bigger struggle ensued: to define the specific meanings and boundaries of constitutionalism in practice, across an empire that had changed significantly since the constitution was abrogated in 1878.[1] The many contradictions of Ottoman constitutionalism came to the fore during the tumultuous period from 1908 through 1913. Out of those contradictions, the meaning of *muhalefet* underwent a fundamental shift, and Refik Halid's satirical persona, the Porcupine (Kirpi), was born. These internal contradictions of constitutional politics—and particularly within the Committee of Union and Progress (CUP)—have been obscured by nationalist recollections and histories. Mainstream nationalist recollections attribute a heroic status to the CUP and conflate that organization with constitutionalism, thereby marginalizing, often to the point of effacing, the liberal opposition within the constitutional movement. Here we can recover some of the gradations of constitutionalism by turning to the concept of *muhalefet* and to the voice of one writer who dissented by writing satire, becoming a *muhalif* in the process.

At the start of 1908 *muhalefet* signified the coalition of groups in favor of restoring the constitution, dubbed *muhalefet* because they opposed the despotism of Abdülhamid II. By 1913, *muhalefet* had come to mean something else altogether; it became synonymous with the opposition *to* the CUP, a body that had assumed the position of power. This was not an instantaneous shift, either in politics or in the meaning of the term *muhalefet*, in response to the restoration of the constitution in 1908. Instead, it was a process of polarization that took place in the span of five years. Here I unpack that process of polarization that made for a new kind of *muhalefet*. By 1913, the endpoint of the chapter, *muhalefet* was defined—as a pretext for their banishment—as a specific group of roughly eight hundred men associated with the liberal opposition coalition, a group that included Refik Halid.

. . .

After returning from Paris to Istanbul in 1910, Refik Halid entered a new and burgeoning scene of literary satire and began a new phase of his career that was shaped by the uncertainty and dangers of Ottoman constitutionalism.[2] Although he was in many ways still ambivalent about the political tumult around him and was not yet an opponent of any one regime or movement, the increasingly sharp tone of his satire earned him the pen name Kirpi, or Porcupine. The bestower of this moniker was none other than his friend Yakup Kadri (Karaosmanoğlu), who was a member of the literary circle at *Fecr-i Âti*, the literary light of dawn that had quickly burned out.

In this phase—roughly March 1910 to November 1911—Refik wrote scores of short satires and essays and even a satirical chronicle in the style of Naima, the famous Ottoman chronicler (*vakanüvis*) of the eighteenth century, titled, "History of the Era of the Parliamentarians" ("Tarih-i Devr-i Mebusan"). In a short span of time, he had gone from intern to newspaper publisher to noted satirist. He wrote for a range of outlets that included *Şehrah* (a liberal-royalist paper) and *Cem*, the longest-running and most prominent satirical newspaper of the era.[3] In 1911, thirty of these works were compiled and published as *Kirpi'nin Dedikleri* (The Porcupine's utterances), in a volume that provides us with a series of snapshots of Refik Halid's preoccupations during the Second Constitutional Era, specifically in the period from the 31 March Incident in 1909 through the outbreak of the Ottoman-Italian War and formation of the Freedom and Accord Party in the fall of 1911.[4] Writing in a period marked by relative peace in the empire and intensifying conflict within the CUP and Senate/General Assembly, the Porcupine hit on topics that resonated with the reading public of the Ottoman capital of Istanbul as well as among its political elite.[5] In fact, the Porcupine's utterances had garnered the attention of both the liberal leadership and the CUP, with Sabahaddin (the maverick Ottoman prince who headed the coalition of liberals) commending him for authoring the most "European" stories of the era—and the CUP exiling him to Sinop.

BACKGROUND: THE DILEMMAS
OF OTTOMAN CONSTITUTIONALISM

The five years between July 1908 and July 1913 were among the most momentous the empire had ever seen. Once the Young Turk coalition had achieved their unifying goal of restoring the constitution, differences of opinion proliferated regarding the application of that relic from 1876, the Ottoman Constitution (*Kanun-ı Esasi*), and the meanings of constitutionalism. Whereas the ambiguity surrounding the idea of a constitution and of freedom (*hürriyet*) had enabled disparate actors to cohere in loose coalitions forged prior to 1908, those same ambiguities would foster fragmentation among these groups once constitutionalism unfolded in reality.[6] Questions cascaded among those who were trying to determine the contours of the postrevolutionary order: How would the existing Ottoman government or executive accommodate the reconstituted Ottoman legislature, now reopened after twenty-eight years? Who would be responsible for military, fiscal, and foreign policy, and for domestic administrative decisions? What role would the new cabinet play, and who would have the prerogative to appoint ministers? What place, if any, would non-Muslims and non-Turks have in governing the empire? Divergent answers to these questions escalated existing tensions and within a year resulted in open conflict between factions that were defined as much by their divergent political agendas as by diverse socioeconomic backgrounds, generational differences, and ethno-confessional identities.

Driving—and complicating—the unfolding of the constitutional movement was the CUP, the key player in the Young Turk coalition. In many ways the very existence of the CUP was antithetical to the idea of a liberal, constitutional order. Formed as a secret society in 1889, after 1908 the CUP continued to operate as such, only a few years later declaring itself an organization and then a political party. At the same time, members claimed a special role as guardians of the constitutional order they had helped bring about. Comprising an internal wing of junior military officers who had been politicized in the course of their education in the new military academies of the Hamidian regime, and an external wing formed abroad by intellectuals in exile, the CUP leadership had both the capacity and strength to articulate and enforce their vision—through force when needed. As recent studies by Nader Sohrabi and Bedross Der Matossian have shown, while the CUP had to adhere to the language of constitutionalism to maintain credibility, the leadership saw the constitution not so much as a supreme legal framework for the empire as an instrument to achieve their goals. That goal—broadly articulated as "saving the empire"—meant to preserve Ottoman territorial integrity through forced programs of centralization and modernization. This, in turn, would augment the CUP's own power, increasingly set against the existing Ottoman establishment.[7] So, in effect, association with the CUP signaled an impulse that was both deeply conservative and radical: they were striving to save the empire, and at the same time they deeply resented the class associated with that empire's establishment. Making matters more complicated, they did not have the numbers, and perhaps they even lacked the will, to completely dispense with that establishment. The Second Constitutional Era saw the unfolding of these contradictory impulses, making for a situation that was full of irony and therefore, as we will see, ripe for satire.

The CUP's path to consolidating power was marked by setbacks. As the secret society/organization infiltrated the executive and began to dominate the legislative branches, many who had initially been affiliated with the CUP protested these developments by leaving and joining liberal opposition coalitions, including the Ottoman Liberal Party (Osmanlı Ahrar Fırkası) in 1908–9 and the Freedom and Accord Party (Hürriyet ve İtilaf Fırkası, informally known as the Liberal Entente) in 1911–12, only to be shattered by 1913.[8] As the CUP evolved from a secret society into an organization circa 1911, and then into an open political party in 1913, the body's de facto internal structure became less transparent and increasingly concentrated in the hands of a few. By the time of the Raid on the Sublime Porte in January 1913, three figures dominated the CUP. The so-called Triumvirate of Paşas—Talaat, Enver, and Cemal—both demonstrated the concentration of power within the CUP and signaled the polarization within the larger Young Turk movement between 1908 and 1913.

In the period between the Constitutional Revolution of July 1908 and the Raid on the Sublime Porte in 1913, two different but inseparable processes were underway. The first entailed a struggle to work out formal questions of governance, jurisdiction, and administration. It included the separation of power in the top echelons of the government, as well as the question of how to administer the diverse populations that remained within Ottoman realms after a succession of territorial losses. The two broad factions involved in working out answers to these questions were (1) the Centralists, headed by Ahmed Rıza, which included but was not limited to the CUP, and advocated for centralized administration and Turkification, entailing the minimizing of autonomy for non-Muslim communities; and (2) the Federalists, or liberals, represented by Prince Sabahaddin, a maverick member of the Ottoman dynasty who advocated for decentralized administration and more autonomy for non-Muslim communities. The second process involved conflict between the CUP and factions that opposed what they saw as the former's anticonstitutional aspirations and tactics, which the CUP employed under the guise of guarding the constitution itself. For example, the perception of anticonstitutional tactics drove Ahmed Rıza—who had been an intellectual leader in the Young Turk movement abroad before 1908—to lead the parliamentary opposition to the CUP after 1909. The decision to join, remain in, or defect from the CUP often had to do with a calculus of means and ends. It hinged on questions having to do with the lengths one was willing to go to realize the Unionist (CUP) vision, and at what point one would choose constitutionalism as rule of law over the constitution as an instrument.

There were several key turning points as the Young Turk coalition fragmented and the unbridled euphoria and "freedoms" of 1908 turned into a CUP dictatorship. The brief counterrevolution and its violent suppression in March/April 1909 was the first violent conflict to break out under the new regime—only nine months after the restoration of the constitution—and it proved to be formative. In a nominally "Sharia-ist," movement, the counterrevolutionaries called·for the restoration of Islamic law and were supported by the liberal wing of the Young Turk coalition. Some argue that it was more a revolt against the involvement of the CUP than against the constitutional order itself.[9] The CUP-led "Action Army" (Hareket Ordusu) suppressed the revolt and restored the constitution (again), marching into Istanbul from the CUP base of Macedonia. This action signified the lengths the CUP leadership were willing to go to in order to guard the formal supremacy of the constitution—and the Committee's own power. Purges of civil and military officials and personnel followed, and career bureaucrats and military men were replaced with less-qualified men who were loyal to the CUP. Two years of relative calm were followed by the outbreak of war with Italy in Libya between September 1911 and October 1912, then the catastrophic First Balkan War of October 1912 through April 1913. During this time, a new liberal party formed in opposition to the CUP in the summer of 1911. The party, known as the Freedom and Accord Party/Liberal Entente, took the reins of government in July 1912 and ushered in a period known as the Great Cabinet (Büyük Kabine), ruling as the empire was driven into the Balkan War by the states of the Balkan League. As a direct response to the military's failures in the Balkans, the Liberal Entente was forcibly removed from power in the Raid on the Sublime Porte. The CUP leadership then proceeded to consolidate their hold on power, garnering mass support when they were able to mitigate the empire's losses in the Balkan War, principally by taking back Edirne from Bulgaria.

The motor propelling the CUP as a force in politics and society throughout this period was the generational rebellion of the young military men from modest backgrounds in the Balkans, who resented the old guard of military and civilian leadership in the metropole. But owing to the small numbers of men with expertise in governance—and the lack of a revolutionary ideology to justify destroying the system and the empire in toto—the CUP leaders suppressed their own resentments and opted to use rather than overthrow the existing structures, personnel, and constitution. Instead, they sought to infiltrate the state and to take command from within, creating an empire within the empire. While they did not attempt to destroy the government and existing establishment wholesale, their tactic of taking over from within did not preclude purging and replacing sectors of the government at certain points. As this chapter shows, the tension between saving the empire and destroying its establishment would shape politics in the last decade of the empire's existence, and the politics of the early republic as it supplanted the empire.

ENTER *MUHALEFET*

Owing to its conspiratorial and secretive nature, it can often appear that the CUP leadership were carrying out a master plan from the start. Many historians impute an inevitability to the 1913 coup and its concomitant consolidation of power, assuming that it was a foregone conclusion as far back as 1908.[10] This involves positing that there was a clear polarization between the Unionists and their opponents before one had emerged. At the same time, it takes for granted that there was an instant shift in the concept of *muhalefet* circa 1908–9—from a position of opposition against Sultan Abdülhamid and the despotism associated with his reign to opposition against the CUP—an assumption that rests on the false notion that Hamidian hegemony was instantly replaced by Unionist hegemony. It also ignores the fact that before the CUP became the preeminent power in 1913, their rise to power was brimming with contestation from within and without. (See figure 1.)

During this period—which Refik Halid would, for his own reasons, look back on as marked by continuous and clear polarization—contestation was the norm, but the meaning of *muhalefet* was still evolving. As the CUP

FIGURE 1. Political cartoon from *Alem* in 1909 depicting the ills of the Ottoman Empire: "The Constitutional Struggle," or the battle between the Committee of Union and Progress and the Liberal Entente Party, occupies center stage. Courtesy of Palmira Brummett, *Image and Imperialism in the Ottoman Revolutionary Press* (Albany, NY: State University of New York Press, 2000), p. 138–9.

penetrated Ottoman politics and structures of governance, *muhalefet* was shifting from a broad meaning that encompassed all constitutionalist opposition to the Hamidian regime, to a more specific and complex one with at least two connotations. I refer to the first as "political/parliamentary opposition." This understanding of *muhalefet* included opposition *to* the CUP, rather than opposition to Abdülhamid's "despotism," an opposition of which the CUP had been a constituent part prior to 1908. The repurposing of the word *muhalefet* signaled none other than the breakdown of the constitutional coalition. That coalition was recombining as an opposition between the CUP on the one side, and on the other the various and sundry others who were opposed to them, on constitutionalist grounds or not. Early in the period examined here, *muhalefet* also returned to its old meaning of dissent and disagreement, an ideal that was seen by proponents of the constitution as a defining feature of a constitutional regime. One can see this connotation as more in line with the nineteenth-century meaning, in the academic discussions of the Young Ottomans during the Tanzimat era.

Refik Halid's writings in this period, which were simultaneously reporting on parliamentary debates and opposition and providing commentary on them, allow us to trace both of these meanings from the perspective of a keen observer who was not always aligned with the liberals but was nevertheless outside the CUP. By paying particular attention to his satirical writings between early 1910 and late 1912, we see that the usages of *muhalefet* slowly unfolded alongside broader political polarizations. Noting the processual nature of *muhalefet* is important for understanding how the Second Constitutional Era would be remembered in 1919 and after, and how the ideal of *muhalefet* would later be imagined, both for those who identified with it and for those who were in power. Despite his later assertions, the Porcupine was hardly a courageous and consistent *muhalif.* But he was a particularly talented and popular writer of satire, whose writings help us grasp the tumult of these years.

WRITERS AND JOURNALISTS:
CRUCIBLES OF OTTOMAN CONSTITUTIONALISM

The press sat at a crucial juncture of the dilemmas and contradictions of Ottoman constitutionalism. After the long period of surveillance and censorship under the Hamidian regime, the revolution restored freedom of the press and touted it as a central right guaranteed "within the limit of the law"

(Article 12 of the original 1876 Constitution). Within days after July 24, 1908, a flood of newspapers hit the market.[11] Among the hundreds of new publications were titles that operated from both partisan and nonpartisan positions. Some newspapers (e.g., *Tanin*, *Volkan*, and *İkdam*) were organs of a particular faction (or even the mouthpiece of an individual) and were directly bound up with the political struggles underway. Others claimed to be independent (such as *Aşiyan*), and many of those were satirical (*Cem*, *Karagöz*).[12] As Palmira Brummett writes, the press "addressed both the anxieties created by the disestablishment of the old regime and the underlying forces and conditions that had produced the revolution in the first place."[13]

Despite the important role they played and the proliferation of titles in the early days after the revolution, the wave of newspapers crested in late 1911; by spring 1913, the government had placed severe restrictions on journalists and the press. By June of that year, the Unionist (CUP) regime had exiled dissenting journalists and writers—along with hundreds of others associated with the political opposition—en masse to Anatolia. As the pendulum swung from near total freedom in 1908 to state censorship and exile in 1913, journalists and editors were subject to two opposing and simultaneous legal regimes. On the one hand, the law that guaranteed the constitutional freedom of the press and spelled out its legal limits, the Press Regulation of 1909, had made its way through the two chambers of the fledgling Assembly in the spring and was promulgated in July of that year. On the other hand, martial law (*idare-i örfi*)—declared as part of the response to the 31 March Incident—remained in effect until the fall of the Unionist regime in 1918. While rule of law existed on paper for the press and was guaranteed in the constitution, in practice, journalists had to contend with arbitrary limitations and penalties.[14] Newspapers were regularly shut down, often on the basis of having published material that was insulting or slanderous to prominent individuals or the government—a holdover from the censorship in the Hamidian era.[15] They would then reopen—sometimes as soon as the following day and under a new name—per a loophole in the Press Regulation. And while the Liberal Entente also closed newspapers such as the CUP organ *Tanin*, during their brief hold on power, the fate of journalists was more precarious under the Unionists.

In three assassinations that were catalysts for the polarization already underway, the CUP used paramilitary elements (*fedai*) to murder liberal journalists. In spring 1909, Hasan Fehmi of *Serbesti* (Freedom) was murdered on the Galata Bridge; the resulting public outcry became a catalyst for the 31 March Incident. In June 1910 Ahmed Samim, who wrote for *Seda-yı*

Milli (National echo), *İştirak* (Partnership), and *Osmanlı Gazetesi* (Ottoman gazette), was also shot.[16] And in July 1911 Zeki Bey, a secretary in the Public Debt Administration and an investigative journalist for the liberal *Şehrah* newspaper—who was in the process of uncovering a scandal involving finance minister and CUP member Cavid Bey and the European banker Ernest Cassel—was gunned down near his home in Bakırköy.[17]

The press became not only a venue for the development of a public sphere in which to work out the application of constitutionalism but also a violent theater for the contradictions within the post-1908 order. Those contradictions were by 1913 choking off the possibility for contestation in all of its forms, the press included.[18] For a brief moment the circumstances were ripe for satire, and there was a space in which to express it. It was in this context that Refik Halid began writing under his nom de plume, the Porcupine. The collected stories of the Porcupine, *The Porcupine's Utterances* (*Kirpinin Dedikleri*), provide us with a fascinating running commentary on these fraught years of Ottoman constitutionalism, as well as with a barometer for the changing meanings and usages of the word *muhalefet*. That same work—and in particular one joke— would eventually be the cause for Refik Halid's exile to Sinop, as he assumed his place within the newly specific category of *muhalefet*. And the Porcupine's silences provide us with valuable clues about the partisan affiliations that he harbored, despite his claims to nonpartisanship and independent thought.

THE PORCUPINE SPEAKS

While he was generally silent about events throughout the first year of the revolution, Refik Halid wrote one story about the 31 March Incident and its suppression, "Dervish Hasan's Conscience" ("Dede Hasan'ın Vicdanı"). The story appeared in *İştirak* (Comrade) in February 1910, just after his return from Paris and before he began publishing in *Cem*. Although it was not included in any of his published volumes, the story illuminates the author's transition from writing the Maupassant-esque stories discussed in chapter 1 to new forms of social and political satire, as well as the deep ambivalence of his outlook. At the heart is a moral dilemma reminiscent of his 1909 story "Ayşe's Destiny," but with a political-social critique that made it appropriate for publication in the empire's first socialist newspaper. The protagonist of this tale is an old dervish named Dede Hasan, who struggles with his conscience over whether to report his foster son, Memiş, for involvement in the insurrection. When the dervish decides to go to the authorities, Memiş is promptly arrested. But as he sees that the government has started executing people, he fluctuates between denial that they would do this to Memiş and the desire to find and save his son. After witnessing mass hangings and hearing and seeing that Memiş is among those who have been executed, Dede Hasan becomes distraught, feeling responsible for his foster son's death. Little does he know that the authorities had intended to arrest Memiş on the very night that the dervish denounced him.[19] Dede Hasan's moral prison—which he would have been condemned to for either reporting his son or not doing so—is reminiscent of Ayşe's moral prison as a common woman repeatedly victimized and with little or no recourse to justice.

The story suggests a reference to "Dervish Vahdeti," who played a leading role in the mutiny and was executed accordingly, and the timid reference shows how Refik Halid was beginning to dabble in politics but without taking a firm stand. It also points to the complex ways that Refik Halid was grappling with the inner conflicts caused by the external political situation. The relationship between father and foster son suggests the kind of unfinished patriotism among the empire's subjects that characterized the politics of the Second Constitutional Era. The heterogeneous Ottoman "family" of multiple millets, ethnicities, and confessions, despite the aspirational language of brotherhood, was never bonded as completely as a homogeneous blood family would be. After several months—or decades, if we count the nationality reforms and Ottomanist projects of the nineteenth century—of trying to will an Ottoman political family into being through discourses of freedom and brotherhood, the 31 March Incident demonstrated that when push came to shove, divisions trumped commonalities. Perhaps the most painful realization was that people were voluntarily choosing this path; like people in the panoply of factions who were denouncing each other to the authorities as "reactionaries" (mürteci), Dede Hasan had made a deliberate, if conflicted, moral decision to turn in his foster son.

"Dede Hasan's Conscience" was the first of many stories in the prolific period between March 1910 and November 1911, when Refik Halid penned works later published as The Porcupine's Utterances (Kirpinin Dedikleri). As mentioned previously, these stories provide a window onto his preoccupations and make clear that the targets of his humor were not always people we would expect. The picture of Ottoman society that he paints is interesting in that it is not always one wracked by polarization and violent conflict, even though this is how Refik Halid would later portray this period. The stories also do not focus on the singular plight or repression of journalists, presented as one of many failings of the period. Moreover, the CUP's members are one among many targets of satire in a variegated political and social landscape that he wrote of with much more nuance.

At center stage are manifold contests among the bureaucracy and citizenry; individuals, social classes, and parties; and the ideals and realities of constitutionalism. The Istanbul landscape was full of such absurdities, many of them stemming from the contestations between the old and new establishment that shared the political and social landscape and the unfulfilled expectations of *meşrutiyet* (constitutionalism) and *hürriyetler* (freedoms). This landscape was also rich in targets that included other "secret societies" (*cemiyât-i hafiye*) comprising elements opposed to and within the CUP. The Porcupine jokes with sarcasm about the gunning down of journalist Ahmet Samim in July 1910 in *Cem* and that of Zeki Bey in 1911. In December 1910, in the "Weekly Chatter" column written under the name "Vakanüvis" (the Court Chronicler), he parodied the Press Regulation, listing the articles of a kind of gag press law:

> Article 1: The press is free . . . and because of that, every gazette or daily newspaper must have a director that is not affiliated with any party or a member of any association (*cemaat*). Article 2: Any director violating Article 1 will be fined 1740 lira (in cash); or will be imprisoned for between 6 and 40 years. Anyone who is found to have such a newspaper in their possession will be arrested and deported from the country. Article 3: It is not necessary that the language in which an editor publishes a newspaper be written correctly by everyone. [*Müdir-i musevelin gazetenin intişar ettiği lisanda kitabet edecek kadar beheresi olmak şart değildir*].

In January 1911, in "The Secrets of the New Year" ("Yeni Senenin Esrarı"), published in *Cem*, the Porcupine even makes fun of the legal catch-22 in which the press found itself. In the context of a conversation between his alter ego and a fortune-teller making predictions for the new year, the Porcupine asks, "Will *Cem* be shut down?" In response, the fortune-teller states, "Fear not! As long as there is martial law [*idare-i örfi*] it will not be shut down. But beware of the new Press Regulation!" Porcupine concludes, "And with this warning, it was easy to discover the secret of the new year!"[20] Contemporary readers would have grasped the ironic commentary on authoritarian democracy: a newspaper would be protected under martial law but be in danger of being shut down under the supposedly liberal Press Regulation—precisely the opposite of what one would expect in a constitutional regime.

The hazards of writing and journalism—and with that the contradictions of constitutionalism—were as obvious as they were absurd.

In late October 1910 the Porcupine was already reflecting on his short-lived internship from 1908 to 1909, yet obscuring the political context of his dismissal. This was his first, and failed, post in government financial administration—a position that was cut short by CUP-led purges—prior to his move to Paris. The experience provided fodder for a witty story titled "How Did I Become an Intern in a Bureau?" Rather than contrast himself with the Unionists, he compares his European sensibilities and upbringing with his colleagues in the Ottoman bureaucracy, whom he sees as mired in tradition and medieval formality. The message is that he is a modern, Western, beer-drinking youth who cannot fit into the Ottoman bureaucracy and who promptly departs. As mentioned in chapter 1, it is more likely that he was purged by the CUP in the wake of the counterrevolution.[21] Refik Halid's choice not to mention his dismissal would undermine his claims to independent, nonpartisan journalism and concede his membership in the establishment that he later claimed to oppose.

Perhaps more important, the story highlighted how the idea of contestation for its own sake was coming to be at odds with his vested class and partisan political interests. This was a theme in his hugely popular and most famous story, "How Do They Collect Taxes?" ("Vergiyi nasıl toplarlar?"), published in Cem in early December 1910. Here, the Porcupine again comments on the ironies of the new rule of law. In a parody of a Socratic dialogue, he writes,

> The other day I was walking slowly by the Ministry of Justice, when I ran into a friend. After asking me whether the cabinet would fall or not, and whether the Interior Minister would get violent and beat the opposition MP's during his speech, he then said: "Where to? What are you doing here?"
>
> The narrator responds to his friend, "People were saying that the Ayasofya mosque was going to be torn down, so since I thought this might be my last chance I figured I would come down and have a little look; I've got nothing else to do and a lot of time." He continues, "My friend took me by the arm and led me through the threshold of the Justice Ministry, saying, 'if that's the case, then come on, let's go listen to the court cases and have a good time!'"
>
> Once through the door, they find their way through the dark corners where boot-wearing petition-writers are standing, writing petitions for their squatting customers, all amidst the sickening stench of a tannery, with cigarette smoke, bad breath, and body odor. At that point they heard names being called—"Nadir Efendi! Fevzi Efendi! Şakir Bey! Hasip Efendi!" and they knew a court case was about to be heard, so they went in.

The accused was being addressed by the judge: "Look, what are they saying about you? Last November 1st, when taxes were due, you obstructed the civil servants Nadir, Fevzi, and Hasip Efendis from coming into your house to carry out their duties and collect the taxes you owed! How did this happen? Tell us, then!"

The defendant stood up; he was about 50 years old; he stood for a while, gulped, looked first at the judge, then at the sultan's seal (*tuğra*) on the wall, then at the ceiling, like a man coveting a dead man's possessions [*terekeden mal beğenir gibi*], and finally said:

"Your Honor, let me ask you first, how do they collect taxes? Have you seen?"

The judge shot back, "You have no right to ask me questions! Get on with it!"

The accused didn't pay any attention, and went on:

"Yes, how do they collect the taxes, have you seen? They shouldn't even call it collecting, they should call it breaking and entering. . . . The toll collector on the [Galata] bridge collects his 10 *kuruş* more politely, a bear cuts his pear off the tree more pleasantly, a dentist extracts a tooth, a horse-shoe maker removes a horse shoe, and a storm rips an oak tree out of the ground more politely, more humanely than that. . . . Let me start from the beginning:

"About 20 days ago, I was sitting at home with the family talking, when we heard a rapping at the door. I stuck my head out the window and looked—my God! Coaches had surrounded our house, people had gathered outside, *imams, muhtars*, everyone from the neighborhood had come into the square, they were looking into the [police] cage, pointing at our doors and windows, shaking their heads, mumbling things. What was it? Was there a fire? A raid (*baskın*)? A hanging (*askın*)? I didn't know what. . . . I opened the window and asked:

"'What do you want, sirs?'

"In response to my polite address I got about 70 buzzing, threatening moans, the street heaved like the seas bringing up their depths, and finally the imam's voice was heard:

"'Open up, sir, we're coming in!'

"A policeman added, 'In the name of the law!'

"People murmured to each other:

'In the name of the law, huh? Oy, in the name of the law!'

"When my wife heard this, like a hanged man on a rotten rope she dropped, 'boom!' on the floor; the kids, yelling like new army recruits, ran and enveloped her; the cook grabbed me by the skirts like a white-shirted toll-collector on the bridge; the butler slipped away with all the skill of a policeman. Which one would I look to? Of course I left everyone in the state they were in and went downstairs and opened the door. . . . As soon as I unlocked it, the brave fellow in the front pushed it open, and with a noise heard around the neighborhood, the door swung open and into the wall, he hopped over me like a trapeze artist and flew up the stairs. . . . The other officials (*memurlar*) followed suit. There were 25 people in the courtyard; people were waiting outside, the coach-drivers were cracking their whips; the neighbors had climbed all over the police cages, and were watching us. I approached one of them: 'What is it, sir,' I said, 'to what do I owe this visit?' He looked me right in the face: 'Who are you?' he said.

"'The owner of the house!'

"'Prove it!'

"I froze in astonishment. My wife had fainted, my servant had fled; as for my cook, she didn't even know Turkish, let alone whether I was the owner of the house. . . . Finally the imam came to my aid; then they explained:

"'You owe taxes! You haven't paid, should we confiscate your things?' However, Your Honor, you know that they are supposed to send three warnings, and they didn't, so how was I supposed to pay the money. . . . I wanted to appeal it, I proposed paying in installments, they wouldn't let me, the news went down to the station, and then the sound of soldiers marching was heard! They started coming to the house and looking around. . . . My God! Why was it necessary to have so many people? Twenty men, twenty civil servants (*memur*), between the ages of 18 and 55, skinny, fat, bearded, clean-shaven, some with embroidered collars, some with beribboned trousers, but all of them dirty, looking for things to confiscate. They tracked mud in from the street, all the way up to the ceiling in the kitchen, they got their dirty paws on everything, they straightened their ties and arranged their fezzes in the mirrors, and in the middle of all this confusion I looked and this man (tall and thin, with sunken cheeks, with a scar under his moustache) had climbed onto my daughter's wedding couch (*gelinlik kanepesi*) with his muddy feet, batting around the dirt like a cat, and staring out at the Bozdoğan Kemeri [an aqueduct in Istanbul, implying that the house is in Old Istanbul; home to established and respectable Muslim families]: 'What are you doing, sir?' I said, 'this is a sin, this is where a person will sit later on!'

"He didn't even pay attention. . . . He even called his friend over, inviting him to enjoy the view of the aqueduct with him. This was the last straw. The blood had risen to my head, and I said: 'This furniture that you've stepped all over with your hooves isn't a pile of manure in front of the prefecture, you know!' At that moment a sharp hammering sound came to my ears, and I ran to the next room; three men were squatting down, doing something, I looked: Are they hammering nails into a piano?!

"'What are you doing!' I shouted, 'Have you gone mad?'

"One of them, in perfect calm, answered:

"'In order to sequestrate the piano we're going to nail the piano to the wall and stamp it—that's the procedure!'

"With every strike of the hammer, each string of the poor instrument was making a separate sound, the poor thing was bellowing like a duck being strangled. The men were hammering as if they had learned the skill from Istavri, the [Greek] carpenter that built our house. I couldn't bear it any longer, I took the hammer from the man's hands (the fat one with the chubby cheeks and the scarred whiskers) and I said, exactly as I'm telling you now: 'Get lost, you scoundrel (*Defol buradan haydut*),' I said, 'even if a bandit breaks into my house he's not going to drive nails into my piano, whose gang are you part of, anyway?'

"At this, the men all stopped their searching and surrounded me: 'We are civil servants, constitutional servants (*meşrutiyet memuruyuz*)! We're going to report you to the Security Directorate, send you to the Court Martial, and throw you in the *Bekirağa Bölüğü* prisons!' they yelled; had I continued my tirade any longer, these so-called "constitutional servants" would have decided to have me hanged. By this point they were frothing at the mouth, putting all of their heads together over my things and pointing their fingers at me, saying, 'Reactionary! Reactionary! (*Mürteci*)' and with their hot wax, putting their seal wherever they happened upon, like right in the middle of my daughter's dowry mirror, right on the beak of the stork on our lacquer screen, right on the signatures of our oil paintings. The house reeked of candle wax.

"Finally they wrote something on some papers, they started signing like crazy, must have been 30 times, they made me stamp everything, and they left. . . . I closed the door as they were getting into their coaches, sitting in their seats, puffed up with pride and self-importance in front of the shocked crowd still gathered on the street; I flew down to the kitchen with the aim of finding the butler and sending him to the judge, thinking Mehmet must be there, since I could hear the clinking of copper pots and pans.

"I opened the door. . . . Oh, Your Honor, what do you think I saw? This kid (18 years old, puny, pale) had gotten to the stove, and was popping bites of every food he found from the pots and pans there, filling up his stomach. . . . 'What are you looking for here?' I said, and he got startled. And then again, 'What are you looking for? What?!' And he responded, 'something to be confiscated!' . . . He wasn't looking for things to be confiscated, but only food to be digested (*haczolunacak eşya değil, hazmolunacak yemek arıyordu*). I took him by the tail of his riding coat and threw this imbecile out onto the street, and that's the end of my story!"

The defendant, in accordance with article 113 of the penal code, was made to pay a penalty of 3 gold *mecidiye*s. On the way out I approached him, and said:

"You should file a suit against them, see, they slandered you by calling you a reactionary (*mürteci*)!"

My interlocutor looked at me, and said: "Why should I sue them? . . . Let them be the liberals (*Hürriyetperver onlar olsunlar*), as long as I'm not one of those who drive nails into pianos!"

This rich story raises the question of what exactly the Porcupine was lampooning: not the political platform of the CUP per se, but both sides of a sociopolitical encounter. On one side were Young Turk civil servants, with their utter lack of culture and manners, philistine tactics, and hypocrisy in using the language of liberalism and constitutionalism to coerce upstanding, middle-class citizens of Istanbul into submission. On the other side stood the rather ridiculous members of the middle-class establishment itself. The civil servants come in and make a mockery of bureaucracy and the rule of law, using their seals and signing a flurry of documents while mindlessly turning a respectable middle-class household upside down. And the man of the household, with his accoutrements of the Westernized Ottoman bourgeoisie, stands appalled and defenseless, unable to even make his case effectively in court. At once a critique aimed at the constitutional regime, it also addresses the absurdities of the establishment. The unfinished nature of the CUP takeover comes through in the terms Refik Halid uses: *mürteci*, or reactionary, the name deployed by the Unionists to discredit their opponents; and *Hürriyetperver*, or liberal, since there was still a liberal camp to speak of, implicitly opposed to the CUP.

Despite his open disdain for the CUP types, Porcupine did not neglect targeting the liberals, either. In his late November 1910 piece, "Individual Initiative? Alas!," he takes aim at Prince Sabahaddin's concept of "Individual Initiative and Decentralization" (*Teşebbüs-ü Şahsi ve Adem-i Merkeziyet*), a doctrine and party/movement established in 1906 that was supposed to be the answer to centralist modernization.[22] Porcupine takes up Prince Sabahaddin's view that if each person could have more initiative, then society would modernize. This is shown as the narrator, speaking with his old classmate, gets in an argument about such "individual initiative." At the mention of this phrase, the narrator's friend—who had been nodding off—jumps to attention and launches into a tirade about how he has applied for thirty different jobs in the two years since the revolution. He has been trying to practice individual initiative, but to no avail. After acquiring a bureaucratic post earning 400 kuruş a month, he finds that

"one day freedom came out, the flags unfurled, and the people poured into the streets. I saw young and old, children and families, rich and poor, candidates for office, neighborhood *muhtar*s, people pawning mattresses, selling children's talismans, and everyone started getting guns; walking around all cocky with knives in their belts . . . saying, 'I belong to the Unionists! I belong to the liberals (*İttihattanim, Ahrardanım!*).' I applied here, I asked for help from there, and finally I opened up a gun shop. Business was so good that 5 or 10 times a day I was throwing my fez up in the air, shouting, 'Long Live Freedom! Long Live Individual Initiative!'"

But then one day they banned weapons longer than 10 centimeters; then 5 centimeters; then it was no longer possible to earn a living like that. Out of work, he "started looking everywhere, and even applied to clean the offices at the Patriarchate and to be a ticket collector on the tramway"; finally I "decided to found a newspaper. . . . *Mecmuai Havadis*" [similar to Refik Halid's own *Son Havadis*]. That was a flop, too. So I went into journalism, thinking that surely I would become rich and famous that way. But soon enough, another order:

"mentioning this, conveying that is unacceptable, caution should be exercised, and a week later: a fine of 40 lira. . . . Oh man, there is no way out; then it became 5, 10 days in prison, we get into a coach, and are taken into custody! Now the people accuse me of being a reactionary because I wrote against their spring waters, and they boycott my newspaper . . . of course then the newspaper offices close, take their sign down, and we are out on the streets!"

Searching around again, even applying to be the interpreter for a Greek (*Rum*) parliamentarian [a minor absurdity], he decides to become a farmer. When that does not work out, as a last resort he becomes the governor of a province in Anatolia, planning to use his individual initiative to turn it into a veritable Swiss village. His hopes are dashed when thousands of people show up at his office protesting, with flags that say, "Freedom or death! Crete or war!" "What are these?" he asks, "is this about Crete?" "No," they say, "those are old flags. We are having a protest against you!" When he tries to speak, they shout him down, saying: "Damn the governor! Long live the Committee of Union and Progress!" (*Cemiyet*). After trying arms-dealing, journalism, farming, and public service, he concludes, "so much for individual initiative!"[23]

Alas, the alternative to the CUP—the liberals with their doctrine of individual initiative—only creates more absurdities, as we see in this story. Reflecting already in late 1910 on the previous few years, and thinly veiling parts of his own experience (in a post in 1908–9, as a newspaper publisher and then journalist), the Unionists were certainly an element in Refik Halid's story, but not yet the sole force to oppose in politics. And contestation is everywhere, even in the unruly Anatolian town. Within this indeterminate landscape, we do see the term *muhalefet* used, but in several contexts and with several connotations, even in this one volume of the Porcupine's stories. At times it is used to mean opposition, as in disagreement and dissent as a constituent part of a constitutional regime. In "Ramazan, the Drum, and the Cabinet," from August 1911, Refik Halid opens his allegorical essay with the line, "Just like you cannot have Ramazan without a *davul* [the drum that wakes people in the morning to rise and eat before the fast at sunrise], so you cannot have constitutionalism without *muhalefet*." In other contexts, being a journalist is dangerous, such as in the individual initiative story; the danger lies not yet in the risk of offending the CUP exclusively, but in inadvertently eliciting the ire of the people by insulting something they hold dear, even something as innocuous as their spring water.

The last story to be written in the original collection of *Kırpının Dedikleri* is "Advice to the Chinese Constitutionalists" from late 1911. It is fascinating, betraying the disillusionment Refik Halid and others felt three years into the Second Constitutional Era, framed as cautionary advice to the Chinese constitutionalists, whose adventure had just begun that October. This is also the story that would be the cause for Refik Halid's exile two years later. Writing that he had heard ("and, as they say, the sound of the drum is nice from afar") that China had risen up and "decided to show its ability and talent by opening a National Assembly," he declares his wish to help by offering the Chinese words of wisdom that he has gleaned from his own experiences. He wishes them well, sending a prayer that they won't have to go through what his own land has gone through in the last few years. His intent, tongue in cheek, is to share his experience, as a humble servant "in the name of humanity," to warn them of what they should avoid and what not to avoid.

His address contains twelve points (repeatedly making a play on words between Huda, the Persian-Ottoman term for God, and Buddha, writing, "I hope that Buddha protects you from things ending up the way they have here!"), many statements of which are references to particular figures in politics whom he does not name, but whom readers at the time would have recognized. In point 4, he declares sardonically, "Constitutionalism means martial law. The court martial is the guardian of the constitution." Point 5: "Do not do purges with the goal of taking the hat that is on Ahmet's head and putting it on your Mehmet's ... and don't boast, "we are saving the government by chopping up the map of the homeland (*vatan*) into little pieces." This was nothing less than a frontal assault on the contradictions of the CUP and the constitutional regime.

Point 10 is a series of seemingly vague pieces of advice that refer to specific events and people, ending with what everyone seemed to understand was a joke about CUP leader Talaat [Paşa]: "Do not dress those suddenly in a European frock coat (*frak*) who are used to wearing robes (*hırka*). It is ridiculous." And Point 11: "For the *memleket* to progress on the road to justice, first the notables/senators (*ayan*) should not shrink from publishing their *jurnal* (spy reports), parliamentarians from falling into their old needs, *journalists from taking bullets in the head* [a reference to Zeki Bey, gunned down a few months earlier], and the people from being subjected to the rod [referring to the CUP's violence and intimidation tactics]."[24] By late 1911, then, Refik Halid's criticism was coming to focus more specifically on the CUP and the contradictions between their violent, extraconstitutional tactics and the constitutionalism the party's adherents were claiming to guard—even if the liberal opposition was also not above using violence to advance their cause.

The CUP leadership, in their own party newspapers, took note of Refik Halid's criticisms. Like his three friends who had been gunned down—Hasan Fehmi, Ahmed Samim, and Zeki Bey—Refik Halid later recalled that he had routinely received threatening letters "with a picture of a *tabanca* or Mauser [types of guns] instead of a signature at the bottom."[25] *Tanin*, the CUP party organ, ran many violent diatribes against him, some as lead articles; prominent Unionist Süleyman Nazif also published pieces critical of him in *Hak*.

THE PORCUPINE 2.0

After a hiatus starting in late 1911, the Porcupine resurfaced again in July 1912, penning six stories that would be collected along with most of the original thirty in a second edition of *Kirpinin Dedikleri*. In 1920 the publication was issued under very different circumstances and toward a different end, which I take up in chapter 4. The six stories merit examination because they reflect the polarization that took place between late 1911 and mid-1912: namely, the period when the nominally nonpartisan Great Cabinet (Büyük Kabine) under Ahmed Muhtar Paşa was formed, which allowed the CUP opponents to have their turn in power, and when the Balkan War broke out. These stories are much more pointedly directed against the CUP. They criticize the Unionists' violent tactics and hypocritical program at a time when it was safe and opportune to level direct criticism. The stories were the last pieces of political satire Refik Halid would pen until after World War I.

In general, the pieces from 1912 are much more pointed in their humor and much more focused in their criticism of the CUP. In "Until the Second 10th of July" (July 10 was the date of the revolution in the old calendar), written in July 1912, just before the Great Cabinet took over, Refik Halid reflects on the last few years, arguing that the empire is in fact living through a "second tyranny" (*istibdad*), the term ordinarily reserved for Abdülhamid's reign. He likens the situation to one in which the "house of government, as if on fire on its uppermost floors is being looted by those attempting to save themselves." He highlights the hangings, beatings, and torture that went on in the Bekirağa prison-barracks in the wake of the 31 March Incident in 1909 and the "caravans" of those exiled for being in a "secret society" (the societies uncovered by the CUP in the ranks of the military).[26] He mocks the recent elections (in April 1912), known as the *sopalı seçim*, or stick elections, because of the beatings and violence that preceded them: "Fill the prisons to the gills with newspaper publishers, and the journalists, throw them in prison one at a time, trickling like the faucets of Kırkçeşme, and lock them up with the court martial's key—and oh these elections were really by the books!" He adds that these elections were "a page straight out of the book of evils belonging to the trial of Zeki Bey [the third journalist who had been shot down, in July 1911]."

In "If Union and Progress Wins" ("İttihat ve Terakki galebe ederse") from September 1912, he imagines what would happen if the CUP were to win the next election (which never took place due to the outbreak of the Balkan War). He begins with an address: "Citizens! In these elections, keep your mouth shut and your eyes wide open!" and proceeds to predict the absurdities that will happen if the CUP were to win. Among other predictions, he says that the "'*muhalif muharrirler*' or *muhalif* writers will be annihilated, not in the uncivilized way, with bullets and knives, but with electric power . . . and in this way it will have more blessed (*bereketli*) and beneficial (*faydalı*) results," mocking here the CUP's adulation of technological modernization.

And finally, in "What Must the Unionist Committee Do?" ("İttihat Cemiyeti ne yapmalı?"), from late September 1912, he provides advice, facetious of course, to the CUP candidates to assure their victory in the next election. They should, according to him, circulate a proclamation that promises the "poor people" that they will, among other things, bury Talaat Bey (Paşa) up to his waist and stone him; close down *Tanin* (the CUP organ), set Cavid Bey (Salonican *dönme*, or crypto-Jew, and former CUP finance minister) in the shop window of the Salonica Bonmarché and leave him there for forty days and nights as an example, and even strip Halacyan Efendi (an Armenian parliamentary deputy and member of the CUP) naked and shave his head so it (i.e., his head and mind) can be truly "enlightened."

What we see in these pieces from 1912 is the *idea* of *muhalefet* taking a more consolidated and partisan shape. It is used not just to mean parliamentary opposition or the dissent voiced by journalists in the press. Rather, it is opposition expressly directed at the CUP as a force antithetical to the ideals of constitutionalism. Now, under the Grand Vezirate of the nonpartisan cabinet of Ahmed Muhtar, it was safe to attack the CUP. But even as he did so, Refik

Halid did not criticize the so-called Savior Officers (Halaskâr Zabıtaları), an informal assemblage of anti-Unionist military men whom the Liberal Entente used for the sort of extraconstitutional tactics that they had criticized the CUP for. This decision betrays the fact that the burgeoning imagination of *muhalefet*, or contestation, was one in which one's own partisanship had to be downplayed. Refik Halid could contest the CUP's tactics and call out the party's hypocrisy, but it was not in his interest to reveal his own partisan affiliations or material interest in voicing such criticisms. Instead, he had to maintain the stance of an independent and persecuted journalist.

It is telling, then, that Refik Halid, at least in his persona as the Porcupine, seems to have written nothing about the Balkan War as it was taking place. This is striking, first because the war was such a significant propaganda event, at least for the CUP, given the victimization of Muslim communities in the Balkans and the significance of the Balkans in the CUP imaginary. The Ottoman defeat is portrayed by historians as having galvanized mass sentiment against non-Muslims and thereby serving as a point of unity for an incipient and extreme nationalism.[27] Refik Halid was associated with the liberal opposition to the CUP, and because of his class and Istanbul origins he was not particularly attached to the Balkans in the way the Unionists were. For him, the defeat was likely just as much of a disaster, but a disaster for the liberals as much as for any incipient nation. He seems to have refrained from criticizing them for their mismanagement of the war, at least at the time. Was it beyond the limits of his *muhalif* journalism to draw attention to the defeat and the liberals' role in bringing it about? Was partisanship starting to consume the space of independent journalism and political commentary? Or was he already so compromised by his associations with the Great Cabinet and the liberals that he did not have a leg left to stand on?

On January 7, 1913, in what turned out to be the final weeks of the Great Cabinet, Refik Halid was appointed to his second government post, that of Serkâtib, or head clerk, in the Beyoğlu prefecture of Istanbul. Presumably this appointment was a reward for his scathing anti-CUP articles. Once again, his patron was Ahmed İhsan (Tokgöz), liberal and now the Beyoğlu prefecture director under Mayor Cemil Paşa (Topuzlu). Just as his first appointment had been suddenly terminated in the staff purges following the 31 March Incident in 1909, his second would also be short lived due to the January 23 Raid on the Sublime Porte. Refik Halid retreated to his family's villa in Erenköy and reportedly ceased writing. But he seems to have continued collecting a salary for what turned out to be a sinecure. This was yet another indicator of the ways the members of the establishment were able to remain in place with their privileges, even under a supposed CUP dictatorship.

THE CRYSTALLIZATION OF *MUHALEFET*

Muhalefet as a coherent form or idea of opposition expressly against the CUP did not instantly spring forth in 1908. Rather, its shape and meanings evolved as the role of the CUP, the inability of opponents to rule or provide a viable alternative to CUP authoritarianism, and the problem of contestation unfolded throughout the Second Constitutional Era. As the CUP leaders consolidated power, they added extensive restrictions to the 1909 Press Regulation regarding licensing, circulation, and penalties, most severely in the spring of 1913. While the constitution was still formally in effect, the "limits of the law" were becoming more and more restrictive.[28] Journalists and writers like Refik Halid were caught in the crosshairs between the freedoms and rational regulation of the 1909 Press Regulation on the one hand and the exigencies of martial law on the other. By late 1911, the polarization between the Unionists and liberals began to crystallize. Both factions started referring to *muhalefet* as something expressly directed at the CUP. Opposition and contestation became intrinsic to politics; the problem was that there was no space for dissent in the authoritarian order established by the CUP; opposition, as far as the Unionists were concerned, was tantamount to conservative, anticonstitutional reaction.

A treatise from this moment demonstrates the ways *muhalefet* was crystallizing as something directly opposed to, and in fact the polar opposite of, the CUP. In 1913 a *muhalif* and Sufi, Sehbenderzâde Filibeli Ahmet Hilmi, wrote a treatise analyzing the dynamics between the Unionists and their opposition, *Muhalefetin İflası: Hürriyet ve İtilaf Fırkası* (The bankruptcy of *Muhalefet*: The Freedom and Accord Party).[29] This might be considered the first narrative analysis of *muhalefet* in the Second Constitutional Era. In it, Filibeli Ahmed Hilmi enumerates the seven accusations against the CUP that prompted Miralay Sadık Bey to split from the organization and spearhead the formation of the Freedom and Accord Party—an attempt to collect diverse opposition groups together—a few years earlier, in 1911. The seven accusations, negated in order to form the seven principles of the opposition, were as follows:

1. [The Committee of] Union and Progress interferes in government affairs.

2. They give preference to their own people for national posts (*milli vazifeleri*).

3. Their leaders [unlawfully] attach to government ministries.

4. They issue orders according to their whims rather than law and order.

5. Some of the Committee's esteemed members have formed a secret society/cabal.

6. They do not seek official sanction for their authorities and dignitaries.

7. In place of lawful arms and reason, the principles of revolution and the Committee are used to justify the army and the government's use of overpowering force.[30]

The program for *muhalefet*, to the extent that a coherent program can be said to have existed—and for the Freedom and Accord Party in particular—was defined in direct opposition to the perceived violations of the Unionists. This occurred just as Refik Halid and so many others in the press were honing their satirical skills as an expression of *muhalefet*. It is evident, then, that between 1911 and 1913, *muhalefet* was evolving both as a coordinated partisan opposition to the CUP *and* at the same time as a more diffuse space in which to exchange diverse views and analysis—a holdover of the Young Ottomans' notion of the concept. *Muhalifs* included journalists and writers who were independent; practiced *muhalefet* as part of their profession in a constitutional order; and discussed the merits and flaws of partisan *muhalefet*, as Filibeli Ahmed Hilmi was doing, as well as the partisan opponents of the CUP party-regime, such as affiliates of Prince Sabahaddin. Refik Halid was participating in *muhalefet* in both its partisan and idealistic/intellectual meanings.

The CUP targeted the opposition in both of its forms after fully realizing power through the Raid on the Porte on January 23, 1913. After the assassination of Mahmud Şevket Paşa—the elder statesman and military figure who had lent credibility to the CUP by serving as the Grand Vezir—in June, the CUP took the full reins of power. And within days of Mahmud Şevket's death, Cemal Paşa had more than eight hundred men associated with the *muhalefet* arrested. Four days later, they were deported en masse to Sinop. The Porcupine was number 834 on the list. He was rounded up, held in Bekirağa prison barracks, and then deported. Refik Halid claimed that he was on the list for insulting Talaat Paşa in the story "Advice to Chinese Constitutionalists." By mocking the pasha for looking ridiculous in a European suit, he took aim at his lower-class, Balkan background and no doubt struck a deep nerve. Certainly the personal animosity between the two—the patrician, who resented his own political marginalization, and the provincial who, still insecure, was taking over the political arena—must have been part of the motivation. But one might also surmise that Refik Halid's close association with the liberals—particularly his writings in the service of the Great Cabinet—would have been enough to place him on the list of deportees. The divergence between his account and his actual role in the opposition might be understood as an attempt by Refik to downplay his partisan associations and loyalties and to emphasize his opposition through more subtle satirical critiques. Regardless of why he had been exiled, he was now at a safe remove from the capital, at least from the perspective of the Unionist leadership, and in the camp of *muhalefet*. The next chapter follows him to Sinop and shows the extent to which the Porcupine fulfilled this new role, as well as the extent to which identification as a *muhalif* still contained deep contradictions.

THREE

The Joke
(1913–1918)

THE DEPORTATIONS TO SINOP in June 1913 were the final blow leveled by the Unionists to *muhalefet* in the capital. Cemal Paşa, then the military governor of Istanbul, described in his memoir how in the days after the January 1913 Raid on the Sublime Porte he had already met with those whom he considered the "brains" of the opposition. He wrote:

> On my second day after entry into office [January 1913] I went to the garrison headquarters, and visited Ali Kemal Bey as well as Rıza Nur and Ismael Bey of Gumuldjina, the deputies for Sinope, who were interned there.[1] I gave them the . . . assurance that they were in no danger if they abandoned all idea of untimely opposition. I remarked that in these unhappy times the country needed the help of all reasonable and well-disposed men, and that if they believed in my good intentions I could give them an honorable field of labor. Ali Kemal wanted some post in Europe. Dr. Rıza Nur asked for the money necessary to prosecute his medical studies in Paris. Ismael Paşa gave me his word of honor that if he were allowed to remain in the country he would refrain from any opposition to the Government until normal conditions were restored.[2]

With Dr. Rıza Nur in Paris, Ali Kemal in Vienna, and Ismael (Gümülcineli İsmail Hakkı Bey) under what was effectively a gag order in Istanbul, the Unionists turned their attention to the press. In March 1913 addenda were added to the 1909 Press Law, including unprecedented restrictions on printing, importing, and circulating press material. The press "was forbidden to publish, under penalty of suppression and expulsion of editors, any references to reported differences in the Cabinet or rumours of its resignation."[3] But in his dealings with the editors of the major papers, Cemal Paşa reached another gentleman's agreement, writing that

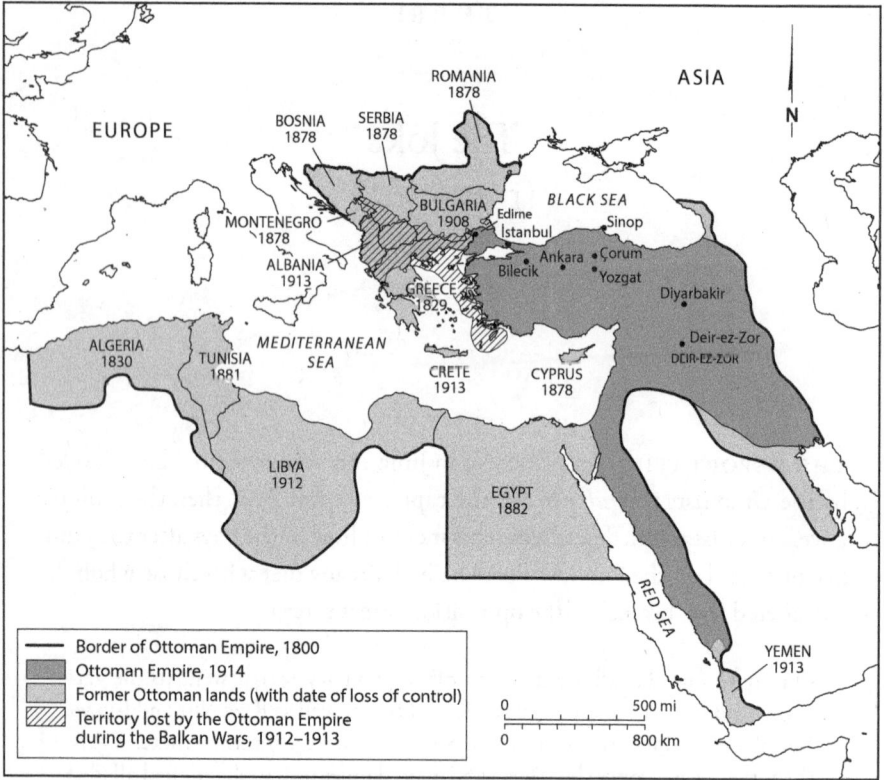

MAP 2. The Ottoman Empire by 1914, including territory lost over the course of the previous century

I invited the editors of the principal newspapers of the capital to call upon me, and told them that their papers would be subjected to a very mild censorship only if they would undertake to publish no articles of a kind to imperil public order. I asked them to write articles of a general and helpful nature, to enlighten public opinion and rouse the new forces which the Fatherland needed for its salvation. I desired to allow even the most violent organs of the Opposition to continue publication, organs which dated from the time of the previous Ministry. The latter certainly exceeded on occasion the instructions given them, but I confined myself to making representation to their editors or responsible directors.[4]

When Grand Vezir and elder statesman Mahmud Şevket Paşa was assassinated a few months later, Cemal Paşa had already compiled a list of individuals he deemed dangerous:

Anticipating some such occurrence, I had previously made the officials at the Police Prefecture draw up a list of all persons of every class who might be expected to exploit the situation and start riots in the different quarters of the city. I had given instruction to the Prefect of Police, Azmi Bey, to arrest offhand everyone on this list at the first serious attempt at a rising. Azmi Bey reported to me that this order, given long ago, had just been carried out, and asked where the persons arrested should be taken to. Said Halim Paşa, the Interim Grand Vezir, Hadji Adil Bey [sic], Minister for the Interior, and I decided that in order to keep the capital quiet it was necessary to send the prisoners to Sinope and supply them with sufficient money. I asked the Shipping Administration to fit out a ship to take them, and asked Azmi Bey to have all the arrests carried out in the course of the night so that they could be put on board and sent away by the next evening. I also had Damad Salih Paşa and others whom I knew to be involved in the plot arrested and examined by the police.[5]

The government swept through and arrested the *muhalif*s from their homes across the city. This raised alarm among onlookers such as Lütfi Fikri Bey, the noted lawyer and liberal opposition figure, who was spared deportation and promptly fled to Paris.[6] After a few days at the Bekirağa prison barracks in Istanbul, the detainees were sent by steamship to Sinop. One among hundreds, Refik Halid spread out his sleeping mat on the ship's deck next to the likes of Mustafa Suphi, a former Unionist who had split from the party relatively late.[7]

While many of these eight hundred deportees would be set free and allowed to return to Istanbul two years later, Sinop was but the first stop in a succession of Anatolian cities and towns where Refik Halid and about thirty others would be exiled. He moved in this period from Sinop (June 1913–July 1915) to Çorum (July 1915–July 1916), to Ankara (July–October 1916), and finally farther west to Bilecik (late 1916–January 1918) before returning to Istanbul. These cities were peripheral in the context of Ottoman imperial culture and political power and at a safe remove from the fields of battle. For the erstwhile Porcupine, these years were the least productive of his life. When he was finally allowed to return home, it was early 1918, and Istanbul was in the last months of the long, bitter war. When he returned to the capital, he was still treated with deep suspicion, and Ottoman documents from this period refer to him as "Refik Halid Bey, known under the sobriquet 'Kirpi,'" a figure "[who] is not at all to be trusted." And yet, as we shall see, he had hardly been an outspoken or consistent *muhalif* while in exile. His experiences and writings during this period make it possible to chart the significance of being cast out of the capital—and from his career in politics and journalism. As we follow Refik through Anatolia, we see the ways in which he was insulated from both the privations of the war in Istanbul and the dangers of war at the front. At the same time, against the backdrop of an important episode in the Armenian Genocide, we also see his complicity in Unionist-led state violence, a complicity that was integral to how he maintained his position of privilege in the larger Ottoman establishment. While his words, before and after the war, were words of opposition and defiance, his literary writings in exile were social realist, and his actions during the war tell a story of silent complicity with the worst of Unionist crimes. This in turn exposes the limits of *muhalefet* as opposition: it may have been opposition to the Unionists, but it was an opposition that fit safely within the confines of the broader establishment.

SINOP

Roughly four hundred miles from Istanbul, the picturesque Black Sea port town of Sinop is located at the tip of a narrow peninsula, "bound to Anatolia by an isthmus as fine as a cotton string."[8] At the time of the Porcupine's exile, it was home to about eight thousand inhabitants and a recently renovated fortress, as well as shipyards that had been used as a prison since 1885.[9] The town had a sizable Christian population, mainly Rum, and several drinking establishments that would later feature in stories inspired by Refik Halid's time there. Since it suddenly became home to so many Istanbul opposition figures, one can imagine that it must have felt like something between an extended intellectual retreat and an alienating and stark exile. This is indeed what Ahmet Bedevi Kuran, a personal secretary to Prince Sabahaddin who later became a historian of the Young Turk era, suggests in his vivid description of the people and places of Sinop, written in the 1940s.[10]

A town squeezed between a fortress and the sea, Sinop was the perfect open-air prison. Among the range of various figures contained there, Kuran mentioned Refik Halid as well as Refii Cevat, İsmail Hakkı, and (Doktor) Celâl Paşa by name. "The Sinop exiles were such a collection of characters," he writes, "it resembled a concentration camp. Here it was possible for one to find people selected from all classes back in Istanbul [as Cemal Paşa had claimed when describing the assortment of those being exiled]. *Hacıs* and *hocas*, from military men to civilians, from MP's to small-time civil servants." While the city was "very dingy and cramped next to the grandeur and magnificence of Istanbul" and devoid of excitement, Kuran wrote that the highlight was the trip to the quay on the day when the mail boat arrived from Istanbul.[11] Exiles were allowed to move freely about town but had to check in at the police station every morning and evening. Among the various cliques that formed, one group spent their days "monotonously" in a waterside café opened by one of their fellow exiles. The intellectuals among the group kept to themselves, immersed in study and research. Ahmet Ferit (Tek), member of the liberal opposition and future interior minister in the republic, rarely left his house, choosing to seclude himself with his family. Refik Halid Bey, Kuran says, socialized with a variety of people including fellow *muhalif* Dr. Celâl Paşa, whose daughter Nâzime he married while in Sinop. İsmail Hakkı lived at the house of Rıza Nur, a prominent Young Turk who had become a *muhalif* and was a native of the town, and gathered regularly with a small group of friends. Despite giving them relative freedom, the Unionists also went to great lengths to monitor the *muhalefet*. According to Kuran, they sent spies and hired some from within the exiled community to report on their fellow opposition figures. Kuran was particularly sensitive to this surveillance, since he and his friends were plotting their escape via the only possible route: the sea.

Though Kuran escaped to the Russian Black Sea port city of Sevastopol and continued to Paris, Refik remained in Sinop, where he passed his days in relative comfort. According to Şerif Aktaş's biography, he had ample time for hiking and hunting and for smoking nargile and socializing in the town's coffeehouses.[12] Refik also managed to get married, to Nâzime Hanım, the daughter of one of his closest friends in exile, Dr. Celâl Paşa.[13] But in his own recollections, Refik Halid emphasized the losses. "I settled in a pension owned by an elderly Rum couple, leaving everything behind—my chief clerk's position with a salary of 2000 kuruş, my spacious house, my fun-filled life," he wrote. "I felt absolutely empty; utterly helpless and discouraged."[14] He neglected to mention that his father was sending him money; despite the financial hardship Mehmed Halid sent five *altın* every month. And at some point he resumed collecting his salary for the chief clerk's position he had left behind. In fact, in June 1917—four years into his exile in Anatolia—his representative (*vekil*) petitioned for a salary increase associated with the position of Beyoğlu Başkâtibi, which he still formally held from 1913.[15]

By the fifth month of his exile, Refik tried to obtain a pardon so that he could return to Istanbul. He directed his efforts toward those still affiliated with the dynasty. In November 1913 he sent a request for pardon to Prince Abdülmecit, who was an admirer of his work.[16] He also wrote to the Grand Vezir and Foreign Minister Prince Said Halim Paşa. When Cemal Paşa ultimately received the petition, he rejected an appeal to the authority of the government—rather than to the CUP—as a violation of the de facto predominance of the Unionists within the Ottoman government. Cemal Paşa contended that "Refik Halid made a wrong maneuver; if he had given it straight to me I would have pardoned him."[17] Later, likely around early to mid-1915, when many others were receiving pardons, Refik Halid inquired again of Cemal Paşa, this time through the district governor (*mutasarrıf*) of Sinop, but to no avail.[18]

"THE JOKE"

Refik Halid wrote very little during the war, and even less during his two-year stint in Sinop. In fact, when he wrote to request a pardon, he declared that he had not published anything—political, satirical, or literary—for over a year and a half. This meant that the last time he had published anything substantive was circa June 1912. This was when the Freedom and Accord Party, with which he was informally aligned, came to power.[19] "Because I found myself in exile," he would later recall, "I could not even pick up a pen. Why would I write if it couldn't be published? I got used to the laziness."[20] But at some point he did again pick up a pen, and he tells us, "Then from there [Istanbul] they asked me to write a piece for an almanac called *Nevsâl-ı Millî* (National New Year). I sent an article entitled, 'İneğe buzağıya dair' (Of cows and icebergs) and my photograph. Somehow it got published. That's it."[21] After testing the waters and seeing that he could be published under his own name without drawing the attention of the censorship office, Refik wrote another article under a new pen name, Aydede (Grandpa Moon). This was in 1914, when Ali Kemal (one of the three opposition leaders sent to Europe in January 1913 after the Raid on the Sublime Porte) asked Refik to write for his Istanbul newspaper, *Peyam*. But as soon as authorities learned that Ali Kemal had given Refik a forum to write, *Peyam* was shut down until the end of the war, a testament to Refik's pariah status.[22]

Refik would not publish anything else until he arrived in Bilecik in late 1916. Shortly thereafter, censorship had started to ease up. But this does not mean he didn't write, and a handful of social realist stories that provide subtle social commentary were later published in a 1919 collection called *Homeland Stories* (*Memleket Hikâyeleri*). The one that I focus on here, "Şaka" (The joke), was written in Sinop—presumably in the first half of 1915, since we know he left in July 1915 for Çorum—and touches on themes related to gender and interconfessional relations. In contrast to the Anatolia that Turkish nationalists would later promote as the nationally pure bosom of the Turkish nation, Refik depicts it as a space populated by Christians and Muslims who coexisted and even fraternized, although at their own peril. It is worth recounting in detail.

"Şaka" turns on the fascination of three Turkish gentlemen—two from Istanbul (presumably fictionalized characters from among the exiles) and one local merchant—with the local Rum (Greek Orthodox) women, particularly one, Despina, whom they nickname Pandispanya (*Pan di spagna*/sponge-cake).[23] During one of their nights out at a seaside taverna in the Greek quarter, the three friends begin waxing nostalgic about the nightlife in Istanbul, particularly the Rum and Armenian neighborhood, Samatya, which Servet Efendi had frequented before being exiled. They then take a stroll through the Rum quarter, where Servet Efendi sets his sights on Despina, "a tall, well-built girl wearing a black apron." Refik writes that she wore "a long, broad, honey-colored kerchief, almost a turban," that was "wound decoratively around her charming hair, which was of the same color." As she passed them, she "carelessly and playfully expos[ed] her large thighs which protruded from her narrow skirt a bit too much, with the air of one who knows they would be appreciated. On her neck there was a tiny silver crucifix, attached to a delicate chain which shone bright red like a coral in the last redness of the sun."

When Servet Efendi learns that Pandispanya likes to take late-night dips in the sea with her friends, the three drinking buddies—who have been out until the tavernas closed their doors for the night—head to the beach in the hopes of catching a glimpse of the women: "Suddenly, the three friends heard sharp women's laughter, a few sentences in Greek, a splashing and fluttering in the water. With a drunken intelligence, Servet Efendi immediately reminded his still uncomprehending friends of his secret of the evening. 'Pandispanya is bathing!' he said." Now drunk, Servet Efendi decides to play a prank on Pandispanya and to sneak up on her and pinch her thigh. As he "strip[s] very quickly in the darkness" and dives into the dark water, his friends wait on the shore and the story continues:

As though waiting for a cannonball to explode, they looked over there, toward the point where the opening and closing rings of light were playing. This Servet was such a bad street character, what a bold and unconventional man; how did this roguishness enter his head? How wonderful it would be; something like a crab in the water, he will grab the girl so quickly, and who knows how she will scream, how terrified she will be, how she will flee, struggling toward the wharf!

After quite some time had passed, but the expected scream had not rung out, Şakir Efendi said: "He didn't do it. He must have turned back." However, he hadn't turned back. . . .

Nedim Bey muttered, "Where is he? Let him take care and not have an accident!" Now the sea appeared frightening in the threatening darkness. Like a deceitful intelligence, it made their innards insecure and mistrustful.

The two friends waited for a while [around] the little pile of clothing and underwear. Then, when they understood that there was no longer any hope of his turning back, each of them ran straight toward the police station, like a sacred horse pursued by a demonic nightmare, not seeing the ground under him, torment in his heart and fear in his eyes.

At the dawn after this night during which they had wandered in lantern-lit boats, searching the sea, they found the corpse of Servet Efendi wrapped up in the fishermen's nets. It was clear that, while going under the water, he had wanted to get out, but wherever he tried, the great net obstructed him; it panicked the poor wretch and killed him.

The commissioner who gave the description of the night's searches to his friends, turned to the wet corpse, wrapped in a gendarme's overcoat. He scolded him as though he were a suspect who had been brought before him, and asked: "My dear fellow, what did you think you were looking for at the bottom of the sea in the middle of the night?"

The prank that went awry was the joke that gave the story its title. The real-life irony, however, is that Refik likely penned "Şaka" precisely as Armenians and other Christians were being deported and massacred nearby—during the very last moments of coexistence between Turks and Greeks, Muslims and Christians, in Sinop and across the empire. As Refik described the edge of the sea that Servet Efendi plunges into, the war was raging on several fronts and the empire was on a similar precipice. Yet in this little corner of Anatolia, Greek taverns were still open for business and Rum girls were still splashing about in the Black Sea, unwittingly providing entertainment for Turkish male voyeurs. The dreadful end that Servet Efendi met is telling—and perhaps even emblematic of the dreadful effects the war was about to have on local, multiconfessional communities. The story, however, asks us to empathize with Servet—a Turk lured into the dark sea by the elusive laughter of a

Greek girl. We are left entirely in the dark about the fate of Despina and her friends—those who were, in fact, facing increasingly lethal violence as the Unionist regime entered the Great War.

Refik's Halid's perspective on the war, which the Ottomans entered in late 1914, was consistent with his background as a privileged intellectual from Istanbul living in provincial exile. Years later he would recount it from the vantage point of Sinop, a city that was not in the direct theater of conflict:

> In 1914 I witnessed the first unnatural image that stays in my mind from World War One: The ship "Gülcemal," while bringing the post from Istanbul to Sinop, before setting down anchor, suddenly turned away from the mouth of the harbor and reversed course as if it were startled; belching out its black smoke in the darkness, it hurriedly departed from the Black Sea's famous Karaburnu and dissolved into the night.[24] ... The flight of Gülcemal was heard about everywhere immediately, and made everyone's hair stand on end. ... [T]he people stood at attention waiting to hear, and one could say there was anxiety for Anatolia. The only news we got from the world was from "Milli Ajans" [National News Agency] on the şapiroğraf, with its runny ink and stained pages, but everyone waited for it to be distributed. Finally we learned it: Germany, Russia, and France had declared war.[25]

The war thus began for Refik Halid when he saw a mail boat reversing course. The empire had entered the war after a period of armed neutrality (August 2–late October 1914). For Refik Halid, it was not the widespread images in the press of dreadnaughts in the Bosphorus, but the image—trivial and nearly comical—of a mail boat in the Sinop harbor that signaled the start of the war. Insulated from the mortal dangers of the war, he had the space to joke and use irony about his marginal position.

The next summer, the CUP would transfer Refik from Sinop to Çorum, a landlocked town near Yozgat. By July 1915, only about fifty of the original eight hundred exiles remained. The rest had been released, with some set free so they could serve in the army.[26] Refik was among a group of twenty-eight sent to Çorum, alongside İştirakçi Hilmi (Hilmi the Socialist) and Refii Cevat (Ulunay).[27] "The few and the monstrous," as Refik jokingly called the group, were kept in exile because of "public opinion" (*efkâr-ı umumî*); that is, doublespeak for whatever the CUP wanted to justify as legitimate policy.

"Because of this 'public opinion,'" Refik writes, "the then-Minister of the Interior [Talaat Paşa] took us from Sinop and sent us packing to Çorum. And he really sent us packing. . .they gave the order 'get them there!' to the gendarmes, they got some carts, put the exiles in them. One morning our convoy set off, and for days we went, until one day we stopped at the bank of a river. Why? As if we were at the border between two countries and they brought us to that point and then dumped us. We continued on horseback."[28] As Refik would write later, "abstract words" like public opinion were useful for the opportunist politicians of the time. "Bombastic, loaded, and flamboyant," the perverse logic of the term "made an impression, concealed shame, and hid flaws." In the constitutional period, he writes, one would have to translate "public opinion" as "my own idea"; as in, 'This is what I think, this is what has settled in my mind; this is what I feel like, this is what my friends' desire is,' in place of, 'Public opinion demands it!'"[29] "The history of the [Second] Constitutional Period is the witness," he says with hindsight in 1940, "for how much real 'public opinion' suffered at the hands of this fake 'public opinion.'" In short, he laments, "Oh, public opinion, what crimes are being committed in your name!"[30]

The twenty-eight men—hardly hard-core criminals or enemies of the state—traveled approximately 250 kilometers in nine days. Refik jokes that "rather than a procession of exiles, we looked more like an American film crew, a gold rush convoy, or some kind of military expedition exploring in newly-discovered continents; the only thing missing was for us to encounter red- or black-skinned natives, to throw dynamite into mountains, or to build bridges across rivers."[31] He describes arriving in Çorum in positive terms. Decades later, his good friend and fellow exile, Refii Cevat, would also reminisce about the journey, how they celebrated the end of Ramazan with villagers in Boyabat, a town between Sinop and Çorum, and the locals treated them to a celebratory afternoon meal.[32] Despite the war, Refik said of his time there: "They put me all the way in Çorum—that safe place, with no clamors of war to be heard, and no sounds of cannons, oh Çorum, what a peaceful place it was."[33]

Refik's emphasis on peace, however, may have been tongue in cheek. During his time there—where he had his "first serious contact with poor, Inner Anatolia"—he suffered a personal tragedy when his parents came to visit Çorum and his mother fell ill and died there (she is reportedly buried in Hıdırlık cemetery there).[34] More significant for late Ottoman and Turkish history was that the period between July 1915 and July 1916 overlapped with the worst period of "deportations and killings" (*tehcir ve tektil*), known today as the Armenian Genocide. Nowhere did Refik Halid expressly condone the mass killing of Armenians or any other Christians. In many instances, after the fact, he provided subtle but scathing criticisms of such policies, and often surprising empathy for Armenian suffering. Given that the Liberal Entente was often portrayed as an alliance of Ottoman liberals and non-Muslim groups, one might think that those Ottoman liberals might have felt some pangs of sympathy and regret during and after the genocide. Refik's stance, not of vocal opposition to but of silent complicity with the genocide, points to the limits of *muhalefet*. Liberal *muhalifs* like him may have been inclined toward alliances with non-Muslim groups of the empire in the Second Constitutional Era, but once the killing of Armenians started, many remained silent or chose to resist in only subtle ways.

THE ROAD TO ANKARA

In order to understand Refik's changing stance toward the genocide, we must first establish how close he might have been to the violence against Armenians as it was unfolding between spring-summer 1915 and fall 1916. According to Raymond Kevorkian's *Armenian Genocide: A Complete History*, there were more than five thousand Armenians in the *sancak* of Sinop on the eve of the war. The town of Çorum, in the sancak of Yozgat, had roughly thirty-five hundred Armenians.[35] The Armenians around Sinop did not live in town, but there were four communities nearby. The largest was in the inland town of Boyabat, which had over thirty-five hundred Armenian inhabitants, and was where their convoy of exiles celebrated the end of Ramazan en route to Çorum. Eight hundred from that community were arrested, interned at the mosque, and then "disappeared" on the way to Ankara, where they were ostensibly to face court-martial. The rest of the population was deported via Çankırı (roughly 280 km inland from Sinop and also in the Kastamonu vilayet) in mid-October and were all slain near Yozgat later that month.

In late April 1915, while the opposition members were still at Sinop, "a good part of the Constantinople Armenian elite" was exiled to Çankırı.[36] Like the *muhalefet* (who implicitly were all Muslim), Armenian intellectuals and elites were placed under house arrest and had to provide their own subsistence and rent lodgings from locals. But there the two stories diverged, showing the privilege that went with the status of being Muslim *muhale-fet*; according to an Armenian survivor, fifty-six of the Armenians exiled to Çangırı were put on the road in mid-July 1915 and "slain to a man shortly thereafter." The second convoy set out on August 19. They were interned briefly in Ankara and killed a few days later near Yozgat.[37] Kevorkian notes that the local Armenians of Çangırı (as opposed to those who were exiled there from İstanbul) escaped the first wave of deportations by raising a sum of 460 Turkish pounds and turning it over to one Cemal Oğuz and his coworkers. But "early in October... 2,000 men were deported. These deportees (including 21 from the Istanbul Armenian elite interned in Çangırı) were moved along a route that brought them through Çorum while Refik Halid was there, then on to Yozgat, and ultimately to Syria."[38]

Refik might not have seen any firsthand evidence of the genocide in Sinop, as the events in Çangırı and Kastamonu were geographically distant enough to make this possible and the deportations from nearby Boyabat occurred after he had passed through the town. Çorum and Ankara were a different story. His journey to Çorum in late July 1915 coincided with deportations through the same region—likely along the same roads, within days or weeks of each other. And by October, when he would have been comfortably settled, hundreds if not thousands of Armenians were regularly marched through the town on their way to be killed in nearby Yozgat. So far, we can reconstruct what he might have witnessed in Çorum based only on circumstantial evidence, since he does not make mention of the genocide in his recollections of exile in Sinop or Çorum. Shortly after his arrival in Ankara in summer 1916, however, we know that Refik came face to face with some of the horrific violence the Unionist regime perpetrated against Armenians in Anatolia, with their scorched earth policy.[39] We know this because he penned a detailed eyewitness account five years later, which I take up in detail in chapter 4.

Before it became the home of the Grand National Assembly and the capital of the new Republic of Turkey, Ankara—or Angora as it was known in English—was a small, dusty town in central Anatolia. Refik Halid never had much affection for it, and he was relieved to leave after three months. Years later he recounted that the only reason to endure the suffering of being in Ankara was to be back on the railway line connecting him with Istanbul.[40] He had requested a transfer there from Çorum, which was approved by Dr. Reşit, the provincial governor (*vali*) of Ankara. He may have sought the transfer to have better access to medical resources. If so, this would have been an important benefit, since he contracted the flu upon arriving in Ankara, and people were dying of typhus and flu all around him.

Refik Halid arrived, amid the notorious heat of the city, "by coincidence" on Constitution Day in July. He takes the opportunity to describe in retrospect the ironies, and indeed the disappointments of Ottoman constitutionalism, a mere eight years after the revolution:

> There were all different kinds of straggly, half-hearted flags hung in the half-empty shops of the marketplace, from the color of sour orange to the green of a saint's tomb [*türbe*], some with 3- or 5-cornered stars, with the crescent a little too open or too closed. The *Meşrûtiyet* didn't even teach us how to do flags; hadn't even been able to impress upon us how to revere the flag. It couldn't even get us to show the unity of the flag itself. A foreigner who didn't know our homeland [*memleket*], had he passed through the marketplace, wouldn't have noted the resemblance of these to any flag in Larousse; these brought to mind more the decorations from some kind of traveling circus than from the anniversary of a nation winning its freedom; he would think they were the little flags [*alamet*] in front of each shop in the old Spice Market in Istanbul [Mısırçarşısı]. Let those illiterates find the peddler they are looking for by looking at these flags! And I encountered slogans written in ink that was running—crying—on cotton fabric, hung above each street, like: "The Final Victory is Ours!"... And signs: "Freedom, Justice, Equality!"[41]

The ambivalent dissident was both disappointed by the unfulfilled promise of constitutionalism and repulsed by the perversion of constitutional values he was seeing around him. Yet he was willing to consort with all manner of officials within the Unionist regime while in exile.

Refik had no acquaintances to speak of in his new place of exile, but he remembered that the old commissioner from Çorum had been transferred to the central commissariat in Ankara and somehow made his way to his house. It was a weekend, and this "imposing figure"—whom he described in terms that were reminiscent of a Circassian irregular—"with his *kalpak* hat, black beard, bare chest, in repose in his corner window . . . got dressed for my sake, put his sword on, and together we set about searching for a pension among the Catholic Armenian families that had been left without men in the Castle (*Hisardibi*) district."[42] They could not find a spare room there, despite their best efforts, and he ended up renting a narrow room above a gloomy, small restaurant. He would "perch" there until he found a suitable dwelling.

Those Armenian Catholic households "left without men" were a direct result of Unionist violence. The Armenian community of Ankara had contained just over eleven thousand people in 1914, and it was unique, according to the historian Kevorkian, because about 70 percent were Catholic, having been converted by French missionaries in the early eighteenth century.[43] The only ethnic tensions in the town seemed to date from 1913, when roughly ten thousand Muslim refugees (*muhacirin*) from the Balkans were settled there. Kevorkian notes that "here, perhaps more than elsewhere, the discourse that sought to paint the Armenians as a seditious group remained most unconvincing," since they were not only Turkish speaking, but Catholic, not highly politicized, and under the protection of Austria-Hungary (the Ottomans' ally in the war) and the papal nunzio—unrelated, that is, to Russia.[44] The provincial governor who had been appointed in June 1914 resisted orders to deport the community when he received them from the Interior Ministry in summer 1915. This prompted his immediate dismissal and replacement with twenty-seven-year-old Atif Bey, a member of the CUP Central Committee and an important player in the Special Organization (Teşkilât-ı Mahsusa), the secret paramilitary organization under the control of the CUP's inner circle and attached to the Ministry of War.[45]

As interim district governor (July 14–October 3, 1915), Atif Bey proceeded to liquidate the Armenian communities of the province, including its capital, Ankara, save for the Catholic contingent, which he said would be spared. After telling them there was no need to appeal to Istanbul for help, he had approximately fifteen hundred Catholic men rounded up in late August 1915. They were then forcibly marched toward Syria, with their survival guaranteed to the papal nunzio and the German embassy. After a month-long march, those who were still alive ended up near Aleppo and were sent on to Ras ul-Ayn and Deir ez-Zor; reportedly only four priests and thirty laymen survived.

A few weeks later the remaining Catholic women, children, and elderly were expelled from their homes and interned at the railroad station for about a month. Most of them were ultimately stripped of their property, deported to Syria, or persuaded/forced to convert and marry Muslim men in the town. A few hundred families—the households "without men" that Refik Halid referred to—were allowed to remain in Ankara "as the families of military men," although the men in question had been 'massacred or deported.'"[46] Such was the tattered state of the Armenian Catholic community when Refik Halid arrived.

The fire in September 1916, then—for which Refik Halid's later account, dealt with in the following chapters, is the sole narrative eyewitness account, and therefore an invaluable source—took place a year after the main wave of deportations, and seems to have been part of a systematic arson policy designed to facilitate the seizure of assets and real estate from Armenian communities that had already been stripped of most members and almost everything else.[47] Kevorkian notes that the record books of the Registry of Abandoned Property (*Emval-ı Metruke*) "were indeed opportunely consumed by the flames," making it impossible to trace the assets of those killed and deported.[48]

DR. MEHMED REŞİD (ŞAHİNGİRAY) (1873–1919)

Most of the deportations and killings of Armenians in Ankara were perpetrated by the Unionists over the course of 1915 under Atif Bey. But in the words of Dr. Mehmed Reşid—the provincial governor of Ankara in 1916–17 who approved Refik Halid's request to be transferred to Ankara from Çorum—there was still some "unfinished business" to attend to in 1916.[49] Refik would bear witness to that unfinished business during his time there. In the next chapter I explore in detail his account, focusing here on how, despite his disgust with the Unionist leadership and its decision to enter the war, Refik was on familiar, even warm, terms with some Unionist officials—including some of the most notorious war criminals. His cordial relationship with Dr. Mehmed Reşid (Şahingiray) is a prime example of this, and demonstrates solidarities across party lines, despite the rhetoric of *muhalefet* and the rivalries between Unionists and *muhalif*s in this period.[50]

Also known as Çerkez (Circassian) Reşid, the *vali* was fifteen years older than Refik. He was also known by the name Şahingiray, suggesting he might have been, like Refik, of Crimean Tatar ancestry. He had earlier approved Refik Halid's request to be transferred from Çorum to Ankara and would, in 1916, arrange for his expedited departure to a comfortable stint in Bilecik. Refik was said to have enjoyed telling the story about Dr. Reşid giving him a basket of fresh Angora pears, which signified his hospitality and warmth.[51] In his memoirs, Refik claimed that the *vali* did not abuse his influence and that he "treated the exiles, and me most of all, very well." In particular, he apparently protected Refik from the reports of the police chief, a "crude partisan" (*kaba bir partici*) who was always trying to level "meaningless charges against me" (*manasız vesilelerle aleyhimde*).[52]

Dr. Reşid had been a founding member of the CUP but was universally acknowledged not to have been the group's brightest intellect. Interestingly, in the Hamidian era he had vocally criticized the Ottoman leadership for the 1896 massacre of Armenians and put up posters in Istanbul to the effect that all Ottomans were brothers.[53] Although he had flirted with Prince Sabahaddin's liberal constitutionalist/federalist wing, after the 31 March Incident in 1909 he returned to the fold of the CUP.[54] In the Second Constitutional Era he proceeded through a series of insignificant provincial posts, which included *kaymakam* of the tiny island of Kos, in October 1909, followed by district governor of Homs in Tripoli (Lebanon) province in February 1910; in the summer of 1911 he moved to Kozan, then soon afterward to Rize in northeast Anatolia. He was finally removed in September 1912 for "belligerent behavior," but was returned to that office again in November 1912 during the Great Cabinet period. Despite this rather unimpressive curriculum vitae, contemporaries such as Süleyman Nazif described him as a legalist (*kanunperest*), saying that "his incorruptible character inspired personal respect, and promoted discipline within the administration."[55] When the CUP took over as a dictatorship in January 1913, Dr. Reşid was assigned to Northeast Anatolia again, and by July of that year he was district governor of Karesi in Western Anatolia, where he remained until July 1914.

It was in these years—which overlapped with the losses in the First Balkan War and the flood of Balkan refugees escaping violent, mass expulsions of Muslims—that the doctor seems to have undergone a radical change of heart with respect to Ottoman brotherhood and turned to large-scale violence against Christians. Yet Dr. Reşid seems to have gone to more extremes than most, becoming one of the frontline henchmen—first against Greek populations in the Aegean region and then against Armenians in the interior. While in Karesi he was "one of the protagonists of illegal expulsions of the Greeks from the Aegean coast, a violent policy hardly concealed from diplomatic circles, and executed by party and government organs." According to historian Hans-Lukas Kieser, "the İttihadists [Unionists] saw it as retaliation for the evil which, according to them, the Muslims under Greek domination had been suffering since the Balkan Wars." By summer 1913, Dr. Reşid was "a high [Unionist] functionary who, in his private notes, no longer considered the Ottoman Rum as compatriots (*vatandaşlar*), but as 'foreigners' and internal enemies against whom the severest measures needed to be taken, including expropriation and expulsion."[56] Watching the class structure and power relations in the Aegean region, he "appeared to conceptualize late Ottoman society in sweeping antagonistic categories of Islam and Turkishness versus Christianity, Greek-ness (*Rumluk*) and Armenian-ness (*Ermenilik*)."[57]

By the time of the Great War, Dr. Reşid had become one of the most zealous killers of Armenians; by his own estimate, he "removed" 120,000 Armenians from Diyarbakir after July 1915. The majority were massacred; the rest died from exhaustion. In a conversation he had with fellow CUP functionary Mithat Şükrü [Bleda], he said, "Either they us, or we them. . . . My Turkishness triumphed over my identity as a doctor. . . . The Armenian bandits were a load of harmful microbes that had afflicted the body of the fatherland. Was it not the duty of a doctor to kill the microbes?"[58] According to Süleyman Nazif—a Unionist turned opponent who was a vocal defender of Armenians during the genocide—Dr. Reşid was "solely responsible for the tragedy of the massacres and deportations in Diyarbakir. . . . As a reward for his 'patriotic services' there, he was promoted in rank and salary to become provincial governor (*vali*) of Ankara." Nazif notes that "as soon as he set foot in the center of the Ankara province, which was his last post, the city was burned from top to bottom [*şehir serapa muhterik oldu*]." "Only after finishing with his work of massacres and deportations did he come to Istanbul."[59]

The relationship between Dr. Reşid and Refik raises important questions: How could the "butcher of Diyarbekir," who was so "well-integrated into the CUP power structure during the years 1913–1916," be close friends with and even an advocate for Refik Halid, an intellectual whom the CUP had exiled for his oppositional writings and activities?[60] It also leads one to ask what it meant to be a dissident intellectual, if "the opposition" was silent in the face of the genocide.

Part of the explanation for their friendship, I contend, lies in the fact that during his time in Ankara (March 1916–March 1917), Dr. Reşid "turned against the system then in place, which was full of corruption and war profiteers." As Kieser writes, "his intransigence and straightforwardness began seriously to upset the regime."[61] According to his daughter's recollections, Dr. Reşid did not last long in his position in Ankara because he had "declared war on all manner of corruption and injustice," and "after removing the go-betweens [war profiteers and corrupt officials] would turn them over directly to the administration. When the administration refused to remove them," he got into a conflict with them."[62] Despite efforts by his daughter to highlight his attack on corruption and war profiteering, the fact was that Dr. Reşid not only played a major role in the confiscation of Armenians' property and wealth, but he also profited from it. He was said to have left Diyarbakir with forty-three boxes of jewelry and other valuables taken from Armenians.[63] But it is possible that Refik and Dr. Resid found common cause against Unionist corruption at that moment in 1916, something that might even have enabled Refik to look the other way as the Armenians were being stripped of property and life around him.

RETURN TO ISTANBUL

The last place Refik journeyed to on his exile was Bilecik, a city about 120 miles east of the capital. Thanks to Dr. Reşid's directives, Refik was allowed the privilege and dignity to travel there freely by train, rather than being escorted by police. When saying his farewell, Dr. Reşid admitted that he had even tried to intercede to get Refik Halid permission to return directly to Istanbul instead of Bilecik, to no avail. Refik arrived in Bilecik in early October, on the day of the Feast of the Sacrifice (*Kurban Bayramı*). He recalls that it was the first "refreshing" *bayram* he had experienced in exile and that Bilecik was one of those sweet towns that, even though it was objectively nothing special, with its "ramshackle houses and broken pavements," seemed "bright, new, and clean."[64]

In Bilecik, Refik found several people he knew. As he went to submit his transfer papers to the district governor (*mutasarrıf*), he received a warm welcome from the accountant (*muhasebeci*), Hakkı Behiç. Hakkı was a friend from his days as a clerk at the Finance Ministry, whom Refik held in high esteem, writing, "He knows language well, loves reading, is a clear writer, is an enemy of bribers and war profiteers, and even though he was a Unionist he was an intellectual who did not hesitate to complain about bad administration."[65] He also encountered the former district governor of Sinop, Müştak Bey, whom Refik Halid had asked to allow his return to Istanbul early on in his exile. Refik noted Müştak Bey's transformation since they met in 1914 in Sinop, when he was a "solid" CUP appointee to a locality where he was entrusted with hundreds of exiles. Now, in 1917, he was beleaguered and raging against the Unionist regime. Having seen the CUP's corruption and war profiteering, Müştak Bey had become "troubled and depressed, and wasn't looking after his job." He eventually resigned. The war was taking a toll, not just on civilian populations and soldiers, but also on those within the wartime administration.

If the tattered day-to-day administration of the provinces was prompting one kind of shift in the politics of the empire's ruling class, another movement was underway in Istanbul among the intellectuals who had been effectively cut out of any political or partisan debate during the war. This movement—a literary one—would propel Refik back to Istanbul finally in early 1918. Yakup Kadri, Ömer Seyfettin, and Ziya Gökalp, for example, had started a new literary project, known as Millî Edebiyat (National literature). Under the auspices of the CUP, they had started publishing *Yeni Mecmua* (The new journal), in July 1917, even before the war had ended. The Millî Edebiyat movement, which had begun around 1910 and resumed toward the end of the war after a hiatus, was, among other things, a way to build a Turkish national culture beyond party lines. While inherently political, the project entailed the promotion of seemingly apolitical or at least nonpartisan portraits of Turkish society. The sociologist and litterateur Ziya Gökalp was the main ideologue behind this project of cultural Turkism. Like the short-story writer Ömer Seyfettin, he had close ties to the CUP leadership, particularly to Talaat Paşa, who was interior minister during the war and had to approve all publications.

Ziya Gökalp's Millî Edebiyat movement was emblematic of two major shifts. First, it signified that a move toward nationalist literature required consensus; its authors had to somehow bridge, transcend, or otherwise blur the partisan divides that had made a Turkish literature so difficult to imagine before 1914. It was also a way for the Unionist administration to sponsor a type of literature that turned to more abstract themes and concerns that were unifying and that distracted the public from the failings of the government. Second, it marked a moment of inclusion for *muhalefet*. Refik Halid, still branded as unreliable and part of *muhalefet*, was nevertheless allowed to participate from his exile in Bilecik. He sent two anodyne short stories, "Küs Ömer" (Sulky Omar) and "Boz Eşek" (The brown donkey) to his old friend from *Servet-i Fünun*, Celâl Sahir. Sahir liked the stories but had to appeal twice to Talaat Paşa, who first refused them publication, then relented after he was persuaded to read them. Talaat agreed to allow them to be published, but only under the initials "RH." After Refik Halid's return from exile, Ömer Seyfettin asked him for more stories, this time for Ziya Gökalp's *Yeni Mecmua*; Refik sent "Sarı Bal" (Yellow honey) and "Şaka" (The joke).[66]

What finally made it possible for Refik Halid to return to Istanbul was a combination of personal and political serendipity.[67] His wife, having returned to Istanbul with her father in 1914 and then gone to stay with Refik in Bilecik in 1917, was back in Istanbul about to give birth, so he requested a ten-day leave to visit her in the capital. He then took advantage of the fact that Talaat Paşa, who had a personal grudge against him, was out of the country attending negotiations for the Treaty of Brest-Litovsk. Cemal Paşa, who had sent Refik Halid into exile nearly five years earlier, was the acting interior minister, and he personally approved Refik Halid's return in late January 1918. Ottoman documents confirm that this was still a controversial move: "There is no way that Refik Halid, given his past actions and his notoriety, is deserving of trust."[68] When Talaat returned from Brest-Litovsk, he demanded that the decision be reversed and Refik Halid be sent back to Bilecik; this time, his new friend and patron, CUP ideologue and Central Committee member Ziya Gökalp, stepped in and persuaded Talaat to allow Refik Halid to stay in Istanbul for good.

Refik's experiences between 1913 and 1918 illustrate the fissures between Unionists and the Ottoman establishment as well as the lines of solidarity between them. Recall that Refik's exile had been prompted by the publication of a joke that poked fun at Unionist Triumvir Talaat's lower-class origins, aggravating an already deep social rift. One of his major stories from that period of exile was written under the title "The Joke"; it turned on the ambivalent relationship between Muslims and non-Muslims that was driving the empire apart. In the course of his exile he, with his actions, associations, and silences, exposed the joke, or at least the deep irony behind *muhalefet*, demonstrating that he could close ranks with the most extreme of Unionist elements. The experience of a *muhalif* who rubbed elbows with Dr. Reşid and other Unionists laid bare the shared interests of the opposition and the ruling power in the face of genocide. The next chapter turns to the profound reconfiguration, of both Unionism and the concept of *muhalefet*, after the Ottoman defeat in the world war. Unionism would metamorphose into the national independence movement over the course of 1919; the concept of *muhalefet* would then be retooled by the likes of Refik Halid into opposition against that national movement until the nationalist victory in late 1922. And the new battles lines, between nationalists and their *muhalifs*, had everything to do with the question of continuity from the recent, wartime

Unionist past detailed here. Refik Halid, whose strongest gesture of *muhale-fet* to date had been his satirical Porcupine stories of 1910–12, emerged in the Armistice period to construct a bold imaginary of *muhalefet* in his writings and to oppose Mustafa Kemal himself at a key moment in his bid for power in 1919.

FOUR

The True Face of Istanbul
(1918–1922)

REFIK HALID RETURNED TO ISTANBUL in January 1918 to find a city profoundly exhausted by the privations of war. He began publishing anodyne stories in *Yeni Mecmua* that spring, and by summer, when military censorship was lifted, he was dabbling in satire again—this time in a novel about war profiteers in cahoots with the Unionist regime. Refik's send-up of a particular war profiteer prompted talk of another exile, which was only prevented from coming to fruition by his Unionist defender, Ziya Gökalp.[1] Unchastened by the incident, Refik set to work writing his first novel, *İstanbul'un İç Yüzü* (The true face of Istanbul), which was serialized in *Zaman*.[2] Refik's new work, written in a social realist style, reflected the zeitgeist of the last months of the war, at once conveying the feelings of profound existential malaise and crisis in Istanbul, and in doing so leveling a social critique against the Unionist regime, war profiteering, and the moral collapse of the empire.[3] At the heart of the novel were İsmet (Chastity) and her long-lost childhood friend, Kâni. Born during the Hamidian era to household servants of an aging pasha, by war's end both had chosen what were common paths for those with few options: İsmet had become a prostitute, Kâni a war profiteer. After years of not seeing one another, the two crossed paths on a boat to the Prince's Islands, the site of many excesses during the war years. Their subsequent trysts in different parts of the city provided Refik opportunities to reflect on Istanbul society and to convey the sense of the inhabitants of a city unmoored, from which all life and vitality had been wrung out.

The Ottomans' final political demise—which was fully intertwined with that of the CUP—was likewise a kind of unmooring. After five years of dictatorship, the Unionists had come to represent not only a political party but also a shadow entity reaching deep into the Ottoman military and civil administration and a force that had started to shape mass politics and Ottoman Turkish identity. Under the direction of the triumvirate of Cemal, Enver, and Talaat Paşas, the CUP had played out the contradictions between the twin goals of saving the empire and destroying its establishment. This was readily apparent in the period I take up here, between the signing of the Armistice of Mudros in October 1918 and the triumph of the National movement that would abolish the Sultanate in November 1922—a period of political (and historical) purgatory referred to as the Armistice period (*Mütareke dönemi*).[4] During this period the view from inside Istanbul was grim: the Ottomans faced occupation of the capital by Allied forces and of parts of Anatolia by Greece, Italy, and France, as well as a series of treaties that would dismember most of the empire and then partition what remained. The Paris Peace Conference of 1919–20 forsook self-determination in the Middle East for mandatory rule and new forms of colonialism. With the signing of the Treaty of Sèvres on August 10, 1920, representatives of the Ottoman government agreed to renounce all non-Turkish territory and to cede their administration to the Allies. The treaty also created zones of foreign influence within the remaining rump state.

Outside the negotiation chambers of France and Switzerland, facts on the ground were changing. By June 1919, a national resistance–cum–independence movement under the leadership of Mustafa Kemal (Atatürk) began to challenge what remained of the Ottoman regime and, the following year to establish an alternate government based in Ankara. Inspired by Woodrow Wilson's call for self-determination and the twelfth of his Fourteen Points—which ensured "secure sovereignty" for the "Turkish portions of the empire"—the national resistance openly defied the terms of the emergent Treaty of Sèvres. After defeating the Greek army and driving out Greek civilian populations and expelling British, French, and Italian forces in Anatolia, the presumptive national government abolished the Sultanate in November 1922. By 1923 it had forced a new international settlement, and on July 24 the Treaty of Lausanne superseded the Treaty of Sèvres and recognized the territorial sovereignty of an independent Turkish state in all of Anatolia. It also guaranteed minority rights to Greeks, Armenians, and Jews who remained in the new nation and mandated the exchange of populations between Greece and Turkey.

The empire, the Sultanate, the Caliphate, and much of the establishment would meet their end, and the purgatory of the Armistice period would give way to the inception of a new nation-state: the Republic of Turkey, established on October 29, 1923. But despite the nationalists' renunciation of the CUP as a party—which was a crucial part of their bid for domestic and international legitimacy and the basis for their struggle to establish a sovereign state between 1919 and 1923—important elements of the CUP had recombined under the banner of the national independence movement. Even Mustafa Kemal had been a member of the CUP, though his relationship to the party's leadership, and particularly Enver Paşa, had been conflicted. Once in power, the nationalists doubled down on renouncing their connections to the CUP and swept aside the contested history and transformation of *muhalefet* itself, as we shall see. While there was no room in the ensuing official history of the republic for the range of opposition and contestation within late Ottoman politics in general and *muhalefet* in particular, *muhalefet* became a driving concept for Refik Halid's writings and imaginary at precisely this moment.

The subsequent "official history" of the republic focuses on the mobilization of the national resistance in Anatolia at this moment and its eventual triumph over the Ottoman government in Istanbul and the European occupying forces, leading to the establishment of the republic. This chapter offers a counternarrative that is centered in Istanbul, and informed by Refik Halid's political and literary itinerary between late 1918 and late 1922. Rather than telling a story in which the center of action was in Anatolia and the struggle for national salvation was solely against the Ottoman government in Istanbul and the Allied occupation, the chapter traces how *muhalefet*—both as a concept and a political entity—became retooled in response to the national movement as the empire was in its final death throes. It argues that as the Unionists regrouped into the nationalists, *muhalefet*, which was previously in oppositional relation to the CUP (in 1912–13), became transposed and defined as a movement against the nationalists. In Istanbul, Refik held the position of head of the General Directorate of Post, Telegraph and Telephone Service (PTT)—which placed him in the service of Damad Ferid Paşa's government— just at the moment that the remnants of Unionism were recombining and coalescing into the nationalist resistance movement in Anatolia. The position provided him with a front-row seat to the transformation from Unionism to nationalism and to the irreversible breach between the Ottoman Empire and the Turkish nation-state. The so-called Telegraph Episode—an incident that involved direct opposition to Mustafa Kemal and served as a trigger for the national movement in June 1919—was the moment when Refik made a direct attempt to foil military and political resistance to the Ottoman government and, by extension, the Allied occupation. In doing so, he was motivated by personal enmity and the logic of *muhalefet* from the preceding era.

Refik's opposition to the nationalists did not begin or end with the Telegraph Episode. That event featured in the official history as one of the first internal acts of treachery against the Turkish nation, however, making it a fascinating point of overlap between official history and the counternarrative I explore here. Working in the employ of the Ottoman government under British occupation, after all, meant tacit acceptance of the occupation: a stance antithetical to the goals and interests of the national movement. It would be a difficult position to justify once the nationalists emerged victorious; in the eyes of Unionists-cum-nationalists and now nationalists, it was nothing short of collaboration and treachery. Thus, a second goal of the chapter is to show how, between 1919 and 1922, Refik went on to stage a different kind of opposition, not on the battlefield or even at the telegraph machine, but in the literary imagination. He elaborated a new imaginary of *muhalefet* in his writings to stake out a heroic position for himself rather than to accept the label of traitor or collaborator. This new *muhalefet* involved condemning the national movement for its ties to Unionism, ties that the nationalists expressly denied. But it also went further, constructing a historical narrative for the idea of *muhalefet* and depicting an archetypal *muhalif* as tragic hero. Through this active period of literary production, writings from which were later excised from the record in the Republican era, he tried to carve out a principled position of opposition to what he insisted were morally and politically bankrupt Unionists in nationalist disguise.

This arc of history, as told through the experiences of Refik Halid and *muhalefet*, involves three distinct phases of Refik's career in the Armistice period: a period of soul-searching and indeterminacy, for him as for the larger Ottoman establishment, which lasted from the end of the world war until his first appointment to the Directorate of Post and Telegraph (late 1918–April 1919); the period of his first tenure as general director of Post and Telegraph, when the Telegraph incident took place and his active attempts to foil the nationalist movement unfolded (April–October 1919); and the period in which he opposed the nationalists by other means, writing prolifically about their ties to the Unionists and valorizing the concept of *muhalefet* after stepping down from the post for the first time, including his second term in March–September 1920 (the entire period covers October 1919–November 1922). Featured in this chapter is one of the most striking examples of his transposition of *muhalefet* from the Unionist to the nationalist period: the story he composed in 1921 about the Ankara fire of 1916. The fire itself was an episode associated with the Armenian Genocide, which he witnessed during his wartime exile. In contrast to his choice to remain silent about the genocide, which transpired around him during his time in Anatolia, he chose to speak up about it in Istanbul, when the Turkish nationalists' war with the Greek occupiers was in full throttle, using that tragedy to condemn the Unionists for it as part of his campaign to discredit the nationalists. The chapter concludes by tracing how, just days after the nationalists' triumphant entry into the city, Refik, an incorrigible *muhalif* and now a national traitor to boot, fled Istanbul and closed out a chapter of *muhalefet* that accompanied the formal death of the Ottoman Empire.

BETWEEN THE PAST AND THE FUTURE

In the months between the end of the war in November 1918 and his appointment to the Directorate of Post and Telegraph in mid-April 1919, Refik's political stance was not consistently oppositional, in large part because the entire basis of political authority was in flux. The empire was in free fall after its defeat in the war. Refik, like everyone else, was struggling to make sense of the recent past and to envision some kind of future for the empire. In his writings he took on the voice of an embittered *muhalif,* a humanist, and a spokesman for the Ottoman government, all in a few short months.

Refik's first move was to publish three essay-stories in *Zaman* (Time) that gave voice to a flood of critical and pointedly political sentiments. The first, "Be Careful Not to Get Cheated, Don't Believe, Don't Get Duped!," was a stingingly cynical condemnation of politics, written in verse. The second, "There's No One Guilty Around Here!," marked a return to his classic ironic style, poking fun at the fact that everyone conveniently claimed at war's end to have been antiwar, and that no one wanted to be held accountable for its catastrophic toll. Refik cheekily wonders if he himself could have been the one that caused the war, since no one else has stepped forward to claim responsibility. The third story, "Where to, Gentlemen?," took aim at the CUP leadership. In a stinging indictment, Refik wrote:

> The dinner party is over, gentlemen, but where are you going without wiping your mouths, washing your hands, or drinking our bitter coffee . . . ?
> For five years you've feasted everywhere like crows pecking at a human carcass; like vultures and eagles raised on the death of whole families you've finally had your fill of human flesh. . . . Is he a member of the opposition (*muhalif*)? Take him down. . . . Is he a writer? Shoot him in the head. . . .

Is he a Turk? Send him to his death.... Is he a Greek (*Rum*)? Get money from him.... An Armenian? Cut off his head.... An Arab? Hang him.... A woman? Send her home.... A robber? Press him for a cut of his action.... A ruffian (*külhanbeyi*)? Come here next to me.... A Jew? Ask him what he thinks [*sor fikrini*] ... and beat anyone else who's left over.... [P]ut their money in your pocket.... [T]here, that's your "programme"!... [T]hey recognized neither sultan [*padişah*] nor rule of law [*nizam*], they knew no mercy nor conscience [*insaf*].... [T]he people were wasting away from hunger on the streets and they were in their villas eating partridge brains and drinking bird milk [dining luxuriously on rare and expensive delicacies] ...so let them make sure they've killed off the entire nation [*millet*]; because if there had been one drop of blood left in our veins, one ounce of strength left in our arms, we would have grabbed them by their collars and taken our revenge.... *However they left waving their arms at us and spitting in our faces.* (emphasis added)

The animus Refik expresses here is often dismissed in national historiography as an example of the emotional, irrational anger of the liberal opponents of the CUP at the war's end, as if there were no reason for such sentiments and therefore no reason to dwell on or analyze them.[5] His invective, though, was a warranted, and understandable response to the forces—collective and individual—that had brought about the current situation. Not only had the CUP and their supporters thrown the empire headlong into a self-destructive war, but the leaders had then fled the country rather than face punishment for their crimes.[6] For Refik and many others, this was just the most prominent example of pervasive moral bankruptcy, initiated and encouraged by the Unionists, which had crippled politics and brought the empire to its current impasse. Hinting at how it continued in a new guise, he wrote:

Yes, don't get cheated, don't believe, don't get duped; this world is a world of lies and deception.... [T]he one who looks like a shepherd passes for a pasha, then the wolf comes and swallows up the flock; with peace another politician comes before us and sets up his campaign tent to play the money box; while on the corner, it's politics at knifepoint; he'll sing of "liberty" (*hürriyet*) to all the smiling faces, he'll loudly explain the meaning of justice—then gather money from the crowd; new crooks are constantly popping up, thinking, "it's neither witchcraft (*sihir*), nor a miracle, it's a talent for sleight of hand!" He'll steal what's left in our hands and put it in his hat; in short, it's the same pantomime, the same trick! Don't get cheated, don't believe, don't get duped: not by the Pied Piper's flute, luring you away with promises of love, nor the words of an MP, nor the talk of a pilgrim (*hacı*), nor the idols of the priest.... I felt burned by all of them, my trust was lost for all of them. Again someone will come out: "Equality!" he'll shout, five years later he'll buy land from Çamlıca to Kanlıca [i.e., across all of Istanbul] and make his own apple orchard, and leave the people thirsty.... [A]nother one will pop up: "Justice!" he'll say, then the next day he'll burn the harvest, destroy the farms, and hang the men! Then another one will come: "Freedom!" he'll shout; then he'll sew my mouth shut, tie my hands, climb onto my back and have his way with me (*keyfini gettirecek*)!

Let's see, after this whose head are they going to pawn, whose coach are they going to get on and yell out a folk song (*türkü*).... [Y]ou'll think it's a policeman but it will turn out to be an outlaw; you'll think it's a favor but it will turn out to be a trap; it will look like an angel but turn out to be Satan.... [I]f you don't open your eyes the eggs are all going to break! So don't think every bearded man is a holy man, don't listen to every empty word. Enough with the bravado! Don't get carried away by someone's posturing.... [M]y main advice to you is:

Open your eyes, stay on your toes, don't get cheated, don't believe, don't get duped!"

The reception of the essays was overwhelming, and all three were translated and published in the city's French, Greek, and Armenian newspapers. Refik would later claim that they were so popular the newspapers they appeared in sold for many times their original price.

Days after publishing these three essays, Refik composed another essay of a different type, one that transcended the partisan CUP-*muhalif* divide. In an article titled "Sulh" (Peace), which he wrote for *Yeni Mecmua* just days after the Armistice of Mudros, Refik positioned himself as a humanist above and outside politics:

In this essay I will not discuss the national election, the structure of the state, nor the reasons or conditions for the peace. Leave that to the politicians, the statesmen, the parliamentarians, and the daily newspapers, let them look at the political side of the peace ... *[H]umanity*, which has endured such misery during this five-year war, *has the right to finally read a true history* ... [F]inally peace will fall to its knees before us, caressing our faces, taking our heart, and putting our worries to rest, like a mother taking us into its bosom.[7] (emphasis added)

He described poignantly how "the marching armies stopped; the booming cannons went silent, even the waves of smoke from the gunpowder in the mountains was erased." "No more fresh wounds would be opened in brave chests," he wrote, "no more shadows of Izrail would be in pious heads; the Armistice that was being signed was giving the order to *humanity* running toward death: Stop and Live!" (emphasis added).[8]

Refik's humanist moment, while poignant, was fleeting. When members of the CUP Triumvirate fled to avoid prosecution for leading the empire into the war and for the many crimes committed therein, his tempered and circumscribed criticism of the regime and its collaborators gave way to a flood of emotion and soul-searching.[9] While it suddenly became safe to condemn—and thus expressly contest—the CUP, assessing its culpability and eradicating the secretive and complex organization from the political sphere were much more difficult. The Unionist regime had permeated governance from top to bottom and garnered support from multiple strata of society that reached deep into Istanbul and Anatolia.

After the cathartic condemnations of the CUP's leaders and the attempt to rise above the divisions and see the common plight of humanity, the hard work of mapping out a way forward for the empire began. Ottomans of all stripes braced themselves for the peace negotiations in Paris, scheduled to commence in January 1919. The core dilemma facing the Allies and Ottomans was how to disentangle the CUP from the Ottoman government to punish those who were culpable and to preserve some form of sovereignty. Three questions came to center stage in public debates about the future in Istanbul's press in late 1918 and early 1919: (1) What should be preserved and what should be shed from the hollowed-out empire? (2) How could the perceived state of moral and political bankruptcy be reversed in order to rebuild the state, with however truncated a territory? and (3) What form and extent of Western involvement could and should be accepted going forward? The Unionists were no longer seen as guardians of the constitution, much less the nation. It was clear that they had done nothing less than eviscerate the state, in fact. Debates in the press at this time refer to a homeland (*memleket*), constituted of "commoners" and "intellectuals," that was not only separate from the CUP but victimized by the party and its policies. The CUP were coming to be imagined as disaggregated from state and party as intellectuals and statesmen debated ways of expunging them from politics. Also implied in these debates was some kind of implicit, bedrock identity that imbued the Ottoman Sultanate with profound historical and cultural significance.[10] Who and what constituted the nation (*millet*) absent the CUP, after all? For all of the CUP's atrocities, it was a challenge to reimagine the empire without the force that had taken over the state and started to shape a notion of Turkish identity for the past decade. Such an effort would not last long. The circumstances within and beyond the empire's borders shifted, and CUP elements began to regroup in Anatolia as a national resistance movement.

Most important was the question of whether it would be possible for the preexisting so-called *muhalefet*, unified only in their opposition against the CUP, to run the empire were it to be expunged of the CUP. While the Freedom and Accord Party—which had come to be synonymous with *muhalefet* against the CUP before the war—attempted to regroup in late 1918/early 1919, it was clear that it comprised such disparate elements and obsolete leaders that it lacked the vision and the political capacity to fill the power vacuum left in the wake of the CUP's dissolution. Liberal *muhalifs* looked outside the empire for guidance as they sought to imagine a way forward, and Refik seems to have been part of at least two efforts that pinned their hopes on England and the United States.[11] He was a member of the Wilsonian Principles League, founded in late 1918, and the Friends of England Society, which was established in January 1919. The latter included leading liberal intellectuals such as Dr. Adnan (Adıvar), Halide Edib (Adıvar), Ali Kemal, and Ottoman statesman and *muhalif* Sait Molla.[12] Neither organization lasted long, and neither achieved much. The main claim to fame of the Friends of England Society was its vilification in the opening pages of *Nutuk*, Mustafa Kemal's official history of the War of Independence.

Refik, for all of his claims to being above partisan politics, seemed very much a part of the patronage network, if not formally a member of the political party of the Liberal Entente. When Tefvik Paşa's cabinet resigned and Damad Ferid Paşa's was formed in early March 1919, Refik threw in his lot with the latter and joined the liberals in their bid to run the Ottoman government. His associate Ali Kemal, editor of the liberal *Sabah* newspaper, was appointed interior minister in Damad Ferid's government, itself made up of vehement opponents of the CUP and the nationalists. Refik Halid stepped in as editor of *Sabah*, serving there for a month before being appointed to the post of general director of Post and Telegraph. During that month, just as the Paris peace talks were getting underway and he was poised to enter government service, we see Refik taking on yet a third voice: the erstwhile humanist and angry *muhalif* was now writing as a veritable spokesman for the embattled Ottoman government. In a March 20 front-page editorial titled "After the Armistice, Before the Peace," he appraised the situation the government faced as "terribly uncertain" and described how the homeland (*memleket*) was "feeling a powerful current, a force [pressing] against us from all sides" (*aleyhimize her tarafta kuvvetli bir cereyan, bir galeyan hiss oluyordu*). With reference to the genocide, he noted that "the entire nation (*millet*) is being accused because of actions that were in violation of the laws of humanity and the laws of war." "Without any investigation, but purely based on perceptions and partisanship," he noted, the future of "some of our provinces (*vilayet*) in Asia, and even the status of the capital itself is under discussion." As he put it, even an "Istanbul Question" had "sprung out of nowhere and entered into the discussion."

Refik nonetheless expressed hope because the new government had undertaken initiatives to increase its esteem among the public and to reinstitute order, including arresting and investigating "those suspected of having been influential in the 'massacre and deportations disasters' [the Armenian Genocide]."[13] Refik argued that the government should be seen as solid, "the old committees and organizations (*cemiyat ve hey'at*) having been utterly obliterated because of the fearful war." He contended that new ones were being constituted as the Council of Ten, or the High Council in Paris (i.e., the Paris Peace Conference) formed ideas and judgments without objections, even for Germany. Refik was optimistic that this Council of Ten, made up of two representatives from each of the five Entente Powers (England, France, Italy, the United States, and Japan), was preparing to shape a new kind of peace and world. He concluded by exhorting "every concerned Ottoman" to do their duty and to protect their conscience by supporting and aiding the government in its efforts to protect the rights and properly judge the movements of the "other Ottoman elements" (i.e., non-Muslims)—even in light of their alleged unworthiness.

"After the Armistice, Before the Peace," surely a propaganda piece for the Ottoman government and perhaps even his honest personal opinion, took note of the same alarming developments that were then spurring nationalist counterparts to form scattered resistance movements. He had not written off the Ottoman government, but still viewed it as a legitimate (if embattled) political authority that could find a solution to ensure the empire's survival. Whether in earnest or not, the article expressed faith in both British protection and the Paris system. Refik the *muhalif*, opponent of the CUP, was a defender of the Ottoman government and establishment, even under de facto colonial occupation. And there was still hope that the real problem in his view—the CUP—could be eradicated from politics and a settlement for the empire could be reached. This faith in the eventual triumph over the CUP would turn to deep anxiety in the next phase, as he entered state service on the one hand, and the CUP recombined into a national resistance movement on the other.

Damad Ferid's government, made up of many older *muhalifs*, assumed the reins of government in spring 1919. It was only a matter of time before Refik would be drafted into a government post; finally, the self-identified *muhalifs* would have their day in power. And indeed, his former *Sabah* editor Ali Kemal called him up to serve the government in mid-April.

Nationalists would accuse Ali Kemal of being a sellout and a tool of British interests. Indeed, he was a longtime Anglophile, liberal, and self-proclaimed *muhalif,* who had been exiled several times (including to Aleppo in the Hamidian period and to London during the Second Constitutional Era).[14] His staunch opposition to the CUP went way back; he had been actively involved in the 31 March Incident in 1909, in fact. He and Refik had met at the Publishing Congress (*Matbuat Kongresi*) in late 1918, shortly after the Armistice of Mudros, and again at the meetings of the Wilsonian Principles League shortly thereafter.[15] And now he was minister of the interior, appointing Refik Halid to the post of general director of Post and Telegraph at the suggeston of Dr. Adnan (Adıvar), a prominent intellectual who would later join the national forces in Anatolia and go on to become a major figure in the national government.

Since the inception of the offices of post (1840), telegraph (1855), and telephone (1909), the directorship had been a highly sensitive position, one possessing strategic value and power. As the sole medium of rapid communication across Anatolia, the telegraph assumed even greater importance after the war's end, when former Ottoman territories were occupied by the French, Italians, Greeks, or British, and sometimes subject to Armenian and Kurdish control. The official in charge of the telegraph directorate was also crucial in upholding censorship policies, which sought to control not just publication within the empire but the smuggling of newspapers and books from outside. It was emblematic of the vacuum in political authority that in the crucial transition from war to peace in late 1918 to mid-1919, the position had been vacant for months. Refik described in later memoirs what he saw as the government's main priorities at the moment: to establish connections to the leaders of the occupation powers, to remove the threat to public security that had sprung up with the "brigandage" of the Rum and Armenians in Anatolia, to accelerate the peace agreement process in Paris, and to punish the instigators of the war.[16]

On April 15, 1919, he assumed the position at the head of the General Directorate of Post and Telegraph, in what was his third government

FIGURE 2. Refik Halid as general director of the Post and Telegraph Service (1919/1920). Courtesy of the Taha Toros Archive.

position—all in non-Unionist administrations (see figure 2).[17] Refik served in this post until the fall of the Damad Ferid government on October 1, 1919, when the more nationalist-friendly Ali Rıza government was formed and a new phase of the Istanbul-nationalist rivalry began. This also ended a phase of Refik's own political career in which he and his fellow liberals were in the paradoxical position of *muhalifs* in power. In the space of six months they had to contend with a series of momentous changes. Under British pressure, the newly reconstituted War Crimes Tribunal (Divan-ı Harb-ı Örfi) in Istanbul was handing down indictments regarding CUP war crimes, specifically acts associated with the Armenian Genocide; in May the Greek army landed at İzmir and commenced its occupation of western Anatolia with British approval; and, most fatefully, shortly thereafter Mustafa Kemal landed at Samsun with the goal of uniting the scattered resistance movements into a national movement against foreign occupation.

THE TELEGRAPH EPISODE: THE BOW AND THE ARROW

Refik's first days on the job were both overwhelming and mundane; he wrote of discovering sacks full of *jurnals* (spy reports for the government) and making new appointments. By his own admission, he viewed every

MAP 3. Proposed settlement for Ottoman lands in the Treaty of Sèvres (1920)

development through the lens of his hatred and enmity toward the Unionists. When news first came of the Greek landing at İzmir, his first thought was that it was Unionist misinformation aimed at provoking chaos. And yet in his retelling of the event, he claimed to have been so busy trying to keep up with ministry business that he had not even gotten around to hearing about Mustafa Kemal's arrival in Anatolia—the fateful and famed opening moment in *Nutuk*—or to studying the circular that kicked off the national movement.[18] This was the Amasya Circular that announced Mustafa Kemal's plans to call a congress of resistance movements in Sivas in mid-September, after a plenary of the Eastern region's movements in Erzurum in July.

What became known as the Telegraph Episode occurred in late June 1919, when Mustafa Kemal, sent to Samsun on a military mission from the Ottoman government to suppress brigandage in the region, began sending telegrams to the Istanbul government instead, proclaiming his intention to unify the scattered resistance movements under his direction. Telegraphic communication had already become an issue weeks earlier, when the Ottoman government forbade telegraph operators in Anatolia from transmitting telegraphic appeals from the İzmir Defense of Rights Committee to those in Anatolia to arm themselves and march on İzmir to oppose the Greek occupation there. The Istanbul government was not interested in fomenting popular resistance, but rather in cooperating with its British overlords in the hopes of surviving another day.

When Mustafa Kemal began sending word around in the Amasya Circular via telegraph of his intention to mobilize the scattered resistance movements into a national resistance movement, the Istanbul government was alarmed, to say the least. Under orders from Ali Kemal and his British superiors, Refik blocked Mustafa Kemal's telegrams, forbade telegraph operators in Anatolia from receiving or transmitting them, and ultimately called for Mustafa Kemal to resign his position for failing to fulfill the mission he had been charged with carrying out. Mustafa Kemal, as far as the Istanbul government was concerned, was also acting in defiance of official Ottoman government policy, which was to work with the occupiers and try to keep order in Anatolia.

Mustafa Kemal resigned his post, and the Istanbul government issued an order for his arrest on charges of rebellion. The Telegraph Episode was not the end of the story of Refik's opposition to Mustafa Kemal and the national movement, however. Refik for his part continued his efforts to block Mustafa Kemal and to derail the Erzerum and Sivas Congresses later in the summer. He became such a target of opprobrium for his hostility and open opposition throughout the summer, not just to Mustafa Kemal but to the nationalist movement, that by the time the Sivas Congress met in September, the attendees were publicly calling for his arrest and execution. The events at the Sivas Congress made clear that there was no possibility of the Istanbul government—at least the one run by Damad Ferid as Grand Vezir—and the national movement joining forces to resist occupation, and relations between the two ceased. The National Pact (*Misak-ı Milli*) was declared to proclaim the borders of a Turkish sovereign entity, and the presumptive national government in Ankara was established. By late 1919 the expressed goal of the nationalists was to supplant the Ottoman government, which they would accomplish in stages over the next three years.

The June Telegraph Episode was only one event in the longer conflict involving the nationalists' challenge to the political authority of the Istanbul government, and vice versa. Even so, it receives inordinate attention, both in official history—Mustafa Kemal's 1927 rendering in *Nutuk*—and in Refik Halid's memoirs of the Armistice period, which were written in 1924 but only published in their entirety in 1948. Both men included exhaustive, verbatim transmissions of the telegrams exchanged, although each focused on different ones to bolster his respective case.[19] For both it was a watershed moment. Refik, trying both to exculpate himself and to take some credit for shaping history, likened the episode to "an arrow shot out of a bow," by which he meant that his actions in opposition to Mustafa Kemal triggered the "political revolution" (*inkilâb-ı idarî*, lit. revolutionary transfer of political authority) leading to the republic.[20] Through this framing, he portrayed, retrospectively, his contestation of Mustafa Kemal's early bid for authority as a heroic act and catalyst leading to the greater good: the new, independent nation-state of Turkey, to which he much later became a loyal patriot. For Mustafa Kemal, the Telegraph Episode was the moment when the Ottoman government in Istanbul defied him, by extension betrayed the Turkish national will that he embodied, and thus ceased to be the legitimate sovereign authority of the Turkish nation. According to his account in *Nutuk*, Mustafa Kemal's only allegiances from that point on were to the sultan directly and to the Turkish nation.[21] Because of Refik Halid's rejection of his authority, Mustafa Kemal reasoned that he was compelled to replace the Ottoman government as the executor of national sovereignty on behalf of the Sultanate.

The Telegraph Episode was surely a turning point in the Turkish War of Independence, although the path to national victory three years later was determined by many other contingencies. In the genealogy of *muhalefet* we are tracing here, too, it was nothing less than a crossing of the Rubicon. The resulting breach between the Ottoman government and Mustafa Kemal gave way to a new framework of opposition, between the Istanbul government on the one hand and the presumptive national government on the other. Tellingly, the nationalists did not situate themselves as *muhalefet*, even though they were very much in opposition to the legal political authority, the Istanbul government. The fact that they did not position themselves as *muhalifs* shows that in its vernacular usage the word remained reserved for those who had opposed the Unionists, even though those opponents were now running the Istanbul government. The *muhalifs*, even when they were in power, still identified and were identified as *muhalifs*. It was as if both sides—the CUP and their opposition—were still tacitly accepting CUP dominance and the impotence of the formal structures of the Ottoman government.

This is a curious phenomenon, particularly because the category of *muhalefet* was necessarily in flux. Those who had opposed the CUP, on

whatever grounds and whether vocally or not, became caught in this pro-
longed power struggle between "Istanbul" and "Ankara." Istanbul, the seat of
the Ottoman government, was under British occupation, the consequences
of which were still unclear. Ankara, eventual seat of the national movement,
was being represented as a political authority that was qualitatively new, and
yet it was well known that CUP elements were animating that movement.
And because of this knowledge of the association between the CUP and the
nationalists, not everyone was eager to jump on the nationalist bandwagon
from the start. The nonaligned—disgusted at the CUP, balking at colonial
occupation, and well aware of the impasse that lay ahead for Ottoman sovereignty—would sooner or later have to choose: accept British occupation or
join the nationalists—a retooled Unionist movement—in Anatolia.

The decisive question for those who clung to *muhalefet* in this new era had to
do with the continuity between the CUP and the national movement. Despite
nationalists' oaths of renunciation of the CUP, many *muhalifs* did not believe
they were in earnest. They regarded the nationalists as Unionists in disguise,
with the same agenda, the same illiberal tactics, and the same gang-like men-
tality, and often described them metaphorically as wolves in sheep's clothing.
They shared early British skepticism, and saw the nationalists' renunciation of
the CUP as a charade meant to sidestep culpability for war crimes and recoup
power. The nationalists had to struggle not merely against the Western occupying forces but also for the hearts and minds of Anatolia's exhausted Muslim
population, to persuade them to take up arms once again—this time against
the Greek invading forces—as well as of the Ottoman-Turkish establishment
in Istanbul, to persuade them to defect from Istanbul and Ottoman political
authority and join the national movement. Those who chose to persist in the
role of *muhalif* remained dead set against Ankara.

The nationalists eventually accomplished their goal of winning over the
population and much of the Ottoman establishment—and the category of
muhalefet shrank considerably. By late spring 1920, a critical mass of Istanbul
intellectuals, many of whom had been outspoken *muhalifs*/liberals in the
previous era, departed for Anatolia, prompted by the formalization of the
British occupation over the Ottoman government. By late summer 1921,
the tide in the Greco-Turkish War turned toward the Turkish nationalist
forces, and the following autum they swept west across Anatolia, driving out
the Greek army and much of the Greek (Rum) civilian population in the process. Refik Halid and a handful of other prominent figures—Ali Kemal, Refii
Cevat (Ulunay), and Rıza Tevfik among them, stayed the course in Istanbul.

In sharp contrast to his later claims to downplay his opposition to Mustafa Kemal—that he was simply in the wrong place at the wrong time and that he was following orders when he refused to accept Mustafa Kemal's telegrams in June 1919—when we look more closely at his actions and his writings, we see that Refik continuously and actively tried to stymie the nationalist movement throughout the Armistice period. He was, in fact, one of the most prominent and vocal antinationalists even after their triumphant arrival in Istanbul in October 1922.[22] His actions had not gone unnoticed in Ankara; the national movement had begun calling for his arrest in late September 1919, and on July 3, 1920, he was condemned by the Ankara Court of the First Instance. He was charged with being "guilty of treason against the homeland" and sentenced to execution in absentia.[23] He then served a second term as general director of Post and Telegraph when the Damad Ferid cabinet was formed anew in March 1920—the critical juncture when the British occupation became de jure and the Ottoman parliament closed and reopened in Ankara as the Grand National Assembly of Turkey. He served until September 26 of that year, stepping down a few weeks before the Damad Ferid cabinet fell for the last time. During that second tenure, he claimed to be neutral, but we find him—two days after the opening of the Grand National Assembly in Ankara—issuing assurances to the Interior Ministry that publications by the nationalist forces circulating in Istanbul had all been collected and destroyed.[24] He was continuing to oppose the national movement in every way he could, even after the pivotal moment when the British occupation of the Ottoman government became de jure.

IMAGINING *MUHALEFET*

Refik Halid, out of political power in fall 1919, continued to pursue his campaign against the nationalists—undertaken with the sanction of the British and from the safety that came with his privilege, but now took his campaign to the literary realm. In early October 1919, after stepping down from his post, he retreated to his older brother's residence in the suburb of Yeşilköy (San Stefano) and began to resurrect his old persona, the Porcupine. While there was continuity with his old writings, the Porcupine had a new preoccupation: the construction of a new literary and historical imaginary of *muhalefet* and an accompanying archetype of the *muhalif* as tragic hero. In addition to taking up the continuities between the Unionists from the 1910–12 period and the "wolves in sheep's clothing"—Unionists disguised as nationalists—that emerged after the war, he began to reconceptualize *muhalefet* through the construction of a clear binary between the *muhalifs*/liberals and Unionists-as-nationalists.[25] Throughout the War of Independence, Refik voiced his opposition to the nationalists via this imaginary, deploying it as a tool to highlight the enduring political connections between the politics of the recent Unionist past and the emergent Turkish national movement. Because the denial of these links was at the crux of the national movement's claim to legitimacy, he put the onus on the nationalists to demonstrate that they were a new force, fighting a new struggle for a Turkish nation. The nationalists' response, formulated in the context of a humiliating and unjust foreign occupation, was to redefine and sideline all who opposed them as traitors to the national cause—as the Unionists had smeared all who opposed them as reactionaries (*mürteci*).

Refik began his series of condemnations of the nationalists by challenging their decision to make Anatolia both the political base of operations and the heart of the new nation's homeland. In the first of two connected stories he wrote in Yeşilköy, "Anatolia Says" ("Anadolu diyor ki"), he writes as a personified Anatolia, protesting the nationalists: "I am not Rumelia!" (the Ottomans' former Balkan territories), he states, alluding to the Balkan background of many of the Unionists and their willingness to subject Anatolia to even more suffering under another of their ill-advised plans to make it into their "national homeland." Anatolia is *not* the Balkans, it is not the nationalists' birthright because they are from the Balkans, and they are not welcome to instrumentalize it for their own ends, as they had done, first with the constitution and then with the Ottoman government and state.[26] In the second story, "The Unionist Says" ("İttihatçı diyor ki"), Refik speaks through a Unionist to express seething resentment: "I am not a liberal (ben itilafçı değilim!) [i.e. member of the Freedom and Accord Party]!" of course. The "Unionist" tells us:

> My unclean heart does not warm to the [soothing] milk of peace ... [N]either water nor soap can wash away the stain on my sullied forehead; my savage heart cannot enter Europe ... [L]et those who are unaware learn: ... Talat Paşa is nothing like Sadık Bey [founder of the Freedom and Accord Party]; our associations do not bring benefit to the homeland (*memleket*).[27] ... We neither feel shame before others, nor fear Allah!

He continues:

> Beware: do not be deceived by my writings or my speeches; do not invoke the name "Union" without my permission; do not think I am human just because

you see me without a tail. . . . In one swipe I would take down a *muhalif* for no reason, slap a white shirt on him and hang him. . . . Let me see to what I know, I'll engage in some [war] profiteering, and I'll hawk patriotism in the wake of massacres and deportations [the Armenian Genocide]!

And as for the *muhalifs*:

> Let the *muhalifs* blow over us like the wind: May they neither settle into the palace, nor find support in the army, and may there not be a whiff of them in the party (*fırka*). . . . [L]et them get down from their horses tomorrow and get on donkeys; may they be extinguished in their graves like lamps that have burned the last of their oil.[28]

An existential battle was indeed taking shape, but not the one between the Turkish nation and its foreign occupiers. Instead, it was the internal battle between *muhalifs* and Unionists-turned-nationalists, the latter taking over Anatolia the way the Unionists had taken over the empire, to drive it into the ground.

It was at this time that Refik published *Memleket Hikâyeleri* (Homeland stories), a volume of collected stories he had written while in exile that included "The Joke," the tragic story of the sexual desire of a Turkish man for a Rum girl discussed in chapter 3. In publishing this collection in 1919, Refik was subtly challenging the nationalists' appropriation of Anatolia as their partisan-national homeland through a series of social realist snapshots of peasants and everyday life. In contrast to the then-emerging didactic, patriotic literature valorizing Anatolia as the bosom of the Turkish nation, *Memleket Hikâyeleri* offered a restrained counterpoint to the emerging nationalist imaginary. While they were not overtly political or oppositional, the stories reinforced assertions Refik made elsewhere that Anatolia did not match up to the nationalists' projection of it.

In addition to republishing earlier works, Refik produced hundreds of new writings that tackled the evolution and reinvention of the Unionists as nationalists.[29] An example is "The Story of Two Sons" ("*İki Oğlun Hikâyesi*"). In this deft attempt to grasp the empire's predicament, the story follows a man who walks to Çamlıca (a village outside Greater Istanbul), where he encounters an emaciated figure with a sunken face and sallow skin who seems to have suffered terrible misfortunes. Just as the narrator is taking pity on him, the man looks back and says, "Don't you recognize me?" The narrator then realizes that indeed "only eight or ten years earlier" (ca. 1912) the gaunt man before him had been famous and infinitely wealthy. He recalls that the man used to own land "on three continents." In a clear reference to the Ottoman Empire, which only a decade prior enjoyed sovereignty on three continents, Refik writes that the fallen man had once had "farms in the Balkans from Işkodra to Edirne, endless land in Anatolia, date groves in Basra, orange groves in Jaffa, rose gardens in Trablus, coffee plantations in Yemen, every kind of land of inestimable value."

Next, the narrator asks about the man's misfortunes, and the latter blames his losses on his two sons, setting up a parable about the Balkan War and World War I; the story involves a younger son who was cruel and violent by nature (the CUP), and an older son, who was kind but naïve and pliant (the establishment/liberal *muhalefet*). The cruel son talked his father into letting him manage lands in the Balkans, which he promptly destroyed. He tortured the animals, tore apart the furniture, and beat up the neighbors' children. Hoping to salvage their patrimony, the father then put the elder son in charge, but this resulted in their being swindled and losing property (the Balkan War). When the father turned again to the cruel younger son, soon all that remained was "five or six farms in Anatolia." Then, when he asked the elder son to manage the land—but allowed his grandchild by the younger son to manage it—all was lost (the Armistice-era government). The grandson (the nationalists), who had the same cruel nature as his father, started burning and looting, gambling and drinking, torturing and hanging just like his father had done, until there was nothing left. Ultimately, the old man's story ended with the lament, "So, my dear, my two sons finished me off, emptied all that wealth down to the last, one with his boorishness and unruliness and the other with his clumsiness and naivité. . . . But I will never excuse my younger son. . . . [W]hatever happened, my God, if one of them had ever done something to make me happy, would I have had so much grief?"[30] In this parable of the empire's final collapse, Refik depicts the dynamic between the liberals/*muhalefet* and the CUP, indicating that the nationalists were the spawn of the CUP; his story was focused not on foreign oppression and occupation (which would have been central to the Unionist-cum-nationalist rendering), but on internal contestation and failings. It was a view of history that the nationalists characterized as treasonous, and the fact that it was espoused by someone in the employ of the British-occupied Istanbul government only made it more suspect.

In another story written during his Yeşilköy residence, Refik also implicates the nationalists in the political violence of the previous decade. "On Vines and Trellises" ("Asma ve Çardağa dair") is an artful commentary on the ravages of partisan politics after 1908. In it he writes about the dramatic increase in political violence—particularly hangings—since the Young Turk Revolution and the restoration of the constitution. Playing on the words *asma*, which can mean both "vine" and "hanging," and *çardak*, which can mean both "trellis" and "gallows," Refik recalled that until 1908, the two words only brought to mind grapes and quince. It was after the 1909 counterrevolution that they took on the grim association with the gallows. In the story, Refik reminisced about his 1916 exile in Ankara and described how he and his fellow exiles became acclimated to violence. Shocked and sickened the first time they witnessed a public hanging, they quickly became so desensitized that they would continue to drink their coffee in Ankara's central square—then still the center of a provincial town, not yet the national capital—as executions went on nearby. Refik emphasized that these executions included the hanging of at least one innocent man. He referred specifically to an incident during the 1909 counterrevolution, when novice excecutioners failed at their task and one of his acquaintances narrowly escaped death when the white shirt he had been dressed with for his execution tore. After removing it and escaping through the crowd, he made his way from Beyazıt Square to the Unkapanı docks, where he hopped on a boat and left Istanbul.

Refik did not just stick to narrating how history did unfold; he also ventured into counterfactual outcomes as a thought exercise and a means to express his critique. In the story "What Would Have Happened If It Hadn't Happened?," written around 1921 (and among those stories excised from the record during the Republican period), he speculated about the trajectories, both historical and individual, that might have taken shape if the 1908 Constitutional Revolution had not taken place. This was entering forbidden territory, since for all their flaws and transgressions, the Unionists were still credited with having restored the constitution and with ending the despotic reign of Sultan Abdülhamid II. Refik conjectures that not only would Bulgaria not have declared its independence, but Bosnia-Herzegovina would not have been annexed by Austria-Hungary, and thus perhaps World War I would not have broken out. He imagines the newspaper articles announcing promotions of government officials and envisages that, for instance, Mustafa Kemal would still be a regular soldier, and thus "the nation would be bereft of their great hero in Anatolia." There would have been no need for him, he writes, since Greece would not have occupied Anatolia in the first place. Refik even imagines that he himself would have risen to the top of the Ottoman bureaucracy, rather than having been purged by the CUP in 1909. He thinks of all the medals and honors he would have garnered and laments, "If only I could give all those up and not be that way, and if only the government wasn't this way!"

As they watched the CUP regroup and the nationalist mobilization taking place in Anatolia, Refik and other *muhalifs* must have felt a profound sense of powerlessness. By imagining different outcomes, as he did in these stories, Refik was able to recoup a sense of power and agency, however imaginary. In "The Last Days of the Constitutionalist Dignitaries" ("Rical-ı Meşrutiyet'in Son Günleri"), he continued in this vein, now imagining the just forms of death for the most prominent wartime CUP figures.[31] After frantically traveling to the Caucasus, Moscow, and Germany, Enver Paşa cannot find any friends. Bewildered and disoriented, he gives up his vision of world conquest in favor of piety and becomes a reciter of the Qur'an (*hafız*) and a pilgrim (*hacı*). When he dies, he is remembered as "Hacı Hafız Enver Efendi." Cemal Paşa, who finds he cannot drown his sorrows with alcohol, women, or gambling, wanders the streets, wailing, and decides to become a poet. He establishes a following with his demonstrably terrible poetry and is declared the national poet. "The hanging, repressing, burning, looting dictator of Arabia" ends his life reciting patriotic and melancholy poetry, drinking champagne, and smoking Cuban cigars. Talaat Paşa's fate is perhaps the worst: after failing at every profession he takes up, he ends up in abject poverty. The local policeman finds his corpse dressed in rags and is not able to identify him. After he is buried in an unmarked grave, no one even notices his death. He is gone without a trace.

For all three, who in any case ended up dead within a few years of Refik's writing these stories, justice involves a total withdrawal from politics and the world. Refik seems to imply that they had failed so miserably at saving the empire and used their power so perversely that it would only be fitting for them to separate from each other and from the political authority they once enjoyed. As in the previous story, Refik condemns the careerism of those who benefited from the wartime situation through rapid advancement and war profiteering. He evokes a yearning that those profiting from such human suffering receive justice, even if only by fantasizing about their deaths. Again, the power of imagination is the only power he has to express opposition in the present moment, when he could already see that in real life there was little hope of triumphing over the Unionists/nationalists.

Having roundly condemned the nationalists for their Unionist pedigree in the past, and for their denial of that pedigree and their kidnapping of Anatolia for their partisan cause in the present, Refik went on to satirize Ankara's future and nationalist utopianism in "This Must Be a Dream…" ("Hülya bu ya…"). The story, subtitled "Observations of an American Traveler Regarding Ankara," was dated February 11, 1921, and centers on an American journalist marveling at the achievements of the presumptive national government.[32] In Ankara, he proclaims, "there is no need to walk, use an automobile or a coach," because "now the road itself moves and brings you to whichever quarter you'd like!" He continues: "Despite it being winter, the trees were lush and green, leafy, and the flowers were blooming" because "in Ankara there are no seasons." The American is guided by a local, who shows him the empty Grand National Assembly and explains that the members of parliament need not waste their time attending in person, since they are all busy with their day jobs as ministers, directors, commanders, and provincial and district governors. In the chamber of the Grand National Assembly there is instead a telephone (sesli telefon) in the place where each deputy would be seated. In what seems like a commentary on the fact that the legislative branch of government—which should be the heart of a constitutional order—was merely window dressing for the nationalists, the ministers would literally phone in from their real offices.

As the guide introduces the new ministers—familiar figures like Adnan Bey (Adıvar) as health minister and Ziya Gökalp as the singer of a "national hymn [beste]" written by Halide Edib—the "wonders" of the new Ankara continue to unfold. Refik writes about how a recording of the song is played on an apparatus (cihaz) that is used to lull citizens to sleep. In this new utopia, the nationalists have even conquered death: "One of our doctors has invented a machine," he writes, "that reads your future cause of death and corrects it!" Ankara, he writes, "is not like a city on the surface of the Earth, but like one on Mars.… Here, everything, everyone is always: Machines, again machines, always machines!"[33]

Refik was skeptical, to say the least, of the nationalists' utopian project, and dismissive of their adulation—even worship—of technology. Not only was their Unionist past worthy of condemnation; their vision for a future society was also far-fetched and unattainable. Like many others, he even saw in the nationalists a distinct resemblance to the Bolsheviks, whose vision also seemed far-fetched and who were also in the midst of a—far bloodier— revolution and civil war. Certainly the tactics the nationalists employed, their class backgrounds, and their Jacobin ambitions would have supported that view.[34] In January 1920, Refik explicitly compared the situation in Ankara to Moscow, in an article for *Alemdar* called "Girinin in Place of Lenin." He argued that just as Lenin can be replaced by Girinin [Mikhail Kalinin], Enver was being replaced by Kemal. The message was that in essence, they are all—whether Lenin and Girinin, or Enver and Kemal—the same, and in both cases, the recent past and present were blurring into one. The problem, in his view as in Ali Kemal's, was that the nationalists, like the CUP before them and the Bolsheviks across the border, were functioning like gangs in politics, a criticism he and Ali Kemal reiterated time and again in these years.[35]

As Refik Halid was drafting all of these imaginative critiques of the nationalists, he was also carrying out a direct and heated correspondence with them. He published one such exchange, which provides us with a vivid and devastating image of the antagonism. In "Correspondence with Mr. Mehmet Ç," ("Mehmet Ç Bey ile Muhabere") he includes the full text of two threatening letters to the editor, written by a nationalist partisan in Anatolia in late 1920 (when Refik had already been sentenced to death in absentia for treason to the nation) and early 1921, as well as his responses in the summer of 1921. The writer of the letters, identified only as "Mehmet Ç," attacks Refik both on a personal level and for his work as editor of *Peyam-ı Sabah*, the main organ of the liberal *muhalefet* in Istanbul at the time. Mehmet Ç writes: "Are you still talking about me? Do you suppose I've forgotten that you likened me to a murderer in your writings, during my absence in the Armistice? Refik Halid: It is impossible for me to forget you! Not because of my individual dislike toward you, [it is] because I know that my country is holier than anything else [that] I cannot forget you! *To forget you would amount to treason against my country.*" He goes on to say that he would not only like to kill Refik Halid, but to come to Istanbul and hack his children to pieces, and hopes that no one else will kill him before Mehmet Ç himself has a chance.

Refik responds by addressing Mehmet Ç as "Üsküplü [from Skopje; in today's Macedonia] Mehmet Ç Bey, in the Hacı Bayram-ı Veli quarter of Ankara." On one level this is meant to remind Mehmet Ç of his provincial location in Ankara and of his provincial, non-Anatolian, Balkan origins. On a second level, we can read it as a broader jab aimed at Unionist-*cum*-nationalists, who hailed from the Balkans. At the same time, by specifying the quarter where the Grand National Assembly lay, the Hacı Bayram-ı Veli quarter—which ostensibly took its name from the shrine of an early fifteenth-century Sufi saint—Refik contrasts the rich philosophical and moral traditions of Sufism and the early Ottoman dynasty with the philistine Mehmet Ç, and the morally and spiritually bankrupt CUP and national movement.[36] After making these erudite digs at the letter writer, Refik writes, "I could not answer your previous letter (in which you congratulated me for my new post) due to my *not* being very busy [meaning 'I am not giving you the time of day']. But this time I am sending an immediate answer because it would be impolite to leave it unanswered [meaning 'Because I am a gentleman I am deigning to give you a response']. First, the sentence 'Are you still talking about me?' straight away as an opening to a letter really comes out of nowhere, and I found it quite unattractive." He then gets more serious and responds to Mehmet Ç Bey's threats and accusations, questioning his notions of patriotism and his bravado. He asks why Mehmet Ç's name never appears in the nationalist newspapers' lists of heroes in Anatolia, when one even sees women's names on those lists. Refik ends his response with the wish that "God willing, one day, the readers of our correspondence may see us walking across the bridge [Galata] and say, 'Look, there are two valuable citizens one next to the other!'" He confesses that two months earlier the lock on his door at home had broken, but that he has yet to fix it. Writing that he has no protection against anyone who might come to kill him, he says, "I put a cane against the door to prop it shut at night and I sleep like a baby. I trust not in that cane, but in God." Effectively, Refik dares Mehmet Ç Bey to come to Istanbul and kill him.

The story highlights the depths of hatred that CUP-turned-nationalists harbored against their opponents and the violent and vindictive feelings nationalist partisans felt toward writers and intellectuals in Istanbul. The object of Mehmet Ç's vitriole extended beyond Refik to Ali Kemal, who would be lynched, and to Refii Cevat (Ulunay), who was forced to flee the country in 1922. Refik published the letters to expose the vicious partisanship of the CUP-turned-nationalists and to contrast it with his vision of a pluralist political arena (he hopes they can one day walk hand in hand). The exchange highlights once again the class character of the rift between *muhalifs* and the national movement, populated by provincial Muslims, often of a military background, recently expelled from the Balkans and Russian lands. It also highlights the continuities, both of individuals and more broadly of political and martial culture and of mafia-like intimidation tactics, between the CUP and the nationalist movement. Refik Halid and Ali Kemal, among others, viewed the CUP-turned-nationalists as a gang rather than a legitimate popular movement aimed at establishing lasting justice.

These stories, each in a different way, lay bare the partisan realities of the nationalist movement on the one hand and the continuities between the Unionists and the nationalists on the other. Both points were taboo from the perspective of the nationalists, who were marketing themselves as qualitatively new and as representing a unified Turkish nation struggling for self-determination and against colonial occupiers and their local collaborators. And in fact the rivalry between nationalists and *muhalifs* was coming to revolve around these two points held over from the recent Ottoman past: partisanship and continuity of power from that past. In one last example that illustrates this pattern, Refik published a refutation of the national movement in the form of an eyewitness account of the Ankara fire of 1916. Prompted by the events in and around Ankara in 1921, he approaches the red line of calling out culpability for the Armenian Genocide to level a subtle but profound condemnation of the nationalists.

"THE ANKARA FIRE"

In August 1921, when the nationalists were still highly vulnerable both on the battlefield and in the propaganda war, Refik Halid decided to write an account of the 1916 fire that he had witnessed during his exile in Ankara. At the time he wrote it, the Battle of Sakarya—a key juncture in the Greco-Turkish War—was raging. In a story titled "The Ankara Fire," he wrote about what he saw as the real origins of the nationalists' relationship to the new capital and shed light on how the Armenian Genocide—the memory of it, the question of accountability for it, and the fraught question of restorative justice to right it—was embedded in the rivalry between CUP-nationalists and liberals-*muhalifs*. His evocative piece is the only eyewitness account we have of the fire, and for that reason, in addition to its value in Refik Halid's campaign against the nationalists, it merits verbatim reproduction here:

> Don't think, looking at the title, that this is a pun or an allusion related to the latest events in Ankara [i.e., the Battle of Sakarya and the fires near Ankara as part of the national movement/Greco-Turkish War in August 1921]; in this article I am only going to discuss one terrible fire that I witnessed while I was in Ankara in the old days (*fi tarihinde*) [although only five to six years before he published this piece], instead of trying to cover a difficult and tiring ground by way of invention today I am simply going to recount for you a memory (*hatıra*). I don't think this "Ankara fire" article will be out of step in a time that Ankara is so much in the news.

Here he begins his eyewitness account:

As for me, I am desensitized to Istanbul's fires, a wise and astute man, having gotten used, since my birth, to seeing fires, flames, smoke, charred debris; no calamity or conflagration would be able to scare me.[37] . . . Especially since the restoration of the Constitution I have often been looking for a sight of fire in my surroundings; as I was completely accustomed to looking upon the threshold of fire, full of loud cries by rowdy men, it was obvious that I was not going to be seized by anxiety and grief[; rather it was] as if I were watching a sunset, an illumination [of a city during a festival], or a movie when facing the fire.[38] But the Ankara fire turned out to be more enormous and ferocious than any of the fires I had heard about or known; lasting a full two days and three nights, it burned three-quarters of the town—and the best part of it—reducing a huge provincial center into a tiny township, transforming it into a village.

It was in an August, just like this; that is, as it is customary, in the season for eggplant [i.e., when people would smoke eggplant over fires]. In the middle of a burning hot night, stupefied by the heat, we were tossing back and forth, just as we were almost falling asleep, we heard voices on the street and bells in the distance; our neighborhood was an Armenian Catholic one, whose men had been deported, yet its women were kindly [he is being ironic, given that the men were killed en masse] left. I opened the window and asked, "What's going on?" of the flat shadows speaking with each other fearfully in the half-darkness.

"Fire!" they said.

Fire? Come now! . . . On this night? So still that not even a leaf was stirring? How easy would it be to quell it? And I had no doubt that we would get news soon after that it had been put out altogether. However, since leaving Istanbul I hadn't seen, hadn't been able to see a fire, and so could not resist the desire to see a sharp light, a straight flame, even if only once in three and a half years, so I climbed onto the terrace, driven by habit and curiosity. Ever since the war was declared, petrol had become as expensive as rose water, was sold by the *dirhem*, and pained us when it was burned. I opened the door of the closet next to me, and, using my hands and feet to climb the staircase, which was bolt upright and narrow like a corkscrew, I emerged onto the glazed [tile] roof: in the distance, deep in the belly of the city was a part of a flame, no more than a fistful, like the lanterns behind the Karagöz shadow puppet theatre curtains, waving calmly, spurting out soot now and then and ready to go out on its own, simply being quelled, being consumed, becoming darkened.

"You call this a fire?" I said. "This is a lantern!"

I came down from the roof and went to bed. But in the morning, I woke up early to a hubbub the likes of which I had never heard until then. The fire was still going on. They were even saying that, if the mansion of I-don't-know-which Hacı Misak or Karabet Çakşıryan [both Armenian names] catches fire, then it would be difficult to stop it. Naturally I rushed up to the terrace again; this time it looked like a real fire; pitch black smoke, sparks, pieces of wood on fire, with flames waving in the wind, and a reddish heat like an oven.

After seeing this I got to thinking how narrow and crooked Ankara's streets were. . . . In some places the street was so narrow that you could reach your hand across from one window box/balcony (*cumba*) to the one across the street; and because under there the sun never shone, no matter the heat, and despite it being July [*sic*], there was a dampness that would never dry. And the houses were all wooden and without gardens. And then there was the fact that there was no water in the city; we could only manage to get water to wash our faces begging and pleading and paying 5 kurush for a clay jug full of water. There was a very good chance the fire would become a calamity, having been given the time to grow under these conditions. . . . I got dressed and shot out to the street.

It was burning; it was burning with a terrible might, devouring and burning, stretching and expanding ahead, rustling and wheezing. As if under every house there was a separate bellows, fanning the flames, ratcheting up the violence of it. Before this, the people in the surrounding area were busy trying to save their belongings and those like us in the distant quarters were content with watching it all. Most people during this season had moved into their gardens/orchards anyway. Such mansions burned so quickly that no time was found for its doors to be opened; those who didn't know Ankara before this fire might think that the houses that were burnt consisted of small ones and the [burnt] things [consisted] of junk [i.e., remnants of things]. But it wasn't like that; mansions with twenty rooms and marble staircases, grand pianos, extravagant carpets, and crystal chandeliers were burning. It wasn't just straw-filled cushions, cooking grills, and remnants of things that were burning, *but the possessions that rich Armenians had obtained by working with an unbearable effort over the course of many years* [emphasis added].

And that which had been saved caught fire on its own in a single moment, a heap of things spread out in a wide square. Among those things I counted exactly 14 pianos; all 14, groaning, burned and turned to ash in a painful melody. The narrow streets were choked, full of carts and bales of things. It was no longer possible to curse, even to escape; the fire had spread in 5 or 6 different directions and was simply ricocheting forward haphazardly, as if it was thinking, "I can't burn everywhere at the same time, it takes too long, let me hurry up"; It was springing [forward], like the trains going in different directions at the railway station, smoke billowing right and left, huffing and puffing, it was hurrying ahead.

And the wounded and dead began to appear. They were carrying the stretchers around, shouting, "Make way! Move aside! Out of the way!" And there you go, in the midst of all this pandemonium, in this hot and ferocious time, a friend freshly arrived from Istanbul pops up in front of me. We hugged each other, and we had so much to tell to each other that we ran into whatever was the closest place, a building. It was the old Frères School, now a hospital. It was being evacuated. We found two chairs and started to talk. There was no limit to the tears, moaning, cries for help and shouting around us. What tumult, heat, buzzing, rushing [here and there]. But we didn't notice. . . . *He was conveying to me the scandals [being carried out by] of the Unionists in Istanbul in the [Princes'] Island[s]—the small steamboats being sent to get ice cream, their whores wrapped up in heaps of banknotes in their beds, the corruption, the bribery, those shameful acts. It was making me so hot under the collar [lit. roasting my mind] that I wasn't able to think of anything else* [emphasis added]. Then a minute later

"Hey get out, you're going to burn!"

we heard a voice saying, and two people grabbed us under the arms; we flew out; we looked back and [saw] the building had caught fire. It was then that I was able to examine the circle of the fire's expansion. What do I see, but a roof four houses down from the one where I was, crackling and burning. . . . When I got back, safe and sound, I learned that they had been afraid that I was trapped under debris, [or] had been injured or burned.

I shouted, "Oh God, my things!" I started to pack my things and tie them in bales, wrap my carpets with the skill and readiness that life gives to some-one who has been on the road for three-and-a-half years straight. I was ready in 20 minutes. A military doctor sent a cart, we got on and said "Giddyup!" to them; it was as if the house was waiting for that cue and immediately caught fire. Someone for whose friendship I will be forever grateful, who lived in a quarter far enough away that the fire was unlikely to reach him, opened his home to those of us exiles who were victims of the fire. We were saved. But the fire; it burned all day, all night, and the whole next day and night. Oh what a horror it was! The narrow streets, the city burning day and night, that fire and that hubbub reminded me of ancient Rome. And the governor [Dr. Reşid], in the face of this terror, with a countenance dull and frozen like Nero, going around with his retinue slowly and calmly. But the poor fellow, what else could he do? If I were in his place, . . .[illegible] they were spread out in the fields outside the city. They had neither a drop of water nor a bite of food. The bakeries of Eskişehir were supplying bread to Ankara, so bread came to us from the road. In the market town [*kasaba*] neither shop nor caravansaray, nor bathhouse, nor any other roofed structure remained, no instruments or tools for any craft.

And here, the punchline to the story, the connection to the CUP, and to the present:

This fire saved me from Ankara forever. At that time Talaat was still Minister of the Interior. I was made homeless, and sent a telegram asking permission to be transferred to Bilecik. Somehow, he ordered it, and thus I, dear and sweet, narrowly escaped pitch black and scorched Ankara.

I was unable to bear Ankara to such a degree that I was simply thrilled when my political enemies [the nationalists as of 1920/21] *chose it to be their center/headquarters; "they deserve it!" I thought.*[39] (emphasis added)

The story of the fire—in all of its painstaking detail—was the story of how the nationalists, like the CUP, were a force of destruction rather than salvation. The CUP saw to the destruction of Ankara once, with the fire, and the nationalists were not, despite their claims, creating something redemptive, but rather destroying the town again by making it their capital. In pointing out the grim continuity between the two, Refik is calling out and condemning the metamorphosis of the CUP into the national movement then underway. Bound up with this condemnation of the nationalists is the violence wrought against the Armenian civilian population, exemplified by the Ankara fire during the war. It should be recalled that he, like several other prominent *muhalefet* figures, not only refrained from vocal condemnation of the genocide but maintained close relations with at least one of the major perpretrators, Dr. Reşit, the governor of Ankara at the time of the fire. Even here, writing in 1921, Refik stops short of direct, explicit condemnation of the genocide, showing us that there was a line that even he, as a self-proclaimed *muhalif*, would not dare to cross. And yet the gesture of empathy alone toward the Armenian victims, even identified by name, whose hard-earned wealth was going up in flames, was further than Unionist or nationalist would go.

It is fascinating, in that light, that the description draws sustained attention to the fire and the extent to which Armenians were targeted and affected by it. He uses the event to condemn the nationalists, yet makes no explicit placement of blame or explanation. Presumably the reader in Istanbul in 1921 would know exactly to what and whom he was referring. The fire does not seem like a mere accident, yet the question of culpability is intentionally left hanging. The fact that it appeared to be such a small fire, seemingly easily extinguished at the outset, and yet had somehow become an inferno by the next morning points to suspicious agents. And the passing comments about the quarter being Armenian Catholic, the deportations, and the opulent, hard-earned wealth that was going up in flames would indicate to a contemporary reader the political nature of the fire. The details of Refik Halid's conversation with his Istanbul friend add further weight to the accusations against the Unionists of wrongdoing on many levels. But perhaps most puzzling and fascinating is the reference to the provincial governor, likened to Nero, standing by and watching coldly as the city was turned to ashes. That governor, Dr. Reşit, who had reportedly been so fond of Refik Halid, had committed suicide in early February 1919 after having been arrested in connection with the genocide, and readers would surely have known that.

Refik Halid started to sketch the outlines not just of a historical pedigree and literary imaginary for *muhalefet*, but of a *muhalif* political and social identity, as well. In the collection *Ay Peşinde* (In pursuit of the moon) (published by Sabah Press in 1920–21), Refik published a story called "Metampsikoz" ("Metempsychosis") wherein he confesses to being preoccupied with that theory and uses it to reaffirm his credentials and identity as a *muhalif*.[40] In all the successive epochs of human history, he writes, he would have been in the opposition: his soul would have been in the body of someone scolding Adam and Eve for eating the forbidden fruit, someone criticizing the construction of Noah's Ark, and someone condemned to the pharaoh's dungeons, all the way up to the French Revolution, where he would have been a Girondin, condemned to the guillotine before 9 Thermidor. Before settling into his current body, his soul was in that of a Janissary enemy of Alemdar Paşa, separated from that body during the martyrdom of Selim III (1807–8) or the time of Alemdar's death, and put into his current body, as a *muhalif* against the CUP! In other words, his identity as a *muhalif* was something essential to his nature and would remain constant as the metempsychoses of history went on around him; it was not simply contingent on whether his party was in power or in the opposition at any given point. The other key point here is that souls and bodies—structures and contents—were in flux all around him. The CUP was transmigrating from the Ottoman government to the new national government in the making. Only his identity, even his soul, if you will, as a *muhalif*—and the *muhalifs*' perennial defeat—was to remain fixed.

And perennial defeat for *muhalefet* would mean chronic anguish for the *muhalif*. "The Suicide of a *Muhalif*" ("Bir Muhalifin İntiharı"), dated January 8, 1921, and subtitled, "A Bitter and Didactic Drama in One Act," is a monologue set in a dingy hotel room on a back street of Sirkeci, near the train station in Old Istanbul. A thoroughly demoralized and broken *muhalif*, driven to muttering to himself and on the point of insanity, bemoans his fate as he prepares to commit suicide. Dressed in tatters, with only the "quivering light" of a candle down to its last dregs, the *muhalif* mutters to himself, "Ah *muhalefet*, ah! You have finally completely destroyed us! Look at the state we are in! Who would have [guessed] that after the Armistice the opposition (*muhalefet*) would again face such a fate, again like an orphaned child, head hung low, stomach empty, eyes full of tears, heartbroken, sneaking into corners and crawling from door to door." He ruminates over the past ten years, setting up a historical narrative for *muhalefet*. Paraphrasing, the *muhalefet* as an opposition force was defeated before the war, but its members were novices, so it was alright; they suffered through the war, pinning their hopes on emerging triumphant over the Unionists at the end of the war. Alas, disappointment and defeat again, within six months (i.e., the time it took for the Unionists to regroup as the nationalists in 1919), and now? "We are stuck in Istanbul; but the arena for the Unionists is again a wide one; those who are hungry here [in Istanbul] can fill their stomachs there [in Anatolia], the one who here sees danger can there find peace; and the one who here without a position can there find employment." Taking out a rifle from under his pillow, he loads it with the one bullet he could afford to buy, saying, "The Anatolia path is closed to us, but the road to paradise you [the rifle] can open for me! The *muhalif*s have made me weary of my dear life, I will die! Goodbye, incompetent *muhalif*s!" And with that, he shoots the gun—and misses. The *muhalif*, it seems, lacks even the capacity to end his own life.[41]

Finally, "A Perfect *Muhalif*" ("Tam Bir Muhalif"), from his collection *The People I Have Known* (*Tanıdıklarım*), published in 1922, we get a portrait of Veli Bey, the quintessential *muhalif*, a relentless underdog. The author begins by saying that "one would never expect to find in such an unassuming, pure, and clean heart such a degree of enmity, so solid and deep-rooted, which never loses its power with time or events, and such a deep, sharp, dark hatred." But the "extraordinariness" of Veli Bey is his unshakeable opposition to the Unionists and attachment to the "opposition party" (*muhalefet fırkası*). He had started "in the first days of the struggle between Unionism and Freedom and Accord, and full of hope, threw himself with zeal into the fight, the first in his neighborhood to sign up for the opposition party, the first to get a beating, the first to be thrown out of his post, and because he was poor anyway, the first to fall into abject poverty, the first to be sent into exile; in short, he got first place in all the adventures of harassment and abuse suffered by the *muhalif*s." With each blow, he maintained such a faith in the ultimate victory of the *muhalefet*—when being shipped off to Sinop, for instance, he would say, "This won't last six months! We'll be in Istanbul, in the government soon!" When the Armistice happened, and "the *muhalefet* came into power" (*muhalefet iktidara geldi*), and he still could not find a semblance of a job and could not realize any of his hopes, he still walked around as he had under the Unionists, destitute and wronged. "But he was still hopeful, and still attached to the party. His conviction was as solid as iron." The punch line? He finally died "of poverty, cold, and deprivation," his last wish being that his funeral procession pass by the party offices. "But even this last wish could not be granted to poor Veli Bey. The order (*cemaat*) changed the route so as not to attract the attention of a lot of people were they to turn from Kumkapı to Parmakkapı lane, so they continued with the coffin on the straight road." The author ends with the lament, "So, Veli Bey is the only person I know who is a perfect *muhalif*, this poor political martyr!"[42] If Veli Bey was the quintessential *muhalif*, Refik's depiction of him reveals the tragic paradox of the concept. It seems to entail at once an uncompromising and principled stance, the hoping against hope for justice against the Unionists, and yet to lack any party or grounding upon which to rely.

Even as he mocks Veli Bey, there is something of Refik Halid in his depiction of that "perfect *muhalif*." Refik Halid contested the national movement in every way he could—first using the authority he had in his government post and, failing that, the power he wielded as a writer to construct an imagination of *muhalefet*. At a certain point this must have seemed futile, as the Ottoman government sank into decrepitude and the nationalists gained political and military momentum. He continued, though, all the way to the bitter end of the conflict with the nationalists, when the *muhalif*s, now branded *hain*, or traitors, were driven out of the political arena and out of the country entirely in late 1922. In elaborating on the concept of *muhalefet*, he was elevating it—almost—to an ideology, complete with a historical narrative connecting the recent past with the present and future, and infusing it with criticism of the nationalist agenda, the social background of nationalist partisans, and the cynical modus operandi they were using to further their agenda. At the core of this *muhalefet* was not the renunciation but the explicit recognition of and attention to the continuity between the Unionist past and the nationalist present. The stories recounted here all confirm that *muhalefet* in the Armistice period was in direct continuity with *muhalefet* as it had taken shape before World War I.

As is well known, acceptance of a Kemalist paradigm in the 1920s and long after was premised on the insistence of a total political and cognitive rupture—indeed a complete break—with the "Ottoman past," and that rupture was later dictated as having occurred in the spring and summer of 1919 with Mustafa Kemal's landing at Samsun. Adherence to the official history set out in *Nutuk* entailed the suppression of any public memory of the actual politics of the Armistice period, and in particular, the vilification and suppression of those voices contesting the national movement.[43] Politics persisted, however, and there was much at stake in the reconceptualization of *muhalefet*. It meant calling out the continuities between the Unionists and the nationalists as the movement was taking shape and as the movement was claiming to eschew its Unionist past. Once the republic was established, Turkish political authority had to be portrayed as monolithic and unified and to be reconceptualized so as to appear somehow above politics. Turkey would be a politically undifferentiated nation—even if a deeply partisan nation at its core—as that authority became subsumed into the singular vision and then legacy of Atatürk. The memory of contestation, then, and *muhalefet* as the articulation of that internal contestation, had to be suppressed first and foremost. Even as late as 1922, when most of his associates had joined the nationalist movement, Refik insisted on violating this taboo and pointing out the association between the pre-1918 CUP and the nationalist movement. In a feature for the new year (1922) in his newspaper *Aydede*, a number of prominent figures offered their one-liners about what they expected for the year, and the quotation he printed as his own was: "Refik Halid (thinking)—'this year shall I rejoin the Unionists? From there to the nationalist forces is so easy!'"

Refik Halid was not simply a victim of bad timing, as he claimed in retrospect, when as PTT director he rejected Mustafa Kemal's telegrams in June 1919. His activities throughout that summer and his writings after he stepped down from his post—as well as when he assumed and subsequently resigned from the same post the following year—demonstrate that he, along with Ali Kemal, Refii Cevat, Rıza Tevfik, Sait Molla, and a few others, was actively and vocally opposed to the nationalists down to the day they entered Istanbul in late 1922.[44] This was partly because a nationalist victory remained unimaginable for him. It was also partly motivated by his resentment at having just spent years in exile thanks to them. More important, it was because he saw them as practicing a base form of power similar to that practiced by the CUP before and during the war. Having collaborated with some of them, he knew them, and seems to have distrusted too many of them as they tried to shed their Unionist identity and repackage themselves as nationalists. And yes, it seemed to him that the lesser of two evils was not the Unionist-nationalists, but British occupation, as he kept alive his naïve hope for justice through the arbitration of the newly founded League of Nations.

The continuity of political and military personnel from the Unionist to the national period has been demonstrated in scholarship since the 1980s, and the continuity of tactics of state violence has more recently been illuminated.[45] But the case of Refik Halid's career and writings from the Armistice period illustrates what was at stake in speaking aloud the political legacies of the recent Ottoman past in the emergent Turkish Republic as the transformation was taking place. The cost of his opposition turned out to be fifteen more years of exile, this time to Syria and Lebanon.

By the time he was preparing to flee Istanbul in 1922, Refik Halid wrote of wanting to wash his hands of politics—another trope that *muhalif*s used. In his "Farewell, Politics!" ("Elveda Siyasiyat!"), a piece that would also be excluded (likely by him) from later Republican-era editions of his work, he wrings his hands over his involvement in politics and the price he is about to pay—separation from his beloved Istanbul: "If only I had kept quiet, if only this and only that, if only I had not listened to my mindless friends, . . . I could run around without fear, following my pleasure, far from worry and pain, and I would taste these sweet days [of winter] and dip into the pleasure of spring."[46] Unlike his "perfect *muhalif*" character, who was also a product of 1922, he claimed to finally be ready to give up on politics, which to him was tantamount to the struggle to oppose the Unionists turned nationalists. As it turned out, it would be several more years before he was really ready.

FIVE

Muhalefet from Abroad
(1922–1927)

THE OTTOMAN SULTANATE was a dead letter in late 1922. In October of the following year the Republic of Turkey was proclaimed, with the formal international recognition of the Treaty of Lausanne. Mustafa Kemal would go on to make the claim, ex post facto in official history starting in 1927, of total rupture from the Ottoman past and total unity within the Turkish nation under his leadership, and that claim was foundational to the legitimacy of the Kemalist Republic. This chapter takes up the lost half decade between the formal establishment of the republic and the consolidation of political authority under Mustafa Kemal, capped off by his *Nutuk* speech, itself the basis for the official history of the War of Independence and origin of the republic.

The republic under Mustafa Kemal, once it was proclaimed in 1923, did not of course spring forth a new and indivisible entity devoid of contestation. In *Nutuk*, he narrated the process of consolidation of power as a story of his struggle and successive triumphs over traitors, imperialists, and other enemies of the nation. He thus dealt with the differences of opinion among the ruling elite and military by marginalizing and vilifying any who opposed him.[1]

For our purposes as we trace the genealogy of *muhalefet* and Refik Halid's relationship to the concept, the central process involved in the consolidation of power under Mustafa Kemal was the closing off of opposition—within the establishment—between 1922 and 1927. One need only consider that the Caliphate was abolished in 1924, after the establishment of the republic, and that furthermore, the Independence Tribunals, held in 1925, were in part an effort to cleanse the republic of vestiges from the past, including those CUP elements that were deemed threatening. As we will see, the press, overwhelmingly centered in Istanbul, also constituted a bastion of elite opposition and contestation to "Ankara," which came to be synonymous with Mustafa Kemal and his circle.

It was only after Mustafa Kemal's power had been consolidated within the establishment, and the contours of that establishment had been clarified, that the "state" can be spoken of as a coordinated entity with the capacity to generate and enforce Kemalist reforms, thus institutionalizing the vision of Mustafa Kemal, between 1927 and the latter's death in 1938. The better known Alphabet Reform (1928), Surname Law (1934), sumptuary laws, and remaking of the education system and the economy followed these initial years of the struggle for hegemony on the part of Mustafa Kemal and his circle in Ankara. The first several years of the republic, then, were decisive in the formation of structures of power in modern Turkey, and yet they have been little discussed in historical literature. To the extent that they have been discussed, the opposition therein has generally been dismissed as a momentary political encumbrance that had to be cleared in order for Kemalist modernization to take place.[2]

In this first half decade of the republic, the dynamics of *muhalefet* from the late Ottoman period did persist, albeit in a new and changing context—whether the word was used to signal an aspiration, as a trope, or as a fleeting political reality in the new republic. Between 1922 and 1927 alone several forms of contestation animated politics, both against the Ankara regime and within it. Some of those forms of contestation continued the conflicts of the Armistice period, and others grew out of the dynamics of the transition itself, within the national movement as it metamorphosed into the new state of Turkey. This chapter considers some of these changing meanings of *muhalefet* in the formative years of the republic in light of Refik Halid's predicament as a *vatan haini*, or traitor to the nation, and in a different light, as a *muhalif* in exile.

Refik Halid survived the transition from Ottoman Sultanate to Turkish Republic in 1922–23 by escaping the country to avoid retaliation for his acts of treachery against the national movement, which he would have called his acts of *muhalefet* against the Unionists-nationalists. From his exile in Beirut and Aleppo in the new French Mandate state of Syria/Lebanon, he continued to contest the republic, engaging in *muhalefet* from afar for its first few, formative years by launching a new form of political critique of Mustafa Kemal and his national movement—a history in the form of a memoir. The memoir, which he wrote in 1923, and the controversy its publication generated in Turkey in 1924 became a bombshell, thrown into Turkish politics at a volatile moment. He attempted to cast the recent Ottoman past in a kind of preemptive counternarrative, from the point of view of a *muhalif*, before even the establishment of the master narrative, which would happen with *Nutuk* in late 1927. In order to undersand the importance of the memoir and the controversy surrounding it, I first trace his flight from Istanbul and arrival in Beirut. His own personal experience of transition as a *muhalif* provides a rare bridge across the larger rupture—political and epistemic—between empire and republic. It was from the other side of that rupture that he wrote his memoir of the Armistice period. I then consider the content of the memoir and controversy it engendered in Turkey, ending with his perceptions of the new republic through 1927, as he remained perched in opposition to the republic from French Mandate Syria/Lebanon.

PASSAGE FROM ISTANBUL

The nationalists entered Istanbul with General Refet (Bele) in command on October 19, 1922, sealing the final defeat of the Ottoman government and the empire's British and Greek occupiers.[3] The antagonism between the nationalists and their opponents in Istanbul, the latter typified by Ali Kemal and Refik Halid, had been building for three years. In a fascinating indication of the urgency behind the nationalist-*muhalefet* antagonism, one of the first acts of the nationalists after entering the city was to take over the *Sabah* offices, thereby assuming not just editorial but physical control of the press that had been issuing Ali Kemal's paper, the mouthpiece of the British-aligned liberals.[4] *Sabah*'s owner/publisher, Ottoman Armenian Mihran Ağa, had announced that "official relations with" *Peyam*, Ali Kemal's newspaper, had come to an end a few days earlier, on October 16. Mihran Ağa explained that this was because *Sabah* was a "genuine and warm defender of national ambitions."[5] So when nationalists took over the press a few days after that, they issued a chilling front page on the new "nationalized" *Peyam-ı Sabah*, on October 20, 1922 (see figure 3).[6]

The caricatured heads on stakes in the figure, from left to right, are Ali Kemal (dubbed "Artin Kemal, the man himself"), Damad Ferid (Damadı, his son-in-law), The Other One (Öteki), Rıza Tevfik (Filosof Artini, Artin the Philosopher), Cenabettin (Cenabidis), and Refik Halid (Aydede, his pen name and the name of the satirical newspaper he published in the course of 1922). Artin is a stereotypical Armenian name, referencing the *muhalifs'*

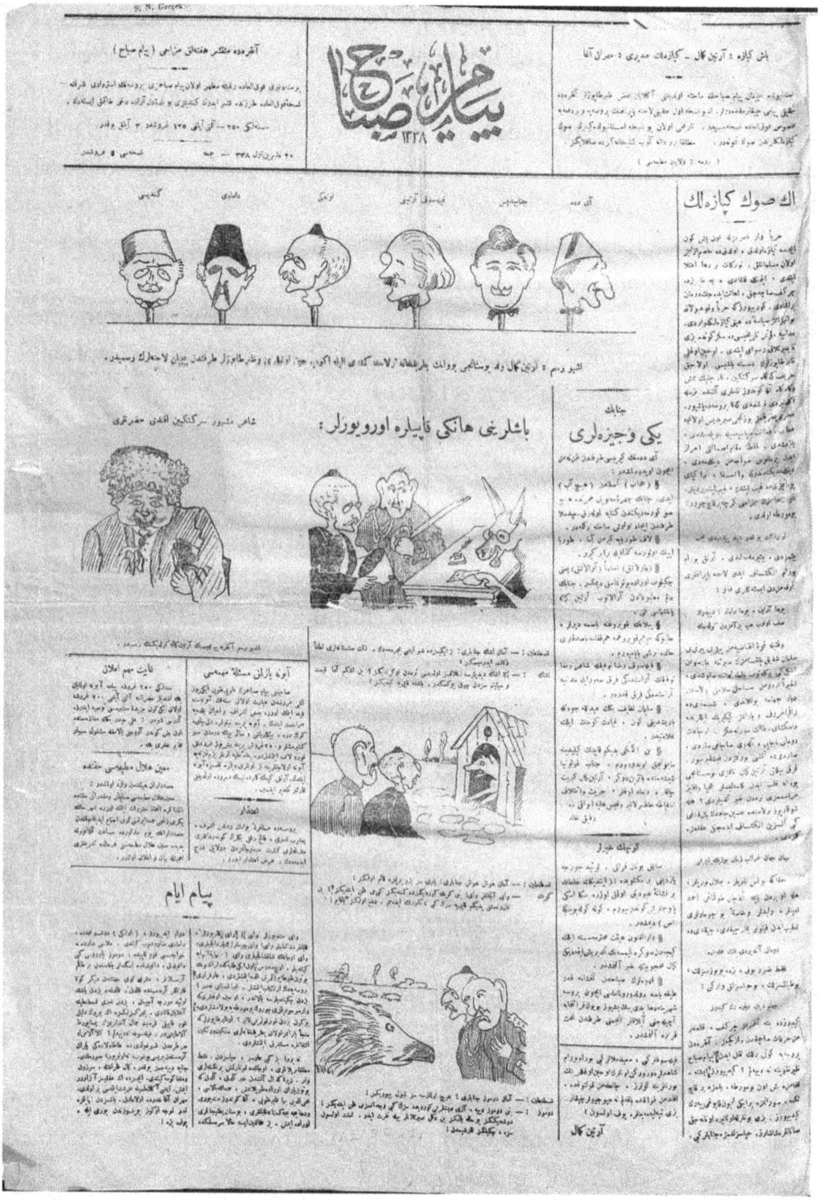

پيام صباح

١٣٣٨

پيام ايام

FIGURE 3. Front page of *Peyam-ı Sabah* from October 20, 1922, the day after nationalist forces took over the capital. Nationalists, having taken over the newspaper, depict the heads of Refik Halid (far right), Ali Kemal (far left), and other prominent *muhalifs* on stakes. Courtesy of the National Library of Turkey (Millî Kütüphane).

perceived tendency to defend the Armenians. The suffix "-idis" is a stereo-typical ending for a Greek Orthodox Christian (particularly from the Pontus, or Black Sea, region), again, conflating liberal *muhalifs* with non-Muslims and therefore traitors. This is a further demonstration of the ways that not only was association with non-Muslims an offense in the eyes of the nationalists, but the Armenian Genocide and culpability for it were also deeply embedded in the contestation and mutual antagonism between the nationalists and their *muhalefet*. Ali Kemal's and Refik Halid's accusations against the nationalists, as being the CUP in disguise and of operating like a gang rather than a political party, were only validated by the nationalists' bilious response to—and ad hominem attack on—them. As discussed in chapter 4, theirs was a kind of contestation that could not be tolerated once the nationalists had won the contest. Ali Kemal, for his part, was reportedly called "Artin Kemal" as he was being lynched in İzmit, on the road to his court martial in Ankara.[7]

Here I pause to consider the way Refik Halid wrote about the experience of that moment as a *muhalif*. Fortunately he provided a characteristically moving description of his last days in Istanbul in the wake of the nationalist takeover of the city and the press. This account also stands in sharp relief to the narrative of "Büyük Zafer," or "Great Victory," of the nationalists:

> At that time [mid-October 1922] I was a guest in the house of one of my friends in Beyoğlu. One Saturday night, we went, three families together, to the French Theatre. Gunfire, shots being fired, Armageddon on the Istanbul horizon.[8] We didn't pay any mind. Not only did we not pay any mind; we took part in it. From the roof of the house we were staying in we shot off 20 or 30 rounds. It was getting to the middle of the night. We left the theatre. Saying goodbye to my friends and their wives we came home. We didn't know anything. Even the police action on Beyoğlu Avenue didn't grab our attention.
>
> However, at that moment, the Babıali [Ottoman] Government fell. Refet Paşa [Bele] showed up [in fact he arrived officially a few days later], and took over (*rapt ve ilhak*) Istanbul and the parliament.
>
> I figured this out the next day, when I read it in the papers. In my pocket I had a Turkish passport [*sic*] ready. Police Director Esat Bey, on my request, had called it in and given the order for it at the 4th Branch and the issue of my passport had been resolved one month earlier [around the time of the İzmir fire]. My intent—if possible—was to pass to Rhodes, or if not, then to Italy. Some people approached me from Refet Paşa saying that he had "Aydede" [Refik Halid's newspaper and pen name at the time] and they suggested I appeal to him. I found that to be useless. The best was to get into my coach

and go. I called home. I told them to get my things ready. I wouldn't be able to stay in Istanbul more than 5 or 10 days longer.

During this time I was considering rashly crossing to the Anatolia shore. All afternoon I was sitting in my apartment looking out at Istanbul's beautiful sweet harbor full of melancholy and the anxiety of impending separation, and it was starting to burn my heart, when they called me to the phone. I can't remember the exact time. Who was on the other side? I'll tell you.

"Refik," they said. "Ali Kemal has been arrested; or, is about to be."

"Oh boy," I said. "Is that what's in store for me, too?"

"No. In cipher from Refet Paşa in Ankara there was only Ali Kemal's name. But God please keep that a secret!"

Did I turn pale? Did I turn red? Did I turn white as a sheet? Did my eyes lose their color? Did my lips turn purple? Ashen-gray? I didn't even know. The only thing I knew was this: For a short time, I froze and I had to lean on the table . . . then I thought that I had to remain calm, serious and very cautious in front of those around me . . . they asked:

"What is it? What's wrong?"

"Nothing, they called from the newspaper. They censored a piece". . . . I talked about this and that, then I went back to the phone and called Ali Kemal's house. The servant answered.

"Is the master there?"

"No, they went out an hour ago."

"The Lady?"

"They went out with the wife of the Tramway Director."

What would I do now? I rang the Serkldoryan [Circle d'Orient Hotel, where Ali Kemal and other liberals/*muhalifs* often gathered] but the answer I got was:

"No, he's not here yet."

I was dying of worry. I went to a friend. With great courage, actually disproportionate courage, showing defiance, I went out into the street. We were on Beyoğlu Avenue. The lights of a warm fall evening were aglow, with crowds of people. . . . [W]e entered the current of people. We got as far as the Bon Marché. I lifted my head. I looked at Ali Kemal's apartment building. There was light in the windows and there didn't seem to be anything to indicate a flurry or a conflict. We continued on our way. We walked to Taksim Square. We froze. We examined his building again. The same silence. The same state, of course. . . . As a consolation, I said to myself, "he's not really there," I said, "a bluff . . . or he escaped, went into hiding; saved. . . ."

We bumped into some friends at Tünel Meydanı [Tramway tunnel plaza]. We were chit-chatting: from the next street over a servant woman appeared. She was frantically making gestures at me. What was it? They were looking to arrest me at home, too? My heart got so tight that it was like I had a forceps inside me. My windpipe constricted, got blocked, I was dying. How I walked and asked, I can't even tell you.

"They called from the press; they've arrested Ali Kemal."

There was no longer any doubt. There was nothing else to do but go straight home and consult with my friends. This night, this long, frightful, stressful night was torture!

The next morning I got fresh courage. I would get up as if nothing had happened, go to the press and get to work on the newspaper. In the afternoon, like I said, I went into the office. It was Monday. My newspaper came out. Sales were not affected by the situation. I sat at my desk. When the *Sabah* workers saw me they were startled. Or they had been advised to hide it. I didn't pay any mind. But in a bit the situation changed. The police correspondent (*zabıta muhbiri*) came running in. He whispered this in my ear:

"I was just at the police station. The order was given for your arrest!"

I stood up straight away. The weather was rainy. I put my cane down and took my umbrella. I went out to the avenue. I was waiting at every step for someone to come up behind me, in front of me, or next to me, and grab me by the collar, saying, "Let's go, we're taking you to the station!"

However I did not veer from my usual way. I crossed the bridge, pitter pattering as if carefree. I took the Tünel train up the hill and went up to Ali Kemal's apartment building. They took me into his office.

There were 5 or 6 people sitting there. They told me all the *muhalifs* were taking shelter at the British Embassy and urged me to join them there. I came to the embassy. The guards didn't even ask. . . . [A]s I was entering, the garden was filling up as men filed in, 1, 2, 3, 5 at a time.[9]

He continued the story in an interview with his biographer in the early 1940s:

The *muhalifs* [note its use here to indicate a specific and self-evident category] attached to the English embassy were brought straight to Taşkışla [barracks]. They were brought as "guests" of General Harrington, the commander of the [British] occupation forces in Istanbul. But Refik Halid was only thinking of the situation on the ship that night seven [*sic*] years before when he was being exiled to Sinop. There were even many of his old friends from exile [in 1913] in this wretched crowd, and he felt his heart tighten. A giant, empty dormitory with broken windows. . . . Inside, this place, with neither mattress nor stool nor rug, his eyes were darkening and his muscles tensing and he thought of throwing himself out the window. And he decided to get out. But getting out was contingent on Harrington's order. Refik Halid raised the question. The answer that came from Harrington was that permission to leave would be given to those who wanted it on the condition that they would no longer be under [British] protection. And out of that entire crowd, Refik Halid was joined by one beturbaned man [i.e., a member of the ulema] and one civilian police officer, making for a total of three.

Refik Halid spent that night at the house of a friend, and remained in hiding the following day. Finally, the director of Security for the French personally escorted Refik Halid to the dock and put him on the Pierre Loti ship, and the ship set sail.[10]

And in the final chapter of his memoir *Minelbab İlelmihrab*, he capped off the story of his departure from Istanbul:

> After a long ordeal, I stepped onto the ship.... I could not believe it. It felt like a dream. But since I had already passed the night so mixed up between dreams and reality, I thought this was just a continuation. I hurriedly raced up the steps. I was inside. I had managed to eek through alive, by a hair's breadth.
>
> And of course I cannot even explain to you the rest, like how the ship pulled up anchor, how it passed by Sarayburnu so slowly, with what pain I looked out at Istanbul, etc.
>
> I will only record the following so as not to forget it: that day was Thursday, the 9th of November 1922.[11]

PASSAGE TO BEIRUT

Refk Halid's departure from Istanbul also coincided, down to a matter of days, with the end of the Ottoman Sultanate (November 1) and the abrupt shift to a new political reality; the Turkish Grand National Assembly in Ankara was recognized by the parties working toward the Treaty of Lausanne on November 11. The specifics of what that would mean in Istanbul were still unclear. How fitting it is, then, that Refik Halid has supplied another account, thinly fictionalized—lost between dreams and reality—of his arrival in Beirut. He wrote the account in a novel called *Sürgün* (Exile), which he began writing as he prepared to return to Istanbul in 1938. The book opens with a depiction of the novel's main character, Hilmi Efendi, arriving in Beirut by sea in late 1922:

> At daybreak Beirut appeared. This journey, which had taken almost a week, entailed stopping at the small ports, that little old, worn-out boat, loaded with timber, a repurposed freighter—even if it were going straight, it could run into trouble in 10 days. Hilmi Efendi, hitting all the seasonal squalls of the Aegean Sea, for a while had lost hope, saying, "I think we're going to sink," and "I'll be saved from this!" But unfortunately in front of Rhodes the winds dropped; and as they got into the open sea near Cyprus a warm

breeze started; around it a pleasant and ripe smell, like the smell of freshly cut watermelon, wafted up. The Damascene (*Şamlı*) traveler who was arranging the beds side by side out on the deck was saying that the smell was coming from the orange trees in Tripoli; the trees were in bloom, the fruits would ripen to perfection, and the new buds would open, the whole of the Lebanon coast now being turned into oranges.[12]

Retired Captain Hilmi Efendi, Refik Halid's military alter ego, had been banished from his homeland (*memleketinden sınırdışı edilen*) with the nationalist victory in late 1922—due to a silly personal grudge between himself and a local police commissioner in Sivas.[13] While Syria/Lebanon were not totally unfamiliar to the novel's protagonist—he had traveled to Beirut on the way to Yemen in 1911 as an Ottoman soldier—this time the circumstances were quite different. The empire had dropped off the map, his military uniform was gone and in any case meaningless, and the "land had become foreign to him" (*memleket de artık onun yabancısı olmuştu*). So much had happened in a long decade of war. This, combined with the fact that he had only a few obsolete and worthless Ottoman coins on him, made him realize that he would be a "beggar in a foreign country." "He noticed his eyes burning, filling up, and getting moist; to swallow back his tears and not show those around him he turned his head toward the breeze at the front of the boat."[14]

Refik Halid, too, arrived in Beirut in late November 1922—also because of what he often claimed was a personal grudge, albeit of a different order—to face an uncertain future in a land that was more foreign than ever before. He settled in Jounieh, a seaside village on the outskirts of Beirut, and would reside there as well as in Aleppo throughout his exile, for a period that coincided with nearly the entire Kemalist era in the new Republic of Turkey (1923–38).

Refik Halid's first impulse in Beirut was not to learn Arabic—which he did not know—or engage in the politics of Mandate Syria. He seemingly took no notice of the Great Rebellion there in 1925 or the burgeoning issues of colonialism and nationalism that grew out of French Mandate rule. Instead, he turned to composing his memoir of the immediately preceding Armistice period. The intention behind writing this memoir was, I contend, nothing less than an extension of his Armistice-era project—of constructing a historical and literary imaginary for *muhalefet*. It was still crucial to him to stake out and justify a position and a profile for himself as a *muhalif*, now by recasting the recent past through his perspective. It was still his only hope of exculpating himself and of evading the label of colonial collaborator or national traitor. To be a *muhalif* was dicey, but it was more respectable than accepting the label of *hain*, or traitor.

Casting the past in this way was also a way of refuting the very basis for the republic, before Mustafa Kemal had even had a chance to construct the story from his own perspective and therefore that of the central state. Once again, as Refik had done in the Armistice period, he went about contesting the national movement (and now the republic) by connecting it back, in vivid detail, to Ottoman politics, particularly the existential battle between Unionists and *muhalifs*. Drawing attention to these continuities, and insisting on maintaining a perspective from the Istanbul Ottoman government, was still a frontal assault on the nationalist movement and thus the new republic, premised as it was on a break from that past. The political landscape in Turkey, furthermore, was changing in ways that raised even further the stakes of drawing attention to the recent past. To understand what was at stake for the politics of *muhalefet* in the new republic, and for Refik Halid's attempt to participate in them from exile, I first consider the larger changes underway back home.

BACKGROUND: *MUHALEFET* AND THE NEW REPUBLIC

Muhalefet within Turkey did not go away with the abolishment of the Ottoman Sultanate.[15] Between 1922 and 1927, in fact, contestation was so intense that the future of the state, and of Mustafa Kemal's hold on it, was far from clear. Istanbul, as the home of what was left of the Ottoman establishment, the base of important CUP elements that were not supportive of Mustafa Kemal, and a hotbed of the *muhalefet* press, was deemed particularly dangerous, and Kemal avoided it. He called representatives of the press to meet with him in İzmit in January 1923 rather than enter the city, for example.[16] He only made his first visit to the former capital in 1927, when his power was more solidly established. In 1925-7 in the course of the Independence Tribunals in Ankara, which were key in establishing his power more solidly, many figures from the Istanbul press and intelligentsia were tried. There, Mustafa Kemal would refer aspirationally to the "new" press as the "iron fortress" that would protect the regime. The "old" press in these early years was far from that and thus was likely the impetus for Kemal's aspirations for the new press. Refik Halid's old stomping ground, the Istanbul press represented all that was threatening from the recent past: the Ottoman bureaucratic and intellectual elite and their defense of tradition, which could not be roundly dismissed as reactionary but was often considered reasoned and liberal.[17]

Within Ankara, too, there was serious contention among the former partisans of the nationalist movement regarding the form that the new state should take. The partisans of the War of Independence had put aside their earlier differences to achieve their common goal of resisting colonial occupation. Once that goal was achieved they soon split into two factions. On one side was the "First," or "Eastern" group (including Mustafa Kemal, İsmet [İnönü], and Kılıç Ali); Eastern referring to the Eastern flank of the resistance movement in Anatolia. On the other was the "Second," or "Western" group, referring to the resistance movement on the Aegean coast and in Western Anatolia. Kâzım (Karabekir), Rauf (Orbay), and others were in the "Western" faction—which contained a diversity of views, similar in some ways to the *muhalefet* of the Young Turk movement of the previous era.[18] While the Westerners, at least initially, broadly advocated saving the institution of the Caliphate and moving toward a liberal democracy, they were more concerned with the circumvention of process that was involved in the decision to abolish the Caliphate, not the religious/spiritual significance of closing down the institution.[19] As historians John Vanderlippe and Erik Zürcher underline, they were worried about process, whereas the Easterners were concerned with outcomes; the rift thus echoed the liberal/Unionist split of the Second Constitutional Era, yet the individuals populating the two factions had recombined.

The "Second Group" lost out to Mustafa Kemal in the short run, and once his supremacy was established, to İnönü, who, like the other figures from the "First Group," was opposed to colonial mandates and in favor of a republic, albeit a republic with questionable safeguards for freedom and separation of powers. In 1924–25, during and after the negotiations leading to the new constitution, the Westerners formed an opposition party, the Progressive Republican Party (PRP), led by Kâzım (Karabekir) and Rauf (Orbay), which was aborted by Mustafa Kemal in the wake of an alleged assassination conspiracy against him. The timing of and controversy over Refik Halid's memoir signaled that he was not outside these politics altogether. Instead, he was an extension of the Second Group, and in any case an extension of the oppositional Istanbul press scene. Although he did not express formal identification with or allegiances to this partisan internal opposition (Second Group/PRP) until after his return to Turkey in 1938, the timing and nature of the controversy over publication of his Armistice-era memoir were bound up with this factional struggle.

The move to authoritarianism—after the Şeyh Sait Kurdish rebellion, the shutting down of the PRP, the Independence Tribunals in 1925, and the İzmir assassination conspiracy incident in 1926—would ultimately drive out some key players from the War of Independence. Several figures who had been national heroes in the War of Independence were made *muhalifs*. Escaping execution for the alleged plot to assassinate Mustafa Kemal, they went into voluntary exile, including Halide Edib, Adnan (Adıvar), Rauf (Orbay), and Kâzım (Karabekir). Their departure from the movement and the state brings to mind the earlier polarization within the CUP between 1910 and 1913; some members left the committee—now the republic—allowing others to concentrate ever more power.[20] After 1926, Mustafa Kemal would neutralize or otherwise eliminate organized parliamentary opposition and opposition in the press, clearing the way for his unique "one-party republic"—and the second party congress of his Republican People's Party was held the following year, the occasion for his *Nutuk* speech.[21]

The boundaries and terms of power and *muhalefet* were in flux along with the terms of the new republic in these first few years. As the state itself was in formation—as the constitution (1924) and the civil code (1926) were taking shape—three official measures were promulgated that were aimed at delineating the boundaries between political belonging and exclusion. These measures, which I discuss in turn, also helped to push what was once deemed *muhalefet* as internal opposition into the realm of treachery (*hıyanet*). Each was also related to Refik Halid's own story in these years: the List of 150 (1923), which designated 150 "Traitors to the Nation" who were to be banished and stripped of citizenship; the Law on the Maintenance of Order (1925), which severely curtailed the space of free expression, setting up martial law anew; and the Independence Tribunals (1925–27), which prosecuted all manner of threats to the nation, imprisoning and executing hundreds. Refik Halid was a member of the List of 150; according to his own claims, the controversy engendered by his memoir was part of the impetus for the Law on Maintenance of Order (Takrir-i Sükun). He watched, aghast, from afar as some of his fellow *muhalifs* from the Liberal Entente and the Istanbul press, such as (Ömer) Lütfi Fikri Bey, were put on trial in the Independence Tribunals.[22] Refik Halid was even mentioned in absentia in the course of those Tribunals. We can assume that it was only because he had already been banished from the country and condemned as a traitor that he was not expressly tried and sentenced.

The List of 150 (1922–1923)

The so-called List of 150 was enshrined as a protocol appended to the Treaty of Lausanne, which itself set out the terms and boundaries for the Republic of Turkey. As the treaty was being negotiated, İsmet (İnönü) (a hard-line Kemalist to the end) and his delegation (which included onetime and future *muhalif* Rıza Nur) negotiated the right to make a list of 150 individuals who would be excluded from the general amnesty being negotiated for the wartime period—an amnesty covering August 1, 1914, to November 22, 1922. These "personae non gratae" would be banished from the new state of Turkey (or barred from reentry, since many, like Refik Halid, had already fled) and denied Turkish citizenship and nationality. By late April 1923 the names to be included on the list had been fixed through discussion in parliament. The list was pared down from 600 to 300 and then, after discussion in parliament, to the requisite 150. By early June it was published in *Resmi Ceride*, the official newspaper.[23] The Treaty of Lausanne was finalized on July 24, 1923, and the republic was declared three months later, on October 29.[24]

There was no further public explanation or specific accusations against those on the list beyond their being labeled "traitors to the nation." The prerogative to exclude specific individuals deemed threatening had long been a desideratum of the nationalists. The idea had been floated as early as February 1921, before the establishment of the republic and in the midst of the battle between "Istanbul" (the Ottoman government) and "Ankara" (the national movement). Discussion became more specific in September/ October 1922, when the nationalist victory was de facto complete.

There is evidence of this in Refik Halid's "Farewell, Politics!," penned on the eve of the nationalist victory in the autumn of 1922, months before the List of 150 was being formally negotiated. He writes that the reason for his "heart being in ruins" was that *the National Forces had reportedly decided to strip the* muhalifs *of citizenship, and they would no longer be considered citizens*! Ah, is this disaster really going to befall me? Am I really going to have to undergo this punishment? Did I not go through enough? No longer would anyone call me a citizen, no longer would this sublime epithet be applied to me, would I remain for the rest of my life crushed and dispossessed? . . . Let's see for how many more days you will be a guest in Istanbul, how many days free, how many days will be you able to be out and about?" (emphasis added).[25] By 1922 the term *muhalifs* had become a transparent category and a political identity, transposed along with the shift in political authority from the Unionists to the nationalists. The pedigree of *muhalefet* had been constructed during the Armistice, and not only did it date back to 1909, but its continuity from the Unionist to the nationalist period was assumed by both sides. Here was a distinct line of continuity between the recent Ottoman past and the Republican present, and from the national movement to the new republic. Based on the unspoken premise that those who opposed the national movement would go on to contest, and therefore endanger, the security of the republic, the List of 150 seemed to be none other than a settling of scores from the War of Independence.

Refik Halid's last days in Istanbul in 1922 were shaped by the very apparent and fluid realities of this vendetta between the nationalists and the *muhalifs* later enshrined in the List. Ali Kemal did not survive long enough to make it to the List of 150. He suffered a worse fate when he was lynched on the orders of Nurettin Paşa in İzmit, on the way to being brought before the Independence Tribunal in Ankara. From writings such as "Correspondence with Mehmet Ç Bey" and the issues of the "Anatolia" version of *Peyam-ı Sabah*, the visceral nature of that antagonism is clear. Indeed, the front page of the issue of *Peyam-ı Sabah* shown in figure 3 is evidence enough. The List of 150 was an institutionalization of nationalist score settling and an indication in turn of the partisan core of the nationalist movement and the new republic. Like the CUP before them, many nationalists saw themselves not as a political party but as the guardians who would carry out the will of the nation. This enmeshing of the party and the emergent state made partisan opposition tantamount to treason. *Muhalifs* became traitors (*hain-i vatan*) and were deemed a threat—not to partisan interests but to national security in the fledgling republic.[26]

Refik Halid watched this score-settling from a safe distance in Beirut, having already left in late 1922. The raw hatred and drive for vengeance that had developed in the course of the War of Independence was channeled, transposed, and entrenched into political institutions and legal conventions as the infant Grand National Assembly debated the names that should go on the list. All agreed that such a list was needed. The only question was who would be forced to leave and who deemed safe enough to stay within the borders of the new Turkey. Which betrayals, and how early or late in the War for Independence, would mean excommunication? How long should those being expelled be given to dispose of their property? What if they were already outside the country? What kind of surveillance over those who stayed would be sufficient to keep them from presenting a threat? And just as important, who would be given the power to make up the list, and what was his personal agenda?

Along with the pain of loss, Refik Halid must have felt the rage of betrayal the spring after he left Istanbul. His former best friend and witness at his 1914 wedding in Sinop during his first exile, a fellow former servant of the Istanbul government in the Armistice period, Ahmet Ferit (Tek), was now interior minister in the new national government. He was the official in charge of drawing up the List of 150. And he had put Refik Halid's name on the list.

The new role of Ahmet Ferit (Tek) is a concrete example of the partisan—and personal—dynamics at play under the surface of the new republic. Ahmet Ferit himself had been deemed a *muhalif* in 1913 and deported along with Refik Halid to Sinop. He himself had opposed the nationalists at an early moment in the Armistice/War of Independence period, writing a letter urging Mustafa Kemal to obey his recall from Samsun by Istanbul and give himself up. At the time, Ahmet Ferit had been minister of public works in the Istanbul government and had enthusiastically engaged in discussions about non-nationalist possibilities for the Ottoman government going forward.[27] Later in the game, in late 1919, Ahmet Ferit had taken part in plans to forcibly obstruct the nationalists. Now that the nationalists had won and were establishing a republic, he found himself not only on the other side but with tremendous power as the official making up the list of those to be stripped of Turkish citizenship—and he had more to hide than most. Nationalist loyalty was the key credential for inclusion in the new Turkish state, and his past loyalties were questionable at best. One can already begin to imagine the kinds of personal grudges—and in this case, personal anxieties, of those on the inside with checkered pasts and imperfect nationalist pedigrees—that were played out in the process of compiling the List of 150.[28]

The final composition of the List of 150 also reveals much about boundaries of belonging in the new Republic of Turkey. Diverse in terms of educational, professional, and regional background, the men on the list were united only by their opposition—to Mustafa Kemal, to the national movement, and now to the Republic—and thus the danger they were perceived as representing. They had crossed the line from dissent to treason (*hıyanet*) and were presumably deemed capable of crossing it again in the future.

It was a heterogeneous group, broken down into several distinct categories: those in Sultan Vahideddin's retinue (dynasty members were expelled from

Turkey via a different law and were not part of this list); cabinet members who had served in the Kuvve-i İnzibatiye, the short-lived military opposition to nationalist forces; delegates to the Treaty of Sèvres (for their betrayal of the nation); civil (Mülkiye) and military (Askeriye) officials; Çerkes Ethem Bey and his Circassian associates, who had mutinied against the nationalist forces; members of the Circassian Congress (Çerkes Kongresi); police officials; journalists; and "unclassified others."[29]

Once the *muhalifs* who presented the most clear and present danger were eliminated, beyond the List of 150 the biggest threat to the legitimacy of the new state was, ironically, some former Unionist elements themselves. A chief example was Kara Kemal, who had directed the—very corrupt— wartime food provisioning of the capital for the Unionists and continued to wield power through his gang-like network.[30] The simultaneous inheritance and renunciation of Unionism was reflected in the selective inclusion and exclusion of former Unionist figures. This sorting process—of what to reject and what to keep about the Unionist past—was bound up with much of the political turmoil in the early years of the republic. The process of retributive justice from wartime in the Divan-ı Harb (Military Tribunal) in the Armistice period was abruptly aborted by the nationalist victory and had been compromised in any case by being a British-led initiative. There remained confusion about which former Unionists were implicated in past crimes, and which crimes, as well as which Unionists could be rehabilitated. Furthermore, given the networks to which men like Kara Kemal had access, the political power they wielded on the ground could be leveraged for or against Mustafa Kemal and the republic, which made them seem dangerous and unreliable.

While the List of 150 was being finalized in the spring of 1923—even before the formal establishment of the republic—Refik Halid was writing the memoir that would make him more controversial and more reviled by those trying to cement their power in the fledgling state. While supposedly removing himself from politics and from the country, he set to work on his very political, personal memoir covering the period between the empire's defeat in 1918 and the nationalist victory in 1922. He began writing his memoir of the Armistice period in 1923, four years *before* the establishment of the master narrative of the period by Mustafa Kemal in *Nutuk*.[31] His memoir might be thought of as a counternarrative of the Armistice, before the master narrative of the War of Independence and the establishment of the republic had had a chance to be devised.

MİNELBAB İLELMİHRAB: THE MEMOIR
AND THE CONTROVERSY (1923–1925)

Refik Halid's reminiscence about the moment he first decided to put pen to paper for his memoir, within a few months of his arriving in Jounieh, serves as an antidote to the scene back home in Turkey, where the elections for the new Assembly, in which the Second Group was almost voted into oblivion, were being held at the same moment:[32]

[I]t was 1923, I think the month of April.... I had just turned 35. I'm in a farmhouse overlooking the sea in the town of Jounieh, near Beirut in Lebanon. The country houses there are, like their city houses, made of stone, solid, well-protected buildings in their own style, mosaic-floored; windows with their heavy wooden shutters to protect against the rain, sun, and hot wind called the "shuluk." Lebanon's April is like Istanbul's July.... I woke up early in the morning, as had been my custom since childhood; in keeping with my custom, too, I made my coffee myself and drank it; and waking up to (adapting to) the custom of this land, I dipped my bread into some olive oil with oregano added to it and had my breakfast; I went out into the garden.

Rose, jasmine, lilac—surrounded by the color and scent of their eternal blooming, under the influence of the climate, the shore, the sea, without even looking at it—nice, but how is the time going to pass?

My flatmate Sabih Şevket was not up yet.[33] Were he up he would be smoking. He would have to light up just to start speaking, sitting in his corner for hours, he would come out of his sleepiness, and only after that would he understand what you were saying and be in a state to find the view of the countryside!

I said to myself: maybe if I write my memoirs, I'll have something to do with my mornings, and enjoy myself. But what are my memoirs, and what could they be? Am I a former prime minister or something? If I bring all of my memoirs together, they wouldn't even fill up the seed of a fig.... But it's not like that. It would be its own sui generis kind of thing [*nevişahsına münhasır bir şey olur*], if it's kept light, resembles a chat, and isn't written in a true political nature or very serious way, not so as to advance a claim, nor to defend an idea, nor even to illuminate history [*tarihi aydınlatmak*]. If it is that way, then it would always be read [i.e. it would be timeless], would bring the past to life a bit, and would nail down the things that, in time, I would forget.

"OK, I'll give it a try!"

I came in from the garden. I put a bunch of paper and my reed pen (reed pens were still used for writing in those days; pens (*stilo*) you'd keep in your pocket as an accessory) on the dining table I had had the carpenter on the corner make for me. How would I begin?

I stared out the open window, half-seeing the village girls going to the stream, with earthen jugs on their shoulders, pine tree groves here and there, the open sea. Finally I began like this:

"I can't say what day it was exactly; but I remember well, it was a very bright, sparkling fall afternoon. . . ."

I filled up five or six pages in one sitting. When my friend woke up, he found me writing furiously. He asked what it was I was writing.

The title itself is telling; *Minelbab İlelmihrab* is an Arabic phrase, literally meaning "from the gate to the *mihrab* (~pulpit)." Figuratively it means something like "the whole kit and caboodle," and it is probably not coincidental that he chose an Arabic phrase, given that he was exiled in Syria/Lebanon. He began writing it in April 1923, stopped during the heat of the summer, and started up again in the fall. It was intended to be written in installments, or *tefrika*, like virtually everything was at that time, to be published in the newspaper. Refik Halid received a telegram on November 28, 1923 from Necmettin Sadak, an owner of *Akşam*, an Istanbul newspaper founded in 1918, requesting that he send the installments to be published, and another in January 1924, requesting subsequent installments.[34] By that point the Treaty of Lausanne had been ratified, the republic had been established, and Mustafa Kemal's People's Party had been formed. Still at issue were some important matters: the form of the constitution for the new republic, the issue of the Caliphate, and the place, if any, for an opposition party to the People's Party.

Only two installments of *Minelbab İlelmihrab* were published in 1924. They sparked so much controversy, prompting the question of whether Refik Halid or any "traitor" from the List of 150 should be allowed to publish at all in Turkey, that publication was ceased. The issue increased the antagonism between the "Istanbul" press and the "Ankara" press (the latter consisting of *Hakimiyet-i Milliye* [National sovereignty], the official newspaper; *Tanin*, the former CUP organ; and *Yenigün* [New day]).

Anticipation was building even prior to publication. *Akşam* published front-page teasers in advance; one detailed the names of the more than eighty personages who would be mentioned in the first section, while another listed all the chapter titles. The day before publication, *Akşam*'s front page featured an advertisement promising that Refik Halid Bey's memoir would appear the following day and would "tell the secrets that have remained unknown inside the Freedom and Accord party and the Istanbul governments." The teasers repeatedly posed the rhetorical question of whether the memoir was a political ploy to protect him and his friends and incriminate their enemies or a "literary" work, and added that the editors had judged it to be the latter and were publishing it out of the desire to include all "corners" of the nation's history. The final teaser claimed that the memoir was "without any doubt the most important and most interesting of all the memoirs that have been published until now."[35]

The first installment tells the story of how Refik learned of the Ottoman defeat at the CUP/*Yeni Mecmua* headquarters in the fall of 1918. But he sets the scene with a poignant evocation of how it felt to be a *muhalif* at that world-historical moment, writing with only five years of hindsight. And one can imagine what it must have felt like for someone in Istanbul to read this poignant recollection in 1924. He was freshly in exile again, and the Turkish national state and society were still sorting through the fundamentals of their past, present, and future:

1. Where and from Whom Did I Learn the News of the Defeat?
I cannot know now which day of all days it was; but I remember well that it was a bright, crisp autumn afternoon. When I arrived in front of the Union and Progress headquarters, I found the street full of automobiles. All of the ministers were surely there.

"Another meeting!" I said; I turned left in the garden, shying away from showing my face and, heading to the back of the building, went into the *Yeni Mecmua* offices. Any time I would go through the door of the "Red Villa," even though my feet had had more than five months to get used to it, I always felt a strange excitement, between two opposite feelings. First, a sense of shame felt at doing something so ugly. . . . What business did I have under the same roof with those men who had exiled me from place to place for five years just because I wrote "The Porcupine's Utterances" and I was neither a "fırkacı" [partisan liberal] nor a "komiteci" [Unionist]? If someone were to come up to me from outside just as I walked through the door, grab me by the arm and say, looking into my face:

"Sir, doesn't what you are doing weigh heavily on your self-respect?"
[W]hat answer would I be able to give other than hanging my head in shame?

Or from inside, what if a Unionist, appearing in front of me and raising his eyebrows were to say:

"God, how do you find in yourself the right to insert yourself among us?"
What else would I be able to do but shrink back in fear and turn away?

This is how it was every time, as if fearing reprimands from within and without, I walked in bashfully, revolted by myself. But—despite feelings, actions, and ideas, I am going to write everything as it happened and as it was—at the same time I felt a strange kind of pride. Because the people who had harmed me, with the rousing of friends that know my value, now show me veneration; those that had looked at my papers as they were sending me to my exile, now were giving me a position in the same building. Actually, there is no need for exaggeration.... This was a literary post [not a political one]. But anyway I was not striving for anything more than that in status; yesterday they had exiled me for my writings, and today: they were keeping me because of my writings. So for that reason it was with a strange pride and all of these thoughts that I entered through the door of the central headquarters, always in a state between the two opposing feelings, half pride and half shame.

So it was that on that day, even though I walked with even more anxiety than usual due to the Central Committee meeting that was happening (and knowing that Talaat Paşa, with whom I shared a mutual dislike and with whom I came face to face only one time, was up there would pain me even more), I did not notice any difference in the situation when I entered the room where the writers' meeting was happening. As always, people were chit-chatting about all kinds of things that were not related to politics. Köprülüzade (Fuat Köprülü), Necmettin Sadık (Sadak), Yahya Kemal and a few other young people were there. At that moment was heard the revving of an automobile. We—as usual—were awaiting the arrival of Ziya Gökalp Bey; because Ziya Bey, would come out of party discussions and throw himself into discussions about literature and knowledge, and these returns always gave me the feeling of a fish that had been caught with a net that escaped back out into the open sea and was free again. We waited, he didn't come; Küçük Talat Bey came in. It was he who came in, but I took him for someone else—his face was that changed; smiling, like always:

He did not forget to say "Maşallah, Beyler!"; but neither did his voice resemble his ordinary voice, nor did his smile resemble his customary smile.... In fact this could not even be considered a smile; if it were possible to take an x-ray of the feeling known as anguish, that is what this picture resembled, a frightful shrinking back was being illustrated. Yahya Kemal, either because of the power of his understanding, or because the hearsay of the night before, delivered the first political question at *Yeni Mecmua*:

"What's happening, Talat Bey?" he said. So something was happening.... I had no idea myself. I was so busy writing articles for *Yeni Mecmua*, teaching at the College [Robert College], and finishing up "The True Face of Istanbul" for *Zaman* newspaper, that I was no longer, in fact could not any longer think about this war that I was so sure would end in catastrophe. My ears pricked up. Yahya Kemal continued with this:

"What's happening, Talat Bey?" and with him saying that, one sensed a reproach and reprimand. And there was yet another facet to it: for Yahya Kemal to have had the audacity to address him in this way, as if to say, "Look what you've done, see? Now how are you all going to weasel out of this one?," it meant that the government party (CUP) must have been shaken from its place. Without even hearing the answer, I immediately understood what was going on just from the way the question was asked, and was sure that the catastrophe had happened without even listening to the answer. Talat Bey:

"Those whores, the Bulgarians left the front and escaped!" he said. Ah, so, a defeat . . . and not one that belonged to our army, either. . . . Our allies will come and straighten it out. That is what I first thought but he continued with this:

"Our line with the Germans has been cut."

We all froze. I got a shiver up my spine.

"There is no other solution than to sue for peace!"

So, that meant that the Great War had reached an end. We were disengaging. Suddenly, I imagined a terrible, terrible sight: the Allied armies coming in from Macedonia and entering Istanbul, passing right through Beyoğlu. . . . Among the thousands of terrible results of the defeat, my mind was only zeroing in on that, bringing that to life. As if there was only one result of our collapse, and that was it. The Europeans, exhuberant with pride, taking revenge centuries after Fatih [Mehmed the Conqueror], entering historic Istanbul with its billions in wealth, and they with their brass band playing music of victory as they enter. Tomorrow a victorious officer will come into this room, a Frank; cracking his whip as if he is chasing chickens, cats, or mice, with the expression of a fop that wants us far away even in times of friendship, let alone times of enmity:

"Pist!" he would say; and we would scatter. I was nailed to my seat, thinking of all of this. Among us, there were those who just a moment before had wanted to run out of this annihilation of the headquarters. It was as if Talat Bey, sitting right across from us, in one instant had lost all of his wisdom, his reason for being, his meaning, and his very existence; he suddenly looked unrecognizable, like a criminal. Ah, the torment on the poor guy's face. . . . Who would have said that I, who was seeing him now, would a little while later, show something so close to torment on my face, because of the failures that I will talk about in detail [in subsequent installments of the memoir], because of a partisan and political defeat he would fall in station.

Everyone suddenly got up. That day would be my last time entering the Red Villa, my last bashfulness. . . . We left in a state of deep anxiety. It would not be my lot to ever even pass by in front of, let along set foot inside it during the Armistice period. Nevertheless, if I live, and if the building doesn't burn down, who knows if I won't ever by a strange turn of events enter again, after a short or long period, or in sweetness or bitterness?

Before turning into the *Zaman* offices, I turned and looked back. That majestic, decorated, shiny building already looked like a Caesar's palace, a ruin lying in place, with spiderwebs on the walls and bats in the hollows. As if a moment later an earthquake would happen right there and knock it all down. It was standing like an apparition in the terrible stillness that comes before such catastrophes.

In great fires, I would see big mansions, the red starting from deep inside, in a red light, the flames not yet reaching the eves. The possessions long ago removed, the people long ago having fled, the mansion transformed by the fire despite all of its grandeur and splendor. What a wretched sight for a person to behold! Such a countenance had the headquarters taken on.

I looked more closely: within it [the burning mansion] an ugly but very just consolation shone: Union and Progress had been annihilated! To me, after what I had suffered, to be able to see this from the center, to hear it at the center, to read it on the face of one of the central committee members, was Divine Providence. . . . But, together with Union and Progress, the state (*devlet*) was also being annihilated. We would finally be saved, but only on the condition of giving it all away! There was no consolation to be found.[36]

This was published on January 15, 1924, and the controversy began in the same issue of *Akşam*. In the very same column on the same page, in fact, was an unsigned article titled "Just Wait a Second! Let the *Ferman* Be Read!," later identified as the work of Falih Rıfkı (Atay). The controversy around the publication had already begun, with the first volley—to which Falih Rıfkı was responding—launched by none other than *Akbaba* (Vulture), the aptly named satirical newspaper that replaced Refik Halid's *Aydede* after he fled the country. Rıfkı defends *Akşam* against the accusation that by publishing the memoir, they, as Refik Halid's friends, are trying to exculpate this "national traitor." He accuses *Akbaba* of having scavenged the carcass of *Aydede*, which indeed they had—co-opting the same staff and appealing to the same readership—and ends with the caveat that "Babıali Caddesi" (the avenue, and quarter of Old Istanbul where the publishing and newspaper industry was based) was "not so labyrinthine," being instead a place where "everyone knows each other" (so presumably *Akbaba* should be careful about who it is accusing of deficient patriotism). He ends, "[L]et this be a lesson in patriotism! We cannot tolerate this! '*Akşam*' is thinking about service to our nation (*millet*) in everything it does, including the publishing of Refik Halid Bey's memoirs!"[37]

Necmettin Sadak then published an editorial wherein he laid out the controversy, which appeared alongside the second installment of the memoir, on January 16, 1924. While Ankara suspected that Refik Halid's only motive was the desire to exonerate himself and his friends who had passed the years of the National Struggle in "weakness and dissimulation and were connected to the Freedom and Accord party," Sadak underlined that, having read the memoir from start to finish, he found it to be beneficial (*fayda gördüğü şey*), and that publication "*reinforces the national struggle which has been going on for 5 years and which we are convinced will continue for many years to come*" (emphasis added).[38] Furthermore, Sadak revealed that none other than

Interior Minister Ferit Bey (Ahmet Ferit Tek) (the official in charge of the List of 150) had sent a secret, encrypted memo to the governor of Istanbul forbidding the publication of the memoir. Thus, Sadak explains, he and his colleagues at the newspaper had decided to temporarily suspend publication. This was *not* out of deference to the interior minister's order, he insisted, since they were responsible only to the law (*kanun*), and there was no law prohibiting the publication. Instead, "we are taking a break so as not to put more pressure on the government, in which we see a thousand troubles, by adding our own reasons to them." Indeed, he states, "for us it is a matter of dignity that we will one day resume publication of this series." He concludes with a "request" to the "patriots in Ankara": "[A]bandon all of your delusions, and don't think that the duty of measuring your actions against your concern for the homeland is limited to a small circle of people [i.e., you are not the only ones who care about this country]. You should investigate very closely the sources and inspirations before making any decrees, especially regarding Istanbul and Istanbul's establishments, and most especially including the Istanbul press." Sadak's was a stern, and surprisingly bold, warning to the new government elite in Ankara: "leave the Istanbul press alone."

Minelbab İlelmihrab, then, became the occasion for and a crucible of the confrontation between "Ankara," or the new government elite, and "Istanbul," where the press was spirited and challenging in its criticism and earnest in its calls for freedom of expression and input into the form the new state would take and the procedures it would follow. In trying to shutter the publication of his old friend's memoir, after having ensured his banishment from the country, Ferit Bey had his own shaky reputation to protect and little but his own claims to authority to rely on. His authority and that of the Ankara government in toto was far from unchallenged; the constitution for the new republic would only be ratified on April 20 of that year, and the first opposition party, the PRP, would be established later that year under Kâzım (Karabekir) and Rauf (Orbay). Not only did Necmettin Sadak and Falih Rıfkı not hesitate to undermine Ahmet Ferit Bey's authority and call attention to the fact that there was no law in place prohibiting the publication of such memoirs, but even some on the Ankara side of the feud, such as İsmail Müştak (who had known Refik Halid since his Sinop days, when the former had been an administrator while the latter was in exile there), weighed in on the side of rule of law and press freedom.

A former Unionist partisan and now a figure in the Ankara government, Müştak pointed out that even though Refik Halid was a national traitor and it was possible that his memoir should be banned, to do so without a legal basis was wrong. In the absence of any law against publishing the memoirs of those on the List of 150, he defended the principle of press freedom, cautioning that "there may be some people who will not be pleased with Refik Halid's memoirs. *Refik Halid might show the faces behind the masks if he divulges some realities that are thought to have been buried in the past.* But we believe that, between us, things should not remain like this. However, even if there are some people like this, to prohibit publication for their sake is a sin and would awaken the worry that freedom of expression (*hürriyeti lisana sansür*) could be censored" (emphasis added).[39] In a separate letter, İsmail Müştak wrote, "I am not saying that Refik Halid Bey's memoirs should not have been banned; what I am saying is, let's find out why they were banned. Laws must be known in order to be obeyed. *Our wish to judge whether our freedom is based on politics or on law* (kanun) *is not in opposition to the spirit of the revolution* (inkilabın ruhuna *muhalif* değil) *but is the ultimate service to it*" (emphasis added).[40]

So what was so controversial about the memoir's first two installments? The answer is as simple, and as elusive, as the larger nature of *muhalefet* under examination here. Certainly there were personal-political insecurities at play: Refik Halid maintained that what made people in Turkey so nervous about the memoir is that it would point out not the big wrongs, but all the little wrongs, hypocrisies, lies, and slipups of the middling figures—the group that had the most at stake and was most vulnerable in the new, formative stage of the republic. It was the men who were posturing, distancing themselves from the CUP and the recent political past, and trying to gain a foothold in the new power structure who were depicted in Refik's memoir. The stated aim of the memoir—to show the realities within what was essentially the liberal *muhalefet* (the Freedom and Accord Party and the Istanbul government), that is, to display the view from another perspective on the War of Independence—was a litmus test for the elites of the new republic. Which ones would see this aim as threatening and want to block this other perspective in favor of "national unity," and which would see its publication as not just desirable but necessary for a republic in which freedom of expression—and the space of constestation—was real and the rule of law was taken seriously? This issue lurked under the surface of the political tension between "Ankara" and "Istanbul": What kind of state, and what kind of republic, would this be? Would politics go the way of the Second Constitutional Era again, with the ruling party using democratic trappings to cloak authoritarian control? Or would there be a real dialogue, with space for different voices and points of view?

These were both *ideological* and *tactical* differences among the ruling elite in the new republic, and the ghosts of the CUP and their *muhalefet* were very present. This brought the question of history—and multivocal histories—to the forefront. In the absence of an official history in these early years, keeping alive the memory of past conflict and opposition exacerbated the legitimacy crisis of the new regime, which was struggling to enforce and solidify its authority. Since no one knew where the chips would land, so to speak, surely the best thing to say about the recent past was nothing. And the last thing anyone with anything to hide wanted was for the Porcupine, Refik Halid, who had vocally and continually opposed Mustafa Kemal and the national movement from his telegraph office and his press offices in Istanbul, to start naming names and dredging up the messy past. There was a world of difference between the feuds and grudges within the political and cultural elites, on the one hand, and the official history that would ultimately be disseminated to the masses from the late 1920s onward, on the other. The official history managed to obliterate alike the memory of actual experiences of common people and political elites, recorded in the pages of *Akşam* and other newspapers for posterity.[41]

What did Refik Halid's self-proclaimed "sui generis" memoir aim to accomplish, beyond influencing the internal power struggles of the new republic? Publicly, he repeatedly wrote of wanting only to "bring the past to life," not to defend any particular idea or dogma, exonerate himself or his friends, or incriminate his enemies. In his private correspondence, however, Refik Halid confided in his dear friend and fellow member of the List of 150, Rıza Tevfik, that he was emulating his great idol, Victor Hugo. He extolled Hugo's virtues, comparing his own and Rıza Tevfik's predicament to that of Hugo and other exiled French intellectuals like Louis-Gabriel Michaud, who had published anti-Bonapartist books about the French monarchy. He pointed out that the two were eventually pardoned and allowed back into the fold of French politics and culture. Hugo's memoirs were an important catalyst for his pardon and for a kind of expansion and consolidation of freedom and national unity in France. Thus one strong motive for Refik Halid was the (self-important) hope that his memoir would prompt a kind of national reconciliation and even lead to his pardon. He was looking forward to a day when the leaders of the Turkish Republic would be able to tolerate contestation, when freedom and Turkish national unity could be expanded—and he certainly seemed to have allies in the Istanbul press with similar aims. That day never quite came; when Refik Halid was finally pardoned and allowed back into Turkey, it was instead for his unsavory service for Turkish interests on the contested Hatay/Alexandretta region, as we will see. And the publication of the first installments of *Minelbab* sparked the opposite reaction: a severe crackdown on press freedom and a reinstitution of a kind of censorship with the Law on the Maintenance of Order.

In the meantime, in Turkey the process of legal prohibition of publications by those on the List of 150 began. The issue was discussed in the press, with appeals made to the public prosecutor's office, the parliament, and the Committee of Justice. When the public prosecutor's office deemed it illegal to publish works of those on the List of 150 on the basis that although they had been expelled from the country, they were still subect to its civil laws, one newspaper even called for putting a final end to the question by asking readers their opinion, rather than letting the matter rest with the public prosecutor.

This state of legal ambiguity and public contention in 1924 existed in the context of other momentous developments. The constitution for the new republic was being completed and would be promulgated in April 1924. And the opposition leading to the formation of the PRP was growing, as were the anxieties of the Republican People's Party leaders that they were under siege even as Mustafa Kemal grudgingly permitted the experiment.[42] The development that finally closed any possible space of contestation was the Takrir-i Sükun Kanunu, or the Law on the Maintenance of Order, inspired in part by the controversy over Refik Halid's memoir.[43]

The Law on the Maintenance of Order (March 1925)

The Law on the Maintenance of Order gave the government extraordinary powers over freedom of expression and assembly—familiar from the martial law of the Second Constitutional Era. The immediate pretext was the Şeyh Sait rebellion in the heavily Kurdish southeast of the new Turkey, a rebellion which was gaining momentum in late February 1925, thanks in part to the recent abolishment of the Caliphate. Martial law in the Kurdish areas in the east was proposed, along with amendments to the High Treason Law. But the ongoing threat was much closer to the center of power: the Istanbul press, indeed, the expansion of martial law to Istanbul, was proposed "because of the supposedly subversive attitude of the Istanbul press."[44] There was a lively debate going on in the press in those first few years of the republic, and one can imagine that some of Refik Halid's friends who were still in Istanbul had not forgotten about him or his potential to critique and comment on the politics of that moment and the recent past.

On March 5, 1925, İsmet (İnönü)'s new government passed the Law on the Maintenance of Order, which "gave the government practically unlimited powers in every part of the country for a period of two years."[45] At the same time, the Independence Tribunals that had operated during the War of Independence since 1920 were reinstituted. As Zürcher puts it, "the two years following this fateful decision saw the silencing of all political opposition in the press, the start of brutal suppression of the Kurdish ethnic and linguistic identity and, in 1926, the elimination of all potential competitors for power from outside the leading Kemalist circle in the political trials in İzmir and Ankara."[46]

And some of the most marked effects were on the Istanbul press. Of the major papers, only the government organs, *Hakimiyet-i Milliye* (in Ankara) and *Cumhuriyet* (in Istanbul), and the former CUP organ *Tanin* remained in circulation. At the same time, those who had been opposed to publishing Refik Halid's memoir, and who were in any case pitted against him and his friends in Istanbul, began trying to conflate him and Rıza Tevfik, in exile further to the east and south of the Kurdish areas, with the Şeyh Sait supporters, accusing them of spreading reactionary (*irtica*) propaganda to the Kurdish tribes on the Turkish side of the border.[47]

The Independence Tribunals (1925–1927)

The last major step in silencing opposition, and therefore contestation, in the new republic was the reopening of the Independence Tribunals in 1925–27. They had been held during the War of Independence from 1920, were resurrected after the Şeyh Sait Rebellion in 1925, and then continued to prosecute an alleged assassination conspiracy against Mustafa Kemal in İzmir in 1926 before being officially closed in 1927. This time the Istanbul press was an important target of the Tribunals. The Law on Maintenance of Order, effectively a gag order on the press, was set to expire in two years; within those two years, the Independence Tribunals set in place more permanent repression of opposition elements.[48] Refik Halid was not tried directly because he had already been banished, but he watched with disgust as many of his associates from the Istanbul press were put on trial. He also maintained that there was a second attempt to publish his memoir in the Istanbul press just days before the passage of the Law on the Maintenance of Order in March 1925, which implies once again the threatening nature of his history-as-memoir.

THE REPUBLIC OF TURKEY,
FROM THE OUTSIDE LOOKING IN

The space for *muhalefet* as partisan opposition, and then *muhalefet* as internal dissent, was closed off as the republic took shape between 1923 and 1926. How did all of these events and controversies look to Refik, watching from exile across the border? In his personal correspondence, Refik Halid was candid and direct, and often brutally honest about his views toward Turkey and its new batch of statesmen. His correspondence with Rıza Tevfik is particularly illuminating. Rıza Tevfik, also known as Filosof, or the Philosopher, was a widely revered and accomplished poet and philologist in addition to being a prominent *muhalif*. He was also on the List of 150, due to his role in negotiating the ill-fated Treaty of Sèvres for the Ottomans and his continuing opposition to and disdain for the nationalists. He was in Amman and Jounieh while Refik was in Jounieh, Beirut, and Aleppo, and he stayed on voluntarily for several years even after he and most other 150ers had been pardoned in 1938. The letters the two exchanged during their fifteen years of exile fill in many gaps about Refik Halid's perception of and the motives behind his literary works and his view of political and social developments in Turkey.

In the first years of the republic and after his arrival in Jounieh/Aleppo, Refik Halid struggled to make sense of his place; a writer who wrote—and only wanted to write—in his native Turkish, he was now severed from his readership and his home. As those who remained in Turkey were struggling to define the structure and boundaries of the new polity, so Refik Halid was struggling to come to terms with his relationship to home. What did it mean to write literature in Turkish while displaced from the new Turkey? Who would his audience be?

His personal life was also turbulent. He told Rıza Tevfik that he had officially split up with his first wife, Nâzime, in late 1924. They had married during his first exile, in Sinop, and had been let back into Istanbul in 1918 thanks to the birth of their son. She and their son, Ender, had initially joined him in his new exile, but after she suffered a breakdown, the two parted ways and divorced, and she and their son returned to Istanbul in 1924. After some trials and tribulations, in summer 1927 Refik Halid married a second time, to the much younger Nihal, the daughter of another fellow *muhalif* and resident in Jounieh, Mahir Said. They remained married until his death in 1965, and their son Ömer Uğur was born in Aleppo in 1933, an event which intensified Refik Halid's desire to return home to Istanbul.

Amid the flux in his personal life, he tried to make sense of how he had gotten where he was. He reflected on the last time he had seen his beloved Rıza Tevfik, in Istanbul in late 1922 just before they both fled the city: "I don't know if you remember, but the last time I saw you was the evening before Ali Kemal's arrest in the Harikzâdegân Apartment building in Lâleli. It was plunged into darkness, the wires had just burned out (*na-tamamdı*); you had just moved in and were in a total state of disarray. Our minds were in ruins, too. Outside, there were demonstrations. 'Kahrolsun! Kahrolsun!' (Damn them! Damn them!) [presumably addressing them] voices were rattling the glass, and rattling hearts as much as the glass. What a gloomy, painful, terrible hour it was!"[49]

Even far away, he stayed connected to his journalism and publishing associates in Turkey and continued, as we have seen, to be a topic of discussion and target of opprobrium in the Turkish press. He even went so far as to stage his own death by meningitis as a prank in late 1924, sending a telegram to the newly established newspaper *Cumhuriyet*, so as to prompt an outpouring of eulogies and kind words in the newspapers of Turkey. His hope was to trigger enough positive sentiment that he would be allowed back into the country, just as the PRP was in full swing and opposition was emboldened. Silly as it seemed, this gag constituted a continuing engagement of sorts with Turkish political and cultural life, despite his physical removal from the country, loss of citizenship, and deprivation of legal belonging. Just what would be the terms of this exile? Refik Halid was continually trying to work this out for himself, and in many ways this not only mirrored but was directly bound up with the larger struggle going on over the terms of rule in the new Turkish Republic and that regime's relationship to the many aspects—political, cultural, and physical remnants—of the Ottoman past.

Poignantly expressing his and Rıza Tevfik's predicament, he wrote in early 1925 (when the PRP was still operating and it looked like formal opposition would be allowed to function, and before the Independence Tribunals were reopened): "I, like you, want so much to go to Istanbul, but there is no way I am even going to try, when there is still the possibility of sacrificing my dignity [even given the way things are going in my favor now resulting from the news of my death, that might have made my return possible]. What would I do there? Go around all sorrowful, in an Istanbul that has lost its soul and where pleasure is not something fun or desirable. If it can straighten itself out then we can get on the road."[50]

In early 1926, after the declaration of the Law on the Maintenance of Order and the political turmoil and crackdown in Ankara, he expressed his disillusionment and estrangement to Rıza Tevfik:

> I am not at all involved in politics, and have decided not to be from now on. This decision is quite categorical. Other than Istanbul there is nothing about Turkey that I think about or miss. When I look at the tribe/assembly of statesmen from afar it's like watching Gog and Magog, and I watch with astonishment but without fear. I cannot even find funny sides to it. To me they look much more unnatural than supernatural. They are more like the inhabitants of Kamer and Mirrih in Wells' novels, and I cannot like them. I even ask myself if they are even really my co-ethnics (*ırkdaş*). How do they speak, what do they eat and drink, how do they dress? They are entirely under foreign influence.

This is indeed a fascinating observation from a Francophile, cosmopolitan Ottoman gentleman.[51] But apparently there was a right way and a wrong way to assimilate European ways.

Despite these feelings of loss, Refik Halid conceded that he had found a comfortable place for himself in Aleppo and Jounieh, with frequent forays to Hatay (Alexandretta sancak) for duck hunting and socializing with the Turks there. He told Rıza Tevfik what he was doing in Aleppo—namely, since 1924, writing and editing for the Turkish-language newspaper *Doğru Yol* (Straight path) with Celâl Kadri and Hasan Sadık. He noted that İskenderun (Alexandretta) and its environs were "all Turks, and [they] have accepted me graciously," indicating that he did have a small readership even outside the bounds of the Turkish Republic, in İskenderun/Alexandretta, which was under special French administration. He wrote that "our *Doğru Yol* is not a dogmatic or fanatical political paper, and not at all on the side of the softas or the Padishah [i.e., not Islamist or Royalist]. *It is only against the revolution and oppressive state made in the name of the Kemalist Republic.* And even this is not manifested with violence, but is moderate" (emphasis added).[52]

In July 1927, eight years after the Telegraph Episode and a few months before Mustafa Kemal's monumental *Nutuk* speech, Refik Halid was still unrepentant. He wrote to Rıza Tevfik: "They threw me out of the country. My offense? One gambling politician [i.e., Mustafa Kemal] at a desperate moment, maybe taking account or maybe without reflection, made a speculative venture, and I was opposed to it. . . . I did not consent to the guy, worried, and instead said, 'and if you lose?' I told the guy to stop and I did not come out on top. That's my only offense!"[53] His resentment was still palpable in 1927 as he continued:

> Don't worry, when they stripped me of nationality I was not in their nationality anyway. In my view it should not be called "casting out of nationality"; liberation from nationality is more like it. *They put a black stamp so that not even children can read my writings, and anything with my signature in the school textbooks and anthologies.* What a medieval and foolish thing. If that child is smart isn't he going to go and ask his dad? Won't he be curious? Does he deserve to memorize it [the banned literature] with all the other names? Didn't we learn the Namık Kemal's and the Şinasi's [i.e., the nineteenth-century writers who had clashed with the regime and suffered banishment]? Let us not make a mistake by comparing ourselves to them. Hadn't we read those who were damned in their eras? Allah cannot remove your [Rıza Tevfik's] poems from the history of literature in Turkey; the angel of death cannot kill my name. There is no artist in the cosmos that has been annihilated with the decrees and decisions of a government in a time of revolution. If they could be killed, then hundreds of people, from André Chénier to Victor Hugo would be nonexistent. Especially Hugo, whose *Châtiments* you have read. I've loved this work for a very long time—in my first exile [in Anatolia 1913–18] I used to keep it under my pillow. (emphasis added)

The year 1927 would turn out to be a watershed for Turkey and for Refik Halid, watching from afar. In that year the new hegemony of the Turkish Republic, the Republican People's Party, and Mustafa Kemal was consolidated. The press had been checked. The "dangerous elements" had been purged: the List of 150 had removed 150 traitors from the country, and the Independence Tribunals had brought to justice old members of the CUP deemed dangerous, thereby publicly cleansing the new republic of that messy past. Social, sumptuary, economic, and legal reforms were getting underway to diminish the control and presence of religious authorities and create a new framework for state and society.[54]

This is the moment when Mustafa Kemal delivered his "Nutuk," or "Great Speech" to the second congress of the Republican People's Party—the party he had founded—in mid-October 1927. In it, he—as president and leader of the RPP—set down the official history of the Turkish War of Independence, beginning with his landing at Samsun on May 19, 1919, and ending with the establishment of the republic, abrogation of the Sultanate and the Caliphate in 1922–24, and elimination of the opposition in the course of the Independence Tribunals in 1925–27.[55] *Nutuk* was, among other things, Mustafa Kemal's corrective to the uncontrollable voices: the memoirs and verbal recollections of individuals, each with their particular vantage point and experience of the messy years between Ottoman and Republican Turkish hegemony. Like the Independence Tribunals that clarified right and wrong in the legal arena, *Nutuk* established the correct, orthodox recounting of events that for decades overshadowed all other accounts, not only in official history but in historical scholarship.

One can assume that Mustafa Kemal knew about Refik Halid's memoir and had read the two installments published in 1924 (not to mention the second attempt in 1925 on the eve of the implementation of the Law on the Maintenance of Order), as well as that Mustafa Kemal grasped the potential significance of having that memoir, and that accounting of events, in the public domain when his hegemony was not yet firmly established.[56] Given that so much of *Nutuk* focuses on the telegrams exchanged between himself and the Ottoman government, and particularly with Refik Halid in Istanbul in the summer of 1919, it also stands to reason that he was going to great lengths to exculpate himself and the national movement from accusations of betraying the Ottoman sovereign authority, which, technically speaking, is exactly what they had done. He was, in effect, still engaged in the effort to justify his role in the power struggle with the no longer extant Istanbul government, and Refik Halid had been the face of that government at a crucial moment. If exile and banishment were not enough to silence Refik Halid, *Nutuk* would put the matter to rest and silence him and other *muhalif*s who threatened the official hegemony—and the new national unity—once and for all. And it did, as shown in the following chapter.

SIX

There Is a World Underground
(1928–1945)

My joy at returning is manifold.
In what state did I leave my beloved homeland? With what
    wonder will I encounter it [anew].
I would recognize only one smokestack mournfully pumping
    smoke out of a factory: Zeytinburnu . . .
The only building in Ankara was Taşhan.
In the banks our language wouldn't pass, in companies our
    words would not get through.
On the train I could not express myself to the ticket collector
    without turning my Turkish into Greek.
At Tokatlıyan [restaurant in Beyoğlu] I could not have given
    my order to the waiter easily if I did not say it in French.
At our beaches I used to look with fear from the shore at the
    swimming foreigners, and I would throw my hat out the
    window at the border when I returned from Europe.
In the homeland, the dry earth was ours, the fertile earth
    belonged to them.
At my age I returned to a state of laughing and crying like a
    baby in the excitement I felt at touching the independent
    and miraculous country that has taken the place of the
    motherland in the state I left it.
I repeat continuously: Long Live Atatürk, Atatürk who gives
    me life and fills my chest even when I am far from home.

—REFIK HALID "Karakayış," telegraph sent to *Tan* newspaper
in response to the question of how Refik Halid felt
to be returning to Turkey, summer 1938[1]

THE RULES HAD CHANGED in the sixteen years since Refik Halid had
fled Istanbul; and so, evidently, had his willingness to follow them. Given
what we already know from the previous chapters about Refik Halid's life,
career, and sensibilities leading up to 1938, the preceding lines alone—for
public consumption coinciding with his arrival in Turkey—raise many questions. Was he being disingenuous, ironic even, in his obsequious praise of

the republic and of Atatürk? How and when did the quintessential *muhalif* undergo this transformation into a Kemalist patriot?

The transformation had been in the works for more than a decade. This public declaration of loyalty and patriotism upon his return to Turkey in 1938 merely signaled a new phase of that transformation. The first phase had begun after 1927 with his "change of sentiments" toward the regime. Through a combination of ceasing his open opposition to the regime and performing political gestures to demonstrate his patriotism and value to the Turkish nation, particularly regarding the contested Hatay/Alexandretta region, as we shall see, he succeeded in gaining a pardon in summer 1938, just months before the death of Atatürk.

With Refik's return to Turkey began the second stage of his transformation: he now had to introduce himself anew to the Turkish public, now as the Kemalist Refik Halid Karay, having added the surname in conformity with the 1934 Surname Law. But to reestablish himself within the new political, literary, and cultural landscape of the Turkish Republic, he went beyond merely adding a surname; instead, he wholly revised the story of his past actions, reworking, reinterpreting, and censoring his past writings accordingly. These vestiges of the recent Ottoman past, and of the culture of *muhalefet* therein, would have to be adapted to fit a Kemalist mold—a task that was complicated enough given that so much about the boundaries of acceptability in politics and thought was implied rather than explicitly spelled out in the single-party regime. And all of this just as Atatürk was dying and the republic he had founded, soon to be bereft of its founder and sole leader, was entering a new phase. Here I trace these phases between 1928 and 1945, first considering Refik Halid's writings and actions as a Kemalist in formation while still in exile, then the role of the Hatay/Alexandretta dispute in his transformation, followed by his reinvention through his redactions and new writings after his return to Istanbul in 1938. Connecting his wartime experience of the 1916 Ankara fire and his Armistice-era writing about that experience with this process of Kemalist reinvention, I highlight the retooling of his 1921 "Ankara fire" essay into a veritable ode to the Republican Ankara of 1939.

As we step into this new phase of Refik Halid's career and writings, the allegory found in his novel *Yer Altında Dünya Var* (There is a world underground) is helpful in allowing us to grasp the complexities of *muhalefet* and, more broadly, the condition of politics between 1928 and 1945. The novel, although published in book form more than a decade after his return, is set in contemporary Syria. The protagonist is a Turk (Nebil, meaning noble), who has come to Syria to claim the land he has inherited from an aunt in Istanbul who has died (symbolizing the Ottoman patrimony in Syria), and ends up also pursuing the elusive object of his desire, Nihan (a Persian word/ name meaning secret, or hidden). Nebil is in desperate pursuit of a buried treasure somewhere on the land he has inherited when he catches glimpses of the mysterious Nihan. As he tries to apprehend her, he has competition from a group of Germans (friends from the Ottoman past) as well as a group of Armenians (the existential threat from the Ottoman past), who are also rushing to find the treasure underground. That Refik was influenced in his employment of symbolism and allegory by the new field of psychoanalysis in the 1930s and 1940s is clear, especially in the last pages, when the narrator/author wakes up from a dream, revealing that the whole story was a hallucination. The novel marks the start of Refik's preoccupation—albeit heavy handed—with excavating the collective unconscious, which in his case means the historical memory and repressed legacy of the Ottoman past. The legacy of past Ottoman connections abounds: Nihan has mysterious origins from Bosnia, the treasure and inherited land is in Syria, and Armenians and Germans are the groups competing for the treasure. All of the old Ottoman passions and rivalries are revived in the quest for the underground treasure.

The allegory of a world underground is widely applicable in Refik's own story, in the politics of the single-party Kemalist Republic, and specifically in the realm of *muhalefet*. While in exile in Syria, Refik was forced to live in one kind of underground world, banned from the republic and branded a traitor. Upon his return and official pardon, in order to live above ground and be accepted back into the fold of the literary and political establishment, he had to reinvent himself. This involved selectively suppressing the memory of and the narrative about his past acts of subversion, effectively driving a part of himself underground. Even in Refik's own writings we see this: on the surface are his emphatic, public declarations of Kemalist devotion, but peering more deeply into his writings reveals a more ambivalent stance toward power, past and present. Mirroring this, in a strictly political sense, *muhalefet* as organized political opposition remained underground, continuing under the surface as factions within the Republican People's Party (RPP); conflict, however, was brewing under that surface. There were many kinds of worlds underground in the single-party republic, as well as a delicate balancing act for all between giving voice to growing factional divisions and containing those divisions so as to keep the appearance of national unity under the RPP.[2]

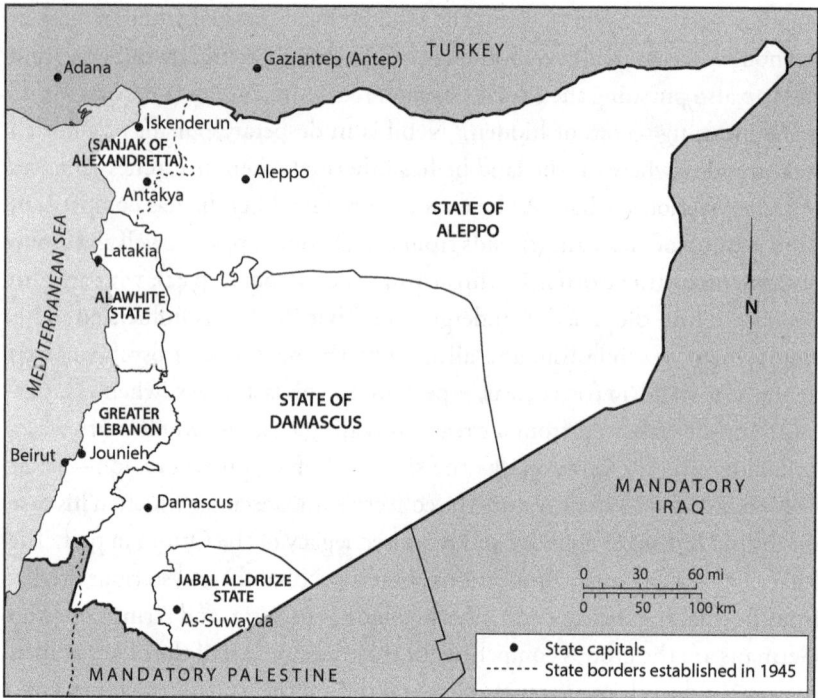

MAP 4. Syria/Lebanon under the French Mandate (1923–39)

REFLECTIONS IN EXILE

In the early years of his Syrian exile, Refik's opposition was vocal and public; his language in public was measured, except for the memoir he attempted to publish in 1924 at a volatile moment for the republic. In private correspondence, his language was less measured. He expressed vitriolic hatred for the regime and particular figures within it. His sentiments expressed from exile against the Turkish regime changed, however, after 1927, a change as dramatic as it was anticlimactic. Mustafa Kemal had succeeded in consolidating a new political order back in Turkey. Several prominent figures in the national movement and early republic, such as Halide Edib (Adıvar) and Ahmet Emin (Yalman), fled the country in protest against his dictatorial behavior. Refik, however, instead shifted his orientation *toward* the Kemalist regime at precisely this time. From his perspective, there was no longer any point to contesting the basis for the republic, and no hope for bringing down the regime. Things were settling down.

Refik Halid would explain his "change of sentiments" not with reference to the consolidation of the Kemalist regime, or to "Nutuk," the speech that announced the completion of that process in late 1927, and in which Refik himself had a cameo appearance as a national traitor. Instead, he explained the motivation for his change of sentiments as a personal one: "[U]nder the influence of his [second] wife, the fifteen-year-old Madame Nihal, he became a partisan/supporter of the new Turkish regime."[3] This conveniently coincided with the bargain struck between opposing factions within Turkey and with the consensus that Mustafa Kemal would be held beyond reproach. He, as leader of the national movement and founder of the republic and its only party, the RPP, would be elevated above politics. The nation, the party, Mustafa Kemal, and the republic would be one indivisible, even indistinguishable whole. It was a new kind of Unionism, or at least a new kind of unity. Rather than the CUP being the guardian of constitutionalism, now Mustafa Kemal was the guardian of the republic and the "arrows," or principles, that the republic and its single party stood for.[4]

Within months of this change of convictions, Refik Halid would help found a new newspaper.[5] *Vahdet* (Unity), based in Aleppo, was not an opposition paper as *Doğru Yol* had been, but was proclaimed to be a neutral paper and was said to have been under the general direction, or at least with the blessing of, Mustafa Kemal from Ankara. And the array of figures involved in the paper indicated a unity of elements indeed. Nuri Genç, deputy in the Syrian Assembly for the Kürddağı district north of Aleppo, sent for Refik in Jounieh and asked him to move back to Aleppo. The newspaper was approved by the Turkish consul of Aleppo, indicating approval from on high in Ankara.[6] Fellow members of the List of 150 were among the founders of *Vahdet*: Ali İlmi Fani (Birgili) and Tarık Mümtaz (Göztepe).[7] According to Refik, the statement of intent for the paper was that "*Vahdet* will have no other aim than to give the news of neighboring states, and will not contain pettinesses such as satirizing or the perversion of reality (*hakikat*)." Refik, when reflecting back to that time, admitted, "Even though it had to be kept half-hidden because of the influence of the French mandate, it was crystal clear that it was the Turkish Republic that was being referred to [as the neighboring state]."[8] *Vahdet* began publication—in Ottoman script, on the eve of the Alphabet Reform in Turkey, which ordered the switch from the Arabic to the Latin alphabet for Turkish—on May 18, 1928. The paper was based in Aleppo and İskenderun, the latter being one of the major towns in the contested Hatay/Alexandretta sancak, just to the west of Aleppo.

Refik Halid's involvement signaled the start of his new, more conciliatory approach toward Turkey. He would later admit that *Vahdet* had helped lay the groundwork for his eventual return to Turkey.[9] Refik Halid started as literary editor of *Vahdet*. His articles were now regularly being sent back to Turkey, even though he formally still had the status of national traitor. In this new chapter of Refik Halid's life and career, his views, as expressed in personal correspondence, also gradually shifted toward support for many aspects of Kemalism. He continued to receive money from his relatives in Istanbul and earned his keep in Aleppo not only by writing for *Vahdet*, but reportedly also in the employ of the French consulate (in his correspondence he claims this is a ridiculous rumor, but other members of the List of 150 were in the employ of French intelligence so it is not so far-fetched), although what precisely he may have done in exchange for this salary, if he did collect one, remains unclear.[10] After 1930 he was routinely portrayed in a positive light in Turkish intelligence reports, confirming that a shift was possible, and that even someone from the List of 150 might be accepted back into the fold.[11]

As the tenets of Kemalism and the republic were steadily taking shape, Refik voiced his approval of various aspects of it, such as laicism (*laiklik*), in his personal correspondence with Rıza Tevfik. He made gestures such as seeking Rıza Tevfik's advice on a good "Öz Türkçe" or "pure Turkish" name for his child—finally landing on Ömer Uğur for his son, who was born in 1933. Such gestures showed his approval, or at least acceptance, of the Kemalist agenda regarding the Turkish language reform, in contrast to his opposition to the politicization of language that he had expressed in the Armistice period.[12] His participation in *Vahdet* signaled his willingness to work for national unity in a broad sense, and perhaps as a Turkish echo of the Syrian "National Bloc" established in the wake of the Great Syrian Revolt in 1925–27.[13] Despite all of that, in private he still expressed his hatred and resentment for particular personalities among the political elite of the republic—İsmet İnönü, for instance—and even some who had fallen into oppositional stances in the early republic, such as Rauf Orbay, Adnan Adıvar, and Falih Rıfkı Atay. In his correspondence with Rıza Tevfik from abroad he continued to discuss and analyze the question of *muhalefet*—in the sense of organized political opposition to the single-party state—and its future possibilities, even into the mid-1930s as he simultaneously expressed hope for a return to Turkey.[14]

. . .

By 1930, Refik was starting to find his footing as a Turkish writer and jour-nalist in exile. Back in Turkey, 1930 was a significant year for the star-crossed story of *muhalefet*. In that year Mustafa Kemal encouraged the formation of an opposition party, the Free People's Party (*Serbest Halk Fırkası*). He appointed Ali Fethi (Okyar), whom he deemed reliable and loyal, as the head, and prominent, perhaps less hard-line figures such as Ahmet Ağaoğlu, Ahmet Emin (Yalman), and Celâl Bayar joined the fray.[15] The party, though, was a victim of its own success. As it started to gain extraparliamentary sup-port among provincial notables and even peasants, it threatened to become a social and political movement that could rival the RPP party-state. Mustafa Kemal quashed the experiment, which in the end lasted only ninety-nine days. Opposition would be reabsorbed into the RPP.

This was the republic's second experiment with partisan opposition. The first had been the Progressive Republican Party in 1924–25, touched on in chapter 5. That earlier experiment had led to severe backlash and increase in repression, including the Law on the Maintenance of Order and the Indepen-dence Tribunals, and to the voluntary exile of figures such as Rauf (Orbay) and Halide Edib (Adıvar) and Adnan (Adıvar). The new experiment with an opposition party in 1930, while brief, caused Mustafa Kemal to implement a range of reforms. In parliament he set aside slots for independent deputies as a gesture toward political pluralism. And in the realm of ideology formation, two more principles of "Kemalism" were added to the four he had set down since the inception of the republic; étatism (statism) and revolutionism were added to republicanism, nationalism, populism, and secularism.[16]

In a broader sense the 1930 experiment with an opposition party was a testament to Mustafa Kemal's conflicted sentiments toward opposition. On the one hand, he appreciated that there should be space for political oppo-sition in a state that claimed to be a liberal democracy, and on the other hand, he harbored a fear that allowing for that space would lead to a loss of control—very much like the contradiction of the CUP with respect to Ottoman constitutionalism discussed in previous chapters. The Free Party episode also exposed the existence of factions within the establishment, the differences between which would have to be expressed behind closed doors and not given institutional expression once the party was torpedoed. Statism, particularly the role of the state in economic policy, would in the 1930s and the 1940s become the issue that divided the establishment. But factional struggles over the role of the state versus private capital in the economy would be contained within the RPP, not the occasion for the formation of a second party. Political pluralism would remain another underground world in the 1930s. As for the intellectual elite, their main preoccupation post-1928 was with the elaboration of Kemalism and Turkish nationalism in the institutional frameworks of education and culture in the republic—the Turkish Historical Society (1931) and Turkish Language Association (1932) being two examples. Political differences would come to the fore over the question of pardons for former *muhalifs* and members of the List of 150, such as Refik Halid. And one can see how those tensions were bound up with the exigencies of national unity at work in the Hatay/Alexandretta episode, which turned out to be the occasion for Refik's ultimate pardon in 1938.

. . .

Refik was undergoing a shift in his writing along with his new political orientation. In his post-shift literary activities, he drew away from direct discussion of the Unionists and the relationships between them and the new republic. He would put that issue aside as part of his conspicuous turn away from overtly political themes, and certainly away from *muhalefet* that could be deemed subversive or treasonous. But politics, for Refik at least, was inescapable; his engagement became more subtle, and the little satire he wrote was less biting and less partisan while still retaining a degree of social critique. Even his avowedly nonpolitical works turned out to have had political value that would help catapult him back into Turkey.

One of Refik Halid's first moves after 1928 was to return to satire, a genre that had always been risky—and despite the fact that *Vahdet* had explicitly rejected satire in its statement of intent. In 1929 he wrote the play *Deli* (Mad), a pithy commentary on the Kemalist reforms that were just reaching a crescendo back in Turkey.[17] It portrayed those reforms as part of a continuum going back to 1908—taking the whole sweep of Unionism, nationalism, and Kemalism as one maddening experience of modernizing reforms. The main character (Maruf Bey, or Mr. Well-Known), was an Ottoman Rip van Winkle who, having gone catatonic on the eve of the 1908 Constitutional Revolution, wakes up an Ottoman gentleman surrounded by Republican Turks in the Istanbul of 1928. He is as disturbed by the changes in dress, behavior, and belief as the Republican Turkish characters are unreflective about the changes. The joke, of course, is that in one sense it is the main character who is disturbed, having suffered a memory lapse, while in actuality it is all those ordinary, healthy Republican Turks who suffer from amnesia, not to mention a kind of brain damage that prevents them from questioning or reflecting on the changes being foisted on them. The butt of the joke here is not so much the reforms or their authors, as would have been the case in Refik's earlier satires, but those being reformed: the urban middle class. Indeed, the funny thing about *Deli* is the lack of self-reflection, lack of consciousness, and even amnesia that the urban middle class exhibited when their world—their clothing, their names, their values—was upended by top-down modernization decrees.

Deli was published in *Vahdet*—in Ottoman characters, despite the fact that the Alphabet Reform had been promulgated in Turkey the previous year. In both form and substance, then, it could have been received as a dangerous act of *muhalefet* by the authorities, or it could have been deemed acceptable humor. Refik later admitted that he was "afraid that it would be interpreted as against Turkey," using the more politically neutral word *aleyhinde* rather than *muhalif* in this case.[18] He continued on to say that his worries were assuaged when he learned that Atatürk received the work warmly. Refik was careful to dedicate the 1938 edition of the play to prove just that: "I am grateful to the favor of 'Atatürk,' who said regarding this work: 'It does not satirize our revolution, it makes it more clear.'" It was even said, Refik claimed, that his "friends in the Assembly, like Fazıl Ahmed and Necmeddin Sadık and others, personally read the play to Atatürk over the course of a few nights."[19] Refik's relationship with Atatürk had certainly shifted since their confrontation in 1919, and it is said that Atatürk himself began to advocate for Refik's pardon in the early 1930s.

Other works from this period display a new kind of ambiguity between politics and literary expression for Refik. His story collection first published in 1931—*A Tall Drink of Water (Bir İçim Su)*—is a testament to this. In "Türk mezarı" (Turkish tomb), a story that was published as part of the collection but written two years earlier, in 1929, he uses his visit to the tomb of Süleyman Şah—grandfather of Osman, who was killed on the Euphrates near Aleppo in 1225 CE—as an occasion for reflection, and more precisely, lamentation. He laments the ruined state of the tomb, the ruined state of the empire that once spanned continents and seas, and the ruined state within himself as he observes the tomb. ("I looked at the tomb from the outside, the inside, and inside myself.") But he then laments something more specific, and more fascinating:

The Turkish tomb . . . is far from the Turkish borders; . . . but this little hand-ful of earth, like the villages that remain on the Danube that were once part of Ottoman lands such as Adakale, this belongs to the land of Turkey. *And I, forbidden from entering the* memleket *by vindictive politicians for the past seven years, I am in Turkey now; but a Turkey where there are no politicians or politicians' police. . . . Neither am I constantly pestering somebody for some-thing, nor does anyone want to throw me down. I am in Turkey. . . . [L]et some small-spirited, fearful journalists and politicians hear this: I am in Turkey! And taking shelter in the imposing shade of the Ja'ber fortress, in this ruined temple, I think comfortably and freely. . . .* [Y]ou did not give way to me, but my tribe is bigger than you, and has sailed the waters of the Danube and the Nile. (emphasis added)

He thus embraces the Mediterranean and the Black Sea. He finishes: *"And I see, as I bend down in the moonlight and scoop up and drink thirstily a handful of water from the Euphrates, the imposing shadow of Süleyman Şah"* (emphasis added).[20]

Refik is still the *muhalif* here, even in 1929, when he claims to have made peace with the regime in Turkey. It is no longer the regime in toto, but certain journalists and politicians, that are his problem, it seems. And it is no longer the continuity from the Unionist past to the nationalist present, but the vindictiveness of some of his compatriots who would forever hold a grudge against him and try to to silence him. But he, too, has taken *muhalefet* into a different realm, struggling to differentiate between the Turkey that he has been cast out of and the greater Turkey—whether in a cultural-national sense or an Ottoman imperial one, in which he has taken shelter in Syria. With this in mind, we can see from his other stories of the same collection the way the natural landscape and the female bodies of Hatay (Alexandretta), for instance, are inscribed with Turkish-ness, showing reverberations of a Gökalp-esque cultural nationalism. Stories such as "Karacaoğlan" recall Gökalp's preoccupation with Anatolian folk legend—but what to make of this when outside the borders of Turkey? That project of cultural nationalism is now used not to appropriate Anatolia as the heartland for a new Turkish nation-state, but instead is transposed onto the space of Aleppo, İskenderun, and Antakya, under French Mandate administration. And this work of Refik's was written before the escalation of tensions between Turkey and Syria over the region, as discussed later.

Interestingly, when these stories were first circulated in the early 1930s, the public's reception of them—especially in the collection *Bir İçim Su*—focused on the apolitical aesthetics of love, sensuality, and beauty. The stories did seem to circulate in Turkey, despite the ban on works by the 150. Refik Halid encouraged this notion that his stories were fanciful and not political, later claiming that "Bir İçim Su" "really does resemble a false (*yalancı*) paradise. I wrote a book that contains no punishment, only reward . . . and this reward I give immediately and fully to the reader. In return I make no demand, threat, or violence. It's like giving 10 francs and entering the 'paradis' of Montmartre in Paris. Fruit, aromas, fairies, everything. Let it be my service to those who know Turkish!" He even notes that the work inspired a new kind of genre, or at least convention, of love letters that common Turks wrote to one another.[21]

This conspicuous turn away from overtly political themes, however, became the pivot to a new kind of engagement in politics. Rather than picking apart the Unionist origins of the nationalists in a bid to undermine the basis for the republic, Refik now put himself in the service of that republic. He did this by using his personal and political contacts in Hatay/Alexandretta and retooling his literary works to bolster Turkey's case for the cultural Turkish-ness, and thus political belonging, of Hatay/Alexandretta to Turkey. And for him, the Hatay/Alexandretta dispute became a golden opportunity and a space of transformation and redemption. Labeled a traitor to the nation, he could redeem himself and rehabilitate his reputation by getting involved on the Turkish side of the dispute.

MEDIATING *MUHALEFET* IN THE HATAY/ALEXANDRETTA SANCAK

Hatay/Alexandretta was a liminal and contested space between Turkey and French Mandate Syria. Containing the major towns of Antioch (Antakya) and Alexandretta (İskenderun), it was home to both Turkish and Arabic speakers; Turks, Armenians, and Arabs. In its demographic diversity it had been a typical Ottoman space. The very diversity that made it typically Ottoman of course made it inimical to the categories of either/or belonging for a nation-state, and this the League of Nations learned firsthand as they tried to arbitrate the dispute between 1936 and 1939.[22] While it fell within the territory claimed in the 1919 Turkish National Pact, it went to the French after the Ankara Agreement between the French and the presumptive Turkish national government in 1921. By 1925 it was attached to the state of Aleppo, itself under French mandatory rule, but still under its own special (French) administration. Its significant Sunni Turcophone population and location, contiguous with Turkey, made it both strategically important and dangerous for the leaders of the republic, since it was under French rule and thus not under their political authority.

The Hatay/Alexandretta sancak had been claimed as rightfully Turkish by Mustafa Kemal in speeches since 1923. It was one of the few irredentist ambitions that Mustafa Kemal, otherwise an isolationist, expressed during his time in power.[23] The Sunni Turcophone community was portrayed as victimized by the other groups in the region, and a campaign got underway to demonstrate the Turkishness of the area. The contestation escalated in 1936 when Turkey began its irredentist campaign to "reunite" Hatay with Turkey, prompting the French to promise to hand the region over to Syria in three years' time, in 1939. A propaganda campaign in the local Turkish and Arabic press between proponents of Turkish and Syrian rule ensued, with Refik Halid representing the Turkish side and Zaki al-Arsuzi, a future founder of the Ba'ath Party in Syria, among those representing the Syrian side. The battle was happening on the ground as well; youth sports associations and literary clubs were leveraged by both sides to build a cadre of young loyalists on either side. Thanks to a Turkish-French Friendship Agreement made in anticipation of the outbreak of conflict that would become World War II, the League of Nations process to resolve the dispute became moot. The matter was resolved in favor of Turkey, leaving Syria out in the cold. On September 7, 1938, shortly after Refik Halid's return and shortly before Atatürk's death, the "Hatay State" was established, under joint Turkish and French military protection; and then on June 29, 1939, after Ataturk's death, a questionable plebiscite was held and the region was transferred to Turkish sovereignty, where it remains today.[24]

In the course of this larger story of the Hatay/Alexandretta dispute, Hatay/ Alexandretta became a site of transformation in the history of *muhalefet* as well. It had of course been an Ottoman province until 1919. Its population, or at least the Turcophone portion of it, had been divided between supporters of the CUP and supporters of the Freedom and Accord Party, showing that the old *muhalefet*, as opposition to the Unionists, had been a presence there. During the Armistice/War of Independence period, the region—because of its Turcophone community and its location within the National Pact boundary but ultimately outside the Republic of Turkey—became a fascinating space of refuge for *muhalifs*. In the early Republican period, too, since it lay just outside the bounds of Turkey and yet was home to a large Turcophone population, it was a hospitable home for *muhalifs* on the outs with the regime.[25] French administrative policies magnified this, as French authorities sought to employ and bolster a range of actors who had grievances with the Kemalist regime, including Armenians, Arab Christians, and even members of the List of 150.[26]

After 1928, however, political authority in the republic became more established and the old *muhalefet*—aimed against the regime as a whole—began to lose its significance. Hatay now held a different world of potential as the site of Turkish irredentist aspirations and a place for old *muhalifs* to prove their patriotism. Old *muhalifs*, even those on the List of 150, could redeem themselves by helping to redeem Hatay for Turkey. And writers were particularly suited to aid the cause, since the contest between Turkey and Syria over Hatay/Alexandretta had to do with proving the cultural identity of the region's population to make a case for its political belonging in one or the other nation-state. The articles that Refik published were—whether in earnest or as a pretext—presented by him and his allies in Turkey as the service to the nation that redeemed him in the eyes of Atatürk and helped pave the way for his pardon and the general pardon of the List of 150 in the summer of 1938.

Refik Halid's visits to Hatay and his interest in Hatay as a subject in his writing began strikingly early, preceding the escalation in tensions over the region by several years. (See figure 4.) He speaks in his personal correspondence of regular forays to Hatay for duck hunting. Already in 1930, he had been cultivating friendly relations with youth literary clubs in Antakya (Antioch); in that year they awarded him a gold pen to honor his contributions to Turkish literature.[27] Looking back, he brags that he was honored by them at a time "when no one knew that the Hatay dispute would happen, or how it would be resolved," nor did anyone know that he would later be invited to Ankara as a guest of Atatürk himself. As noted previously, in 1931 he published *Bir İçim Su*, a collection of pieces romanticizing the landscape and sensual beauty of Hatay's Turkish women, among other things. By that time he was already a literary and cultural icon in Turcophone circles of Hatay. When some of the youths he had befriended in the early years of his exile went on to become leaders of the local Kemalist faction, it seemed a natural extension of his involvement there to use his leverage in support of the irredentist cause.[28]

Lest one think his frequent visits to Hatay in the early years of his exile were politically motivated, his personal correspondence gives no indication of that. According to his personal correspondence with Rıza Tevfik in 1931,

FIGURE 4. Portrait of Refik Halid in Aleppo in 1928, the year his orientation shifted in favor of the Kemalist regime. Note his hat, which in neighboring Hatay/Alexandretta was a sign of support for the Kemalist faction rather than the traditionalist faction within the Turcophone community. Courtesy of the Taha Toros Archive.

Refik Halid did not seem to be anticipating that his involvement in Hatay would bring him any political benefit. Instead, he had resigned himself to permanent estrangement from home and consoled himself with the thought that Aleppo and Beirut and the life he had made for himself there were really not so bad. He likened his experience there to the way the British lived abroad—cut off from their surroundings and clinging to fellow expats and news from home—living in their own bubble.

But when discussion of a general pardon (*Genel Af*) for some or all on the List of 150 became known to Refik Halid in 1933, he did show signs of hoping, and even searching for a path back to Turkey. Once his son was born, his efforts intensified, and he eagerly awaited news from Turkey about the chances and then the legal process of securing a pardon so he could return safely. His efforts, overt and, one might surmise, covert, on behalf of Turkish national interests in Hatay no doubt contributed to the favorable reports he received from Turkish intelligence in Aleppo and to the support he built within Turkey in favor of his pardon.

Was Refik finally in the right place at the right time, situated and influential in Hatay already when it suddenly became politically advantageous for him to be there? He implies that he was, and that his activities as an interlocutor for the Turkish side in the dispute were not mere opportunism. And it seems likely that he was a beneficiary of the transformation of Hatay as a space of *muhalefet* into a space of national unity and irredentism. Refik was likely already respected as a *muhalif* among the Turkish-speaking youth of Hatay, which lent him credibility to argue for the Turkishness of the area. He admits to having been in close contact with the Turkish consul in Aleppo, who was reportedly coordinating the covert irredentist efforts in the area. Whatever the case, his service to the nation on the Hatay issue became in turn a rallying point for the political factions back in Turkey, who were divided not just over economic policy but also over the question of whether to pardon Refik Halid and the other members of the List of 150.

HOME: BURYING THE PAST

Refik stepped into Turkish society and politics, now with the new surname Karakayış (immediately shortened to Karay upon arrival) in June 1938.[29] Refik's allies within Turkey had, after several attempts over the years, finally achieved a parliamentary vote in favor of a General Amnesty for most of

MAP 5. Republic of Turkey as defined in the Treaty of Lausanne (1923)

the 150. This general amnesty remained contentious even after it was signed into law. He was well aware of these crosscurrents, noting in his letters to Rıza Tevfik from summer 1933 the news he was receiving about the possible amnesty: Who within high political circles was for and against? What would the terms be? Would they be barred from government service? Would their assets be restored? Refik Halid was clear that he would not set foot in the country until the legislation had been signed and sealed; informal overtures were not to be relied upon.[30]

Previous attempts had been made—by Atatürk himself and supported by figures such as Celâl Bayar—to get pardons for many of the other 150 as early as 1932, but they failed in the face of significant opposition—and not only from İnönü and other hard-liners in parliament. In June 1938, just days before the parliament voted for the amnesty and Refik returned to Turkey, a scathing editorial was published in *Cumhuriyet*, the paper of record in Ankara, by none other than the editor himself, former Unionist Yunus Nadi, calling the List of 150, including Refik by name, traitors and opportunists. Nadi mocked Refik's newfound adulation of Atatürk, recalling that Refik had been content to praise Enver Paşa to get back home from his last exile.[31] He responded to the contention, presumably made elsewhere, that "17 million Turks" wanted Refik to return, and the argument that the value of his writing should be a basis for his pardon. On May 29, 1938, *Son Posta* headlines focused on the amnesty for those on the List of 150 as well as those imprisoned by the Independence Tribunals and those in the *heyet-i mahsusalar* (special associations) with the provision that they would stay out of state service for ten years. On June 6, 1938, *Son Posta* published a short portrait of Refik Halid as part of the series explaining who the List of 150 was made up of; Refik Halid "Karakayış" is referred to as, along with Rıza Tevfik, "surely the most famous" of those on the List. On June 1, 1938, *Cumhuriyet* declared that those who were returning under the pardon would be back in time to rejoice with the Turkish nation (*millet*) during the celebrations of the fifteenth anniversary of the republic, happening later that year. The same article reported that Şükrü Kaya, then interior minister, had made a speech to the parliament arguing for the pardon, while taking very seriously the "opposition and treachery" that they had taken part in fifteen years earlier. Justice Minister Şükrü Saraçoğlu had also weighed in the previous day, May 31, 1938.

Discussions surrounding the pardon for the List of 150 and for Refik Halid himself might appear as a harbinger of what was to come. Refik was pardoned, against the wishes of İnönü and others, during a moment when Celâl Bayar was prime minister.[32] After Atatürk's death on November 10, 1938, İnönü was elected president and proclaimed "National Chief" (*Millî Şef*). He then began to bring back into political life members of the "old opposition" who had participated in the War for Independence but had later opposed Atatürk's increasing personal power and his political tactics. The "old opposition" forced out of power in the mid-1920s included some of the most prominent names in the republic, including Kâzım Karabekir, Ali Fuat Cebesoy, Rauf Orbay, Refet Bele, Fethi Okyar, Ali İhsan Sabis, Cafer Tayyar, Adnan Adıvar, and Hüseyin Cahit Yalçin. Some of these old allies of Atatürk had been tried by a special Independence Tribunal set up in İzmir in 1926, accused of plotting to kill Atatürk. While none were convicted of involvement in the plot, some, such as Adıvar and Orbay, went into voluntary exile, while others retired from political life. By bringing these men into the government, İnönü created a new stage, surrounding himself with people respected for their past records of patriotism who would support him in confronting many of the "harsh storms on the horizon."[33] İnönü imposed one condition: that there would be no argument in any shape or form whatsoever regarding Atatürk. Atatürk—not the CUP, not the man himself, but the collectively imagined presence of Atatürk—would now serve as the guardian of the nation, the republic, the RPP, and the principles of all, including laicism.

Obtaining legal amnesty was only the beginning. Refik now had to convince his old accusers that he was not a traitor to the nation, but was instead a patriot and always had been. Even *muhalif* was not a safe category, so he had to abandon his association with it, past and present, in order to rehabilitate his reputation. By his own description "half-hidden" from elite society in his early months back in Istanbul, Refik Halid wasted no time reestablishing himself on the literary and publishing scene, determined to reclaim his renown after having been all but deleted from the record in 1922.[34] Judging from the interviews he gave in the first years after his return, he wanted to focus on literature, to discuss his own work and the work he admired from "world literature," rather than return to the thicket of politics. His first professional moves, which I take up later in the chapter, were to (1) recast his life story and past political involvement to fit the new confines of Republican Turkey; (2) republish his older works—with important deletions and revisions—and publish newly collected editions of the works written in his Syrian exile; and (3) publish a series of works in a new genre that stitched together Ottoman past and Turkish present, as he struggled to make sense of all the historical epochs and political regimes he had lived through since the 1880s.

After Atatürk's death, it became safe to broach some aspects of the past and even to voice certain kinds of criticisms of Unionism and its legacies in Turkey. But we have no official proclamation, no official announcement of what those safe topics were, and thus have to rely on what we can infer from the published work of those who claimed the status of *muhalif*, like Refik Halid Karay. Some of the past actions and sentiments that he chose to put underground after his return to Turkey can be traced. The safest course of action was effusive praise of Atatürk, even and especially when the full meaning of "Atatürk" remained ambiguous for the one doing the praising. In Karay's telegraphic response to *Tan* cited at the start of this chapter, we see this ambiguity: "Atatürk" is industrialization, Turkification, and Westernization. Invoking his name is to invoke the miracle of achieving those changes and to imply one's acceptance of a framework of national unity. Beyond that, distinctions within the Turkish nation and Turkish Republic— whether of class, region, or political persuasion—are to be submerged, driven underground, in fact, in favor of that national unity. In that presentation, it is at best ambiguous what space would be left for dissent or opposition of any kind. Once Karay reinserted himself into the scene of publishing, journalism, and politics in Istanbul in 1938, the need to prove his loyalty and credentials as a Kemalist took precedence over any claims to *muhalefet*, past or present.

An important prerequisite to reestablishing himself as a writer in Republican, Kemalist Turkey was the reframing of his narrative and his place in history. He would need to do this for a new generation, for the sake of clarifying the official record and carving out a space to exist and write within the new national order. He first gave a series of interviews to journalist Hikmet Münir Ebcioğlu, which appeared as a book, *Refik Halid Karay and His Own Writings* (*Refik Halid Karay Kendi Yazılar ile*) (undated but published sometime between 1940 and 1943).[35] By interspersing verbatim passages from Refik's literary work with first- and third-person accounts of his experiences, it serves as one inspiration for this present book. In it, his task was nothing less than to reinvent himself and his reputation at a fascinating moment of transition for Turkey.

What he chose to include is as telling as what he left out, and this is true for his life story in *Kendi Yazılar ile* as much as for the works he chose to republish from the late Ottoman period. For instance, while in *Kendi Yazılar ile* he mentions his post as PTT director in 1919, he omits the Telegraph Episode in its entirety, choosing instead to point out that at that same time he was director of the Ajans Press (Agence Presse) wire service, a fact not mentioned elsewhere. He glides over his relationship with Ziya Gökalp, but still rips into the CUP for certain things, demonstrating that it was safe to express certain kinds of criticism toward the CUP in the early 1940s, even when so many members of the current political elite had been members in their youth.

Given his writings and personal correspondence over the years, it is worth relaying verbatim here his fascinating effort to recast his role and political stance during the Armistice era. Full of awkward constructions and elisions that are recognizable to those who know the details of the story, he comes out with the following sanitized rendering:

> In reality, Refik Halid's friends who struggled were the persons that were the most fervent supporters of the revolution and the National Struggle. He even maintained limited contact and relations with them while he was in his PTT post [in 1919/20] and after he began publishing *Aydede* [in 1922]. As is read in various sections of *Minelbab İlelmihrab*, Refik Halid's friends during the time of his *muhalefet* were Kemalists working in Istanbul, like Falih Rıfkı, Yakup Kadri, Rüşen Eşref, and Necmeddin Sadık (Sadak). He

struggled with them. He maintained his own political views. The truth is that he was a bit of an outspoken *muhalif*. Together with these friends he was happy about the Anatolia victory. Before that, he even engaged in a lively discussion with Falih Rıfkı in the newspapers. But a little later, Nemrut Mustafa Paşa's War Crimes Tribunal (*Divan-ı Harb*) arrested Falih Rıfkı. In order for him to be saved from that, Refik Halid made some rather serious efforts on behalf of Falih Rıfkı. The situation that ensued was that his efforts to defend his position would surpass his dignity. But one thing cannot be denied: he was inclined to protect the Istanbul government against the possibility of defeat. But ceasing his active opposition, he could not completely give place to his personal sentiments of opposition [i.e., after stepping down as PTT director]. He would come by the press every few days, chat with the writers. He would come by *Akşam* and gossip; and return. His life from then on [presumably after the Telegraph Episode] would consist of separate, isolated events. Losing his fun friends, he would pass by and finish. He would find himself appointed a member of the City Theatre Council (Darülbedayi Meclisi) [another fact not mentioned elsewhere], and that would occupy him; this was a great distraction. There he would get together with Yakup Kadri [Karaosmanoğlu], Reşat Nuri [Gültekin], İbrahim Necmi, İsmail Müştak, İzzet Melih, and Necmettin Sadık. The City Theatre brought in a lot of revenue that Ramazan [1922, presumably]. Continuing like that, İzmir was then redeemed [i.e., captured from the Greeks, September 1922]. Refet Paşa was in Istanbul [i.e., the nationalist victory in October 1922]. The Babıali/Tevfik Paşa government was still in place. Mihran Efendi [the publisher/owner of *Sabah*] sent Ali Kemal packing after the windows of the *Sabah* offices were smashed, and appointing Abdullah Zühdü as the head writer of *Sabah*, he supposedly nationalized the newspaper [i.e., shifted the sensibilities of the newspaper to a nationalist one].[36]

This is not the most seamless of narratives about his time in Istanbul between 1919 and 1922, given what we know about him. The choppy chronology and the strange diction show how difficult and even impossible it was to put together a coherent story that would be acceptable in the current circumstances. Its disjointedness reflects some of the internal contradictions of the idea and memory of *muhalefet*, not to mention the deeply ambivalent and uncomfortable legacy of the CUP in the republic. What could anyone say about the moment that would in any way differ from the official story of national unity and resistance to foreign occupation and still make sense? In the absence of a counternarrative, the information simply could not add up.

As for his oppositional stance after 1922, Refik Halid concedes, via Ebcioğlu in *Kendi Yazılar ile*, that from 1923 when he started writing in Aleppo for *Doğru Yol* through 1926 his writings were against the "new regime" (note that he avoids admitting opposition to Mustafa Kemal per se), but he says that "these writings included attacks and criticism regarding ancillary (*tali*) personages as much as of the new regime." He tries to mitigate the damage by stressing that the stories he wrote for *Doğru Yol* were reprinted in Istanbul and Anatolia papers (implying therefore that they fit within the confines of political discourse in the early republic), and that particularly *Bir İçim Su*, the collection of stories about sensual beauty and the Turkish landscapes of Hatay, became a cultural sensation in Turkey.[37] By the early 1940s, then, he has erased his past *personal* opposition to Mustafa Kemal and very much downplayed his outspoken political opposition. He could not undo it, since it is already a part of the official history—a history in which his role is that of villain. Instead, he attempts to weave into the account emphatic declarations of his friendships with leading nationalist figures of his generation, thereby repositioning himself within the narrative as having operated *within* the establishment, not outside of it.

Concomitant with that narrative reinvention was the republication of select Ottoman-era works of his in modern Turkish. This was in part a practical necessity because the alphabet had changed in the interim (July 1928); if he did not see that his works were republished in the new Latin script for Turkish, they would be lost to the new generation, and thus from the historical record. Even the works he had published in Syria after 1928 (*Bir İçim Su, Deli, Vahdet*) were published in the old Ottoman alphabet. If the new Turkey was to meet Refik Halid Karay, he would have to issue new editions of his works in the new alphabet. In 1939–40 he published his *Complete Works (Külliyat)* with Semih Lûtfi Press in Istanbul.

If we read closely the new works and compare them with the Ottoman-era publications, we can see not only that he made small changes in terminology and content, but that certain works were excised entirely from new editions—many of them having to do explicitly with *muhalifs* and *muhalefet*. N. Ahmet Özalp attempted a systematic study of these redactions in his 2011 *Refik Halid Karay: Okları Kırılmış Kirpi* (Refik Halid Karay: The Porcupine with the broken quills). Eleven stories from *Kirpinin Dedikleri*, four from *Ay Peşinde*, two from *Ago Paşa'nın Hatıratı*, three from *Guguklu Saat*, and four from *Tanıdıklarım* were deleted altogether from the 1939 and subsequent editions, until Özalp's publication of them in modern Turkish in 2011. There were also scores of changes in phrasing and deletion of sentences and paragraphs from works that did see the light of day in Republican Turkey. Without exception, the content of the deleted stories is political, dealing pointedly with specific personages, political behavior, favorable mentions of Armenians and other non-Muslim groups, and other unflattering aspects of the Unionists, as well as the lionization of the *muhalif* as tragic hero. Among the deleted stories are "Mehmet Ç Bey ile Muhabere," the threatening and violent correspondence between Refik Halid and the nationalist partisan in Anatolia discussed in chapter 4; "Olmasa idi ... Ne Olurdu?" (What would have happened if it hadn't happened?), the counterfactual musing about what would have happened had the Constitutional Revolution not happened (including a disparaging prediction about Mustafa Kemal); "Bir Muhalifin İntiharı" (The suicide of a *muhalif*); and "Elveda Siyasiyat!" (Farewell, politics!), discussed in chapter 5.

We do not know the specific rationale for these decisions or have documentation of conversations that might have happened around these editorial changes. Nor do we know if there was an independent entity at the press or in the government—a person or persons who acted as a censor.[38] We can deduce that certain topics had moved from merely provocative in the Ottoman period to outright taboo in the Republican era. Özalp goes so far as to term these changes made to Karay's work between 1938 and 1943 an *emasculation*, even castration (*iğdiş*) of his writings. They removed, I argue, the *muhalif* dimension effectively sanitizing them for what Özalp terms the new "quasi-fascist" Kemalist state.[39] While Özalp, with his own 2011 political agenda implies coercion and censorship, we also know that Refik Halid was deliberately less belligerent, even conciliatory, toward the regime at this point, saying in an interview shortly after his return that he had become *toleran* (tolerant), "harbored only good feelings and ideas toward everyone," and liked "the political order."[40] It would stand to reason that Karay was at least complicit in, if not the one making, these editorial decisions. Others, such as Halide Edib and Reşat Nuri Gültekin, had also been known to censor their past works.

Most fascinating about the revisions to Refik's past work in this moment of "tolerance" and his stance of goodwill toward all is that the one person he remained *intolerant* toward was his past self as a *muhalif*. In this new order of politics, there is space for all kinds of people except for the virulent opposition or the heroic dissidents and opponents in the past; in effect, no space for the politics of dissent, either. Whether Karay himself made the editorial decision to revise and delete some of his own work or whether he allowed others to make those decisions, the irony of speaking about greater freedom and tolerance on the one hand, and excising unacceptable parts of the historical and literary record on the other tells us much, not only about Turkish politics in the Kemalist period, but about the changing memory of the Ottoman and Unionist past within it.

During this transition period, both for Karay and for Turkey, he also published a number of new literary works that stitched together his experience of past and present, home and exile. These works show his move away from satire and into essays and short stories, still in the realm of social realism, sometimes surrealism, which often take on a tone of seemingly apolitical reflection about past and present. *Gurbet Hikâyeleri* (Exile stories), from its title, is framed as a companion to *Memleket Hikâyeleri*; the latter contains stories written during his first exile, the former from his Syria exile, published in *Tan* in 1938. Many of these "exile stories" are strikingly orientalist and exoticizing of his Syrian/Arab surroundings, including encounters with Bedouin, with thoughts of Lawrence of Arabia, and nostalgic musings contrasting life in Istanbul with exile in the desert. *The Devil's Daughter* (*Yezidin Kızı*), a novel written during his exile in Syria, is a love story between MP Hikmet Ali and a "Kurdish-speaking Argentinian girl" who turns out to be both Yezidi and mentally disturbed. Much of the book is a kind of ethnographic journey to the Yezidi region in Syria, in that sense a recounting of Refik Halid's odyssey from Istanbul to the foreign land of Syria. And *Sürgün*, discussed in chapter 5, is the autobiographical novel he wrote during his transition back from Syrian exile in 1938 and 1939.

Once settled back in Istanbul, Karay set about writing in a genre new to him: historical retrospective. Examples include works such as *Üç Nesil Üç Hayat* (Three generations, three lives) in 1943—a kind of social history that reflects on the ways life has changed across the three eras of the "Aziz Devrinde" (The Abdülaziz Era), "Hamit Devrinde" (The Hamidian Era), and "Şimdiki Durum" (The current situation).[41] It appears harmless and apolitical, and yet the choice of periodization is itself a political commentary. He treats the time since 1909 until the present moment (early 1940s) as the present, presaging revisionist historians such as Zürcher's periodization of the "Unionist period" and disregarding the rupture between the Ottoman and Republican eras. In *Üç Nesil Üç Hayat* he moves through the life cycle with each chapter, considering how birth has changed (from midwifery to the dehumanizing and sterile hospital), through childhood, education, marriage, up to practices around death. There is something healing, or at least restorative, about these attempts to reconnect human experience across the violent ruptures of politics and history—and also something subversive. In contrast to excised and revised editions of his Ottoman-era pieces, Karay's new works show that spaces for reflecting on and connecting to the past were gradually opening in the 1940s, spaces that allowed for a different relationship to politics and the regime.[42]

THE NEW "ANKARA"

By far the most fascinating work from what I call Refik's transitional period was "Ankara," a lengthy essay-memoir published in the 1939 volume *Deli* (Mad). This version of "Ankara" was more than a simple expansion and reworking of the 1921 original "Ankara Yangını" (The Ankara fire). The many orders of change that we can trace between the two versions encapsulate the larger changes in political context and the changing meaning and enactment of *muhalefet* from the event of the republic's establishment to its consolidation and the death of its founder. In the context of his political survival and professional reinvention, it seems to have been imperative that Refik Halid Karay write something to honor Ankara as the new capital soon after his return from exile; it was an opportunity to demonstrate his submission to, allegiance to, and even veneration for the Kemalist project and for the Turkish nation-state, to which his loyalty had been questionable at best in the past. But as was always the case with Refik Halid, it did not turn out to be that simple.

The new "Ankara," like the new version of Ankara the city, has the strange sense of being an *almost* entirely new construction made *almost* entirely out of old materials. Now thirty-three pages long, split into ten sections, the 1939 essay still contains at its core the story of the Ankara fire, a description of which starts halfway through, with section 5. But the tale has been drastically reframed and therefore assigned a very different set of meanings—even the word "fire" has been deleted from the title for the new rendition. The moral of this story is about change and the marvel one feels at witnessing the changes Ankara has gone through across four epochs. Karay speaks of "four Ankaras," of which he has personally witnessed two: not the "Despotic" (Hamidian) Ankara or the "TBMM" (War of Independence) Ankara, but the "Constitutional" and now "Republican" Ankaras.

The thrust of this new "Ankara," then, is Karay's reflection on his last experience of Ankara, in 1916, and his marveling at the transformation achieved by the time he next met the city in 1938. It is about the changed character and the changed reputation of the city, and he opens with a fitting allegory, of the city as person. He compares the experience of meeting Ankara then and now to that of meeting an ugly, unremarkable man one day, parting ways, nearly forgetting about him, and years later having your memory of him transformed when the ugly man suddenly takes on importance and fame. The memory of his rotten teeth and sickly complexion forgotten, you actually start to remember him as important, attractive, and valuable long before he really was, and even start to think of him as an old friend.[43] This malleability of memory is an apt point for him to make just as he himself was in the midst of so much reinvention and revision regarding his own past and legacy.

Karay goes through several digressions about change—for instance, change in alphabet (and now he presents himself as a longtime opponent, using the politically neutral term *aleyhtar* rather than the charged term *muhalif*, of the Arabic alphabet, criticizing and lampooning it letter by letter), change in style of houses and door knockers, and change in habits of dress (the old custom of using walking sticks). He recounts new details about his arrival in Ankara from Çorum in summer 1916, giving us a broader sense of his three-month odyssey in Ankara that year, and pauses to reflect on things such as the amateurish flags commemorating the tenth anniversary of the Constitutional Revolution, which was being celebrated as he arrived in town (cited in chapter 3). He uses this image as a vehicle to lament the unfulfilled promise of constitutionalism under the Unionists—adhering to his criticisms of certain aspects of Unionist rule, even as he is careful to remove others.

When he finally gets around to describing the fire, much has changed in the new "Ankara." Deleted are the ironic comments implying the intentionality behind the fire; he points out the lack of wind the night the fire started but adds that there was also a dearth of water, implying that it was plausible that a fire could rage out of control on its own. Gone is the focus on certain neighborhoods being targeted, in favor of repeated emphasis that three-quarters of the city was destroyed. Gone also is the emphasis that Ankara was turned from a great city into a heap of ruins in the fire; it had always been a nothing town, especially compared to the miracle of Republican Ankara. Gone, too, is the chance encounter with his old friend from Istanbul in the midst of the fire, which had occasioned the appalling revelations about Unionist corruption in the midst of war. Disappeared is the image of the Vali (Dr. Reşit) watching the city burn with his frozen countenance, "like Nero."

Most strikingly, gone is any sign of empathy for Armenians, who were quite clearly identified as the primary target and casualties of the fire in the 1921 rendition. There is no mention of the names of Armenian families who had owned the burning mansions and no mention of the fact that the men had been deported but the women "kindly" left behind (mentioned with irony in the 1921 version), and the lines about the hard work and effort that had gone into achieving all the wealth that was destroyed in the fire have been left out. The image of the burning pianos has survived in the new "Ankara," but in a move emblematic of the larger shift, it is given a new frame. Karay notes that in wandering around, "continuing to watch in the most dangerous places," he happened upon a square. There

> a temporary monument had been built as proof of the Ankara Armenians' wealth: I saw nearly 100 [in the 1921 version it had been 14] pianos that had escaped the fire were lined up one after the other; on top of them were rolled up select, expensive carpets. Suddenly, a giant burning log came and fell among them; there was no one to run and put it out; that log, like a bundle of oily rags, burst into flames and burned the pianos within 15 minutes. And how did it burst into flames? As if it had been doused with gas, kerosene. . . . The burning of those bone-dry, glossy boxes, with a thousand and one melodies coming out from their strings was very strange (*acaip*).

The image of the burning pianos, in fact, occasions the closest thing to empathy that is left in the 1939 description, as Karay likens them to people: "Moaning like people, their strings turning red like fire, their white teeth crackling around the edges and spreading out from the heat, how strangely and disastrously they were burning."[44]

Now, in the new "Ankara," he had removed the agency behind the fire and made the suffering in the fire generic and even universal: "the world had ended that day in Ankara" (*kıyamet o gün Ankara'da kopmuştu*). There were no longer specific, nameable agents, specific authorities, or specific, nameable victims. What remains is a kind of suspended, generic suffering. "Mothers" had lost their children, "girls" were running in the streeets with all they could save—bottles of lavender perfume and pieces of lace—rabbis were running with their robes aflame (because Karay now tells us that the fire extended to the Jewish quarter as well), pregnant women were giving birth in the streets, lovers were embracing each other and making love in the middle of the mayhem. Nero still had a place in the new "Ankara," but no longer as the Vali; now Nero was a generic reference, with the line: "I started to wander around Nero's Rome in flames."

Even in this new, politically sanitized "Ankara," Refik Halid Karay cannot seem to resist ending on an ambivalent note. In the concluding section, after recounting his departure on the train from Ankara toward Bilecik, he shares a final anecdote about Ankara past and present: "an event that happened in Ankara the meaning of which I still cannot grasp."

The first building for the TBMM [Turkish Grand National Assembly] had started being built during the time that I was in Ankara, the building that is now the [Republican] People's Party headquarters . . . of course they were not doing this with the knowledge that one day it would be the National Parliament, they were building it to be the Union and Progress Club. They had dug the foundation and were chipping away at the stones on the lot at the corner of the avenue where the train station was. In those days I was an opponent (*aleyhtar*) of the Unionists, I was young, and passing by this building, I used to get angry and irritated seeing that the political party that had brought disaster on the memleket had extended one of its octopus-like tentacles, hairy, ugly, cold, and clawed, all the way to Ankara.

Everyone believed that the war would be lost within a year; for that reason we were disgusted with the Union and Progress. The building stood there, so unwanted and reluctant; two skinny, pathetic wartime stone-masons, ashen-complexioned, hammering away there with their feeble wrists. And with a slowness as annoying as the Au Ralenti films at the cinema. This slowness that makes a person want to run up, take one of the hammers, and start hammering the stones very quickly so as to show what it means to work and do labor.

So going to the station—I was an expert walker—I would always pass by there in a hurry, both because of having to see this lazy work, and because I did not want to witness the construction of the branch of the party I did not like.

One morning, I ran into a man perched on a stone; his hair was all tangled with his beard, of an unknown age, with eyes shining bright like a baby's, I think he was mad . . . watching the burning city carefully. Seeing me, he gestured with his hand:

"Give me a cigarette!"

Keeping my distance for fear of typhus, I handed him the packet with 4 or 5 left:

"Take them all!" I said.

"Give me matches, too."

I extended the box to him, a little pained:

"All yours!"

I started walking again, and he shouted behind me:

"I have something to say to you!"

I stopped.

"Take a good look at that Engürü" [the archaic/vernacular form of Ankara]!

I looked again at that state I knew too well. I saw that Ankara was now a city without minarets or chimneys, and this chimney-less, minaret-less state showed the flight of so many and the nakedness of the place.

"Is there anything left of Engürü anyway . . ." I said in response.

The madman smiled. With a frozen smile of a mind that is not all there, a smile that does not spread to others around him. . . . I don't know if you've ever noticed, but the most contagious smile is from the one who has the sharpest intelligence and logical mind. I stood and hung my head.

"You don't see it, you can't see it, but before me I see a huge city, huge, huge!"

And he extended his arm, from the Hisar to Çankaya, and to the plain (*ova*), from there straight to the Agricultural School, he drew with his hand a wide, round ring:

"There houses, houses, houses . . ."

In the eyes of this madman talking, the houses in his vision were getting bigger, more majestic, and he added:

"Palaces! Palaces! Palaces!"

In the deserts, as we know, an optical illusion is born out of the heat between the air and earth; there is nothing, and what is very far appears close. . . .

I thought, "in the mind of a mad man, surely, there is a wide expanse, a very bright light, something like the nothingness of the desert; he lives in the nothingness!"

The mad man was still looking into the imaginary ring he had drawn. I understood, from his serious look, his excitement, his smile, that all that he was describing he was seeing, as if he could see behind the curtain at a theatre; let me use the language of buildings for sale and say that he was seeing it in all of its details, even seeing the path to it, with all of its "contents": a big, spread-out city, with tall stone buildings, wide paved avenues, decorated shop windows, balconies with flowers, chimneys puffing out smoke, and a bustling people, with coaches, cars, tramways, clock towers, squares, everything, all of it . . .

These he was, surely, seeing on the horizon, hearing, experiencing, and enjoying.

"Houses! Houses! Palaces! Palaces!" he was saying.

I got a start, and hurried down the lane, quickly, through the ruined buildings and the empty fields toward the miserable station building: I thought, "the vision and dream of a man whose house has burned down, who has been put out on the street, and who has lost his mind (lit. his balance)."

On the bright summer morning, the day when I first saw the new Ankara from the hilltop, I turned into that mad man, on my face pleasure and delight I said with his tongue:

"Houses, houses! Palaces, palaces!"

It makes sense that the madman who envisioned the new Ankara at the end of the new "Ankara" would belong in the collection of Karay's works entitled *Deli* (Mad). The play *Deli*, after which the volume was named, was also about a kind of memory lapse between the Constitutional and

Republican eras. In both cases there is an attempt to grasp a kind of rupture and a sense that only those who are mad have the capability to do so. And it is no coincidence that the madman was the person building the Union and Progress club and thus symbolizing that the foundation of the new Turkey, the new Ankara, and the new republic was none other than the Committee for Union and Progress. The CUP would abide, just below the surface of the republic. By this point in 1939, the meanings surrounding that fact must have been manifold; that continuity itself is not something to be forgotten or buried, but something still very much worth underlining for Refik Halid Karay. Even in this ode to the new Ankara, he cannot seem to help retaining the deep conflict that he and likely many others who had lived through the transition still felt: on the one hand, amazement and veneration for the miraculous progress that was achieved, and on the the other, ambivalence toward the very foundations of the new capital city.

．　．　．

Muhalefet as partisan opposition went undergound in the single-party Kemalist Republic. Political differences persisted within the establishment, with new factions taking shape around issues of economic policy, but they were subordinated to national unity under the banner of Atatürk, a supra-political figure, and kept within the institutional confines of the RPP. In the 1930s, the central preoccupation for intellectuals in the establishment lay in the institutionalization of Kemalist, nationalist ideology, not in questioning it or revising its relationship to the Ottoman past. In order for Refik Halid to become accepted back into the fold of the establishment, now transformed, he had to perform an act in the service of the nation, which he did when he supported Turkey's irredentist bid for Hatay/Alexandretta. He then had to reinvent himself and his literary work, burying his past as a *muhalif*, to the extent possible, and avoiding explicit discussion of politics past and present. No longer interested in contesting the basis for the republic or in contesting the legitimacy of Atatürk, he nevertheless found subtle, low-risk ways to dissent from, or at least to express misgivings about, the Unionist continuities with the Republican present. As discussed in the next chapter, Refik Halid Karay the *muhalif*, or at least his past works as such, would emerge from the underground after 1945, just as the first viable opposition party was born.

SEVEN

Muhalefet in the Free World
(1945–1965)

IN 1945 TURKEY WAS THROWN into a new relationship with an international political, military, and economic order, itself in profound transformation as the Cold War took shape in the aftermath of World War II. Turkey, a single-party, and some would say a quasi-fascist, state in the 1930s and 1940s, was being retooled as a frontline state in the global conflict between capitalism and communism; it was large enough and, thanks to Atatürk, politically and economically powerful enough to have the leverage to decide on which side to position itself. Its neighbor, Greece, was among the first fronts in the Cold War, torn asunder in the midst of the transition in a bloody civil war between communists and British- and American-backed royalists. Turkey was going through no less consequential changes in its internal political makeup to bring it in line with "the Free World." The material and military incentives for this new belonging, in the form of the Marshall Plan, were massive. The consequences were just as significant—the tutelage Turkey had rejected in 1919–22 when the national movement formed in order to avoid colonial occupation now came in the form of guided economic development and a political alliance that was tethered to a template of democratization.

The goal of establishing a two-party or multiparty system had long been the dream of a faction of statesmen and *muhalif* intellectuals within the RPP establishment, and in the late Ottoman establishment before that. Those aspirations were stymied by Atatürk, then immobilized by his successor, İsmet İnönü, due to the outbreak of World War II shortly after Atatürk's death. But the project to create a multiparty regime was given sudden and tremendous momentum, and a new scale of meaning, by the exigencies of the Cold War. Turkey, in order to be a legitimate member of the "Free World" and to fit the template of a democratic country, needed to demonstrate progress on specific indices. In the end, then, it was not so much the internal pressures that produced a true multiparty democracy in Turkey as these nonnegotiable external expectations. Illustrative of this irony, "National Chief" (Milli Şef) İsmet İnönü, long an opponent of the multiparty idea, would ultimately renounce his new authoritarian title and preside over the transition to a multiparty system in the late 1940s.

But what did the establishment of a multiparty system mean from within—within the single-party RPP regime, within the Turkish establishment, and within the long history of *muhalefet* detailed in these pages? After all, thanks to an outside catalyst *muhalefet*, as an organized, sanctioned opposition party, was moving from elusive ideal to political reality. This shift consisted of four separate stages, each with its own internal dynamics and new meanings of *muhalefet*: the transition to a multiparty system (1945–50); the initial term of the Democrat Party (Demokrat Parti, DP), the first opposition party to the RPP to be elected to power (1950–54); the second and third terms of the DP (1954–57; 1957–60); and the period ushered in with the May 27, 1960, military coup d'état (referred to as both coup [*darbe*] and revolution/insurrection [*ihtilal*] in Turkish). Throughout the larger changes and continuities in *muhalefet* since 1945, we find Refik Halid Karay, who already had such a storied relationship to the concept in the late Ottoman and single-party Republican eras, connected to the space of independent, dissident publishing on the one hand and to the emergent second party, the DP, on the other. Once the DP was elected to power in 1950, Refik Halid reaped the benefits of association with *muhalefet* past and present. And once the DP began making the same moves to quash dissent after 1954 that the RPP had done in earlier eras, he seemed to refrain from criticizing it, repeating the same pattern from the past, with the lofty claims of *muhalefet* as principled opposition existing in tension with the partisan realities of *muhalefet* as opposition expressly to the CUP, and then to the RPP.

TURNING POINTS: *MUHALEFET* IN 1945

In the year 1945 alone, the two trajectories of *muhalefet* that we have followed from the late Ottoman era in these pages—the formation of a second party and the space for independent, internal political dissent—both underwent important shifts. In June of that year, Mehmet Fuat Köprülü, Adnan Menderes, Celâl Bayar, and Refik Koraltan resigned from parliament and from the RPP after trying and failing to create an internal opposition (Dörtlü Takrir, or Memorandum of the Four). İsmet İnönü was initially reluctant, but having received encouragement, and even pressure, to allow a second party, ultimately relented, and the DP was established in January 1946. The deal struck for a second party between İnönü and Bayar "served to reinforce the boundaries of acceptable political expression in the multi-party system. As a result, the 'left' and 'right' would be denied a voice, while the two main parties would represent different perspectives on a generally agreed-upon political agenda. As a consequence of the first outcome, the second outcome of [this cooperation] was to ensure that the political debate would have to accept the primacy of the Kemalist reform program, and the secular Republican bases of government."[1] *Muhalefet*, finally employed in the sense of an organized opposition party, was meant to be based on the same consensus among the Turkish establishment that had been in place under the single-party regime. One can see how this played out by looking at the so-called *Tan* Incident of December 1945 to which we now turn, which took place during these six months of negotiation, between the resignation of the four deputies in June 1945 and the establishment of the DP in January 1946.

During the single-party era and particularly World War II, the newspaper *Tan* and its publishing house had been an important space of *muhalefet*, in the sense of dissident journalism within the accepted framework of the Kemalist Republic. Its offices were attacked, burned, and looted in December 1945 by a "fascist" mob, and this incident, which has gone down in infamy as the *Tan* Incident, was not just a dark spot in twentieth-century Turkish history, but a turning point in the history of *muhalefet*. The history and personnel of *Tan*, including at times Refik Halid Karay himself, had been bound up with the larger, fraught story of political opposition in the 1930s and 1940s. Its destruction signified the decimation of one kind of *muhalefet*—independent dissent and critique—just as İsmet İnönü had opened the way for the other kind of *muhalefet*—partisan opposition—initiated from the top and cleaved out of the ruling elite.

THE *TAN* INCIDENT OF DECEMBER 1945

Tan had been established in 1930 as an organ of the Free Progressive Party, the next (ninety-nine-day) iteration of an opposition party after the 1925 closure of the Progressive Republican Party and the institution of the

Maintenance of Order Law (Takrir-i Sükûn Kanunu). In the wake of the global economic crisis, economic policy—and particularly the question of state control of the economy—had assumed center stage in Turkish political discourse; debate, and by extension political affinities in the 1930s and 1940s, centered around the precise meaning of the Kemalist principle of "statism." Celâl Bayar emerged as a leader of the faction embracing a "statist" vision that allowed more space for private enterprise—and indeed, as the director of Turkey's Labor Bank (İş Bankası, est. 1924), he provided the financial backing for *Tan*. The Free Party, to which Mustafa Kemal had appointed Fethi (Okyar) and Ahmet Ağaoğlu as leaders, was intended as an institutional base for those who supported a liberal economic policy. Like the last iteration of an opposition party, it was short lived, but its newspaper, *Tan*, survived the tumult and received a new lease on life thanks to Zekeriya Sertel and his business partner Halil Lütfi.

Zekeriya Sertel, a cofounder of *Cumhuriyet* and a collaborator with hardcore Unionist turned nationalist journalist, Yunus Nadi, on several projects (such as *Life Encyclopedia* [*Hayat Ansiklopedisi*]), had bought the *Tan* newspaper with Halil Lütfi in 1934. While Zekeriya was a leftist and had been imprisoned for his journalistic activities in 1925 and in the early 1930s, he was not as outspoken or ideologically committed to Marxism and socialism as was his wife, Sabiha Sertel, who became a prominent voice at *Tan*. Both had studied at Columbia University during the Armistice period, returning to Turkey with new ideas about journalism and social justice. As Sabiha recalls in her memoirs, in the early 1930s "certain press freedoms" were established, and despite the fact that the Turkish market was not ready for her Turkish translations of Kautsky and Lenin, she and her husband were able to express certain criticisms of the government in the pages of *Tan*. The example of the Sertels and *Tan* shows that the issue of press freedom in the early 1940s was still one in which advocates of an American liberal agenda and of a radical, communist-Marxist one could find common cause. There was still a great deal of ambivalence on the part of the regime regarding safeguards for a free press, in the absence of geopolitical incentives to ensure that freedom.

The personnel at *Tan* included, of course, the Sertels, as well as their close friend and fellow socialist, the poet Nâzım Hikmet. The Sertels also tapped their fellow Columbia University alumnus and liberal, pro-American *muhalif* of sorts, Ahmet Emin (Yalman), to join them at *Tan*. Sertel comments in her memoir that Yalman, who later left the journal, was in charge of the editorials, and as "an agent of American imperialism" he consistently championed those in private enterprise as the "forces of good" and the "left-ists" as forces of evil. He then, according to Sabiha, "filled the paper with reactionaries like [Refii Cevat] Ulunay and caliphate supporters like Refik Halid." By way of background on the latter two, she tells readers: "During the War of Independence, Ulunay and Refik Halid had served the govern-ment of Damat Ferit Paşa. As a result, they were among the 150 people Atatürk had banished from the country for supporting the caliphate." She adds the qualification that "despite his backward ideas, Refik Halid was a forceful writer."

In sum, the "team" at *Tan* "*resembled the famous Tower of Babel and its hanging gardens* [mixing two metaphors, Babel and Babylon]. *Reactionaries were on one floor, fantasists like Burhan Felek on the next, hardcore Islamists like* Ömer Rıza *on another floor, and progressives on yet another*" (empha-sis added). Sabiha fashioned herself just as a "refugee in one corner," being an outspoken and rather dogmatic socialist.[2] The eclectic political space at *Tan* was familiar, even emblematic of the larger, variegated space of political opposition at key junctures such as 1909–1913, in the Armistice years, and even during the brief moments in the Kemalist Republic when opposition took on a formal character. The common basis for *muhalefet* was not one political program but common opposition *to* the dominant power, which in the past was the CUP and in this case the hard-core wing of the RPP. At this point, there seemed to be one common value held by the eclectic team at *Tan*: liberal freedoms. No one would argue that Refik Halid shared the Soviet sympathies of the Sertels or Nâzım Hikmet, but as a dissenting writer, he was on their side when it came to journalism and publishing: the side of open debate, free expression, and multivocality.[3]

The staff at *Tan* had been pushing up against the limits of political criti-cism and debate since the 1930s; Sertel even goes so far as to say that the news-paper's mission was to resist fascism and thus to expose Pan-Turkism, which was growing anew as a movement in direct sympathy and solidarity with Nazism and fascism in Turkey. Refik Halid, we may assume, had no interest in provoking another round of exile for himself by aligning closely with Soviet interests or, by extension, with the Sertels once objections to them became virulent. He seems to have stopped writing his daily column in *Tan* early in 1944, perhaps in an effort to distance himself from the paper, and especially from Sabiha Sertel, who was widely considered to be a liability—a loose cannon and politically dangerous. But even in the summer of 1945, in another venue he wrote pointed critiques of fascism and fascist regimes, articulating again the importance of literature and press freedom. Note, for example, "The Regime That Kills Literature" ("Edebiyat Öldüren Rejim"), published in *Harman* in late July 1945:

There is no longer any doubt that totalitarian regimes kill most of the fine arts, and even literature, which is most necessary to freedom. What has Italy contributed to world literature in the last 20 years? And [in] all of Germany, who was there writing on their own soil in the Nazi era? If any works of value in Italian and German came out, these were written by free-thinking people who had been removed from their motherland, either voluntarily or by force. . . . In totalitarian regimes those who want to make works that express their own opinions cannot go outside of the well-known molds of sculpture and architecture. In fascist regimes that do not value the individual, the art that remains the most barren, the puniest, deficient and stunted is literature. The regime that kills literature constitutes a danger to humanity.[4]

While Karay does not name Turkey per se as a totalitarian regime, contemporary readers would understand that he was indirectly making a statement about the tensions between literature and politics that he himself had experienced and witnessed in Turkey. According to other prominent journalists such as Zekeriya Sertel, İnönü was steering Turkey further toward dictatorship at precisely this time, exemplified by his "one nation, one party, one chief" slogan, which added up to a "police state."[5] It seems likely, then, that Karay was commenting on the dangers then present in Turkey, even as fascism seemed to be defeated in Europe. And he likely did so with the sanction of his allies who were preparing to form the opposition DP.

Paradoxically, Sabiha Sertel notes that "after 1944, progressives were granted a modicum of freedom. This was largely because the Turkish Government had signed the Treaty of San Francisco [the UN charter] and the Atlantic Charter. A number of progressive journals started publishing, and people discussed national issues a little more openly. But the attacks on progressives only intensified. The government employed the fascists as squads to crack down on progressive movements and used many roundabout ways to stifle them."[6]

After the RPP party caucus of April 23, 1945, the opposition came out of the shadows in parliament. The parliamentary deputies Celâl Bayar (İzmir), who had been leading the faction, along with İçel member of parliament (MP) Refik Koraltan, the elder statesman/intellectual, Kars MP Mehmet Fuat Köprülü, and Aydın MP Adnan Menderes, submitted a motion demanding changes to the party charter and laws. Again, as in the

Unionist days, it came down to a question of process. Bayar, however, established connections with *Tan* anew and expressed his desire to build popular support for an opposition party until such time as political circumstances would make such a move possible. The editorial staff of *Tan* was expanded in the course of 1945 in support of this renewed "anti-imperialist, anti-fascist" mandate, to include, among others, leftist figures such as satirical writers Sabahettin Ali and Aziz Nesin—the latter still a household name in Turkey today.[7]

And on the night of December 4–5, 1945, a mob—described as "university youths" (*üniversiteli gençler*) by Zekeriya Sertel, who was their target—attacked and destroyed the *Tan* offices and the ABC bookstore in Cağaloğlu, before going on to Beyoğlu to attack the newspaper of Sabahettin Ali (who would later be murdered as he tried to escape to Bulgaria), and then to Kadıköy to attack the home of the Sertels.[8] All of this was with the knowledge and complicity of Istanbul's mayor, Lütfi Kırdar, with whom the Sertels were in continuous contact throughout the night and who advised them which locations to avoid in order to remain safe. Sertel also recalls that former Unionist Hüseyin Cahit Yalçın was a key agent behind these attacks.

The *Tan* Incident was a turning point and continues to be seen as a dark spot on the history of journalism in Turkey. Journalist Burhan Arpad wrote the following about the context and significance of the *Tan* Incident: "The Second World War just ended. The 'National Chief' of the single-party administration wanted to constitute the appearance of a 'democratic country.'" He wanted to, but *Tan*, for example, could not be tolerated: "The right-wing forces coiled up in the RPP (*CHP'de çöreklenmiş sağcı güçler*), the 'Anatolianists Group' (*Anadolucular Grubu*) hit hard," incited by the Istanbul RPP chapter, which told them that each youth would be rewarded with a new coat (*palto*). This would all indicate deep ambivalence within the RPP, and thus within the single-party regime, toward *muhalefet* in both of its forms. Part of that ambivalence was a very old story. For this was not just the Turkish Republic's first experiment with sanctioned political opposition, but was seen by many as a fulfillment of the Ottoman constitutionalist dream, long deferred, first by Unionist, then by RPP hegemony. The language and associations with *muhalefet* were infused with this longer story. And this meant that invoking the political conflicts of the late Ottoman past could become a new common language through which to comment on and critique politics in the present.

As the landscape shifted and negotiations for the terms regarding a second party and an electoral system unfolded between 1946 and the 1950 DP victory, new kinds of spaces opened in the press in the wake of the destruction of *Tan*. These often had to do with reflection on the Ottoman past of *muhalefet*, which makes sense given that the imaginary of *muhalefet* after 1945 was part of a longer continuum from the late Ottoman era. Underground, and suppressed in official memory for more than two decades, the Ottoman past seemed both remote from official politics of the Turkish Republic and ripe as a terrain in which to imagine counternarratives to official history by this point. Turkey's transition from a single-party to a multiparty republic in the late 1940s was, after all, weathered by some of the same individuals still active from the Unionist generation and still able to retain positions of power in yet another reconfiguration. Falih Rıfkı Atay (by this time part of the hard-line bloc within the RPP) was removed from the establishment newspaper *Ulus* in summer 1947 to be replaced by a more "moderate" editor. Celâl Bayar and Fuat Köprülü were part of the inner circle leading the push for an opposition party growing out of the RPP and were among the founders of the DP, which resulted from that push. Necmettin Sadak (formerly Sadık), the editor of *Akşam*, which had published the first installments of Refik Halid Karay's *Minelbab İlelmihrab* memoir in 1924, and a committed Republican, was appointed foreign minister in 1947. Hüseyin Cahit Yalçın was still editor of *Tanin*, as he had been when that newspaper was the official organ of the CUP in the constitutional period. And of course İsmet İnönü had been Mustafa Kemal's right-hand man since the War of Independence. Ahmet Emin Yalman, a *muhalif* of sorts, chose to write his autobiography—in English—in the 1950s, situating himself as a heroic and pioneering journalist since the dawn of the Second Constitutional Era.[9] In the book he celebrated the 1950 election of Celâl Bayar as the "first democratically elected leader of Turkey," giving his seal of approval to the DP.

In the late 1940s, then, the Ottoman past of *muhalefet* reappeared—on hiatus since 1927—in several forms in cultural and political life. In 1948, for instance, Refik Halid led the way when he resurrected his satirical newspaper *Aydede*, which he had published for the duration of 1922 until he fled for Syria/Lebanon. He used *Aydede* as a venue to finally publish *Minelbab İlelmihrab*, his memoir of the Armistice period—which had been too controversial to publish in 1924–25—serialized as it was meant to be, but this time in its entirety. Both *Aydede* and *Minelbab İlelmihrab* would have been famil-iar to the elder statesmen of the RPP and the emergent DP—they were part of the common language of *muhalefet* past. The gesture of both resurrecting the newspaper and using it to publish his memoir for the first time was thus a signal of the return of contestation, suppressed since the transitional years of the 1920s. It was also a statement that power—whether of the Unionists or the hard-line faction of the RPP—would now have to accommodate *muhale-fet*. That same year, Rıza Tevfik, Refik's close friend and another member of the List of 150, published his memoir, *Let Me, Too, Speak a Little* (*Biraz Ben de Konuşayım*), serialized in the newspaper *Yeni Sabah*. Others who had been vilified by Atatürk, such as Rıza Nur, Kâzım Karabekir, Ali Fuat Cebesoy, and Rauf Orbay, followed suit with their memoirs, which were published in waves in the 1950s, 1960s, and 1990s. In telling their own stories (in some cases publication was posthumous), they were contesting official history, and specifically *Nutuk*, in the form of what Hülya Adak has called "non-official self-na(rra)tions."[10]

1950: A FINAL VICTORY FOR *MUHALEFET?*

In May 1950 the DP was elected in a landslide, unseating the RPP for the first time since the establishment of the party and the republic in 1923. The euphoria that followed was reminiscent of that after the Constitutional Revolution in July 1908. Writers and intellectuals were well aware of the par-allels, and they used discussion of figures from the Ottoman past to amplify them. In doing so, they were also forging a pedigree and imagination for *muhalefet* that one might think of as a reactivation of Refik Halid's project in the Armistice era, which was cut short by the nationalist victory. *Muhalefet* could now be construed—even celebrated—as a virtue, and the euphoria was palpable among the intelligentsia. One minor example comes from Tarık Zafer Tunaya (1916–91), a prominent historian of Turkish political parties, who published an article in *Vatan* on June 18, 1950, just three weeks after the DP electoral victory. In it he offered a biographical sketch of (Ömer) Lütfi Fikri Bey, a journalist, lawyer, and prominent liberal *muhalif* from the Second Constitutional Era and Armistice period. Lütfi Fikri Bey was an editor of the liberal *Sabah* who was put on trial twice and acquitted in the 1925 Independence Tribunals. In the article, "Lütfi Fikri Bey: An Exciting Figure in the History of *muhalefet*"—because now not only was *muhalefet* an idea(l) and a reality, but it had a distinct, and exciting history—Tunaya introduces his hero, Lütfi Fikri: "Not just his words and writings, but really his profession [lawyer] can only be termed, in a word, as *muhalefet*."[11] A student of Tunaya's recalled in the early 1990s, shortly after the latter's death, that Tunaya had long had a fascination with this *muhalif* and had kept not only his unpublished diary but all kinds of writings by and about him squirreled away in a drawer, in the hopes that one day it would be possible to publish a book about him.[12]

· · ·

And here is the good news and bad news about the multiparty system and the advent of DP. The good news is that there was a second party and therefore a space in which to voice differences in policy, political orientation, and critical sentiments toward the regime. There was also an official sanction of *muhalefet* as dissent as a principle with intrinsic value for a democratic regime. The bad news is that the second party was an outgrowth of the RPP and did not signal the entrance of an entirely new elite into the upper reaches of power, even if the support of a new provincial middle class was necessary to their electoral victory. Further bad news was that the new trappings of freedom and democracy were built on the quasi-fascist foundations of the republic and the RPP, creating an arena for *muhalefet*—individual and collective—that was more, if differently, fraught and confusing than before. The institutional foundations of political authority had not been fundamentally altered, after all, and this is what allowed the DP's leaders to literally step into the institutional space the RPP had created—and then use many of the same oppressive tactics. We can see the possibilities and limitations of *muhalefet* in this early multiparty period of the 1950s through Refik Halid Karay's relationship to that opposition party, now in power, combined with his activities both in the realm of literary work and political/social activism.

One result of the contradictions of multiparty democracy in Turkey was that figures such as Karay went from being considered liberal-reactionaries (supposed defenders of the Caliphate who redeemed themselves by happening to be good writers, according to Sabiha Sertel) to liberal-progressives, as they became champions of freedom of expression in a new, liberal democratic framework for Turkey. It became safe to promote freedom of expression and advocate for journalists and writers, as long as one was not a communist. And the DP, at least in the first few years of its ascendancy, was still promoting the values of *muhalefet* even though it was in power, showing once again how sticky that word and its vernacular usages have been. Identification with *muhalefet* was often fixed, and connected to a stance against Unionism and the values it became associated with in the Turkish Republic, specifically in the hard-line faction of the RPP: militarism, illiberalism, extreme statism/ centralism, and intolerance of dissent. For some, *muhalefet* implicitly meant *muhalefet* against the RPP, even if the RPP was out of power—just as it had meant opposition to Unionism whether the Unionists were formally in power or not. Karay seemed to share in the euphoria of the initial electoral victory of the DP as *muhalefet*. He also seemed happy to stay within the parameters of the new elite consensus.

REFIK HALID KARAY:
ELDER STATESMAN OF *MUHALEFET*

Just a few years after the *Tan* Incident, a new space for *muhalefet* as dissident journalism and the casting of historical counternarratives reopened, but all within the new horizons of the elite consensus for a multiparty regime. It was a new iteration of authoritarian democracy—with two parties but one establishment—that also afforded a space for centrists like Refik Halid. Even though his actions had not always matched his words of principled opposition, he could reinvent himself once again as a *muhalif*, this time within the safe confines of the multiparty system. It is possible to track the expansion in the space for *muhalefet* vis-à-vis Refik Halid Karay's work over the course of the 1940s, alongside the broader, more explicit struggles in parliament and the RPP for a formal political opposition. In the early 1940s he had published *Kendi Yazılar ile*, in which he played down, to the point of effacing, his past role as *muhalif*. He did, however, also continue to write for *Tan*, a new venue for dissent, alongside many outspoken dissidents and independent journalists. In December 1945 *Tan* was forcibly closed down, and Karay distanced himself from that circle, and from socialism, which had never presented him with much of a temptation in any case. He looked on as new forms of satire emerged; Sabahettin Ali, Aziz Nesin, and others established *Markopaşa* in 1946, only to be put on trial in 1947, and Karay reportedly testified on their behalf at the trial.[13] And he joined in on the effort to bring new voices to the fore that would challenge the master narrative of official history, as evidenced by his publication in full of *Minelbab İlelmihrab* in 1948, as previously referenced. Now the Telegraph Episode, told through his eyes as Post Telegraph and Telephone (PTT) director for the Ottoman government in 1919, could be discussed in painstaking detail, rather than awkwardly passed over as had been the case in his 1940 narration.

One can suppose that two sets of changes had happened in the interim. First, the boundaries of acceptable opposition in politics had changed, and that opened the space to remember different vantage points on national history (even those that were not just divergent from but antithetical to Mustafa Kemal's) and on the War of Independence. Second, as a result, invoking those events was less dangerous than it had been just a few years earlier. If *Nutuk* had, in 1927, signaled the consolidation of Mustafa Kemal's hegemony over the Republican system he had established and his monopoly over the writing of history, then *Minelbab İlelmihrab*, published in *Aydede* in 1948, signaled something perhaps equally important: the consolidation of a space to publicly express dissent and to narrate the history of *muhalefet* within that system exactly one decade after the death of the republic's founder. If the first installments of *Minelbab İlelmihrab* in 1924 had helped trigger the forging of *Nutuk* as hegemonic narrative, the publication of the memoir in its entirety twenty-four years later helped trigger, or at least signal, the sanction of multiple counternarratives to the hegemonic one.

Karay, by the 1950s, was close not only to Celâl Bayar and Adnan Menderes but also to the likes of his former nationalist rivals, Falih Rıfkı and Aka Gündüz. According to the personal reminiscences of Karay's daughter-in-law and granddaughter, he used to boast of having a close friendship with none other than Kılıç Ali, a member of Mustafa Kemal's inner circle and a presiding judge at the Independence Tribunals of 1925–26. The two used to breakfast together regularly in the 1950s; Karay boasted of all the amazing stories from Kılıç Ali he would take to his grave. Aka Gündüz, who had published the Ankara version of *Peyam-ı Sabah* during the War of Independence and was therefore Refik Halid's mortal enemy at the time, reportedly told Karay in the 1950s that the latter could have been Turkey's "national littérateur" (*millî edib*).

Within this new milieu of national unity and acceptance of former *muhalif*s from within the larger ruling elite, Karay took part in a number of initiatives for journalists and writers. Refik Halid, along with Halide Edib Adıvar, who had returned to Turkey in 1939 and been elected to parliament in 1950, was a cofounder of the PEN Club in Turkey. In addition to helping found the Turkish chapter of that organization, which was aimed at protecting freedom of expression and connecting Turkish journalists to a global campaign to advance and preserve liberal freedoms, he, along with Sedat Semavi—a longtime satirist but less politically provocative—helped found the Journalists Federation, a professional syndicate for journalists. He also obtained funding from the Menderes government to build the Journalists Cooperative Neighborhood (Gazeteciler Kooperatifleri Mahallesi) in Esentepe (Mecidiyeköy) in Istanbul, which became the home and social center for many writers and journalists from 1958 on, including Karay himself.[14] Karay was, furthermore, apparently instrumental in getting July 24 declared Gazeteciler Bayramı (Journalists Day). This is of remarkable significance, because it meant recasting the anniversary of the Constitutional Revolution and celebrating it as a day to honor journalists—the tragic heroes of *muhalefet* and of Ottoman constitutionalism.

.   .   .

Karay's literary productivity between 1950 and his death in 1965 was as dizzying in quantity as it was politically harmless in content. It was overwhelmingly made up of newspaper columns, novels, and his second volume of memoirs, *Across One Lifetime* (*Bir Ömür Boyunca*). The novels he churned out were more or less pulp fiction, often invoking a rather insipid portrayal of the Ottoman past, and they were very popular.[15] He remained popular, entertaining a new and growing middle class, members of which he sometimes depicted as characters in his novels.[16] He was a household name, as the frequency of the female name Nilgün, given to babies born in the 1950s, would attest: his wildly popular trilogy, *Nilgün: A Turkish Princess*, was published at that time, and made into a TV miniseries in the 1970s. He continued to produce about a novel a year, as well as many columns that mused nostalgically about the Ottoman past and the past in general, in an apolitical, whimsical way—evidenced by his second volume of memoirs, which were not arranged in any chronological or thematic order, instead offering random vignettes from different moments in his life and from different eras of the empire and the republic. Three more novels were published posthumously. And in what was ultimately a poetic gesture, his last novel, which was published the year of his death, was entitled, *The Last Glass [of Wine]* (*Sonuncu Kadeh*). These last novels were no longer political in the way his satire and other earlier work had been, perhaps because they no longer needed to be. His modest dream of a liberal democracy, or a close-enough approximation of it, had been achieved with the rise of the DP. Now he was free to play with language, write about his experiences, use his imagination to write about others' experiences, and reflect on past and present in a way that was both apolitical and often ahistorical. His references to non-Muslims in the Ottoman past showed a marked increase in national chauvinism, not to mention misogyny—now as he reminisced about his wartime exile in Anatolia he flippantly referred to two Greek (Rum) girls who had written him love letters from Istanbul offering to visit him in Sinop as an example of "prostitution" (*fuhuş*).[17] Gone was the sensitive portrayal of Suphi Bey's Rum lover İzmaro in his 1910 story "Against Power" ("Kuvvete Karşı"). And gone from his later writings was any mention of the Armenian Genocide, or the Ankara fire, for that matter. On the political front, he did not seem to be bothered by the significant repression carried out by the DP in the second half of the party's reign, starting in 1955—and again, his silences reveal one of the contradictions of *muhalefet* as a trope. In principle, *muhalefet* was about the freedom to oppose power; in reality, it tended to mean opposition to the Unionists, and then to the RPP, which meant an uncritical defense of the DP, even as that party exhibited the same shortcomings as the RPP after a few short years in power.

During these last few decades of his life, Karay also carried on a voluminous correspondence with his base of literary fans. In the 1950s a number of Turks, in the provinces as well as in Istanbul, were avid readers and interlocutors regarding classical literature—schoolteachers and other professionals across Turkey—and they looked up to Karay as a littérateur. One example is Cemil Gökçe, a Turkish Cypriot by birth (b. 1911) who worked in the Turkish PTT administration from 1941 and served as the PTT director in various cities, finally ending up in Buca/İzmir in 1950 and remaining there for thirteen years. He carried on a regular correspondence with Karay, from June 1939 until just a few months before Karay's death in 1965. It is clear from their correspondence that there was a reading public for Karay's work, one that closely followed his and other authors' work.[18] And it seems the two shared a special kinship, having both served in the post of PTT director at different points in Ottoman and Turkish history.

A final connection, which emerged through pure serendipity, makes it possible to connect Karay's claims to *muhalefet* of the older generation, as a supposed defender of the Caliphate and a reactionary, with his newfound role as a progressive of sorts in the 1950s. In the antiquarian bookshops of Istanbul in spring 2013, I came across an original edition of Karay's *Bir İçim Su*, published in Aleppo in 1931, in old Ottoman script despite having been published three years after the Alphabet Reform. It was the author's own copy, with his marginal notes, autographed and given by the author himself, with the inscription: "Selma Sami Çoşar Hanım kızıma suret ve takdirlerimle" (to my girl, Miss Selma Sami Çoşar, this copy with my appreciation). The dedication was dated March 2, 1950 (and still written in Ottoman Turkish, twenty-two years after the Alphabet Reform). Selma Sami Çoşar was the daughter of RPP parliamentarian and *Ulus* writer Hüseyin Sami Çoşar and the sister of Ömer Sami Çoşar, a nationalist-activist and journalist who would later coauthor a book about the 1960 coup with opposition journalist Abdi İpekçi (who would himself be murdered in 1979 while editor of the newspaper *Milliyet*). Selma, who was at the time a young woman (born in the 1920s), would go on to marry and move to England, becoming known as Selma Ashworth. She became an undercover operative for the Turkish Communist Party (TKP) in the 1960s and 1970s, making trips to East Germany to record Turkish radio shows for the Eastern bloc, and later helped to form Amnesty International. These juxtapositions, from the generation of Karay to that of Selma and Ömer Sami Çoşar, not to mention Abdi İpekçi, only make sense after the final transformation in Turkish politics: the 1960 Coup/Revolution.

The emerging landscape of multiparty democracy, then, brought a number of new contradictions to the fore. It shifted the parameters of party politics, provoking an "identity crisis" for both parties; the RPP was the party in opposition for the first time ever, and the DP, leaders of which had identified themselves as *muhalif*s for so long, were now in power. What would this mean for civil liberties such as press freedom? Would the press be free to criticize all parties? Or would the press, traditionally aligned with the *muhalefet* and thus the DP elements, be expected to fall in line and support the DP even though it was now the ruling party? Furthermore, the ascendancy of the DP did not involve an approval of radical leftist expression—communist ideas or sympathies—given that both parties had agreed on a moderate system, and the whole system was encased in the American-supported notion of liberal democracy as a foil against Soviet communism.

Muhalefet, then, was undergoing perhaps its biggest transformation yet in the 1950s. Invoking *muhalefet*, in the sense of dissent and contestation for its own sake, was becoming a signal for the celebration of liberal values and moderate dissent. And yet *muhalefet*, retaining as it did the connotation of *muhalefet* against the RPP and the deep history of *muhalefet* as dissent against the Unionists, became paradoxical when RPP for the first time became the formal opposition party (*muhalefet*). As the DP assumed the reins of power and began to stifle dissent arising from the RPP—even targeting it for suppression from 1954 on—the RPP would start to invoke the concept of *muhalefet* as a way to garner support for its challenge to the DP for supremacy. İsmet İnönü published a volume of his speeches and writings in 1959 entitled *İsmet İnönü in Opposition* (*Muhalefet'te İsmet İnönü*). His handwritten preface, entitled, "The New Phase of the Political Struggle" (*siyasi mücadelenin yeni devri*), was dated September 9, 1959, and opened with the lines, "When one is in the *muhalefet*, one always thinks that the time one is living in is the roughest period."[19] This invocation of *muhalefet* as the condition of the persecuted and downtrodden, of course, would turn out to be disinegenuous to the point of cynical, as İsmet İnönü and other RPP leaders had very close relations with the military, who eventually stepped in to "protect" the multiparty system and effectively reinstate the RPP in power in 1960–61. But it added yet another layer of history atop an already complicated politics and imagination of *muhalefet* in this new multiparty era.

Greek pogrom is external pressure

1960 COUP: THE LAST TURNING POINT

And then the coup of May 27, 1960, took place. Democracy in the "Free World" took a new turn with this coup, prompted by the RPP's and the army's anxieties regarding the Islamist and populist tendencies of the DP and its silencing of opposition against it.[20] This was the final transition in our story, signifying as it did a new era for Turkey and for global politics. The military coup, with its spokesman, Alparslan Türkeş, who had been shaped by the fascist Pan-Turanist movements of the 1940s, was carried out in order to restore a secular, Kemalist order and—paradoxically—to bring about popular democracy, or at least the RPP's vision of it.[21]

The following year (1961) the first new constitution was drawn up since 1924; Adnan Menderes and others were tried and hanged (a method of execution that was a chilling throwback to the CUP suppression of the counter-revolution in 1909 and the Independence Tribunals in the 1920s); and new elections took place, which brought İsmet İnönü and the RPP back to power. The structural significance of this coup was of course that the military, fused with the RPP, came to assume the role of "guardian" of the Kemalist political order and political system, not just of the nation's sovereignty. Although the new constitution, drawn up by intellectuals and academics, proved to be the most "liberal" iteration that Turkey had seen thus far, the ultimate guarantor of this new order would not be the people, but the military—even against the popular will if necessary. The military would continue to have a pervasive and tutelary role in Turkish politics until the electoral victory of Süleyman Demirel's DP successor, the Justice Party (Adalet Partisi), in 1965. Demirel and his party would be forced to step down in the first of Turkey's so-called Coup[s] by Memorandum in 1971 (12 Mart Muhtırası). From 1960 until at least the 1990s, then, there was a cycle of coups d'état (1960, 1971, 1980, 1997). That political pattern was, in turn, inextricably bound up with Turkey's strategic relationship to the United States.

The question of *muhalefet* in this last period is rife with further contradictions, partly because of the new fusing of the military, the legacy of Atatürk, and the RPP. In this context, any dissent or contestation carried a whiff of subversion; opposing the military was tantamount to insulting the legacy of Atatürk, and that was not *muhalefet* but outright treason. The 1961 Constitution was a liberal document, but it was promulgated and protected by the military, which in turn had a privileged and disturbingly nontransparent relationship to the RPP. What valence could any opposition party hope to have given this constellation of institutions and laws? This final synthesis between authoritarianism and democracy could only mean a narrowing of the field of activity for contestation and a deeper entrenching of power, which meant a new level of marginalization for *muhalefet*. As the 1960s unfolded, the introduction of an international New Left movement among students, organized labor, and leftist intellectuals added another layer to the old fissures between power and its opposition.

In one of his last interviews, with a writer from Aziz Nesin's satirical journal *Zübük* in 1962, Karay gave the contradictory answers that continued to typify *muhalefet*. First he critiqued the post-1960 political climate: "When I was writing, freedom of the press was more expansive. This requires some study.... If I were to write as forcefully now as I did then, I would have no hope of receiving a punishment as light as mere exile. In exile we were free, we were better off than in prison [which is, he implies, the penalty for *muhalefet* post-1960]."[22] He then underlined his identity as a *muhalif* even in this climate, saying proudly, "I am a *muhalif*. From the worst government to the best government I will always be a *muhalif* to all of them. I don't practice it anymore. But I like those who do."[23] And then came the necessary reassurance of loyalty: he walked over to the bust of Atatürk on the table in his house, and said, "This thing here . . . it's not here because of flattery, I love him. I am a Kemalist."

Sixty years after the fact, we often forget what a shock and turning point the 1960 Coup was for Turkey and the world. On the eve of the coup, in 1959, despite the fissures and conflicts underway in Turkey politics, the country was lauded by the foremost specialists in the United States for being a paradigm of democracy. Political scientist Dankwart Rustow wrote an article in the late 1950s extolling the virtues of Turkish democracy, noting the restraint shown by the military in staying out of politics and leaving it to civilian statesmen since the founding of the republic in 1923.[24] Karay suffered a heart attack from the distress on the night that the 1960 Coup took place—it was the moment when hopes for a smooth and seamless transition to full democracy were dashed.[25]

Epilogue

MUHALEFET, RECONSIDERED

REFIK HALID KARAY'S LEGACY was recast once again after the accession to power of the Justice and Development Party (Adalet ve Kalkınma Partisi; AKP) under Recep Tayyip Erdoğan in 2002. In the first several years of AKP rule, there seems to have been at the very least a sanction of Refik Halid Karay's work and legacy, if not an active campaign to construct him as a kind of hero of the *muhalefet*. It was implied that he was a forefather of some of the values that the AKP was trying to promote—a kind of Turkish rendition of Christian Democracy in Europe—and the pedigree its members were trying to construct for themselves as they tried to take up the mantle of *muhalefet*, perhaps. And we must recall here something that has already been largely forgotten: that as in the early 1950s, there was a larger opening going on in the first decade of AKP rule in Turkey, this time in part due to exigencies from the European Union rather than the United States. Intellectuals and writers began pushing the boundaries of acceptability in writing about the past and present, revising the Unionist-Kemalist official history, whether motivated by EU imperatives to come to terms with history, and particularly the Armenian Genocide, or because of an internal impetus to acknowledge and consolidate the many voices within the Turkish nation-state. Many of the most illuminating Turkish-language books for the present study, in fact, were published during the 2000s, including the book on the Ankara fire, the publication of Refik Halid Karay and Rıza Tevfik's correspondence in exile, many of Ali Birinci's works on late Ottoman *muhalefet*, and the book on the censored/excised works of Refik Halid Karay. Ali Birinci himself, the top expert in Turkey on Refik Halid Karay and on the larger phenomenon of political opposition in the Second Constitutional Era, the Freedom and Accord Party, was even appointed president of the Turkish History Foundation in the early years of AKP rule. In a sense, *muhalefet*, or those who identified with the concept and the historical imagination that went with it, was finally in power, and an arena opened up in which to examine, grapple with, and bring to light the past efforts and struggles of *muhalifs*—to draw attention to forms of contestation in

Turkey's past and imagine them as part of an integrated history. It was in the midst of that moment, in 2010, that I first began this project, a few years before the issue of *muhalefet* would shift again and burst onto the scene differently, yet again. In 2010, in fact, the topic of *muhalefet* seemed like a nonissue, given that there was little to no organized opposition to the AKP. That changed in 2013 with the Gezi Park protests, and then again with the parliamentary victory of the People's Democratic Party (Halkların Demokratik Partisi; HDP) under Süleyman Demirtaş (imprisoned at the time of this writing) in summer 2015, followed by the brutal repression of that *muhalefet* initiative and the attempted coup in summer 2016. *Muhalefet* is still alive, although who can lay legitimate claim to the concept is unclear: Erdoğan, though in power for almost two decades, because his mission had been to finally triumph over the political and military authority that he saw as Unionist-Kemalist? Or the coalition in opposition to him, given that he had thoroughly stepped into the space of power and enacted many of the same measures to limit liberal freedoms?

Through the tale of Refik Halid Karay, I have tried to provide a prehistory of the present state of *muhalefet*, and by extension a history of the changing structures of power in the late Ottoman and Republican Turkish eras. I have tacked back and forth between Refik Halid's personal itinerary, his own telling and retelling of his experiences, and his perspective on the multiple levels of change he witnessed, his literary imagination, and his role in the history of this long arc of authoritarian democracy, turning on the evolution of political authority from the Ottoman Empire to the Republic of Turkey. My hope has been to illuminate a number of patterns over time, both about the episodic nature of political opposition itself and about the ever-changing memory—historical and literary—of *muhalefet*.

· · ·

It is a funny irony that the banner of *muhalefet* was used first by the Young Ottomans, then taken up by the Young Turks when they were in opposition to the despotism (*istibdad*) of Abdülhamid II. After the restoration of the constitution in 1908, two schools of thought emerged regarding the existence and need for *muhalefet*. In the minds of some Unionists, there was no longer a need for *muhalefet*, since its previous goal of restoring the constitution had been achieved. This view was later assumed by many of the nationalists with the establishment of the Turkish nation-state. Over these decades, however, others, and in different iterations, saw the continuation of *muhalefet* as fundamental to the achievement and maintenance of a constitutional government.

Was *muhalefet* all a big joke? While in the absence of a sanctioned or viable opposition party it was often expressed as a joke, particularly in the form of satire or irony, I have argued that it was anything but a laughing matter. I have argued that by the 1950s, when the term *muhalefet* was invoked to mean the party then out of power at any given moment, it signaled the ongoing but unresolved contestation within the ruling establishment, contestation that was often not accepted as a legitimate part of the political system but was deemed dangerous and even taboo. *Muhalefet* was never fully integrated into the political arena, either in its form as organized partisan/parliamentary opposition or in that of independent dissent through journalism and literature. It was thus a concept that lived half in the imagination and half in political reality as we look across the twentieth century—and that is why Refik Halid Karay has been such a useful guide. Between 1908 and 1950, during which time there were a few brief and unsuccessful attempts at establishing an opposition party, the concept of *muhalefet* took on an array of meanings and connotations, many of which I have explored here. Narrowly defined, it took shape initially to mean the partisan opposition of the liberal Freedom and Accord Party against the Committee for Union and Progress. Out of the shortcomings and failures of that partisan opposition and the undeveloped nature of the constitutional system of political parties, it then took on diffuse meanings that included dissent, often expressed through satire within the larger discursive space of journalism and the press. In the Armistice period the concept of *muhalefet* took on a new value as a means of justifying opposition against the nationalist movement, as the offspring of the CUP, and therefore of justifying collaboration with the British colonial occupiers. As the Kemalist Republic took shape, that form of *muhalefet* briefly coexisted with, but ultimately gave way to, the new dynamics of contestation that grew out of the nationalist movement and War of Independence and around the leadership of Mustafa Kemal Atatürk. The next qualitatively different iteration of *muhalefet* was not until after 1945 with the advent of the multiparty system, when the terms *iktidar* and *muhalefet* became two sides of the same coin, ubiquitous in reference to the parties in and out of power, respectively, in any given moment.

. . .

The word *muhalefet,* as opposition, might lead one to believe that it must be the *opposite* of something: some ideology, some party, or some leader. Refik Halid Karay, indeed, in identifying as a *muhalif* across several eras, often positioned himself against power—against the dominant Unionist or Republican People's Parties, against dominant historical narratives and contemporary partisan propaganda, and against a dominant political culture of extreme partisanship that he likened to organized crime. But Refik's life and work do not reflect the perfect *antithesis* of Unionism, nationalism, Kemalism, or even Islamism, Turkism, or Turanism—ideologies that I have hardly mentioned in these pages. Nor did he offer or identify with some alternative, all-encompassing ideology, beyond that of an elite Ottoman conception of liberal democracy. He was not vocally or explicitly opposed to the Armenian Genocide, although he did seem as disgusted by it as he was by the other atrocities committed under the Unionists, and he seemed to have felt empathy at the time for the suffering endured by Armenians. His stance toward the British occupiers at a crucial moment, during the Armistice era, was ambivalent and complex. He was not explicitly opposed to colonial involvement in the Ottoman government, although he was often annoyed by British arrogance and patronizing behavior, making it difficult to characterize him as an anti-colonial hero by today's standards. His opposition was truly internal, within the arena of a broadly defined Ottoman, and then Turkish, politics, history, and culture.

When we take seriously the political critiques and literary expressions coming out of this internally focused opposition, we can see the internal workings, flaws, and vulnerabilities included, of national politics—and national partisan actors. Refik Halid Karay was not outside nationalism, but within it. For the same reason that he held so fast to his stance as *muhalif*—namely, to provide an internal critique and check on power, even during the times when he in fact compromised with it— tracing his critiques and expressions has made us privy to a different experience of national politics and history. This experience is not radically different from the hegemonic one or the one that revisionist historians have started to excavate, but it is different enough to raise questions about what has been missing from politics and historical narratives until now.

A testament to Refik's place as an opponent, but one always within the politics and history of Turkey, is that at the end of the day, after years of exile during which he never really lost contact with the intellectual and media elite of Istanbul, he was accepted back into the fold of the national political and cultural elite. He was pardoned by Atatürk; he made amends with, or at least earned the respect of, the likes of Aka Gündüz; he became bosom buddies with Kılıç Ali, who had been in Mustafa Kemal's innermost circle; and he seems to have been an enthusiastic supporter of Celâl Bayar (former member of the CUP and particularly the Teşkilât-ı Mahsusa) and Adnan Menderes's Democrat Party—an opposition party, but one that very much grew out of the larger post-Unionist Republican elite. As a *muhalif*, he can be said to have inhabited the space of an "anti-nationalist nationalist," and it is that space I was interested in exploring in this book.[1]

I have tried to present a vivid portrait in words of his experience, and part of that involved the translation of significant examples of his own copious literary expressions of that experience. I have for the most part deliberately refrained from criticizing him, or even really critiquing his version of the momentous politics and history that he lived through, in the interest of exploring his story as a counternarrative to the master narrative constructed by Atatürk. I have used only a smattering of official Ottoman and Republican Turkish government documents, which in the field of Ottoman and Turkish history are often deemed the only unquestionably authoritative source for information. Instead, I have used his literary texts, correspondence, and journals, all of which are unquestionably subjective. Methodologically, my aim has been to use the example of Refik Halid Karay's life and works as a whole to do for Ottoman and Turkish history what he was doing for the dominant powers of his day: to view the events, personalities, and politics from a slightly different angle, but still within an Ottoman arena until the last possible moment, and then, after 1922, from within a broadly nationalist Turkish but not Kemalist arena. Mustafa Kemal's personal and often anachronistic telling of a crucial moment in history—1919, and the 1919–1927 period more broadly—has been the overwhelmingly hegemonic and authoritative version for nearly a century now. In contrast to that official history, Refik Halid's telling, while turning on 1919 and directly intersecting Mustafa Kemal's narrative, is more expansive in its historical scope and has always been seen—quite literally—as a joke. He was a professional joker, taking on the nom de plume Porcupine (Kirpi), thanks to his sharp quills, sharp pen, and sharp wit. "How could a joker offer anything new for our understanding of Turkish politics or history?" an unimaginative historian might ask. But jokes—satire, irony, caricature—and jokers, and journalists, were the antidote to, if not the antithesis of, political authority in the twentieth-century Ottoman Empire and then in Turkey.

Because this has been a story about opposition and authority told from a stance of internal opposition, it also opens up new possibilities for understanding the "transition," which in this light looks more like an evolution—even a transmutation and metamorphosis of power—from the Ottoman Empire to the Republic of Turkey. There were tremendous political stakes in the insistence on total rupture in the official history. Only by insisting officially on total rupture between the Ottoman and Republican Turkish states, for instance, could the question of culpability regarding the Armenian Genocide be sidelined. Only with total rupture could the hesitations, about-faces, and imperfect nationalist pedigrees of the new nationalists be effaced. And only with total rupture could the myriad and possibly incriminating habits, associations, and values of Unionism be expunged from the record. Only with the insistence of total rupture could the resemblances in political culture, affiliation, and habits be submerged. This is not to argue for total reversal in understanding or for any simplistic continuity lying underneath the rupture. But given how variegated and complex the CUP and the organizational structure of the party and movement were, coupled with the incomplete process of retributive/restorative justice during the Armistice, it is very likely that most people did not even know whether their actions during the war had in fact been criminal. And it was that lingering lack of certainty that would surely make the possibility of reckoning with that recent past even more threatening.[2] The process of reckoning with the wartime Unionist regime and the acts committed during that time would never be completed; the half-hearted attempt started by the dying Ottoman government, at the urging of the British, had been aborted with the victory of the nationalists. The Independence Tribunals in 1925–26 under Mustafa Kemal had cleansed the republic of the most prominent surviving remnants of the Unionists, but they would never touch on the larger, far more complicated questions of collaboration and complicity. The ostensible rupture was complete with the Tribunals; Nutuk, composed and delivered the following year, was as much a proclamation of the consolidation of Mustafa Kemal's hegemony as it was an apologia, as Zürcher and others have pointed out.

Beginning with the seminal work of Zürcher in the 1980s, the narrative of total rupture has been undermined and debunked by scholars who have found crucial continuities. We can appreciate the ways that reappraisal and revision of history were far more complex when we view events from the perspective of a *muhalif*. Refik Halid had intimate knowledge of all the personalities of the time, of the shape, habits, and cultures of the social networks, and of the institutional changes, and was deeply skeptical of the claims of rupture between the CUP and the nationalist movement. He was in a perfect position to point out the hypocrisies of those in positions of power in the republic, his own past hypocrisies rendered irrelevant to the outcomes of history. His skepticism disrupts the official history, perhaps more powerfully than modern-day scholars could ever do. His very insistence on continuing to write about the transmutation as it was happening—not to wait until the 1960s, when the big wave of personal memoirs of that generation was published—to tell and retell the story of the recent past over and over in different eras, to not only not hide the continuities and changes but reflect on them and critique them (witness the play "Deli" as a quintessential example), was perhaps his supreme act of *muhalefet*. And his visible collaboration with British occupation authorities was grounds enough to marginalize his vantage point and make him and his work taboo once the nationalists had secured their triumph and hegemony. So, while his work and this book barely scratch the surface of a new appraisal of the evolution and transmutation from the Ottoman past to the Turkish national present, both his life and literary work demonstrate that there are profound historical experiences—underneath the Hat Law, the Alphabet Revolution, Nutuk, and even the revisionist story of continuity of CUP personnel and institutions from empire to republic—that we have been missing. This book, then, is also a call for a new kind of agenda for the study of twentieth-century Ottoman and Turkish life.

None of this story would have the significance it does were it not for the embedded meanings and associations of Refik Halid Karay—his life and his work—in Turkish culture today. He was a quintessential *muhalif* from shortly after the Constitutional Revolution and seems to remain iconic as a *muhalif* in the twenty-first century. As such, his life and works represent a line of continuity between Ottoman and Republican Turkish life. The publication and republication of his works, the excisions, the revisions, the replacement of words and phrases, and his constant recasting of the Ottoman past the deeper he got into the Turkish present all reflect the multiple orders of change and transformation that have been going on under the surface of Republican history. Given that there is no universally recognized national writer per se in or for Turkey, what would Turkey have looked like, and what might it still look like, were Refik Halid Karay to be conceived of as such: the Turkish Kazantzakis, Rushdie, Garcia Marquez, or, as he had hoped, Hugo? Did he capture something about the collective experience of Turks, from their experience with constitutionalism in the late Ottoman period, their formation as a nation-state, and their experience in the republic, and do so in a way that could also transcend partisan divides and capture the universality of human experience? At times, I contend, he did.

What then is *muhalefet*, as a cultural and political space, in twentieth-century Ottoman and Turkish life? Judging from the example elaborated in this book, *muhalefet* is not just political opposition, narrowly defined. It is also the cultural and literary space that is concerned with politics but is not always or necessarily driven by partisan interests and agendas. It is a space of resistance within the constitutionalist establishment and against the political culture and legacy of Unionism. It is a concept that forces us to see party, state, government, and the individual personality of Atatürk as disaggregated from each other. And yet it is also a stance that is, at the end of the day, complicit with the bedrock contradictions of the Turkish Republic. And invoking that space, as well as claiming an identity as a *muhalif*, involves engaging the rather intractable question of what it means to be a Turk who is critical of Unionism and its many and deep remnants in Turkish politics and society, as well as a Turk actively struggling to come to terms with the Ottoman past as it recedes into history and yet echoes in political conflicts even today.

. . .

In his second set of memoirs, *Bir Ömür Boyunca*, Karay included a piece occasioned by his sorting through his old papers and finding the business card (carte de visite) of Mustafa Kemal from 1903, and the letter Refik had written on the back of it to Rıza Tevfik in 1926. He muses that he would like to "write a kind of memoir of the events . . . consisting mostly of the events that were part of my experience/adventure; I thought I should and I must in fact write such a '*monographie*.'" He had thought of writing this two years earlier and had gone through all of his papers, only to realize that he could not begin the task because his

> wound was still fresh. . . . .I preferred to wait and calm my feelings. . . . I wanted to let my nerves calm; let my mind be in control of my feelings. Let my experience of life in exile grow and the ordeal reach completion. I decided it would suffice to just keep notes. Now I feel that I have arrived at a place where the book I wanted to write can be written in an uncorrupted and objective manner, with sound ideas and in a praiseworthy style. For that reason, when the opportunity arises and I decrease my official obligations, soon I will bring that work into being.[3]

To my knowledge, Refik never managed to write such a book.

AFTERWORD

I BEGAN THIS PROJECT IN 2009, at a time when focusing on the topic of *muhalefet* made little sense to anyone, including myself. I stumbled onto and was fascinated by Refik Halid's 1929 play *Deli*, which satirized Kemalist reforms as they were taking place. Scholarship regarding the transition between the Ottoman and Republican Turkish eras, and on the early Republic, was still in its infancy. I was frustrated by the two-dimensional treatment of human experience in conventional political history and the collapsing of what must have been a complex and nonlinear process into a binary between the "rupture" of official history and the "continuity" of revisionist scholarship. And satirical humor was the last thing one would have expected, given scholars' focus on the political, narrowly defined. I wanted to know more about a person who had the audacity to poke fun at Mustafa Kemal (Atatürk) in the midst of a conspiracy of silence—and a seemingly iron-clad censorship regime that prohibited the mere discussion of the recent past, let alone the satirizing of it. I had also long been curious to explore the plight of journalists and writers in Turkey, who had since at least the 1970s worked on a knife's edge, risking imprisonment and torture to report the truth. What would the history of Turkey look like through their eyes?

In Turkish politics, too, in 2009 the concept of *muhalefet* seemed dormant at best, as the Justice and Development Party had managed to absorb a range of constituencies and promised to consolidate democracy, claiming to be a third way between secular democracy and fundamentalist Islamic models for politics. There was no organized opposition to speak of, not because it had been forcibly suppressed but because the ruling party seemed to be at the helm of a thriving economy and the opening of historical archives, even—to some extent—regarding the taboo subject of the Armenian Genocide. There were disgruntled voices and more than a few skeptics, for sure, but they packed little punch in a country with full employment and a ruling party that had the luxury of developing a "neo-Ottoman" foreign policy doctrine. I traveled to Istanbul in April 2013 to interview figures who had been prominent in the leftist and student movements of the 1970s, all of whom (at least the men among them) seemed content enough with the AKP regime and the freedoms afforded to them therein.

A few weeks later, in late May 2013, the Gezi Park protests erupted. Since that time I have watched as the question of *muhalefet* has reached center stage once again; the coalition that had brought AKP to power has come unraveled since the 2016 alleged coup attempt; and journalists, writers, and intellectuals more broadly have come under fire once again. If this book has been delayed, it was not only because my life got busy, but principally because I could not write this history of *muhalefet* in the past without watching to see how this chapter would unfold in the present—and indeed it is still unfolding. The more I read about Refik Halid's experience of *muhalefet* and his construction as a *muhalif* across the twentieth century, the more I could see the patterns repeating, and evolving, in the twenty-first. Official history had dictated historical memory for Turks for decades, requiring Turks to subordinate their lived experience to it in order to be part of the nation. Refik Halid Karay's life and work was now offering me more than just a good laugh and a peek into the experience of transition from empire to republic; it was offering the possibility of an—unlikely—alternative history of the twentieth century, running alongside the making and unmaking of official history, with glimpses onto the continual casting and recasting of the past. This, even just on the small scale of tracking Refik Halid's texts from one era to another, has been a chance to resurrect history—a living, changing history—from the fixed, antihistorical, and dogmatic history that had dominated the imagination.

Finally, I am not a Turk. Nevertheless, this project holds great personal significance for me as someone whose four grandparents, all Greek Orthodox, "Rum" subjects of the Ottoman Empire, emigrated—two from Macedonia and two from Istanbul—to the United States between 1913 and 1920. I was all too familiar with the psychological damage wrought on those who lived through the long decade of war and catastrophe that ended the Ottoman Empire and ushered in the Republic of Turkey. The carnage in Macedonia has rippled through the generations; the atrocities committed against Armenians in the course of World War I, too, were familiar to me from the stories of my grandfather, who was an eyewitness to some of the violence. Greeks (Rum) were not the primary targets of violence the way Armenians were, but they were witness to the deportations and killings of Armenians and were made refugees and exposed to profound deprivation throughout the war years and after. While much recent scholarship has focused on who was directly responsible for the genocide, and to an extent on who might have resisted the killing orders once they were handed down, I instead wanted to understand how a thinking Ottoman Turkish person who was not directly involved in the killing or in the Unionist project, and who might have otherwise identified as a humanist, might have understood the cataclysm and state-perpetrated violence against non-Muslims.

In taking apart the category of "Turk," then, and looking at the fissures within, I was hoping to move beyond a monolithic, generalized understanding of Turkey and of the genocide, both of which were so bound up with the singular telling of the last years of the Ottoman Empire and its metamorphosis into the Republic of Turkey more broadly. And it is important to recognize, as I hope this book forces us to, that non-Muslims were not the only ones to be cast out upon the establishment of the Republic. Instead, some Ottoman Turkish Muslims were cast out—because of their ideas and associations, rather than because of their religion or ethnicity. The difference, of course, was that they could eventually be let back into the fold of the Turkish establishment and the nation. In contrast, Greeks who left would never be welcomed back, and those few who stayed in Istanbul were rendered increasingly invisible, despite their economic importance to the city; they were chronically perse- cuted and for the most part driven out by the 1970s. Such are the realities of national inclusion and exclusion. Nevertheless, the story of *muhalifs* like Refik Halid Karay and the story of non-Muslim minorities are part of the same larger story, and it is that story I sought to understand more closely with this project.

ACKNOWLEDGMENTS

I HAVE INCURRED A DEBT OF GRATITUDE to many individuals and institutions over the course of researching and writing this book. The History Departments at Columbia and at Berkeley provided me with a stimulating intellectual environment, wonderful students, and the time to develop this project—and I am very grateful to all of my colleagues and both departments and universities for affording me these privileges. At the earliest stage, the Middle East Institute at Columbia provided the funds for a research trip to Lebanon and Syria in spring 2010 and afforded me the opportunity to see Beirut and Jounieh, and to catch a glimpse of Aleppo months before the tragedy of the Syrian war would make that impossible. The Shelby Cullom Davis Center Fellowship at Princeton provided me with the space and the community in which to begin to think through the main ideas and the main works of Refik Halid Karay in 2012, and I'd like to especially thank Dan Rodgers, who was directing the Davis Center at the time, for his support and encouragement, and Jennifer Houle, for making the center such a hospitable environment. Shortly thereafter, my colleagues at the Institute for Advanced Study and the Department of History at Central European University (then in Budapest) took a special interest in the topic of political opposition and freedom of expression, a topic with such profound resonance for the contemporary politics of Hungary. I and my family spent a wonderful year in Budapest, thanks to Nadia Al-Bagdadi, Eva Fodor, and Tijana Krstic and Tolga Esmer, for which I will be forever grateful. Several years and several changes later, I was able to find the time to finish writing the first iteration of the book thanks to a year-long fellowship at the Townsend Center for the Humanities at UC Berkeley in 2018–19. Tim Hampton and Rebecca Egger provided the collegial atmosphere and the tea and have been supportive ever since, providing generous funds and the meeting space for a manuscript workshop in September 2019.

Along the way, I presented my work in progress to several audiences. The Ottoman and Turkish Studies Seminar of the University Seminars at Columbia (organized by Zeynep Çelik and Leyla Amzi-Erdoğdular) provided feedback that was immensely helpful to the development of my arguments in chapter 2. I express my appreciation for the Schoff Subvention Fund from the University Seminars at Columbia University for their help with costs associated with preparation of the manuscript for publication. I also presented early portions of this work to the Department of History at UC Berkeley; the conference on rethinking the Middle East Mandates held at Princeton in 2013, organized by Cyrus Schayegh and Andrew Arsan; the Islam in Europe/Europe in Islam working group at Wissenschaftskolleg zu Berlin, for which I thank Georges Khalil and Maria Mavroudi for making it possible; at the History Department of the University of Miami, for which I thank Dominique Reill for being such a wonderful host and interlocutor; and at the London School of Economics, for which I thank Rebecca Bryant.

The project would not have been possible without the help of archivists, librarians, and editors. I'd like to thank the staff at The Prime Ministry Archives in Istanbul (Başbakanlık Arşivleri); the French Foreign Ministry Archives in Nantes, the IISG Archive in Amsterdam, the Hidayet Dağdeviren Archive, and the Ahmet Emin Yalman Papers at the Hoover Institution for their assistance. I thank Oktay Özel for his assistance with documents from the National Library (Millî Kütüphane) in Ankara, and Senem O'Brien at İnkılap publishers in Istanbul for introducing me to Ms. Aslıhan Karay Özdaş, who in turn hosted me at Refik Halid Karay's former residence in Esentepe, replete with his furnishings as they were during his life. It was the closest one could come to meeting Refik Halid Karay in person, and it was immensely helpful in understanding the man and his work.

Çetin Altan and Solmaz Kamuran, Ahmet Altan, Murat Belge, and Halil Berktay gave me important insights on opposition past and present. Ayhan Aktar, Selim Deringil, and Sinan Kuneralp were wonderful interlocutors regarding scholarship as well as contemporary society and politics. Edhem Eldem has provided encouragement, corrections, and necessary skepticism which never borders on condescension, which I appreciate. And I am grateful to Şükrü Hanioğlu for answering key questions about the CUP along the way. Mustafa Aksakal, Jale Boğa-Robertson, Alp Eren Topal, Adam Mestyan, Selim Karlıtekin, Merve Tezcanlı, and Seda Altuğ all helped provide me with important sources, and I thank them for their effort and time. Mehmet Kentel of the Istanbul Research Institute cheerfully and generously provided the image, from the Suna and İnan Kıraç Foundation Photography Collection, used for the cover of this book.

Friends who read one or more of the iterations of part or all of this book include Aimee Genell and Michael Houk, İpek Yosmaoğlu, Roxani Margariti, Veli Yashin, Bedross Der Matossian, Louis Fishman, Rashid Khalidi, Victoria de Grazia, Palmira Brummett, Adrien Zakar, Orçun Can Okan, and Mana Kia. Colleagues in the Department of History at Berkeley provided helpful comments: David Henkin, Tom Laqueur, Maria Mavroudi, Maureen Miller, Michael Nylan, Caitlin Rosenthal, Ethan Shagan, Yuri Slezkine, and Rebecca Herman Weber. The Berkeley Ottoman

Seminar on Crete that I organized in summer 2017 was a productive and intensive discussion of the press in the armistice years, and I thank the following friends and colleagues for joining me there: Züleyha Çolak, Carole Woodall, Lerna Ekmekçioğlu, Amy Mills, Aimee Genell, and Janet Klein. Special thanks go to Baki Tezcan and Ussama Makdisi for reading all of the first iteration of the book, which had a long way to go, and providing very helpful comments on it. Baki Tezcan, in particular, brought my attention to important dimensions I had overlooked in the first iteration of the manuscript, which helped me to overhaul my approach and analysis. Anonymous reviewers at UC Press provided helpful comments, as did those who participated in a manuscript conference I held, again thanks to support from the Townsend Center and the Department of History at UC Berkeley: Peggy Anderson, Janaki Bakhle, Karen Barkey, Houri Berberian, John Connelly, Ben Fortna, Abhishek Kaicker, Hasan Kayali, Anneka Lenssen, Harsha Ram, Caitlin Rosenthal, Jonathan Sheehan, Wen-Hsin Yeh, and Peter Zinoman. Lâle Can did far more than just read and comment on chapters. She provided countless, extensive, and specific suggestions for revision that made this a far stronger and better-written book than it would have been, and for that I am very grateful. Rifa'at Abou-El-Haj has been an unwavering source of intellectual stimulation, moral support, and friendship for twenty-five years, and I cannot thank him enough for his faith and optimism.

I'd also like to thank friends who provided the invaluable moral support to make this and many other things possible over the last many years: Justine Karmozyn, Amy Mills, Caitlin and Guy Dixon, Herro Mustafa, Phoebe and Christos Minias, Abhishek Kaicker and Stacey Van Vleet, Vangelis Kechriotis (who passed away, tragically, in 2015) and Ceyda Arslan, Christina Procopiou and Cristina Mendoza, Magda Dimaki, Cleo Cacoulidi, Thandi Mbityana, Abigail Snyder, and Sally Johnston, as well as extended family members Eleni and Kostas Hainoglou, Dimitra and Dimitris Stogiannis, Alexandra Katsiani and Thanasis Chondros, Menia Spiridonaki, Olga Papadopoulou, and Abbas Yaghobi and Maya Tomaç. Persis Berlekamp, Aimee Genell, and Lale Can provided much needed friendship, moral support, humor, and intellectual engagement across several tumultuous years for all of us. May the coming years be easier than the past few have been.

My editor at UC Press, Niels Hooper, has been, as always, supportive and encouraging even when my ideas were still incipient. I appreciate his willingness to take risks and his enthusiasm. Martha Schulman and Paul Bessemer stepped in at the eleventh hour with wonderful suggestions for revisions that helped me sharpen the points I was trying to make, and that is deeply appreciated.

I owe a special debt of gratitude to Anne and Nick Germanacos, who were there for me and my family like no one else during the most difficult time in my life. Without their support I do not want to think what my or my family's circumstances would be right now. I am forever grateful to them and appreciative of their generosity and kindness.

I thank my mother Helen Philliou, and my father Peter Philliou, who passed away in 2016 after thirteen years of agony and suffering for all of us, and most of all for him. May he rest in peace, finally, and may his memory be eternal. I am forever grateful to my grandparents and extended family for providing me with a strong foundation in the past and a brimming research agenda for life. I thank Jim Philliou and Pat Lee, and Thea Philliou for their humor and camaraderie through many difficult times, and Reza Yaghobi for his friendship.

My children, Daphne and Erfan, mean everything to me and have enriched my life in countless ways. They have never experienced a mom who was not in the process of writing a book; I hope this will be something inspiring and not infuriating for them when they look back on their childhoods. I dedicate this book to them. May the world they are growing up into be one where uncomfortable truths can be told, and where political disagreement turns into opportunity and conversation rather than violent conflict. *Muhalefet* is a universal problem of power. I wrote this book in the hopes of starting a universal conversation, beginning in Turkey.

NOTES

INTRODUCTION

1. *Muhalefet* is derived from Arabic (*mukhālafa*), although, as was often the case with Ottoman Turkish words borrowed from Arabic, its meanings changed as it was adapted into Ottoman Turkish, and then again, as I argue in this book, in response to the specific historical and political experience of the twentieth century. In contemporary Arabic, the word *mukhālafa* means the structural condition of opposition (as in opposite), and opposition as in partisan opposition party; the word *mu'āraḍa*, a word not used in modern Turkish, denotes dissent, disagreement, and opposition. The fact that both meanings are still contained in the same word *muhalefet* in Turkish is testament to the unique history and problem of opposition that I explore in this book.

2. For the English translation of Nutuk, see Mustafa Kemal (Atatürk), *A Speech Delivered by Ghazi Mustapha Kemal, President of the Turkish Republic, October 1927* (Leipzig: K. F. Koehler, 1929). For the modern Turkish transliteration of the original 1927 text, see *Nutuk, Gazi Mustafa Kemal Tarafından* [The great speech/Nutuk, by Gazi Mustafa Kemal] (İstanbul: Yapı Kredi Yayınları, 2011).

3. On Ottoman liberalism, see Şerif Mardin, *The Genesis of Young Ottoman Thought: A Study in the Modernization of Turkish Political Ideas* (Princeton, NJ: Princeton University Press, 1962). On the liberal path not taken in the modern Middle East, including a consideration of Halide Edip as a liberal hero, see Elizabeth F. Thompson, *Justice Interrupted: The Struggle for Constitutional Government in the Middle East* (Cambridge, MA: Harvard University Press, 2013).

4. On the history of the Young Turk movement leading up to the 1908 Constitutional Revolution, see M. Şükrü Hanioğlu, *The Young Turks in Opposition* (New York: Oxford University Press, 1995); and *Preparation for a Revolution: The Young Yurks, 1902–1908* (Oxford: Oxford University Press, 2001).

5. It has been well documented that there was continuity, both in personnel and in political institutions, between the Ottoman Sultanate and the Turkish Republic, and that the "Unionists," or members of the Committee of Union and

Progress, were instrumental in that continuity. Erik Jan Zürcher's *The Unionist Factor: The Rôle of the Committee of Union and Progress in the Turkish National Movement 1905–1926* (Leiden: Brill, 1984) pioneered this revisionist project, and his thesis has been further substantiated and developed by many scholars, Turkish and non-Turkish, over the last thirty years. One point I hope to make in the following pages is that these continuities were hardly unknown to those going through the transition; instead, they were observed and called out as the transition was occurring, and before, during, and after the establishment of official history in 1927. To call out the continuities between the Unionist and the nationalist project, and then the republic, was in fact a defining feature of *muhalefet*.

6. Hülya Adak, "National Myths and Self-Narrations: Mustafa Kemal's *Nutuk* and Halide Edip's *The Turkish Ordeal*." *South Atlantic Quarterly* 102, nos. 2/3 (2003): 509–28.

7. Michael Meeker, *A Nation of Empire: The Ottoman Legacy of Turkish Modernity* (Berkeley, CA: University of California Press, 2002).

8. Refik Halid has been given a place, relatively marginal, in the history of Turkish literature. One of his stories, "The Joke," appears in *An Anthology of Turkish Literature*, ed. Kemal Silay (Bloomington: University of Indiana Press, 1996), 303–8; Erol Koroglu, in *Ottoman Propaganda and Turkish Literature* (London: I.B. Tauris, 2007), devotes part of a chapter to Refik's World War I–era prose.

9. See, for instance, Palmira Brummett, *Image and Imperialism in the Ottoman Revolutionary Press, 1908–1911* (Albany: State University of New York Press, 2000) on political/satirical cartoons.

10. See, for instance, Soner Çagaptay, *Islam, Secularism, and Nationalism in Modern Turkey: Who Is a Turk?* (London: Routledge, 2006); and Carter Vaughn Findley, *Turkey, Islam, Secularism, and Modernity: A History, 1789–2007* (New Haven, CT: Yale University Press, 2010).

11. M Şükrü Hanioğlu, in his *Atatürk: An Intellectual Biography* (Princeton, NJ: Princeton University Press, 2011), argues that Atatürk was at once a pragmatist who was eclectic in his deployment of ideology, and that in many senses his achievement was the fulfillment of a Unionist vision.

12. Debates persist in historiography about the "Islamic" nature, or not, of opposition to the CUP, and specifically regarding the 1909 counterrevolution, which was and is still framed by some as an uprising to reinstitute Shari'a in exchange for the Ottoman Constitution. See, for instance, Erik Jan Zürcher, "The Ides of April: A Fundamentalist Uprising in Istanbul in 1909?," in *The Young Turk Legacy and Nation Building* (London: I.B. Tauris, 2010), 73–83. The Unionists consistently labeled their opposition *irtica*, or conservative/religious reaction, equating opposition to them with opposition to the constitution, and in effect to progress. As we will see, many who opposed the Unionists were very much in favor of constitutional rule but were opposed to Unionist tactics, and thus to the Unionists' understanding of constitutionalism. In the early republic, the brief life of the Progressive Republican Party (1924–25) was bound up with the question of the Caliphate, and that episode of partisan opposition ended with the abolition of the Caliphate. While

there is certainly much work to be done in addressing these issues, my focus here is on the relationship between Refik and *muhalefet*; for his part, he was not involved in the 1909 counterrevolution, and he was already in exile in Syria in 1924, so was not directly involved in the Progressive Republican Party or the debate about abolition of the Caliphate.

13. See Christine M. Philliou, "The Armenian Genocide and the Politics of Knowledge," *PublicBooks* (May 2015) for a discussion of the profusion of scholarship on the genocide in the past two decades. The time is ripe for historians and social scientists to incorporate this new wealth of scholarship into the mainstream scholarship of the late Ottoman Empire and emergence of the Turkish Republic, moving beyond the binaries of denial/vilification and continuity/rupture.

CHAPTER I. AGAINST POWER?

1. Ali Birinci, *Tarihin Alacakaranlığında* (Istanbul: Dergah, 2010), 413. For early biographical information, see also Şerif Aktaş, *Refik Halit Karay* (Istanbul: Akçağ, 2004), 15; and Hikmet Münir Ebcioğlu, *Refik Halid Karay Kendi Yazılar ile* (Istanbul: Semih Lûtfi Kitabevi, ca. 1940), 3.The following sources attest to his having resided in Şehzâdebaşı: Ottoman Prime Ministry Archives (Başbakanlık Osmanlı Arşivleri, hereafter BOA), DH.MKT 2909: 14 d. 1327. Ş. 7 (August 24, 1909); and Refii Cevat Ulunay, "En büyük kaybım" [My most bitter loss], *Milliyet*, July 20, 1965.

2. Yahya Kemal recalled a visit to the Erenköy villa in 1912: "It looked to be one of the villas of the last officials of the Abdülhamid era." Yahya Kemal, *Siyasî ve Edebî Portreler* (Istanbul: Yapı Kredi Yayınları, 2002), 43.

3. Ebcioğlu states that Refik Halid's father's ancestor, İsa Karakayışoğlu, came to Istanbul seven generations earlier from Mudurnu in Anatolia. Since arriving in Istanbul, the family had multiplied and split into several branches in Istanbul and Rumeli, one of which was the Topuzlu family (suggesting that Cemil Topuzlu [1868–1958], the prominent surgeon, one-time mayor of Istanbul, and associate of Refik Halid's, was also his distant relative). Hikmet Münir Ebcioğlu, *Refik Halid Kendi Yazılar ile* (İstanbul: Semih Lûtfi Kitabevi, ca. 1940), 3. Şerif Aktaş mentions the recollection of Refik Halid's sons, Ender and Ömer Karay, that Refik Halid was descended from family members who had come to Istanbul "before the time of Abdülmecit [1839–1861]" (*Refik Halit Karay*, 15). Finally, Ali Birinci, the only biographer to have had access to the General Security Archives (Emniyet Genel Müdürlüğü Arşivleri), cites a source there that gives the family's place of origin even before Mudurnu as Emirdağ, which was in the original heartland of the Ottoman emirate from the fourteenth century. Birinci, *Tarihin Alacakaranlığında*, 414.

4. For more on the Ottoman Bank, see, for instance, Şevket Pamuk, *Monetary History of the Ottoman Empire* (Cambridge, UK: Cambridge University Press, 2000) and *Ottoman Empire and European Capitalism, 1820–1913: Trade, Investment, and Production* (Cambridge, UK: Cambridge University Press, 1987); and

Jacques Thobie, *Intérêts et imperialisme français dan l'Empire ottoman, 1895–1914* (Paris: Sorbonne, 1977).

5. Ebcioğlu, *Refik Halid Karay Kendi Yazılar ile*, 3. One Mehmed Halid Efendi (?–1853) is listed as having been the finance minister (Maliye Nazırı) from June 1850 until August 1851 and minister of pious endowments (Evkaf Nazırı) from August 1851 until March 1852. Sinan Kuneralp, *Son Dönem Osmanlı Erkân ve Ricali (1839–1922): Prosopografik Rehber* [Late Ottoman officialdom: Prosopographic guide] (Istanbul: Isis, 1999), 95. It is possible that this was Refik Halid's paternal grandfather, given that his father was born in 1849, and he, too, worked in the Finance Ministry.

6. Kemal, *Siyasî ve Edebî Portreler*, 43.

7. Kemal, *Siyasî ve Edebî Portreler*, 43.

8. See, for instance, Madeline Zilfi, *The Politics of Piety: Ottoman Ulema in the Post-Classical Age* (Minneapolis, MN: Bibliotheca Islamica, 1988).

9. Ebcioğlu, *Refik Halid Kendi Yazılar ile*, 4.

10. See his family tree in Taha Toros Arşivi, Dosya No. 87 (Refik Halit Karay), doc. no. 001637123019.

11. Ebcioğlu, *Refik Halid Kendi Yazılar ile*, 8.

12. Ebcioğlu, *Refik Halid Kendi Yazılar ile*, 9 (excerpted from *Bir Avuç Saçma* [A handful of nonsense]; and Ulunay, "En acı kayıbım."

13. Benjamin Fortna, *Imperial Classroom: Islam, the State, and Education in the Late Ottoman Empire* (Oxford: Oxford University Press, 2000), 116. On primary education at the same time, see Selçuk Akşin Sömel, *The Modernization of Public Education in the Ottoman Empire, 1839–1908: Islamization, Autocracy, and Discipline* (Leiden: Brill, 2000).

14. On Galatasaray, see Adnan Şişman, *Galatasaray Mekteb-i Sultanisi'nin Kuruluşu ve İlk Eğitim Yılları 1868–1871* [The establishment of the Galatasaray Imperial School and its first instructional years, 1868–1871] (Istanbul: Edebiyat Fakültesi Yayınevi, 1989); İhsan Süngü, "Galatasaray Lise'nin Kuruluşu" [The establishment of the Galatasaray Lyceum], *Belleten* 7, no. 28 (1943): 315–47; Louis de Salve, "L'enseignement en Turquie: Le lycée imperial de Galata-Sérai," *Revue des deux mondes* 5 (1874): 836–53; and François Georgeon, "La formation des élites à la fin de l'Empire ottoman: Le cas de Galatasaray," *Revue du monde musulman et de la Méditerranée* 72 (1994): 15–25.

15. Fortna, *Imperial Classroom*, 102; see also Roderic Davison, *Reform in the Ottoman Empire* (Princeton, NJ: Princeton University Press, 1965), 246.

16. Fortna, *Imperial Classroom*, 104, summarizing Salve, "L'enseignement en Turquie."

17. On Ali Suavi, see Şerif Mardin, *The Genesis of Young Ottoman Thought* (Princeton, NJ: Princeton University Press, 1962).

18. Fortna, *Imperial Classroom*, 108.

19. Fortna, *Imperial Classroom*, 110.

20. Fatma Müge Göçek, in *Rise of the Bourgeoisie, Demise of Empire: Ottoman Westernization and Social Change* (New York: Oxford University Press, 1996),

discusses a bifurcated bourgeoisie that developed in the eighteenth and nineteenth centuries along ethnoreligious lines: the (non-Muslim) commercial bourgeoisie and the (Muslim) bureaucratic bourgeoisie.

21. Fortna, *Imperial Classroom*, 110–11.

22. Birinci, *Tarihin Alacakaranlığında*, 415.

23. Refik Halid Karay, *Bir Ömür Boyunca* [Across one lifetime] (Istanbul: İnkılap, 2009), 204.

24. Refik Halid Karay, "Acı bir bahar hatırası" [A painful spring memory], in *Ago Paşa'nın Hatıratı* [Ago Paşa's memoirs] (Istanbul: İnkılap, 2009), 162.

25. Recollection of İsmail Hikmet (Ertaylan) (1889–1967), in *Türk Edebiyatı Tarihi-Osmanlı Kısmı-Yirminci Asır* [Turkish literature—Ottoman section—twentieth century] (Bakû: n.p., 1926), 38; cited in Birinci, *Tarihin Alacakaranlığında*, 415n18.

26. Aktaş, *Refik Halit Karay*, 17–18; and Birinci, *Tarihin Alacakaranlığında*, 416.

27. Refik Halid Karay, *Minelbab ilelmihrab: 1918 mütarekesi devrinde olan biten işlere ve gelip geçen insanlara dair bildiklerim* [*Minelbab ilelmihrab*: What I know about the people and goings-on of the 1918 armistice period] (Istanbul: İnkılâp ve Aka Kitabevleri, 1964), 202; and Aktaş, *Refik Halit Karay*, 20.

28. Aktaş, *Refik Halit Karay*.

29. Refik Halid Karay, "Kaleme nasıl çerağ oldum?" [How did I become an apprentice in a bureau?], in *Kirpinin Dedikleri* (Istanbul: İnkılap, 2009): 110–16. Birinci, in *Tarihin Alacakaranlığında*, 417, claims he began this job May 3, 1908, and only resigned on May 14, 1909, but does not give a source for this assertion.

30. See, for instance, M. Şükrü Hanioğlu, *The Young Turks in Opposition* (Oxford: Oxford University Press, 1995); M. Şükrü Hanioğlu, *Preparation for a Revolution: The Young Turks, 1902–1908* (Oxford: Oxford University Press, 2001); and Selim Deringil, *Well-Protected Domains: Ideology and the Legitimation of Power in the Late Ottoman Empire (1876–1909)* (London: I. B. Tauris, 1998).

31. Ebcioğlu, *Refik Halid Karay Kendi Yazılar ile*, 18; and Aktaş, *Refik Halit Karay*, 19. Abdülhak Şinasi (Hisar) (1887–1963) was a major literary figure and one-time associate of Prince Sabahaddin in Paris and Yahya Kemal. He returned to Istanbul and took part in the national movement, moving to Ankara in 1931 and working at the Ministry of Foreign Affairs.

32. On the heels of translations of major European literary works: Ahmed Hamdi Tanpınar, *XIX. Türk Edebiyatı Tarihi* [Nineteenth-century Turkish literary history] (Istanbul: Yapı Kredi Yayınları, 2006), 263 passim (first published in 1949). Examples of these imported literary forms include Şemsettin Sami's *Taaşşuk-ı Talat ve Fitnat* [The romance of Talat and Fitnat] (1872) and Ahmed Midhat's *Teehül* [Matrimony] (1870) and *Mihnetkeşan* [Les Misérables] (1871). See Robert Finn, *The Early Turkish Novel, 1872–1900* (Istanbul: Isis Press, 1984), 8 passim.

33. Rüşen Eşref Ünaydın, *Diyorlar ki* [They say that . . .] (Istanbul: Devlet Kitap Müdürlüğü, 1972), 231; and Aktaş, *Refik Halit Karay*, 31.

34. On *Servet-i Fünun*, see, for instance, Attila Özkırımlı, *Tevfik Fikret* (Istanbul: Cem, 1990), 35 passim. Özkırımlı points out that the journal had the support of the "palace" (i.e., Abdülhamid) ("*sarayca da korunuyordu*"), although this did not

mean it was immune to government control and censorship (40). Halid Ziya, one of the key members of the group, would be Sultan Mehmed V's chief scribe (*Başkâtip*) when he assumed the throne in 1909.

35. Hüseyin Cahit (Yalçın) (1875–1957) became a staunch Unionist; editor of the CUP organ, *Tanin*; and after 1922, editor of the official Republican newspaper in Ankara, *Hâkimiyet-i Milliye* (National sovereignty).

36. Karay, *Bir Ömür Boyunca*, 212.

37. Karay, *Bir Ömür Boyunca*.

38. Ebcioğlu, *Refik Halid Karay Kendi Yazılar ile*, 25.

39. See Ebcioğlu, *Refik Halid Karay Kendi Yazılar ile*, 25–27 for Refik Halid's humorous depiction of the atmosphere in which the circle was founded and its name decided upon. The original proposal was "Emel-i Sina," which translates to something like, "Destination: Sinai," as in Mt. Sinai, evoking the biblical Exodus and Moses as prophet. A long discussion ensued about the pros and cons of this as opposed to "Fecr-i Âti."

40. Refik Halid Karay, "Son on senelik edebiyata dair" [On literature of the past 10 years], *Yeni Mecmua* 3 (ca. 1918): 54.

41. Karay, "Son on senelik edebiyata dair."

42. Refik Halid recalls having known Ahmet İhsan since his earliest years and of always having had a fondness for him. Aktaş, *Refik Halit Karay*, 21.

43. Aktaş, *Refik Halit Karay*, 21; and Ebcioğlu, *Refik Halid Karay Kendi Yazılar ile*, 18–19.

44. Ebcioğlu, *Refik Halid Karay Kendi Yazılar ile*, 18–19.

45. BOA DH. MKT 2909: 14 (August 24, 1909; August 15, 1909)

46. Refik Halid himself lamented, thirty years later, that he did not possess a single copy of *Son Havadis* and didn't know if there were any extant copies. *İlk Adım* [The first step] (Istanbul: İnkılâp, 2009), 57. I have found a copy of the first issue held in the Hakkı Tarık Us collection at the Beyazit Library in Istanbul. Birinci, in *Tarihin Alacakaranlığında*, claims the first issue came out on September 11, 1909; he does not provide a source for this information. The copy I located is clearly dated "September 1st, 1909, European calendar" (*1 Eylül 1909 Frengi*).

47. For a hint of the social conditions in Istanbul during the Second Constitutional Era, see Palmira Brummett, *Image and Imperialism in the Ottoman Revolutionary Press, 1908–1911* (Albany: State University of New York Press, 2000); or Nadir Özbek, *Osmanlı İmparatorluğu'nda Sosyal Devlet: Siyaset, iktidar, ve meşrutiyet, 1876–1914* [The social state in the Ottoman Empire: Politics, power, and constitutionalism] (Istanbul: İletişim, 2002).

48. Ebcioğlu, *Refik Halid Kendi Yazılar ile*, 20 (quoting Refik Halid).

49. Translation by Christine Philliou; transliterated modern Turkish version found in Refik Halid Karay, *Memleket Hikâyeleri* [Homeland stories] (Istanbul: İnkılâp Yayınevi, 2009), 185–90. The story is signed as having been written in Erenköy in 1909.

50. Karay, *Memleket Hikâyeleri*, 151–59. The story is signed as having been written in Erenköy, where Refik Halid spent his summers, in 1909.

51. Tropes of frustration and resentment would become commonplace a decade later, when Istanbul was under European occupation; see, for instance, Erdağ Göknar, "Between 'Ottoman' and 'Turk' Literary Narrative and the Transition from Empire to Republic" (PhD diss., University of Washington–Seattle, 2004).

52. March 31, 1909, was, in the new calendar, April 13, 1909.

53. For descriptions in the contemporary press of the initial euphoria in the wake of July 1908, see Michelle U. Campos, *Ottoman Brothers: Muslims, Christians, and Jews in Early Twentieth-Century Palestine* (Stanford, CA: Stanford University Press, 2011). For accounts of the so-called 31 March Incident, see Feroz Ahmad, *Young Turks: The Committee of Union and Progress in Turkish Politics, 1908–1914* (Oxford: Clarendon Press, 1969); Nader Sohrabi, *Revolution and Constitutionalism in the Ottoman Empire and Iran, 1902–1910* (Cambridge, UK: Cambridge University Press, 2011); and Erik Jan Zürcher, "The Ides of April: A Fundamentalist Uprising in Istanbul in 1909?," in *The Young Turk Legacy and Nation Building: From the Ottoman Empire to Atatürk's Turkey* (London: I. B. Tauris, 2010), 73–83.

54. He recalls that he stopped publishing *Son Havadis* and decided to spend his money on his trip to Paris, so we can date the trip to the autumn of 1909. Refik Halid Karay, "İlk Sefer" [The first voyage], in *İlk Adım* [The first step] (Istanbul: İnkılap, 2009), 57).

55. Aykut Kansu, *Politics in Post-Revolutionary Turkey, 1908–1913* (Leiden: Brill, 2000), 185.

56. Kansu, *Politics in Post-Revolutionary Turkey*, 140–42.

57. Karay, "İlk Sefer," 47.

58. Rifa'a Rafi' al-Tahtawi and Daniel L. Newman. *An Imam in Paris: Al-Tahtawi's Visit to France, 1826–1831* (London: Saqi Books, 2011).

59. Al-Tahtawi and Daniel L. Newman, *An Imam in Paris*, 50–51.

60. This disillusionment is nicely encapsulated by a friendship he made on the boat. At dinner the first night he met one Monsieur Théodore Birtch, a writer for *Le Monde Illustré*, whom Refik Halid took to be French (and who recognized Refik Halid as the owner-editor of the short-lived *Son Havadis* newspaper!), until he learned that his real name was Berç Bezirciyan and that his father had been a master craftsman in (Ottoman) Çırağan Palace before leaving Istanbul "for reasons [Refik Halid] can't remember" and settling in Europe. Monsieur Birtch might have been a Paris-born French citizen, but he was also the direct descendant of Ottoman Armenians (Karay, "İlk Sefer," 64). He wasn't as different from Refik Halid as the latter at first expected; similarly, Paris wasn't as different from Istanbul as he had imagined.

61. Karay, "İlk Sefer," 68.

62. Karay, "İlk Sefer," 69.

63. Karay, "İlk Sefer," 77.

64. Karay, "İlk Sefer," 82.

65. Karay, "İlk Sefer," 83.

66. For evidence of lively discussions that included the concept of *muhalefet* (connected grammatically to *ihtilaf,* or dispute), see Alp Eren Topal, ed., *Sürgünde*

Muhalefet: Namık Kemal'ın Hürriyet gazetesi I (1868–1869) [Opposition in exile: Namık Kemal's *Hürriyet* newspaper] (Istanbul: Vakıfbank Cultural Foundation, 2019), 58, 60 passim; see also Mardin, *Genesis of Young Ottoman Thought.*

67. See Hanioğlu, *Young Turks in Opposition.*

68. Hanioğlu, in *Preparation for a Revolution*, 4–6, points out the dizzying array of factions and parties that existed between 1902 and 1908, emphasizing that "each of these organizations and figures could be the subject of a book; no single essay can include all the relevant details."

69. M. Şükrü Hanioğlu, *Preparation for a Revolution* (Oxford: Oxford University Press, 2001).

70. Niyazi Berkes, *The Development of Secularism in Turkey* (Montreal: McGill University Press, 1964).

71. Sohrabi, *Revolution and Constitutionalism in the Ottoman Empire and Iran.*

CHAPTER 2. CONTRADICTIONS OF OTTOMAN CONSTITUTIONALISM

1. For the euphoria, see Michelle Campos, *Ottoman Brothers: Muslims, Christians, and Jews in Early Twentieth-Century Palestine* (Stanford, CA: Stanford University Press, 2011), ch. 1; and for the fading of that euphoria, see Bedross Der Matossian, *Shattered Dreams of Revolution* (Stanford, CA: Stanford University Press, 2016).

2. Palmira Brummett, *Image and Imperialism in Ottoman Revolutionary Press, 1908–1911* (Albany: State University of New York Press, 2000).

3. *Cem* (alternative names in times when *Cem* was forced to close down included *Kalem, Alem,* and *Cemşit*) was run by Salih Cimcoz and Celâl Esad (Arseven), both from pasha families. According to Brummett, like Refik Halid, *Kalem/Cem* "vigorously supported constitutionalism but reserved the right to criticize both the parliament and the dominant CUP." Brummett, *Image and Imperialism*, 30. "Tarih-i Devair-i Mebusan" [History in the times of the parliamentarians] appears in *Kirpinin Dedikleri* [The Porcupine's utterances] (Istanbul: Ahmet İhsan, 1326), 123–165.

4. They were published by Ahmet İhsan, who was a prominent intellectual, editor of *Servet-i Fünun*, member of the liberal coalition, and a long-standing patron of the Halid family.

5. Yakup Kadri (Karaosmanoğlu), *Gençlik ve Edebiyat Hatıraları* (Yenişehir-Ankara: Bilgi Yayınevi, 1969); Yahya Kemal, *Siyasî ve Edebî Portreler* [Political and literary portraits] (Istanbul: Yapı Kredi Yayınları, 2006); and Hikmet Münir Ebcioğlu, *Refik Halid Karay Kendi Yazılar ile* (Istanbul: Semih Lûtfi Kitabevi, ca. 1940), 28.

6. See Campos, *Ottoman Brothers*, and Der Matossian, *Shattered Dreams of Revolution*, for two recent discussions of this ambiguity.

7. Nader Sohrabi, *Revolution and Constitutionalism in the Ottoman Empire and Iran* (Cambridge, UK: Cambridge University Press, 2011); and Der Matossian, *Shattered Dreams of Revolution*.

8. On the Freedom and Accord Party, see Ali Birinci, *Hürriyet ve İtilaf Fırkası: II. Meşrûtiyet devrinde İttihat ve Terakki'ye karşı çıkanlar* [The Freedom and Accord Party: Those who opposed the Union and Progress in the Second Constitutional Era] (Istanbul: Dergâh Yayınları, 1990); and Tarık Zafer Tunaya, *Türkiye de Siyasal Partiler,* c. I, *İkinci Meşrûtiyet dönemi (1908–1918)* [Political parties in Turkey, vol. I, Second Constitutional Era] (Istanbul: Hürriyet Vakfı, 1984), 263–312

9. Sohrabi, *Revolution and Constitutionalism*; and Der Matossian, *Shattered Dreams of Revolution*.

10. Sohrabi, *Revolution and Constitutionalism*, for instance, seems to imply that the leaders of the CUP were premeditated in their actions from the start and only limited by circumstances and contingencies, which they took full advantage of. His analysis focuses on the first year after the Constitutional Revolution, implying that by the suppression of the counterrevolution in 1909 the shift to CUP supremacy had already occurred. Feroz Ahmad's *Young Turks: The Committee of Union and Progress in Turkish Politics, 1908–1914* (Oxford: Clarendon Press, 1969), however, tells us that the CUP fell apart and reconstituted itself a few times within this five-year period, using the Balkan War to catapult itself back to power from near oblivion.

11. Ahmed Emin (Yalman), "The Development of Turkey as Measured by Its Press" (PhD diss., Columbia University, 1914); and Brummett, *Image and Imperialism*, introduction, app. 1.

12. Brummett, *Image and Imperialism*, 30. She lists sixty-eight satirical journals that appeared for varying lengths of time between July 1908 and late 1911.

13. Brummett, *Image and Imperialism*, 5. These included "the lack of political and social freedom, the debilitated economy, the obsolete military, the perceived corruption of officials at all levels of the government, the dearth of opportunity for a new class of Western-educated bureaucrats, the prostitution of the Ottoman economy to European economic interests, and the cultural schizophrenia created by Ottoman reform programs and by European dominance."

14. See İpek Yosmaoğlu, "Chasing the Printed Word," *Turkish Studies Association Journal* 27 (2003): 15–49, on censorship regimes in the Hamidian and constitutional periods.

15. See Yosmaoğlu, "Chasing the Printed Word."

16. Mehmet Hastaş, *Ahmet Samim: 2. Meşrutiyet'te Muhalif bir Gazeteci* [Ahmet Samim: A *muhalif* journalist in the Second Constitutional Era] (Istanbul: İletişim, 2012).

17. For details on Zeki Bey's assassination and its significance, see Aykut Kansu, *Politics in Post-Revolutionary Turkey, 1908–1913* (Leiden: Brill, 2000), 250–51.

18. Bedross Der Matossian, "Ethnic Politics in Post-revolutionary Ottoman Empire: Armenians, Arabs, and Jews During the Second Constitutional Period, 1908–1909" (PhD diss., Columbia University, 2008).

19. See Selçuk Gürsoy, "Refik Halid Karay'ın 1910 *İştirak* dergisinde yayınlanan hikâyesi 'Dede Hasan'ın Vicdanı'" [Refik Halid Karay's story published in *İştirak* in 1910, "Dede Hasan's conscience"], *Toplumsal Tarih*, April 2013, 36–44, for a transliteration into modern Turkish and a contextualization of this story, which originally appeared in February 1910.

20. N. Ahmet Özalp, *Refik Halid: Okları kırılmış Kirpi* [Refik Halid: The broken-quilled Porcupine] (Istanbul: Kapı Yayınları, 2011), 103–6; and Refik Halid Karay, *Kirpinin Dedikleri* [The Porcupine's utterances] (Istanbul: İnkılap, 2009), 62–67. It is worth mentioning that this story appeared only in the original 1911 and 1920 editions, not in the 1939 and subsequent editions.

21. Biographer Ali Birinci claims that Refik Halid was actually employed in the Finance Ministry where his father was a cashier (*veznedar*), beginning two months before the Constitutional Revolution, in May 1908, and "resigned" in May 14, 1909. Ali Birinci, *Tarihin Alacakaranlığında: Meşâhiri Meçhûleden Birkaç Zât* [At the twilight of history: Some unknown famous people] (Istanbul: Dergâh, 2010), 417; and Refik Halid Karay, *Bir Ömür Boyunca* [Across one lifetime] (Istanbul: İnkılâp, 2009), 219; and Ebcioğlu, *Refik Halid Karay Kendi Yazılar ile*, 29.

22. Mehmet Ö. Alkan, ed., *Gönüllü Sürgünden Zorunlu Sürgüne: Bütün Eserleri* [From voluntary exile to forced exile: Complete works] (Istanbul: Yapı Kredi Yayınları, 2007), 270 passim. See also Ahmet Ersoy, "Prince Sabahaddin: A Second Account on Individual Initiative," in *Modernism: The Creation of Nation-States*, ed. Vangelis Kechriotis, Ahmet Ersoy, and Maciej Gorny (Budapest: Central European University Press, 2010), 331 passim.

23. Refik Halid Karay, "Teşebbüs-i Şahsi? Heyhat!" [Personal initiative? Alas!], in *Kirpinin Dedikleri* (Istanbul: İnkılâp, 2009), 14–19.

24. Refik Halid Karay, "Meşrûtiyetperver Çinlilere Nasihat" [Advice for the Chinese constitutionalists], in *Kirpinin Dedikleri* (Istanbul: İnkılâp, 2009), 117–22.

25. Ebcioğlu, *Refik Halid Karay Kendi Yazılar ile*.

26. By secret society here he likely means the anti-CUP groups that had formed within the military in 1910, with Sadık Paşa playing an important role. The society was exposed in late 1910 or early 1911. See, for instance, Kansu, *Politics in Post-Revolutionary Turkey*, 215–16.

27. Ebru Boyar, *Ottomans, Turks, and the Balkans: Empire Lost, Relations Altered* (London: I. B. Tauris, 2007); and Eyal Ginio, *The Ottoman Culture of Defeat: The Balkan Wars and Their Aftermath* (London: Hurst, 2016).

28. See Yosmaoğlu, "Chasing the Printed Word"; and Baykal, "The Ottoman Press, 1908–1938."

29. On Filibeli Ahmet Hilmi, see Amit Bein, "A 'Young Turk' Islamic Intellectual: Filibeli Ahmed Hilmi and the Diverse Intellectual Legacies of the Late Ottoman Empire," *International Journal of Middle East Studies* 39, no. 4 (2007): 606–25. He was poisoned in October 1914.

30. Şehbenderzâde Filibeli Ahmed Hilmi, *Muhalefetin İflası (Hürriyet ve İtilaf Fırkası)* [The bankruptcy of the opposition: The Freedom and Accord Party] (Istanbul: Nehir Yayınları, 1991), 39–40. Originally published as Ahmet

Hilmi Şehbenderzâde, *Muhalifetin İflası* (Konstantiniyye: Hikmet Matbaa-yı İslamiyesi, 1331).

CHAPTER 3. THE JOKE

1. Gümülcineli İsmail Hakkı was not, in fact, a deputy for Sinop. He had been the CUP deputy for Gümülcine between 1908 and 1911 and was in the leadership of the Freedom and Accord Party by this time.

2. Cemal Paşa, *Memories of a Turkish Statesman—1913–1919 by Djemal Pasha, Formerly Governor of Constantinople, Imperial Ottoman Naval Minister, and Commander of the Fourth Army in Sinai, Palestine, and Syria* (New York: George H. Doran, 1922), 16.

3. Feroz Ahmad, *Young Turks: The Committee of Union and Progress in Turkish Politics, 1908–1914* (Oxford: Clarendon Press, 1969), 113–14. In Yücel Demirel, ed., *Dersim Mebusu Lütfi Fikri Bey'in Günlüğü: "Daima Muhalefet"* [Dersim deputy Lütfi Fikri Bey's diary: Always *muhalefet*] (Istanbul: ARMA Yayınları, 1991), 59, Lütfi Fikri Bey noted in his entry for March 26, 1913, two significant developments: first, that the Şevket Paşa government had made it impossible to continue publishing newspapers with their provisional laws and by raising the fees involved; and second, that Edirne had fallen to the Unionists.

4. Cemal Paşa, *Memories of a Turkish Statesman*, 18.

5. Cemal Paşa, *Memories of a Turkish Statesman*, 36.

6. Demirel, *Dersim Mebusu Lütfi Fikri Bey'in Günlüğü*, 102 passim. In his entry for June 11, 1913, he reports the assassination of Mahmud Şevket Paşa, and on June 14 he begins reporting the first arrests among his friends and neighbors in Ayastefanos, naming three specific individuals and going on to state that "many men known as *muhalifs*, hundreds of them, from Ayastefanos and everywhere else," were being arrested. He invokes the violence of four years earlier in the wake of the 1909 counterrevolution, accusing the Unionists of trying to stage a repeat of those events. He points out that the two incidents are qualitatively different, in part because in 1909 "except for the reactionaries (*mürtecis*) everyone was with them [the Unionists]. But not now!" (104–5) On June 18 he reports that those that had been arrested were shipped off to Sinop (107–8).

7. Ali Birinci, *Tarihin Alacakaranlığında: Meşâhiri Meçhûleden Birkaç Zât*. [At the twilight of history: Some unknown famous people] (Istanbul: Dergâh, 2010, 417). Mustafa Suphi had split with the CUP at the Ankara Congress in August 1912 along with Yusuf Akçura and Ahmet Ferit (Tek), also bound for Sinop, and founded the Millî Meşrutiyet Fırkası (National Constitution Party). Mustafa Suphi would eventually be appointed chair of the First Congress of the Turkish Communist Party in Baku in late 1920, and was killed on a boat in the Black Sea in 1921 by supporters of Enver Paşa.

8. Şerif Aktaş, *Refik Halit Karay, Biyografi-İnceleme* [Biography-study] 21 (Kızılay, Ankara : Akçağ, 2004), 40.

9. For details on the history of Sinop, see Alev Çakmakoğlu Kuru, *Sinop Hapishanesi* [Sinop Prison] (Ankara: Atatürk Kültür Merkezi Başkanlığı Yayınları, 2004), 3; and Hüseyin Hilmi, *Sinop Kitabeleri* [Sinop inscriptions] (Sinop: Sinop Matbaası, 1339 [1921–22]), 74.

10. According to Kuran, after the assassination of Mahmud Şevket anyone, rightly or wrongly, deemed by the CUP leaders to be meddling in their policies in Istanbul was sent to Sinop. Ahmet Bedevi Kuran, *İnkılâp Tarihi ve "Jön Türkler"* [History of the revolution and the "Young Turks"] (Istanbul: Tan Matbaası, 1945), 332–34. Kuran had been the personal secretary to Prince Sabahaddin.

11. Kuran, *İnkılâp Tarihi ve "Jön Türkler"*, 334.

12. Aktas, *Refik Halit Karay*, 39.

13. Aktaş, *Refik Halit Karay*, 40–41.

14. Refik Halid Karay, *Bir Ömür Boyunca* [Across one lifetime] (Istanbul: İnkılap, 2009), 202.

15. BOA ŞD. 3146.20; 1335 Ş 13. "Altıncı Daire-i Belediye sabık Tahrirat Başkâtibi Refik Halid Bey'in Sinop'ta ikamete memur bulunduğu sırada vekiline verilmiş olan maaştan artan kısmının verilmesinin talep ettiği."

16. Hikmet Münir Ebcioğlu, *Refik Halid Karay Kendi Yazıları ile* (Istanbul: Semih Lûtfi Kitabevi, ca. 1940), 32–33. 14 Teşrini Evvel 1329 (November 27, 1913), signed "Your Humble Servant, Beyoğlu Municipal Chief Clerk Refik Halid."

17. Ebcioğlu, *Refik Halid Karay Kendi Yazıları ile*, 33.

18. Aktas, *Refik Halit Karay*, 41. He wrote a charming vignette about this district governor (*mutasarrıf*), Müştak Bey, in his later memoir: "Üç mutasarrıf tipi daha" [Three more *mutasarrıf* characters], in *Bir Ömür Boyunca*, 43--46. He ultimately came to express appreciation for his exile, even if tongue in cheek, pointing out that being cloistered in Anatolia saved his life by preventing him from having to serve on any number of war fronts. See "Velinimetim, Sebebi hayatım Cemiyet" [My Benefactor, I owe my life to the Committee], in *Ay Peşinde* [In pursuit of the moon] (Istanbul: İnkılap Kitabevi, 2009), 106–7; and Ali Birinci, *Refik Halid Karay: Ankara* (Istanbul: İnkılap, 2009).

19. Ebcioğlu, *Refik Halid Karay Kendi Yazıları ile*, 31–32.

20. *Bir Ömür Boyunca*, 141.

21. *Bir Ömür Boyunca*, 141.

22. Ebcioğlu, *Refik Halid Karay Kendi Yazılar ile*, 43. *Peyam* (then called *Peyam-ı Sabah*) became, under Ali Kemal's direction, a major voice of the anti-CUP opposition, and then, during the Armistice (Mütareke) period (1919–late 1922) the most vociferously anti-nationalist opposition organ.

23. Setting the scene for the story, Refik Halid would write years later that "before the First World War, Sinop was such a charming and sweet little town in Inner Anatolia, with its Rum quarter, silhouettes of young [Rum] girls floating around, sounds of mandolins to be heard on the streets, and its three hotels and several seaside taverns. It was reminiscent of a village on the Bosphorus, even of those on the European shore." He recalled his flirtations with the Rum girls of Sinop: "In those days Sinop was inhabited by Rum, and Rum girls. We used to go

and flirt with them from afar, watching them in their windows, smiling, making little signs at them and things." *Bir Ömür Boyunca*, 204. The translation of "Şaka" provided here is by Walter Feldman, and appeared as "The Joke," in Kemal Silay, ed. *An Anthology of Turkish Literature* (Bloomington, IN: University of Indiana Press, 1996), 303–8.

24. The *Gülcemal* was so famous as to have been a household name in the late Ottoman Empire and early Republican Turkey. It was analogous to the *Titanic* (it even sank, torpedoed by the British in the Sea of Marmara in 1915, only to be repaired and put back into action). A British/Germanic ocean liner sold to the Ottomans in 1911, it was used to transport Ottoman troops to Yemen that year, to bring Sultan Reşad to the Balkans for his Kosovo visit, and to transport the post between Istanbul and the Black Sea ports, stopping in at each twice a week. Refik Halid wrote about it on several occasions; it was ultimately retired to the Golden Horn in Istanbul; in the Armistice period just after the war, and again in the 1940s, he used it as a symbol for his nostalgic musings and lamentations on the Ottoman past.

25. Ebcioğlu, *Refik Halid Karay Kendi Yazılar ile*, 31.

26. Birinci, *Tarihin Alacakaranlığında*, 419. "Just as we were about to start the third winter of my exile, and the second of the war, all the exiles left Sinop [late summer 1915]. Most of those who had stayed on up to that point were pardoned; it was decided to send a few [28], including us, to Çorum." According to an Ottoman government source, the belongings of those in exile and their families would also be transferred to Çorum. BOA DH.SYS.119 2 (1331 Za 24).

27. Birinci, *Tarihin Alacakaranlığında*, 418; and BOA DH.EUM 5: 1/27 (1332 L 09): "Sinop'ta sürgünde bulunan adi suçluların askerlik yapmak üzere serbest bırakıldığı ve siyasi suçluların hepsinin nakli mümkün değilse serserilerin tefrile edilerek diğerlerinin Çankırı'ya gönderildi."

28. Ebcioğlu, *Refik Halid Karay Kendi Yazıları ile*, 36–37.

29. Ebcioğlu, *Refik Halid Karay Kendi Yazıları ile*, 36–37.

30. Ebcioğlu, *Refik Halid Karay Kendi Yazıları ile* 36–37.

31. Ebcioğlu, *Refik Halid Karay Kendi Yazıları ile*, 37.

32. Birinci, *Refik Halid Karay: Ankara*, 16; and Refii Cevad Ulunay, "En Acı Kayıbım," *Milliyet*, July 25, 1965, 2. According to Birinci, Boyabat would be today's Saraydüzü, although Boyabat is the town in the provincial district (sancak) of Sinop that would indeed have been on the way to Çorum. It was also the town with the largest Armenian community of the region—more than thirty-five hundred people—who were deported and liquidated a few months later. Raymond Kevorkian, *The Armenian Genocide: A Complete History* (London: I. B. Tauris, 2011), 531.

33. *Ay Peşinde*, 108 (according to Birinci in *Refik Halid Karay: Ankara*, 16).

34. "First serious contact with poor, Inner Anatolia": Ebcioğlu, *Refik Halid Karay Kendi Yazılar ile*, 37.

35. Kevorkian, *Armenian Genocide*, 272, 274.

36. Kevorkian, *Armenian Genocide*, 527.

37. Kevorkian, *Armenian Genocide*, 529.

38. Kevorkian, *Armenian Genocide*, 528.

39. See Taylan Esin and Zeliha Etöz, *1916 Ankara Yangını Felaketin Mantığı* [The 1916 Ankara fire: The logic of catastrophe] (Istanbul: İletişim, 2015).

40. *Bir Ömür Boyunca*, 35.

41. Ebcioğlu, *Refik Halid Karay Kendi Yazıları ile*, 39.

42. Ebicoğlu, *Refik Halid Karay Kendi Yazıları ile*, 40. Refik Halid goes on to share a story about this commissioner (*komiser*) that is quite telling: He had also been the censor for correspondence in Çorum and had been in charge of reading/censoring Refik Halid's letters to his family in Istanbul. As he was leaving Çorum for his post in Ankara, he offered Refik Halid a notebook, asking him to look and see if he liked what was inside. His heart sank, thinking he would be subjected to the mediocre literary work of an amateur. He started to read; the sentences were familiar but had no beginning and no end. Then he realized they were from his own letters. The commissioner confirmed this, saying that while he was a censor he copied parts of Refik Halid's letters that he liked. So it was with "this commissioner, who had curiosity about literature, that we were looking for a place for me to live" (Ebcioğlu, *Refik Halid Karay Kendi Yazıları ile*, 40).

43. Kevorkian, *Armenian Genocide*, 485.

44. Kevorkian, *Armenian Genocide*, 495.

45. See Hilmar Kaiser, "Scenes from Angora, 1915: The Commander, the Bureaucrats and Muslim Notables during the Armenian Genocide," in *End of the Ottomans: The Genocide of 1915 and the Politics of Turkish Nationalism*, ed. Hans-Lukas Kieser, Margaret Lavinia Anderson, Seyhan Bayraktar, and Thomas Schmutz (London: I. B. Tauris, 2019), 141–66, for the dynamics then in play within and between the Unionist and provincial administration.

46. Kevorkian, *Armenian Genocide*, 498.

47. See Esin and Etöz, *1916 Ankara Yangını* for an in-depth study of fires throughout Anatolia between 1914 and 1918. As its title suggests, the study focuses on the Ankara fire, drawing in large part on Refik Halid's account.

48. Kevorkian, *Armenian Genocide*, 498. Ali Birinci, in his chapter on Refik Halid Karay in *Tarihin Alacakaranlığında*, provides copious documentation from the Security Directorate and Prime Ministry Archives about the citizenship of the specific individuals affected by the fire and the resources dispatched to help the victims, particularly from the community of Balkan Muslim refugees that had been settled in the town three years earlier.

49. He had cabled the provincial governor of Ankara requesting to be transferred there from Çorum; see *Bir Ömür Boyunca*, 37 passim; for the correspondence between the interior and foreign ministries, security directorate, and Ankara vilayet, see BOA DH.EUM 5 32/3; and Esin and Etöz, *1916 Ankara Yangını*, 105. For a vivid story describing his journey from Çorum to Ankara, see "Kervanda Muaşaka" [Love in the caravan], in *Ay Peşinde*, 19–31.

50. Biographical details regarding Dr. Mehmed Reşid can be found in Hans-Lukas Kieser, "From 'Patriotism' to Mass Murder: Dr. Mehmed Reshid (1873–1919)," in *A Question of Genocide: Armenians and Turks at the End of the Ottoman Empire*,

eds. Ronald Grigor Suny, Fatma Müge Göçek, and Norman Naimark (Oxford: Oxford University Press, 2011), 126–48.

51. Birinci, *Tarihin Alacakaranlığında*, 420.

52. *Bir Ömür Boyunca*, 36.

53. Kieser, "From 'Patriotism' to Mass Murder," 129.

54. Kieser, "From 'Patriotism' to Mass Murder," 131.

55. Kieser, "From 'Patriotism' to Mass Murder," 132.

56. Kieser, "From 'Patriotism' to Mass Murder," 133.

57. Kieser, "From 'Patriotism' to Mass Murder," 135.

58. Kieser, "From 'Patriotism' to Mass Murder," 137.

59. Süleyman Nazif, "Dr. Reşid," appeared originally in *Hadisat*, 8 Şubat 1919; reprinted in transliteration in Nejdet Bilgi, *Dr. Mehmed Reşid Şahingiray Hayatı ve Hatıraları İttihad ve Terakki Dönemi ve Ermeni Meselesi* [Dr. Mehmed Reşid Şahingiray's life and memoirs: The Union and Progress era and the Armenian issue] (İzmir: Kanyılmaz Matbaası, 1997), 167–71. The quotation appears on p. 170.

60. Kieser, "From 'Patriotism' to Mass Murder," 145.

61. Kieser, "From 'Patriotism' to Mass Murder," 145.

62. Bilgi, *Dr. Mehmed Reşid Şahingiray*, 30.

63. Uğur Ümit Üngör and Mehmet Polatel, *Confiscation and Destruction: The Young Turk Seizure of Armenian Property* (London: Continuum, 2011), 147.

64. Birinci, *Tarihin Alacakaranlığında*, 423; and Refik Halid, "Üzüm ve İpek" [Grapes and silk], in *Ay Peşinde*, 95–98.

65. *Bir Ömür Boyunca*, 39. Hakkı Behiç had been posted to Syria with Cemal Paşa after their paths diverged in Istanbul; then, according to Refik Halid, he had become the finance minister in the Ankara government, but shortly after assuming that post, "because of his progressive ideas, probably," spent his life in that city (Ankara) in one long exile.

66. Ebcioğlu, *Refik Halid Karay Kendi Yazıları ile*, 43.

67. See Ottoman document BOA EUM I. Şube dosya 9 vesika nu. 27, 31 Kanun-ı sani 334, January 31, 1918, attesting to Refik Halid's still very tainted reputation in the eyes of Unionist/Ottoman authorities: "Refik Halid Bey, known until the assassination of the late Mahmud Şevket Paşa under the sobriquet Kirpi, has played an influential role in the unhappiness of the homeland (*memleketteki adem-i memnuniyet*) by sowing seeds of strife among people with his daily publications under the veil of satire."

"To the greatest extent of his ability by way of invention (*icad suretiyle*), he made various malicious attacks concerning Unionist officials and the government, [and thus] he worked toward his being cast out of influence/standing and honor of the government. He therefore contributed to arousing the passions that gave rise to the incidence of the assassination [of Mahmud Şevket Paşa] and therefore subsequently to the event he was removed to Sinop along with his associates."

"While in Sinop, he married the daughter of Celâl Paşa, who, while the head doctor of the Beyoğlu Police in the time of the Gendarme Ministry was well-known for his sedition.

"Considering his past involvements and his notoriety there is no way he is deserving of trust."

"Especially in Sinop and Bilecik he had the warmest contact with *muhalifs* the whole time and for the period he lived there."

68. BOA DH.EUM I: 9/27:9 (1336 R 18).

CHAPTER 4. *THE TRUE FACE OF ISTANBUL*

1. Soon afterward they gave him a weekly column in *Yeni Mecmua*, "Hafta Muhasebesi," in which he wrote "Harp Zengini," about Bayramzâde (İdzâde— İd as Arabic for Bayram—thinly veiled) and Topal İsmail Paşa. See Erol Koroğlu, *Ottoman Propaganda and Turkish Identity: Literature in Turkey during World War I* (London: Tauris Academic Studies, 2007), 175 passim.

2. He was also writing for *Vakit*, *Tasvir-i Efkâr*, and *Zaman* at this time. Despite the efforts of Falih Rıfkı (Atay), Ahmet Refik (Altınay), and Refik Halid to keep it going, *Yeni Mecmua* ceased publication after the war ended "because of its association with the CUP." Hikmet Münir Ebcioğlu, *Refik Halid Karay Kendi Yazılar ile* [Refik Halid Karay and his writings] (Istanbul: Semih Lûtfi Kitabevi, ca. 1940), 47.

3. See Koroğlu, *Ottoman Propaganda* for discussion of depictions of black marketeering in the press and in novels in the summer of 1918.

4. Andrew Mango, *From the Sultan to Atatürk: Turkey* (London: Haus Publishing, 2009). For a comprehensive listing of works about the Armistice/War of Independence period as of 1999, see Nur Bilge Criss, *Istanbul Under Allied Occupation 1918–1923* (Leiden: E. J. Brill, 1999), ixnl–3.

5. Criss, *Istanbul Under Allied Occupation*, 5–6: "[T]he only thing its [the Freedom and Accord Party's] members had in common was a blind hatred for the CUP."

6. See Mustafa Aksakal, *The Ottoman Road to War in 1914: The Ottoman Empire and the First World War* (Cambridge, UK: Cambridge University Press, 2008) for an exploration into the decision to enter the war. See also Salim Tamari, *Year of the Locust: A Soldier's Diary and the Erasure of Palestine's Ottoman Past* (Berkeley: University of California Press, 2011), for similar sentiments in the diary of Ihsan Turjman in Jerusalem.

7. *Yeni Mecmua*, 10 Teşrin-i Evvel [November 10,] 1918. This must have been in one of the three issues of *Yeni Mecmua* published after the war and before it closed down.

8. Mevlanzâde Rıfat, *Türkiye İnkılâbının İç Yüzü* [The real face of Turkey's revolution] (Aleppo: Necib, 1929), pt. II, 2. It was a passage memorable enough to be invoked years later by fellow *muhalif* Mevlanzâde Rıfat.

9. Ahmet Emin (Yalman) confirms this time and again in *Turkey in the World War* (New Haven, CT: Yale University Press, 1930).

10. Examples of attempts at sorting out the recent Unionist past and the relationships of *muhalifs* to it include the two-part article in Ahmet Emin's *Vakit*, "Ali

Kemal Bey ve İttihatçılar" [Ali Kemal Bey and the Unionists], which ran December 15–16, 1919; and "Hürriyet ve İtilâf Beyannâmesi" [Freedom and Accord Manifesto], *Vakit*, January 25, 1920.

11. Refik Halid also became the director of Turkey Havas-Reuters Telegraph Agency at this time, which served as the Istanbul government's mouthpiece and as a rival to the nationalists' Anadolu Ajans, run by Halide Edib out of Anatolia. Ebcioğlu, *Refik Halid Karay Kendi Yazıları ile*, 52.

12. On the Friends of England Society, see Tarık Zafer Tunaya, *Türkiye'de Siyasal Partiler*, c. 2 *Mütareke dönemi* [Political parties in Turkey, vol. 2, The Armistice period] (Istanbul: İletişim, 1998), 116 passim; on the Wilsonian Principles League, see Tunaya, *Türkiye'de Siyasal Partiler*, 252–70.

13. See Ayhan Aktar, "Debating the Armenian Massacres in the Last Ottoman Parliament November–December 1918," *History Workshop Journal* 64, no. 1 (2007): 240–70.

14. See Orhan Karaveli, *Ali Kemal: "Belki de bir günah keçisi ..."* [Ali Kemal: "Perhaps a scapegoat" ...] (Istanbul: Doğan Kitap, 2009).

15. He and Refik had met in late 1918: Refik reminisced that the two had been living in the same apartment building on İstiklal Avenue [Grand Rue de Péra], Zeki Bey Apt. Refik Halid Karay, *Minelbab İlelmihrab: 1918 mütarekesi devrinde olan biten işlere ve gelip geçen insanlara dair bildiklerim* [From the door to the pulpit: What I know about the work and people that have come and gone since the 1918 Armistice], 3rd ed. (Istanbul: İnkılap, 2009), 106. He says he had only seen Ali Kemal once before this period, in the midst of a dispute with Hüseyin Cahit before the Constitutional Revolution. On page 108 of *Minelbab* Refik Halid recalls that once in 1908 Ahmet Samim had pointed Ali Kemal out from afar to Refik Halid, and early on in World War I when in exile he wrote a few articles as "Nakş-ı Berab" for *Peyam* before it was shut down. On page 109 Refik Halid mentions passing Ali Kemal on the street in front of Kınacıyan Hanı one month before the armistice. Again at the meetings of the Wilsonian Principles League: *Minelbab İlelmihrab*, 3rd ed., 110. Refik notes that they met in the same room in which the Wilsonian Principles League would have its first meeting a few days later.

16. Refik Halid, *Minelbab İlelmihrab*, 3rd ed., 132.

17. Refik recalls it as April 12 (*Minelbab İlelmihrab*, 3rd ed., 168); an anouncement of his appointment can be found in *Takvim-i Vekayi*, no. 3829 (17 Nisan 1336). *Asır*, 10 Teşrin-i evvel [October 10,] 1919, 1, reports on his having left his post and being on the verge of residing in the same location with former minister Adil Bey, Süleyman Şefik Paşa, and Ali Kemal. In his place, Hamdi Bey, the former telephone director, was reportedly appointed. Hidayet Dağdeviren Archive, box 6, file 12. See also Asaf Tanrıkut, *Türkiye Posta ve Telgraf ve Telefon Tarihi ve Teşkilât ve Mevzuatı* [Turkey Post, Telegraph and Telephone history, its organization and regulations] (Ankara: Efem Matbaacılık, 1968), II:756–57.

18. He reminisces that one day he was taken into a room at the ministry that was called "The Museum"; "in it were old telegraph machines and instruments and old stamp books—clean but worthless things—and on the walls were photographs

of the former ministers and directors of the Post and Telegraph Administration. Among these was the aggrandizing photo of Talaat Paşa." Immediately Refik stopped himself from shouting, "Take that down and throw it out right now!" and said, in a low voice, to his employee: "It is not right to reserve a place in museums and other official spaces for those that are still alive; if any among these people are still alive, please take down their pictures and keep them in a closed place" (*Minelbab İlelmihrab*, 3rd ed., 179–80). He also comments that he ran into a number of old schoolmates at the ministry and says that had he not gone into "political tightrope-walking," perhaps he, too, would have ended up like them, just a clerk (180), although of course when he ran into them it was only 1919, six to ten years after they had graduated (179).

19. Refik Halid, *Minelbab İlelmihrab*, 3rd ed., 206 passim; and *A Great Speech Delivered by Ghazi Mustapha Kemal, President of the Turkish Republic, October 1927* (Leipzig: K. F. Koehler, 1929); for the transliteration into Latin characters of the original Turkish text of *Nutuk*, see *Nutuk: Gazi Mustafa Kemal tarafından* (Istanbul: Yapı Kredi Yayınları, 2011); see also Utkan Kocatürk, *Atatürk'ün Toplanmamış Telgrafları* [Uncollected telegrams of Atatürk] (Istanbul: Edebiyat Yayınevi, 1971), 8.

20. "And Behold! The response and the intervention that constituted the first sign and the first pretext for the great political revolution to come—like an arrow from the bow." Refik Halid, *Minelbab İlelmihrab*, 3rd ed., 221 (author's translation).

21. Much of the early part of *Nutuk* details Mustafa Kemal's strained relationship with the Istanbul government, and much of that story is told through the verbatim recounting of telegraphic correspondence. For sections detailing the Telegraph Episode, see, in its English translation, *Great Speech Delivered by Ghazi Mustapha Kemal*, 30 passim. Note that Ali Kemal's article in *Vakit* was published precisely during this time: "Muhalefetin Manası" [The meaning of *Muhalefet*], July 26, 1919.

22. After stepping down from government service in October 1919, Refik even briefly resumed his position at the PTT the following spring during another crucial turning point in the battle between Istanbul and Ankara (see "Refik Halid Bey," *Alemdar*, no. 486-2786 (18 Nisan 1336): 3, for the announcement of his second appointment). On April 25, 1920, two days after the opening of the Turkish Grand National Assembly, Refik informed the interior ministry that publications by the nationalist forces—printed in Ankara and sold openly or secretly in Istanbul—had all been collected and destroyed. BOA DH.İ.UM 16L3/1L18, dd. 6 Şaban 1338H, 25 Nisan 1336 [April 25, 1920]; Erol Baykal, "The Ottoman Press, 1908–1923" (PhD diss., Cambridge University, 2012), 115. Baykal also points out Ali Kemal's editorial in *Peyam-ı Sabah* from a few days earlier, in which he mocked the Grand National Assembly, and Halide Edib by name, accusing them of being shameless, backstabbing charlatans (104).

23. Emniyet Genel Müdürlüğü Arşivi, dosya nu. 12222-100, cited in Ali Birinci, *Refik Halid Karay: Ankara* (Istanbul: İnkılap, 2009), 27n2.

24. Baykal, "Ottoman Press."

25. He published in liberal/Anglophile newspapers such as *Sabah, Peyam-ı Sabah*, and *Alemdar*; in 1922 he published his own satirical paper, *Aydede*. Refik also released a new, expanded edition of *Kirpinin Dedikleri* and several collected volumes, such as a *Memleket Hikâyeleri* [Homeland stories], *Ago Paşa'nın Hatırâtı* [Ago Paşa's memoirs], *Guguklu Saat* [Cuckoo clock], *Ay Peşinde* [In pursuit of the moon], and *Tanıdıklarım* [The people I have known].

26. Refik Halid, "Anadolu diyor ki" (12 Ekim 1919), in N. Ahmet Özalp, *Refik Halid: Okları kırılmış Kirpi* [Refik Halid: The broken-quilled Porcupine] (Istanbul: Kapı Yayınları, 2011), 57–59.

27. Originally a CUP member (1906), Miralay Sadık (1860–1940) became a founder of the Freedom and Accord Party in 1911 and a prominent *muhalif*. His politics and outlook were markedly conservative/traditional.

28. Refik Halid, "İttihatçı diyor ki" (30 Kasım 1919), in Özalp, *Refik Halid*, 60–62.

29. Not even touched upon here are the wonderful social critiques he published in the form of short stories and essays during this time, exemplified by "Bir Guguklu Saat'in Azizliği" [A cuckoo clock's prank]. See Christine Philliou, "When the Clock Strikes Twelve: The Inception of an Ottoman Past in Early Republican Turkey," *Comparative Studies in South Asia, Africa, and the Middle East* 31, no. 1 (2011): 172–82.

30. "İki Oğlun Hikâyesi" [The story of two sons], in Özalp, *Refik Halid*, 153–57; originally published in *Guguklu Saat* [Cuckoo clock] (Istanbul: Sabah Matbaası, 1341 [1922]).

31. "Rical-ı Meşrutiyet'in Son Günleri" [The last days of the constitutionalist dignitaries], in Özalp, *Refik Halid*, 164–70; originally published in *Guguklu Saat* [Cuckoo clock] (Istanbul: Sabah Matbaası, 1341 [1922]).

32. Refik Halid, "Hülya Bu Ya" [This must be a dream] (11 Şubat 1921), in *Ago Paşa'nın Hatırâtı* [Ago Paşa's memoirs] (Istanbul: İnkılap, 2009), 25–37. The word *hülya* has both positive ("vision, reverie") and negative ("daydream, fantasy") connotations.

33. Karay, *Ago Paşa'nın Hatıratı*, 25–37.

34. *Alemdar*, 3 Ocak 1920.

35. See "Lenin Yerine Girinin" for the litany of names the *muhalifs* were assigning to the nationalists, including "Kamarillalar, pansiyon[cu]lar, çeteler, bandolar . . . eşkıya, Kemaliler Celaliler" (Camarillas, padrones, bandits, and Celâli/Kemalists). Ilgar, *Mütareke'de Yerli ve Yabancı Basın*, 22–23.

36. See Ahmet Emin Yalman's anecdote about the importance of Hacı Bayram-ı Veli to the religious nationalists, and Mustafa Kemal's rejection of that in the wake of the Battle of Sakarya: *Turkey in My Time* (Norman: University of Oklahoma Press, 1956), 110.

37. Here he makes a pun on the Persian/Ottoman idiomatic expression *gorg-u baran-dide*, "wolf who has seen rain," and says he was more like a "wolf who has seen fire."

38. The term he uses—*tulumbacı*—can refer to both firemen and rowdy men.

39. For this translation I worked both from the original text, in *Peyam-ı Sabah*, 26 Ağustos 1921, and the transliteration in Taylan Esin and Zeliha Etöz, *1916 Ankara Yangını: Felaketin Mantığı* [The 1916 Ankara fire: The logic of disaster] (İstanbul: İletişim, 2015), app. B, 22528. I thank Baki Tezcan for his assistance.

40. "Metampsikoz" [Metempsychosis], in *Ay Peşinde* [In pursuit of the moon] (Istanbul: İnkılap, 2009), 73–80.

41. Refik Halid, "Bir Muhalifin İntiharı" [The suicide of a *muhalif*], in Özalp, *Refik Halid*, 147–50; reprinted from *Ago Paşa'nın Hatıratı*, original 1921 edition.

42. Refik Halid Karay, "Tam bir *muhalif*" [A perfect *muhalif*], in *Tanıdıklarım* [People I have known] (Istanbul: İnkılap, 2009), 21–26.

43. See, for instance, Michael Meeker, *A Nation of Empire: The Ottoman Legacy of Turkish Modernity* (Berkeley: University of California Press, 2002) for discussion of the "amnesia and prohibition" surrounding the Turkish War of Independence in the republic.

44. According to Orhan Koloğlu, *Osmanlı'da Son Tartışmalar: Mondros'tan Mudanya'ya* [The last Ottoman discussions: From Mondros to Mudanya] (Istanbul: Doğan Kitap, 2008), 184–5, Ahmet Emin, in his newspaper *Vakit*, even targeted "this group that called themselves *muhalifs*" in mid-1922 in the article "Memleketin Muhalifleri" (meaning both The opponents of the homeland and The homeland's *muhalifs*). "In this land, there is a class of men that call themselves '*muhalif*'. But I wonder against whom and what are they opponents, and what are they in favor of? It is doubtful that they themselves could give an answer to that question, but the answer they are giving with the developments happening before our eyes is that the rationale of this so-called *muhalefet* is one against the homeland, its existence, and its future.... They objected to the arbitrary and lawless ways of Union and Progress, but the things they have done make Union and Progress look like fanatical legalists by comparison.... The saddest part is that there are so few of these men that honorable men who love their land cannot even launch a social boycott against them."

45. Erik Jan Zürcher, *The Unionist Factor: The Rôle of the Committee of Union and Progress in the Turkish National Movement, 1905–1926* (Leiden: E. J. Brill, 1984); Uğur Ümit Üngör, *The Making of Modern Turkey: Nation and State in Eastern Anatolia, 1913–1950* (Oxford: Oxford University Press, 2011); and M. Şükrü Hanioğlu, *Atatürk: An Intellectual Biography* (Princeton, NJ: Princeton University Press, 2011).

46. "Elveda Siyasiyat!," in Özalp, *Refik Halid*, 191.

CHAPTER 5. *MUHALEFET* FROM ABROAD

1. Hakan Özoğlu, *From Caliphate to Secular State: Power Struggle in the Early Turkish Republic* (Santa Barbara, CA: Praeger, 2011); Erik Jan Zürcher, *Political Opposition in the Early Turkish Republic: The Progressive Republican Party, 1924–1925* (Leiden: E. J. Brill, 1991); and Amit Bein, *Kemalist Turkey and the Middle East: International Relations in the Interwar Period* (Cambridge, UK: Cambridge University Press, 2018).

2. Metin Heper and Jacob M. Landau, eds., *Political Parties and Democracy in Turkey* (London: I. B. Tauris, 1991), ch. 5. Özoğlu, *From Caliphate to Secular State* is a recent work that highlights this period and takes seriously the notion of power struggle within the elite.

3. For contemporary descriptions of this event and Refet Paşa's activities thereafter, see Stanford J. Shaw, *From Empire to Republic: The Turkish War of National Liberation, 1918–1923, a Documentary Study*, vol. IV (Ankara: Turkish History Foundation, 2000), 1872–76; footnotes 345–53 supply citations for many more descriptions, from the Ottoman/Turkish and foreign press as well as figures who provided accounts, such as Falih Rıfkı. "On 19 October, 1922, a week after the signature of the armistice at Mudanya, General Ref'et (Bele), one of Mustafa Kemal's original companions in the War of Independence, arrived in Istanbul at the head of the force of Turkish gendarmes (in fact soldiers in gendarmerie uniforms) that was to take over Eastern Thrace." Andrew Mango, *From the Sultan to Atatürk: Turkey* (London: Haus Publishing, 2009), 149.

4. Orhan Koloğlu, *Osmanlı'da Son Tartışmalar Mudros'tan Mudanya'ya* [The last Ottoman controversies, from Mudros to Mudanya] (Istanbul: Doğan Kitap, 2008), 192.

5. Koloğlu, *Osmanlı'da Son Tartışmalar*, 192.

6. *Peyam-ı Sabah*, 20 Teşrin-i Evvel 1338/October 20, 1922.

7. The caption reads: "This picture: A picture is of Artin Kemal, son of Yovan the Gardener (Bostancı Yuvan), shorn off from his fields at the Patriarchate by the Agop [Hagop/Armenian] traitors and fellows [in lieu of photo credits to the photographers, who often were Armenian]."

8. This would be October 15, 1922, when an agreement was reached to end the war with Greece and for the handover of Eastern Thrace to Turkey, leading to the Treaty of Lausanne the following summer.

9. Cited as "unpublished section of *Minelbab İlelmihrab*," in Ebcioğlu, *Refik Halid Karay Kendi Yazılar ile* [Refik Halid Karay and his writings] (Istanbul: Semih Lûtfi Kitabevi, ca. 1940), 55 passim.

10. Ebcioğlu, *Refik Halid Karay Kendi Yazılar ile*, 57.

11. Refik Halid Karay, *Minelbab İlelmihrab: 1918 Mütareke devrinde olan biten işleri ve gelen geçen insanlara dair bildiklerim*, 3rd ed. (Istanbul: İnkılap, 2009), 381–32.

12. Refik Halid Karay, *Sürgün* [Exile] (Istanbul: İnkılap, 1998), 11–12.

13. Hilmi Efendi had slapped the local police commissioner in the face in the course of an argument about the Virgin Mary being pregnant (i.e., blasphemy); the locals had taken Hilmi's side, and the police commissioner was transferred elsewhere. But later, having attained a high office, he wanted revenge. One day, while Hilmi was getting a shave at the barber's the authorities came and arrested him and, after detaining him for forty days, threw him on a boat leaving the harbor. "It was a misunderstanding. When everything settled down again he would explain his problem and surely the mistake would be corrected. *The new administration had not yet settled in or come into its own. As was well-known, the government had big problems*

to deal with, the peace issue, and the issue of coming to a mutual understanding with Europe. . . . [L]et them finish up with that first" (*Sürgün*, 16–17, emphasis added).

14. Years later, he said in an interview that in this novel, "I talked about the pain of exile and longing for home (*memleket*). I think I was successful." *Hafta* [Week], August 5, 1959; Refik Halid Karay, "Edebiyatı Öldüren Rejim," [The regime that kills literature], *Memleket Yazıları* 3 [Homeland writings, vol. 3] (Istanbul: İnkılap, 2014), 536.

15. See Tolga Köker, "The Establishment of Secularism in Turkey," *Middle East Law and Governance* 2, no. 1 (2010): 17–42; see also Zürcher, *Political Opposition in the Early Turkish Republic*, for a study of Mustafa Kemal's experiment with creating his own opposition party in the early years of the Republic.

16. For more on this meeting and for a cogent portrait of factions in the emergent Republic, see Jacob M. Landau and Metin Heper, "The Progressive Republican Party," in *Political Parties and Democracy in Turkey*, ed. Jacob M. Landau and Metin Heper (London: Routledge, 1991). The authors argue that the Istanbul newspapers "represented the thinking of a cosmopolitan bourgeoisie and intelligentsia which preferred to maintain the country's international ties to the isolation which the Kemalists were offering" (68); Frederick Frey, in *The Turkish Political Elite* (Cambridge, MA: MIT Press, 1965), claims that the Progressive People's Party, led by such figures, was "the last truly dangerous traditional threat to Kemalist hegemony."

17. Landau and Heper take a hard-line Kemalist view and refer to the attempt by these elites in 1924–25 to form an opposition party (the Progressive Republican Party) as the "last gasp of tradition" that had to be eliminated to clear the way for Kemalist reforms. *Politics and Political Parties in Turkey*, 66.

18. Ahmet Emin (Yalman), in "Muhalefetin vaziyeti" [The situation of *muhalefet*], *Vatan*, May 1923, claimed that those in the "Second Group" were patriotic to the man and loyal to the nation, but because they were unhappy for their own personal reasons were "making *muhalefet*"; because they each had their own reasons, the Second Group was not a homogeneous block. See Ahmet Demirel, *Birinci Meclis'te Muhalefet: İkinci Grup* [Muhalefet in the First Assembly: The Second Group] (Istanbul: İletişim Yayınları, 1994, 2019), app., 3.5.1923.

19. John M. Vanderlippe, *The Politics of Turkish Democracy: İsmet İnönü and the Formation of the Multi-Party System, 1938–1950* (Albany: State University of New York Press, 2005), 15 passim.

20. For the most recent treatment in Turkish on Karabekir, see Cemil Koçak, *Karabekir'in Kavgası* [Karabekir's quarrel] (Istanbul: Timaş Yayınları, 2016).

21. The People's Party (*Halk Fırkası*), established in late 1923, was officially renamed the Republican People's Party on November 10, 1924, making the "single-party Republic" formal.

22. Özoğlu, *From Caliphate to Secular State*.

23. *Resmi Ceride* [Official newspaper], January 7, 1925.

24. Hakan Özoğlu points out in *From Caliphate to Secular State* (23 passim) that despite the prevailing notion that the population exchange and other aspects of Lausanne were religious rather than ethnic, because of British/Western European

assumptions about social and political organization, in actuality the Turkish delegation had repeatedly demanded a religious rather than ethnic delineation. This was so that Kurds, Arabs, Circassians, and other Muslim groups would not be given minority protections, and members of those groups would be subject to exclusion from the general wartime amnesty being negotiated.

25. "Elveda Siyasiyat!" [Farewell, politics!], in N. Ahmet Özalp, *Refik Halid: Okları Kırılmış Kirpi* [Refik Halid: The broken-quilled Porcupine] (Istanbul: Kapı Yayınları, 2011), 190–91. Ever the humorist, Refik Halid continues this piece by telling his readers, "With these thoughts in mind, with this hope [of saving his position] I prepared an example of a non-political article; I don't think it will capture the objections of those newspapers who are opposed to me anymore. If it meets with the approval of my readers, from now on I will write in this way; if it doesn't, what can I do, I cannot sacrifice my life [soul] for the pleasure of four people! They will finally say words of pity behind my back." He continues with a short essay about the process of pickling cabbage and turnips, detailing how to find the best cabbage leaves and which kind of water to use, and so forth.

26. On this, note the Hıyanet-i Vatan Kanunu [Treason to the Nation Law] of April 29, 1920, amended March 29, 1923. Zürcher, *Political Opposition in the Early Turkish Republic*, 26.

27. For more on Ahmet Ferit (Tek)'s role in the Istanbul government at this time, see *Minelbab İlelmihrab*, 3rd ed., 229 passim.

28. Ferit would resign in 1925 in the wake of a scandal having to do with his (along with other hard-liners, Yunus Nadi and Kılıç Ali) secretly permitting wealthy Armenians to return to Istanbul to dispose of their property. See Zürcher, *Political Opposition in the Early Turkish Republic*, 39–40. According to Hakan Özoğlu, Ferit was also a "known pan-Turkist in parliament and was a founding member of the Turkish Hearths (Türk Ocakları)." *From Caliphate to Secular State*, 174n63.

29. Mustafa Kemal opened the new parliamentary year on March 1, 1924, and two days later abolished the Caliphate and expelled the Ottoman royal family from the country in a fait accompli. This was the action that precipitated the split in the RPP and led to the formation of the short-lived Progressive Republican Party. Zürcher, *Political Opposition in the Early Turkish Republic*, 38. "Unclassified others": Benjamin Fortna, *The Circassian: Eşref Kuşçubaşı* (London: Hurst, 2016).

30. See Ahmet Emin (Yalman), *Turkey in the World War* (New Haven, CT: Yale University Press, 1930), ch. 10.

31. Memoirs about the War of Independence period would proliferate, but mostly after Atatürk's death, with more appearing after the establishment of the multiparty system. Some notable exceptions were Halide Edib's *Ateşli Gömlek* [Shirt in flames], published in 1924 in English, but only published in Turkish in the 1950s; and Mevlanzâde Rıfat's *Türkiye İnkilâbının İç Yüzü* [The real face of the Turkish Revolution], published in Aleppo in 1929. Both are exceptions that prove the rule.

32. Landau and Heper, *Politics and Political Parties in Turkey*, 68.

33. Fellow exile and former director of the Tramvay service in Istanbul.

34. *Minelbab İlelmihrab*, 3rd ed., 11 passim.

35. *Akşam*, January 14, 1924, 1.

36. *Akşam*, January 15, 1924 (first installment of *Minelbab İlelmihrab*; this portion of the text was omitted from future editions and only appeared in the 1924 version). Passages in boldface were part of the original text in 1923–24 but were later redacted for Republican-era editions.

37. *Akşam*, January 15, 1924; and *Minelbab İlelmihrab*, 3rd ed., 19–20.

38. "Weakness and dissimulation and were connected to the Freedom and Accord party": *Minelbab İlelmihrab*, 3rd ed., 14.

39. *Minelbab İlelmihrab*, 3rd ed., 32–33.

40. Refik Halid then published an open letter to İsmail Müştak in *Doğru Yol*, a newspaper published out of Aleppo by fellow members of the List of 150. He thanked Müştak for defending him so eloquently and pointed out that his letter in return was less a response than joking around, since "in my view, even the most serious matter carries within it strange and pleasant/funny sides." *Minelbab İlelmihrab*, 3rd ed., 35–36. He then goes on to take Müştak's accusations literally—that is, the accusation that Refik Halid had "turned his back" on his country, with which he takes issue by demonstrating that he was facing the coast when the boat he departed on took off, so he did not technically turn his back, and so forth. The letter was dated February 3, 1924.

41. Michael E. Meeker's *A Nation of Empire: The Ottoman Legacy of Turkish Modernity* (Berkeley: University of California Press, 2002) is an interesting example of this; the amnesia and prohibition surrounding the War of Independence and World War I are for the provincial society in Of. From our case we can see that the elites who had taken part in the transmutation/transition had no such amnesia, but agreed to not discuss it publicly and thus to place the prohibition on the masses.

42. Zürcher, *Political Opposition in the Early Turkish Republic*.

43. Karay, *Minelbab İlelmihrab*.

44. Zürcher, *Political Opposition in the Early Turkish Republic*, 82. Zürcher notes that two journalists, Falih Rıfkı (Atay) and Yakup Kadri (Karaosmanoğlu), supported this idea. Mustafa Kemal eventually weighed in as president and joined the critics of Fethi (Okyar)'s government, effecting a vote of no-confidence and triggering the formation of a new government and cabinet under İsmet (İnönü).

45. Zürcher, *Political Opposition in the Early Turkish Republic*, 84–85.

46. Zürcher, *Political Opposition in the Early Turkish Republic*, 84–85.

47. *Minelbab İlelmihrab*, 3rd ed., 44–45.

48. See Köker, "Establishment of Secularism in the Early Turkish Republic"; and Özoğlu, *From Caliphate to Secular State*.

49. Abdullah Uçman, ed., *Aziz Feylosofum: Refik Halid'den Rıza Tevfik'e Mektuplar* [My dear philosopher: Letters from Refik Halid to Rıza Tevfik] (Istanbul: Dergâh Yayınları, 2014), (10 Mart 1926), 25.

50. Uçman, *Aziz Feylosofum* (10 Mart 1926), 18.

51. Uçman, *Aziz Feylosofum* (10 Mart 1926), 22.

52. Uçman, *Aziz Feylosofum* (10 Mart 1926), 26. Interestingly, French intelligence reports in 1924 noted that Hasan Sadık and Celâl Kadri, editors of *Doğru Yol*, were "nettement partisans du Mandat," and that Kadri in particular was a Francophile who "never missed an opportunity to do good works for the Mandate." French Foreign Ministry Archives, Nantes: Haut Commissariat Beyrouth, Service de Press 1 SL 010.

53. Uçman, *Aziz Feylosofum* (July 28, 1927), 38–39

54. Geoffrey Lewis, *The Turkish Language Reform: A Catastrophic Success* (New York: Oxford University Press, 1999); Gavin Brockett, *How Happy to Call Oneself a Turk! Provincial Newspapers and the Negotiation of a Muslim National Identity* (Austin: University of Texas Press, 2011); and Hale Yilmaz, *Becoming Turkish: Nationalist Reforms and Cultural Negotiations in Early Republican Turkey, 1923–1945* (Syracuse, NY: Syracuse University Press, 2013).

55. Hülya Adak, "National Myths and Self-Narrations: Mustafa Kemal's *Nutuk* and Halide Edip's *The Turkish Ordeal*," *South Atlantic Quarterly* 102, nos. 2/3 (2003): 509–28.

56. The same goes for Halide Edib's memoirs, published in English in 1924 and 1926, which Mustafa Kemal surely knew about; Mustafa Sabri Efendi, the last Ottoman Şeyh-ül-İslam, had also published some memoirs at this early stage from his exile in Egypt.

CHAPTER 6. *THERE IS A WORLD UNDERGROUND*

1. Ali Birinci, *Refik Halid Karay: Ankara* (Istanbul: İnkılap, 2009), 33n3: "A copy of the telegraph can be found in the BYG-KUP file, document 153, in the Atatürk Belgeliği of the Millî Kütüphane."

Dönüş sevincim katmerlidir.
Sevgili yurdumu ne halde bıraktım? Nasıl bir harika ile karşılacağım.
Dumanı yaslı tüten bir fabrika bacası tanırdım: Zeytinburnu . . .
Ankara'da tek bina Taşhan'dı.
Bankalarda dilimiz ötmez, şirketlerde sözümüz sökmezdi.
Trende Türkçemi Rumlaştırmadan biletçiye meram anlatamazdım.
Tokatlıyan'da Frenkçe söylemezsem garsona dilediğimi kolayca yaptıramazdım.
Plajlarımızda yüzen yabancılara kıyıdan korkarak bakar,
Avrupa'dan dönerken hudutta şapkamı pencereden atardım.
Memlekette toprağın kurusu bizim, yaşı elindi.
Bıraktığım haldeki bu vatan yerine istiklal ve mücize ülkesine kavuşmaktan
    duyduğum heyecan içinde şu yaşımda ağlar güler ilan bebeklerine döndüm.
Mütemadiyen tekrarladığım şu: Yaşasın Atatürk, beni gurbette de göğsümü
    kabartarak yaşatan Atatürk.

2. Refik Halid Karay, *Yer Altında Dünya Var* [There is a world underground] (Istanbul: Çağlayan, 1953; repr. Istanbul: İnkılap, 2009).

3. Hikmet Münir Ebcioğlu, *Refik Halid Karay Kendi Yazılar ile* [Refik Halid Karay and his writings] (Istanbul: Semih Lûtfi Kitabevi, ca. 1940), 67–68.

4. See, for instance, Hale Yilmaz, *Becoming Turkish: Nationalist Reforms and Cultural Negotiations in Early Republican Turkey, 1923–1945* (Syracuse: Syracuse University Press, 2013).

5. Yilmaz, *Becoming Turkish*. In his letter to Rıza Tevfik dated Feburary 17, 1928, Refik mentions that he is involved in starting a new newspaper, and that he and his wife had decided to settle down in Aleppo for that reason. Abdullah Uçman, ed., *Aziz Feylosofum: Refik Halid'den Rıza Tevfik'e Mektuplar* [My dear philosopher: Letters from Refik Halid to Rıza Tevfik] (Istanbul: Dergâh Yayınları, 2014), 44.

6. Ebcioğlu, *Refik Halid Karay Kendi Yazıları ile*, 68.

7. He continued to keep company with members of the List of 150, even after his sentiments about the Republic changed. In Aleppo he worked on *Vahdet* with Ali İlmi Fani (Bilgili) and Tarık Mümtaz Yazganalp (Göztepe), and he socialized with Mevlanzâde Rıfat Bey until the very afternoon that the latter died of a heart attack. See Birinci, *Refik Halid Karay: Ankara*, 29–30.

8. Ebcioğlu, *Refik Halid Karay Kendi Yazılar ile*, 68.

9. Ebcioğlu, *Refik Halid Karay Kendi Yazılar ile*, 68.

10. French intelligence services were aware of his presence and of *Doğru Yol*, which received a subvention of 1500 francs from the French administration as of 1924, as well as, later on, *Vahdet*. French Foreign Ministry Archives, Nantes: Haut Commissariat, Service de presse (1SL 010), 1924–28.

11. Beyrut Konsolosluğu raporu, 15 Kasim 1935: Dosya nu. 12222-100; cited in Birinci, *Refik Halid Karay: Ankara*, 30–33.

12. "Lisana Hürmet" originally appeared in *Yeni Mecmua* and was later included in *Tanıdıklarım* (The people I have known), the first edition of which was published in 1922 (Istanbul: Cihan Kütüphanesi, 1922); Istanbul: Semih Lûtfi Kitabevi, 1941), 100–104.

13. On the Great Revolt, see Michael Provence, *The Great Syrian Revolt and the Rise of Arab Nationalism* (Austin: University of Texas Press, 2005).

14. Uçman, *Aziz Feylosofum*, 107–22.

15. Interestingly, Ali Fethi (Okyar) had written the tract *Muhaliflerin Esrarı* [The secret of the *Muhalifs*] (Istanbul: Matbaa-yı Amedi, 1332 [1916]). On Ahmet Ağaoğlu, see A. Holly Shissler, *Between Two Empires: Ahmet Ağaoğlu and the New Turkey* (London: I. B. Tauris, 2003).

16. Walter F. Weiker, "The Free Party, 1930," in *Political Parties and Democracy in Turkey*, ed. Jacob M. Landau and Metin Heper (London: Routledge, 1991), 93–94.

17. For a translation and further discussion of "Deli" see Christine Philliou, "When the Clock Strikes Twelve: The Inception of an Ottoman Past in Early Republican Turkey," *Comparative Studies in South Asia, Africa, and the Middle East* 31, no. 1 (2011): 172–82.

18. Ebcioğlu, *Refik Halid Karay Kendi Yazıları ile*, 76.

19. Ebcioğlu, *Refik Halid Karay Kendi Yazıları ile*, 76.

20. Ebcioğlu, *Refik Halid Karay Kendi Yazıları ile*, 70–71.

21. Uçman, *Aziz Feylosofum*, 60.

22. Sarah D. Shields, *Fezzes in the River: Identity Politics and European Diplomacy on the Eve of World War II* (Oxford: Oxford University Press, 2011).

23. Amit Bein makes an argument that the Kemalist Republic was less isolationist, and more engaged in the politics of the Arab Middle East, than scholars since World War II have contended. See Amit Bein, *Kemalist Turkey and the Middle East: International Relations in the Interwar Period* (Cambridge, UK: Cambridge University Press, 2018).

24. See Shields, *Fezzes in the River*.

25. Two prominent examples were Mevlanzâde Rıfat, author of *Türkiye İnkilabının İç Yüzü* [The true face of the Turkish Revolution] (1929) and Ali İlmi (Fani) from the List of 150, who taught at the French lycée and put out the newspaper *Ferda* (Tomorrow).

26. Seda Altuğ, "Between Colonial and National Dominations: Antioch Under the French Mandate" (MA thesis, Atatürk Institute for Modern Studies, Boğaziçi University, 2002); and Seda Altuğ, "Popular Nationalism and the City: Antioch During the French Mandate," *Chronos* 13 (2006): 231–75.

27. Refik Halid Karay, *Minelbab İlelmihrab: 1918 mütarekesi devrinde olan biten işlere ve gelip geçen insanlara dair bildiklerim* [Minelbab ilelmihrab: What I know about the work and people that have come and gone since the 1918 Armistice], 3rd ed. (Istanbul: İnkılap, 2009), 46.

28. Bekir Sıtkı Kunt, for instance, had as a lycée student met Refik Halid in 1924 when the latter was on a visit to Antakya. Kunt would go on to become the editor of *Yeni Gün* (New day), the main newspaper affiliated with the partisans of the Republic in the region. Ebcioğlu, *Refik Halid Karay Kendi Yazıları ile*, 71.

29. Karakayış indicated his ancestral line from the Mudurnu Karakayışoğulları in central Anatolia (analogous to his old friend/rival Yakup Kadri's choice to take on the patronym Karaosmanoğlu, after his illustrious ancestral line in western Anatolia, for instance), but soon afterward he shortened it to Karay. Rumor still circulates that he took on this name because it spelled, backward, a first-order obscenity in Turkish, making it a one-word satire on the Surname Law and the Alphabet Reform (given that Ottoman script would have been read in the opposite direction to the Latin script). Others contend that he was too much of a gentleman to make that joke.

30. He even told a story in a 1962 interview to the satire magazine *Zübük* that in 1936 he had been invited to visit Ankara by the Turkish consul in Aleppo. He had refused, saying he had a phobia about the Karakol, and that he would wait until he had legal, written permission to return to Turkey.

31. Yunus Nadi, "Yüzellilikleri Affedebilir miyiz?" [Can we pardon those on the List of 150?], *Cumhuriyet*, June 28, 1938.

32. Celâl Bayar was prime minister from November 1, 1937, to January 25, 1939.

33. Vanderlippe, *Politics of Turkish Democracy*, 34–35.

34. Uçman, *Aziz Feylosofum*, 168–70.

35. Note also that Rıza Tevfik did a similar project with Feridun Aydemir, editor of Hatay-based newspaper *Yenigün*, in 1943: Feridun Aydemir, *Kendi Ağzından*

Rıza Tevfik: Hayatı, Felsefesi, Şiirleri [Rıza Tevfik in his own words: His life, his philosophy, his poems] (Istanbul: Remzi Kitabevi, 1943).

36. Ebcioğlu, *Refik Halid Karay Kendi Yazıları ile*, 54.

37. Ebcioğlu, *Refik Halid Karay Kendi Yazıları ile*, 59 passim.

38. N. Ahmet Özalp, *Refik Halid: Okları Kırılmış Kirpi* [Refik Halid: The broken-quilled Porcupine] (Istanbul: Kapı Yayınları, 2011), underlines throughout his discussion of these excised and revised works that we do not and cannot know whose hand it was that was responsible for the changes.

39. Özalp, *Refik Halid*, viii. He goes on to say that he believes Karay was not the only author to be subjected to this emasculation during the single-party period, but aside from the classic work *Çalıkuşu* (The wren) by Reşat Nuri Güntekin, he does not provide other examples.

40. *Yeni Gün*, March 11, 1939; and Refik Halid Karay, *Edebiyatı Öldüren Rejim* [The regime that kills literature] (Istanbul: İnkılap, 2014), 460.

41. He was drawing from a larger trend here, examples of which include the Mithat Cemal Kuntay novel *Üç İstanbul: Roman* [Three Istanbuls: A novel] (Istanbul: Sander Yayınları, 1976); originally published in 1938.

42. Recall that works such as Ahmed Hamdi Tanpınar's *Huzur* (A mind at peace)—at the center of which is the heavy weight of melancholy and loss surrounding the Ottoman past—were written at this time. Ahmed Hamdi Tanpınar, *A Mind at Peace*, trans. Erdağ Göknar (New York: Archipelago Books, 2008); originally published in 1943.

43. At the end of the first section he quotes a poem by Tevfik Fikret ("Kılıç"), which is interesting because at this time Tevfik Fikret had become a crucible in the struggle between fascists and anti-fascists and a heroic symbol for the anti-fascists in Turkey. Because of his vocal opposition to Abdülhamid, he was imprisoned in 1901; this act of heroism and sacrifice became a kind of codeword for the opposition in the late 1930s and 1940s.

44. Refik Halid Karay, "Ankara," in *Deli* [Mad] (Istanbul: Semih Lûtfi, 1939), 48.

CHAPTER 7. *MUHALEFET* IN THE FREE WORLD

1. John M. VanderLippe, *The Politics of Turkish Democracy: İsmet İnönü and the Formation of the Multi-party System, 1938–1950* (Albany: State University of New York Press, 2005), 168.

2. Sabiha Sertel, *The Struggle for Modern Turkey* (London: I. B. Tauris, 2019), 109–10. English translation of *Roman Gibi: Anılar* [Like a novel: Memoirs].

3. Sabiha herself bowed out of writing for *Tan* in 1941, as part of a bargain struck by Ahmet Emin Yalman with Interior Minister Şükrü Kaya to keep the newspaper open. Then, thanks to a chance encounter with Şükrü Kaya and Kılıç Ali at the Marine Club, she was told she could write again, as long as she avoided discussion of foreign policy because her views were too critical of Germany. Sertel, *Struggle for Modern Turkey*, 110.

4. *Harman* 7 (25 Temmuz 1945): 2–16; and N. Ahmet Özalp, *Refik Halid: Okları kırılmış Kirpi* [Refik Halid: The broken-quilled Porcupine] (Istanbul: Kapı Yayınları, 2011), ix.

5. Zekeriya Sertel, *Hatırladıklarım* [My recollections] (Istanbul: Can Sanat Yayınları, 2015), 216.

6. Sertel, *Struggle for Modern Turkey*, 139.

7. Sertel, *Struggle for Modern Turkey*, 165.

8. See Burhan Arpad, "4 Aralik 1945" (1978) in *"Bir Istanbul Var İdi"* ["Once there was an Istanbul"] (Istanbul: Doğan Kitapçılık, 2000), 173–75, for an essay on the significance of the *Tan* events, published on the thirty-third anniversary, in 1978, which was itself a volatile moment for the Turkish press.

9. The 1950s was in one sense a golden age for journalists; witness Ahmet Emin Yalman, who penned his autobiography in English (*Turkey in My Time*) in the 1950s and framed his journey as one of a heroic and pioneering journalist.

In addition, in the 1950s it was finally safe to idolize and praise the United States. Yalman had been pro-American since the beginning, when he had advocated for an American Mandate in the Armistice period. Now, in the 1950s, Turkey's most important strategic partnership was with the United States, and its newfound democratic values, with freedom of expression at the top of the list, were politically safe to promote. Later, in the 1960s, the RPP and the military would again appreciate American tutelage in their efforts to suppress dissent and communism in covert ways.

10. Hülya Adak, "Who Is Afraid of Rıza Nur's Autobiography?," in *Autobiographical Themes in Turkish Literature: Theoretical and Comparative Perspectives*, ed. Olcay Akyıldız, Halim Kara, and Borte Sagaster (Würzburg: Ergon Verlag, 2007), 125–41.

11. Tarık Zafer Tunaya, "Muhalefet Tarihinin Heyecanlı Siması Lütfi Fikri Bey" [Lütfi Fikri Bey, an exciting figure in the history of *Muhalefet*], *Vatan*, June 18, 1950; reprinted in Yücel Demirel, *Dersim Mebusu Lütfi Fikri Bey'in Günlüğü: "Daima Muhalefet"* [The diary of Dersim PM Lütfi Fükri Bey: "Always *Muhalefet*"] (Istanbul: ARMA Yayınları, 1991), 5–12.

12. Demirel, *Dersim Mebusu Lütfi Fikri Bey'in Günlüğü*, 5.

13. Levent Cantek, *Markopaşa: Bir Mizah ve Muhalefet Efsanesi* [Markopasha: A legend of satire and *muhalefet*] (Istanbul: İletişim, 2001). Sabahattin Ali, also a communist, was killed trying to flee the country to Bulgaria in 1947. Çetin Altan (1927–2015), in an interview I conducted with him in Istanbul in April 2013, reported that as a young man of twenty, he testified along with Refik Halid Karay at the trial of Aziz Nesin.

14. See Çelik Gülersoy, "Dostum Burhan Arpad" [My friend Burhan Arpad], in, *"Bir İstanbul Var İdi"* [Once there was an Istanbul], by Burhan Arpad (Istanbul: Doğan Kitapçılık, 2000), 9, for reminiscences about life in the Journalists Neighborhood (Gazeteciler Mahallesi) since 1958, when the "cité"—a "small, quiet, charming place filled, in time, with trees and many flowers"—was built by Prime Minister Menderes because of the necessity to "get along with the press." He recalls Refik Halid as an example of the journalists who had "in the past gotten involved in politics," contrasting him with Sabri Esat Siyavuşgil, a "solid littérateur [*som*

edebiyatçı]." In March 1958 Refik Halid Karay, as copresident (*başkan*) of the Journalists' Cooperative Neighborhood, along with Cemil Cahit Cem, sent a telegram to Adnan Menderes, announcing that the project was almost finished and inviting the prime minister to the grand opening. Devlet Arşivleri Genel Müdürlüğü Cumhuriyet Arşivi S2 30.1.0. 10 Mart 1958.

15. He published five novels before 1950:

İstanbul'un İç Yüzü (1918)

Yezidin Kızı (originally published in Aleppo in 1937; serialized in *Tan* in 1938, 1939, 1972)

Çete (1939)

Sürgün (1941, 1964)

Anahtar (1947)

He also published eleven novels plus a volume of memoirs between 1950 and 1965:

Bu Bizim Hayatımız [This is our life] (1950, 1964)

Nilgün (vol. 1, 1950; vol. 2, 1950; vol. 3, 1952; 3-vol. set, 1960)

Yer Altında Dünya Var [There is a world underground] (1953, 1966, 1973)

Dişi Örümcek [The female spider] (1953, 1964)

Büğünün Saraylısı [Today's courtier] (1964, 1965; serialized as part of the *Hürriyet* series As It Was [*Olduğu gibi*])

İki Cisimli Kadın [Janus-faced woman] (1954)

2000 Yılın Sevgilisi [2000-year beloved] (1954)

Kadınlar Tekkesi [Tekke of women] (1956, 1964)

Karlı Dağdaki Ateş [Fire on the snowy mountain] (1956, 1973)

Dört Yapraklı Yonca [Four-leaf clover] (1957)

Sonuncu Kadeh [The last glass] (1965)

Three novels were published posthumously: *Yerini Seven Fidan* (1977) [The sapling that loves its place], *Yüzen Bahçe* (1981) [The floating garden], and *Ekmek Elden Su Gölden* (1985) [Bread from the hand, water from the lake].

16. *Anahtar* [The key] (1947) (Istanbul: İnkılap, 2009) was the story of a middle-class bank manager in İzmir, suspected by his wife of adultery when she finds a mysterious key in his suit pocket.

17. "Sürgünde Yanıma Gelmek İsteyen Rum Kızı" [The Greek (Rum) girl who wanted to visit me in exile] in *Bir Ömür Boyunca* [Across one lifetime] (Istanbul: İnkılap, 2009), 201–4.

18. Rasih Selçuk Uysal, ed., *Cemil Gökçe'ye, Ali Fuat Başgil'den Münir Murettin Selçuk'tan Yuruf Ziya Ortaç'tan Safiye Ayla'dan Refik Halit Karay'dan Cemal*

Kutay'dan Mesut Cemil (Tel)'den ve Başkalarından [Letters to Cemil Gökçe from Ali Fuat Başgil . . . Refik Halit Karay . . . and others] (Istanbul: Post, 2017), 77. Karay writes in a letter from November 23, 1963, that he has just started writing his memoir, entitled, *Bir Ömür Boyunca*, noting that "there are political facets to it. But my intention with all of it is to make people laugh. May it not make people lose hope" (*iç karartmasın*). Gökçe wrote a touching obituary/eulogy for Karay just after his death in the summer of 1965, reprinted in Uysal, *Cemil Gökçe'ye*, 33–35. In it, he again recounts Karay's trajectory and his involvement in politics as well as literature, emphasizing Atatürk's protection of Karay and Karay's consistent love for the "homeland" (*yurt*) and "nation" (*millet*). Rather than emphasize Refik's opposition to Mustafa Kemal while serving as PTT director in 1919, he notes instead that Refik Halid "fell out with Damat Ferit Paşa and resigned" from the post.

19. *Muhalefet'te İsmet İnönü* [İsmet İnönü in opposition] (Istanbul: Ekicigil Matbaası, 1959), frontmatter.

20. Feroz Ahmad, *The Turkish Experiment in Democracy* 1950-1975 (Boulder, CO: Westview Press, for the Royal Institute of International Affairs, London, 1977).

21. On the possibility of US involvement in this coup and the documented involvement of the United States in hundreds of coups worldwide during the Cold War, see Christopher Gunn, "The 1960 Coup in Turkey: A US Intelligence Failure or a Successful Intervention?" *Cold War Studies* 17, no. 2 (2015): 103–39.

22. *Zübük*, April 16, 1962, 5, 7: "Benim yazı yazdığım zaman basın hürriyeti daha genişti. Bunu incelemek gerekir. . . . Bugün aynı kuvette yazıları yazarsam sürgünle de kurtulacağımı ümit etmiyorum. Sürgünde hürdük, hapishaneden iyiydik."

23. *Zübük*, April 16, 1962: "Ben muhalifim. En iyi hükümetten en kötü hükümete kadar hepsine muhalifim. Şimdi yapmıyorum. Ama yapanlar hoşuma gider."

24. Dankwart Rustow, "The Army and the Founding of the Turkish Republic," reprinted in *Men of Order: Authoritarian Modernization under Ataturk and Reza Shah*, ed. Touraj Atabaki and Erik Jan Zürcher (London: I. B. Tauris, 2004), 164–208.

25. Ms. Aslıhan Karay Özdaş (Refik Halid Karay's granddaughter), interview with author, Refik Halid Karay's residence, Esentepe, Istanbul, April 2013.

EPILOGUE

1. Erol Koroğlu, *Ottoman Propaganda and Turkish Identity: Literature in Turkey During World War I* (London: Tauris Academic Studies, 2007).

2. See Fatma Müge Göçek, *Denial of Violence: Ottoman Past, Turkish Present, and Collective Violence against the Armenians, 1789–2009* (Oxford: Oxford University Press, 2015).

3. *Bir Ömür Boyunca* [Across one lifetime] (Istanbul: İnkılap, 2009; originally published in 1964), 160–64; and Abdullah Uçman, ed., *Aziz Feylosofum: Refik Halid'den Rıza Tevfik'e Mektuplar* [My dear philosopher: Letters from Refik Halid to Rıza Tevfik] (Istanbul: Dergâh Yayınları, 2014), 193–94.

BIBLIOGRAPHY

UNPUBLISHED AND ARCHIVAL SOURCES

Ottoman Prime Ministry Archives/Başbakanlık Osmanlı Arşivleri (BOA), Istanbul

DH.EUM.I. 9/27

DH. EUM I. 45/62

DH.EUM 5. 1/27

DH.EUM 5 32/3

DH.EUM 18/109

DH.EUM 180/34

DH.EUM.AYŞ 45/62

DH.EUM.MH 180/34

DH.EUM.MH 180/109

DH.İ.UM 16L3/1L18

DH.MKT 2909/14

DH.SYS.119 2

İ.DUİT 54/118

İ.DUİT 54/125

İ.DUİT 54/127

HR.IM 147/83

ŞD 3146 20

International Institute of Social History (IISG), Amsterdam

İsmail Hakkı Arar Papers: 517–18, 522, 523.

French Foreign Ministry Archive, Nantes

Service de Presse du Haut Commissariat, Beyrouth: 1 SL 010: reports from Aleppo press (1924–31)

Hoover Institution, Stanford, CA

Hidayet Dağdeviren Archive

Ahmet Emin Yalman Papers

Hakkı Tarık Us archive, Istanbul University, Istanbul

Milli Kütüphane Süreli Yayınları Koleksiyonu [National Library Serial Publications Collection], Ankara

Devlet Arşivleri Genel Müdürlüğü: Cumhuriyet Arşivi, S2/30 passim (1955-1958)

Taha Toros Arşivi Dosya No. 87 (Refik Halit Karay), Istanbul

OTTOMAN/TURKISH NEWSPAPERS/JOURNALS

Akbaba

Akşam (1919–25)

Alemdar (1919–22)

Asır (1918)

Aydede (1922, 1948)

Cem (Kalem)

Cumhuriyet

Doğru Yol (1924)

Hakimiyet-i Milliye

Hürriyet

İkdam (1919–22)

İştirak (1909)

Markopaşa (1946–47)

Milliyet (1950–60)

Peyam-ı Sabah (1920–22)

Resimli Kitap

Resmi Ceride

Sabah (1919–22)

Şehrah (1910?)

Serbesti (1909)

Servet-i Fünun

Son Havadis (1909)

Tan (1938–45)

Takvim-i Vekayi

Tanin

Vahdet (1928–38)

Vakit

Vatan

Volkan (1909)

Yeni Gün

Yeni Mecmua

Zübük (1962)

PUBLISHED AND SECONDARY WORKS

The parentheses around a last name indicate that the patronymic was not used before 1934.

Adak, Hülya. "National Myths and Self-Narrations: Mustafa Kemal's *Nutuk* and Halide Edip's *The Turkish Ordeal*." *South Atlantic Quarterly* 102, nos. 2/3 (2003): 509–28.

———. "Who Is Afraid of Dr. Rıza Nur's Autobiography?" In *Autobiographical Themes in Turkish Literature: Theoretical and Comparative Perspectives*, edited by Olcay Akyildiz, Halim Kara, and Börte Sagaster, 125–42. Würzburg: Ergon Verlag, 2007.

(Adıvar), Halide Edib. *Memoirs of Halide Edib*. New York: Century, [ca. 1926].

———. *Mor Salkımlı Ev* [The house with wisteria]. Original English edition: New York: Century Company, 1926. Turkish edition: Istanbul: Yeni Matbaa, 1963.

———. *Shirt of Flame (Ateshden Ceumlek)*. New York: Duffield, 1924.

———. *The Turkish Ordeal; Being the Further Memoirs of Halide Edib*. New York: Century, 1928.

Ahmad, Feroz. *The Turkish Experiment in Democracy, 1950–1975*. Boulder, CO: Westview Press, for the Royal Institute of International Affairs, London, 1977.

———. *Young Turks: The Committee of Union and Progress in Turkish Politics, 1908–1914*. Oxford: Clarendon Press, 1969.

Akçam, Taner. *Killing Orders: Talat Pasha's Telegrams and the Armenian Genocide*. Palgrave Studies in the History of Genocide. Cham, Switzerland: Palgrave Macmillan, 2018.

———. *A Shameful Act : The Armenian Genocide and the Question of Turkish Responsibility*. 1st US ed. New York: Metropolitan Books, 2006.

———. *The Young Turks' Crime Against Humanity: The Armenian Genocide and Ethnic Cleansing in the Ottoman Empire*. Human Rights and Crimes Against Humanity. Princeton, NJ: Princeton University Press, 2012.

Akçam, Taner, Ümit Kurt, and Aram Arkun. *The Spirit of the Laws: The Plunder of Wealth in the Armenian Genocide*. War and Genocide, vol. 21. New York: Berghahn Books, 2015.

Akın, Yiğit. *When the War Came Home: The Ottomans' Great War and the Devastation of an Empire*. Stanford, CA: Stanford University Press, 2018.

Aksakal, Mustafa. *The Ottoman Road to War in 1914: The Ottoman Empire and the First World War*. Cambridge, UK: Cambridge University Press, 2008.

Akşin, Sina. *İç Savaş ve Sevr'de Ölüm* [Civil war and death in Sèvres]. Istanbul: Türkiye İş Bankası Kültür Yayınları, 2017.

Aktar, Ayhan. "Debating the Armenian Massacres in the Last Ottoman Parliament, November–December 1918." *History Workshop Journal* 64 (2007): 240–70.

———. *Varlık Vergisi ve "Türkleştirme" Politikaları* [The wealth tax and "Turkification" policies]. Cağaloğlu (Istanbul): İletişim Yayınları, 2000.

Aktaş, Şerif. *Refik Halit Karay*. Biyografi-İnceleme [Biography-study] 21. Kızılay, Ankara: Akçağ, 2004.

Alkan, Mehmet Ö., ed. *Gönüllü Sürgünden Zorunlu Sürgüne: Bütün Eserleri* [From voluntary exile to forced exile: Complete works]. Istanbul: Yapı Kredi Yayınları, 2007.

al-Tahtawi, Rifa'a Rafi', and Daniel Newman. *An Imam in Paris: Al-Tahtawi's Visit to France, 1826–1831*. London: Saqi Books, 2011.

Altuğ, Seda. "Between Colonial and National Dominations: Antioch Under the French Mandate." MA thesis, Atatürk Institute for Modern Studies, Boğaziçi University, 2002.

———. "Popular Nationalism and the City: Antioch during the French Mandate." *Chronos* 13 (2006): 231–75.

Anderson, Benedict R. *Imagined Communities: Reflections on the Origin and Spread of Nationalism*. London: Verso, 1991.

Arpad, Burhan. "4 aralik 1945" (1978). In *"Bir Istanbul Var Idi"* ["Once there was an Istanbul"]. Istanbul: Doğan Kitapçılık, 2000.

(Atatürk), Mustafa Kemal. *Nutuk, Gazi Mustafa Kemal Tarafından* [The great speech/Nutuk, by Gazi Mustafa Kemal]. Istanbul: Yapı Kredi Yayınları, 2011.

———. *A Speech Delivered by Ghazi Mustapha Kemal, President of the Turkish Republic, October 1927*. Leipzig: K. F. Koehler, 1929.

Aybars, Ergün. *İstiklal Mahkemeleri 1920–1927*. Cilt I–II [Independence Tribunals]. İzmir: Dokuz Eylül Üniversitesi Yayınları, 1988.

Aydemir, Feridun. *Kendi Ağzından Rıza Tevfik Hayatı Felsefesi, Şiirleri* [Rıza Tevfik in his own words: His life, his philosophy, his poems]. Istanbul: Remzi Kitabevi, 1943.

Aydin, Cemil. *The Politics of Anti-Westernism in Asia: Visions of World Order in Pan-Islamic and Pan-Asian Thought*. Columbia Studies in International and Global History. New York: Columbia University Press, 2007.

Bashkin, Orit. *The Other Iraq: Pluralism and Culture in Hashemite Iraq*. Stanford, CA: Stanford University Press, 2009.

Baykal, Erol. "The Ottoman Press, 1908–1923." PhD diss., Cambridge University, 2012.

———. *The Ottoman Press (1908–1923)*. The Ottoman Empire and Its Heritage: Politics, Society, and Economy, vol. 67. Leiden: Brill, 2019.

Bein, Amit. *Kemalist Turkey and the Middle East: International Relations in the Interwar Period*. Cambridge: Cambridge University Press, 2018.

———. "A 'Young Turk' Islamic intellectual: Filibeli Ahmed Hilmi and the Diverse Intellectual Legacies of the Late Ottoman Empire." *International Journal of Middle East Studies* 39, no. 4 (November 2007): 607–25.

Berkes, Niyazi. *The Development of Secularism in Turkey*. Montreal: McGill University Press, 1964.

Beşikçi, Mehmet. *The Ottoman Mobilization of Manpower in the First World War: Between Voluntarism and Resistance*. The Ottoman Empire and Its Heritage, vol. 52. Leiden: Brill, 2012.

Bilgi, Nejdet. *Dr. Mehmed Reşid Şahingiray Hayatı ve Hatıraları*. [Dr. Mehmed Reşid Şahingiray: His life and memoirs]. İzmir: Kanyılmaz Matbaası, 1997.

Bingöl, Sedat. *150'likler Meselesi: Bir İhanetin Anatomisi* [The List of 150 question: Anatomy of a betrayal]. Istanbul: Bengi, 2010.

Birinci, Ali. *Hürriyet ve İtilâf Fırkası: II. Meşrutiyet Devrinde İttihat ve Terakki'ye Karşı Çıkanlar* [The Freedom and Accord Party: Those who opposed the Union and Progress in the Second Constitutional Era]. Istanbul: Dergâh yayınları, 1990.

———, ed. *Refik Halid Karay: Ankara*. Istanbul: İnkılap, 2009.

———. *Tarihin Alacakaranlığında: Meşâhiri Meçhûleden Birkaç Zât*. [At the twilight of history: Some unknown famous people]. History Series 29. Istanbul: Dergâh, 2010.

Bouquet, Olivier. "Old Elites in a New Republic: The Reconversion of Ottoman Bureaucratic Families in Turkey (1909–1939)." *Comparative Studies of South Asia, Africa, & the Middle East* 31, no. 3 (2011): 588.

Boyar, Ebru. *Ottomans, Turks, and the Balkans: Empire Lost, Relations Altered*. London: I. B. Tauris, 2007.

Brockett, Gavin D. *How Happy to Call Oneself a Turk: Provincial Newspapers and the Negotiation of a Muslim National Identity*. 1st ed. Modern Middle East Series, no. 26. Austin: University of Texas Press, 2011.

Brummett, Palmira. *Image and Imperialism in the Ottoman Revolutionary Press, 1908–1911*. Albany: State University of New York Press, 2000.

Çağaptay, Soner. *Islam, Secularism, and Nationalism in Modern Turkey: Who Is a Turk?* London: Routledge, 2006.

Çalışlar, İpek. *Halide Edip Biyografisine Sığmayan Kadın* [Halide Edip: The woman who would not fit in her biography]. Istanbul: Everest Yayınları, 2010.

Campos, Michelle U. *Ottoman Brothers: Muslims, Christians, and Jews in Early Twentieth-Century Palestine*. Stanford, CA: Stanford University Press, 2011.

Cantek, Levent. *Markopaşa: Bir Mizah ve Muhalefet Efsanesi*. (*Markopasha*: A legend of satire and *muhalefet*). Istanbul: İletişim, 2001.

Çetinkaya, Doğan. *The Young Turks and the Boycott Movement: Nationalism, Protest and the Working Classes in the Formation of Modern Turkey*. Library of Ottoman Studies, vol. 41. London: I. B. Tauris, 2014.

Chatterjee, Partha. *Nationalist Thought in the Colonial World: A Derivative Discourse?* London: Zed, 1986.

Clayer, Nathalie, Fabio Giorni, and Emmanuel Szurek, eds. *Kemalism: Transnational Politics in the Post-Ottoman World*. Library of Modern Turkey 42. London: I. B. Tauris, 2019.

Criss, Nur Bilge. *Istanbul under Allied Occupation, 1918–1923*. Ottoman Empire and Its Heritage 17. Leiden: E. J. Brill, 1999.

Dadrian, Vahakn N., and Taner Akçam. *Judgment at Istanbul: The Armenian Genocide Trials*. New York: Berghahn Books, 2011.

Davison, Roderic. *Reform in the Ottoman Empire*. Princeton, NJ: Princeton University Press, 1965.

de Salve, Louis. "L'enseignement en Turquie: Le lycée imperial de Galata-Serai" [Education in Turkey: The imperial high school of Galata-Serai]. *Revue des deux mondes*, no. 5 (1874): 836–53.

Demirel, Ahmet. *Birinci Meclis'te Muhalefet: İkinci Grup* [Muhalefet in the First Assembly: The Second Group]. Istanbul: İletişim, 1994, 2019.

———. *Tek Partinin İktidarı: Türkiye'de Seçimler ve Siyaset (1923–1946)* [The power of the single party: Elections and politics in Turkey (1923–1946)]. Istanbul: İletişim, 2013.

Demirel, Yücel. *Dersim Mebusu Lütfi Fikri Bey'in Günlüğü: "Daima Muhalefet"* [The diary of Dersim PM Lütfi Fikri Bey: "Always *Muhalefet*"]. Istanbul: ARMA Yayınları, 1991.

Der Matossian, Bedross. "Ethnic Politics in Post-revolutionary Ottoman Empire: Armenians, Arabs, and Jews During the Second Constitutional Period, 1908–1909." PhD diss., Columbia University, 2008.

———. *Shattered Dreams of Revolution: From Liberty to Violence in the Late Ottoman Empire*. Stanford, CA: Stanford University Press, 2014.

Deringil, Selim. *The Ottoman Twilight in the Arab Lands: Turkish Memoirs and Testimonies of the Great War*. Ottoman and Turkish Studies. Brighton, MA: Academic Studies Press, 2019.

———. *Turkish Foreign Policy during the Second World War: An "Active" Neutrality*. LSE Monographs in International Studies. Cambridge, UK: Cambridge University Press, 1989.

———. *Well-Protected Domains: Ideology and the Legitimation of Power in the Late Ottoman Empire (1876–1909)*. London: I. B. Tauris, 1998.

Dündar, Fuat. *Modern Türkiye'nin Şifresi: İttihat ve Terakki'nin Etnisite Mühendisliği 1913–1918* [The cipher of Modern Turkey: Union and Progress' ethnicity engineering 1913–1918]. Cağaloğlu (Istanbul): İletişim Yayınları, 2008.

Ebcioğlu, Hikmet Münir. *Kendi Yazılarıyla Refik Halid* [Refik Halid in his own words]. Istanbul: Semih Lûtfi Kitabevi, ca. 1940.

———. *Refik Halid Karay Kendi Yazılar ile* [Refik Halid Karay and his writings]. Istanbul: Semih Lûtfi Kitabevi, ca. 1940.

Ekiz, Osman Nuri. *Refik Halit Karay: Hayatı, sanatı, ve eserleri*. [Refik Halid Karay: His life, his art, and his works]. Istanbul: Gökşin Yayınları, 1984.

Emin (Yalman), Ahmed. "The Development of Turkey as Measured by Its Press." PhD diss., Columbia University, 1914.

Erdemir, Sabahat, ed. *Muhalefet'de İsmet İnönü (1956–1959)* [İsmet İnönü in the opposition]. Istanbul: Ekicigil Matbaası, 1959.

Ersanlı, Büşra. *İktidar ve Tarih: Türkiye'de Resmi Tarih Tezinin Oluşumu (1929–1937).* [Power and history: The formation of the official history thesis in Turkey, 1929–1937]. Istanbul: İletişim Yayınları, 2003.

Ersoy, Ahmet. "Prince Sabahaddin: A Second Account on Individual Initiative." In *Modernism: The Creation of Nation-states,* edited by Vangelis Kechriotis, Ahmet Ersoy, and Maciej Gorny, 331–40. Budapest: Central European University Press, 2010.

(Ertaylan), İsmail Hikmet. *Türk Edebiyatı Tarihi-Osmanlı Kısmı-Yirminci Asır* [History of Turkish literature—Ottoman section—twentieth century]. Bakû: n.p., 1926.

Esin, Taylan, Etöz, Zeliha. *1916 Ankara Yangını: Felaketin Mantığı* [The 1916 Ankara fire: The logic of catastrophe]. Istanbul: İletişim, 2015.

Evrimer, Rıfat Necdet. "Emin Bülend." *Fecr-i Âti Şairler* [Poets of Fecr-i Âti]. Istanbul: İnkılap, 1958.

Fawaz, Leila. *A Land of Aching Hearts: The Middle East in the Great War.* Cambridge, MA: Harvard University Press, 2014.

Findley, Carter Vaughn. *Bureaucratic Reform in the Ottoman Empire: The Sublime Porte, 1789–1922.* Princeton, NJ: Princeton University Press, 1980.

———. *Ottoman Civil Officialdom: A Social History.* Princeton, NJ: Princeton University Press, 1989.

———. *Turkey, Islam, Nationalism, and Modernity: A History, 1789–2007.* New Haven, CT: Yale University Press, 2010.

Finn, Robert. *The Early Turkish Novel, 1872–1900.* Istanbul: Isis, 1984.

Fortna, Benjamin. *The Circassion: Eşref Kuşçubaşı.* London: Hurst, 2016.

———. *Imperial Classroom: Islam, the State, and Education in the Late Ottoman Empire.* Oxford: Oxford University Press, 2000.

Frey, Frederick W. *The Turkish Political Elite.* Cambridge, MA: MIT Press, 1965.

Gelvin, James. *Divided Loyalties: Nationalism and Mass Politics in Syria at the Close of Empire.* Berkeley: University of California Press, 1998.

Georgeon, Francois. "La formation des élites à la fin de l'Empire ottoman: Le cas de Galatasaray" [The formation of elites at the end of the Ottoman Empire: The case of Galatasaray]. *Revue du monde musulman et de la Méditerranée* 72 (1994): 15–25.

Gingeras, Ryan. *Fall of the Sultanate: The Great War and the end of the Ottoman Empire, 1908–1922.* Oxford: Oxford University Press, 2016.

———. *Mustafa Kemal Atatürk: Heir to an Empire.* New York: Oxford University Press, 2016.

———. *Sorrowful Shores: Violence, Ethnicity, and the End of the Ottoman Empire, 1912–1923.* Oxford: Oxford University Press, 2009.

Ginio, Eyal. *The Ottoman Culture of Defeat: The Balkan Wars and Their Aftermath.* London: Hurst, 2016.

Göçek, Fatma Müge. *Denial of Violence: Ottoman Past, Turkish, Present, and Collective Violence Against the Armenians, 1789–2009*. New York: Oxford University Press, 2015.

———. *Rise of the Bourgeoisie, Demise of Empire: Ottoman Westernization and Social Change*. New York: Oxford University Press, 1996.

Göknar, Erdağ. "Between 'Ottoman' and 'Turk': Literary Narrative and the Transition from Empire to Republic." PhD diss., University of Washington-Seattle, 2004.

———. "Reading Occupied Istanbul: Turkish Subject Formation from Historical Trauma to Literary Trope." *Culture, Theory and Critique* 55, no. 3 (2014): 321–41.

Gunn, Christopher. "The 1960 Coup in Turkey: A US Intelligence Failure or a Successful Intervention?" *Cold War Studies* 17, no. 2 (2015): 103–39.

Gürsoy, Selçuk. "Refik Halid Karay'ın 1910 *İştirak* dergisinde yayınlanan hikâyesi 'Dede Hasan'ın Vicdanı'" [Refik Halid Karay's story published in *İştirak* in 1910, "Dede Hasan's conscience"]. *Toplumsal Tarih*, April 2013, 36–44.

Hanioğlu, M. Şükrü. *Atatürk: An Intellectual Biography*. Princeton, NJ: Princeton University Press, 2011.

———. *A Brief History of the Late Ottoman Empire*. Princeton, NJ: Princeton University Press, 2008.

———. *Preparation for a Revolution: The Young Turks, 1902–1908*. Oxford: Oxford University Press, 2000.

———. *The Young Turks in Opposition*. Oxford: Oxford University Press, 1995.

Hastaş, Mehmet. *Ahmet Samim: 2. Meşrutiyet'te Muhalif bir Gazeteci* [Ahmet Samim: An opposition journalist in the Second Constitutional Period]. Istanbul: İletişim, 2012.

Hilmi, Hüseyin. *Sinop Kitabeleri* [Sinop inscriptions]. Sinop: Sinop Matbaası, 1339 [1921–1922].

Hilmi, Sehbenderzâde Filibeli Ahmed. *Muhalefetin İflası (Hürriyet ve İtilaf Fırkası)* [The bankruptcy of the opposition (Freedom and Accord Party)]. Istanbul: Nehir Yayınları, 1991.

Ilgar, İhsan. *Mütarekede Yerli ve Yabancı Basın* [Domestic and foreign press in the Armistice period]. Istanbul: Kervan Yayınları, 1973.

İskit, Server Rıfat. *Türkiye'de Matbuat İdareleri ve Politikaları* [Press regulations and policies in Turkey]. Istanbul: Tan Basımevi, 1943.

———. *Türkiye'de Matbuat Rejimleri* [Press regimes in Turkey]. Istanbul: Ülkü Matbaası, 1939.

Kaiser, Hilmar. "Scenes from Angora, 1915: The Commander, the Bureaucrats and Muslim Notables during the Armenian Genocide." In *End of the Ottomans: The Genocide of 1915 and the Politics of Turkish Nationalism*, edited by Hans-Lukas Kieser, M. L. Anderson, Seyhan Bayraktar, and Thomas Schmutz, 141–66. London: I. B. Tauris, 2019.

Kansu, Aykut. *Politics in Post-Revolutionary Turkey, 1908–1913*. Leiden: Brill, 2000.

Kansu, Aykut. *The Revolution of 1908 in Turkey*. Leiden: Brill, 1997.

Karaer, Nihat. *Tam Bir Muhalif: Refik Halid Karay* [A quintessential *muhalif*: Refik Halid Karay]. Istanbul: Temel Yayınları, 1998.

Karaosmanoğlu, Yakup Kadri. *Gençlik ve Edebiyat Hatıraları* [Memoirs of youth and literature]. Istanbul: İletişim, 2003. First published 1969 by Bilgi Yayınevi (Yenişehir-Ankara).

——. *Kiralık Konak* [Mansion for rent]. 3rd ed. Istanbul: Remzi Kitabevi, 1958.

Karaveli, Orhan. *Ali Kemal: "belki de bir günah keçisi . . ."* [Ali Kemal: "Perhaps a scapegoat . . ."]. Istanbul: Doğan Kitap, 2009.

Karay, Refik Halid. "Acı Bir Bahar Hatırası" [A painful spring memory]. In *Ago Paşa'nın Hatıratı* [Ago Paşa's memoirs], 162. Istanbul: İnkılap, 2009.

——. *Ago Paşa'nın Hatıratı* [Ago Paşa's memoirs]. Istanbul: İnkılap, 2009.

——. "Anadolu diyor ki" [Anadolu says] (12 Ekim [October] 1919). In *Refik Halid: Okları kırılmış Kirpi* [Refik Halid: The broken-quilled Porcupine], edited by N. Ahmet Özalp, 57–59. Istanbul: Kapı Yayınları, 2011.

——. *Ay Peşinde* [In pursuit of the moon]. Istanbul: İnkılap Kitabevi, 2009.

——. *Bir Guguklu Saat'in Azizliği* [A cuckoo clock's prank]. Istanbul: İnkılap, 2009.

——. "Bir Muhalifin İntiharı" [The suicide of a *Muhalif*]. In *Özalp, Refik Halid*, 147–50. Reprinted from *Ago Paşa'nın Hatıratı*, 1921 ed.

——. *Bir Ömür Boyunca* [Across one lifetime]. Istanbul: İnkılap, 2009. Originally published in 1964.

——. "Dede Hasan'ın Vicdanı" [The Conscience of Dede Hasan]. *Toplumsal Tarih*, April 2013.

——. *Deli: Fantezi piyes 1 perde: yirmi senelik içtimâi panorama bir saatte* [Mad: A one-act fantasy piece; a 20-year panorama in 1 hour]. Halep: Solakzâde, 1929.

——. *Deli* [Mad] (Istanbul: Semih Lûtfi, 1939).

——. *Edebiyatı Öldüren Rejim* [The regime that kills literature]. Memleket Yazıları vol. 3. Istanbul: İnkılap, 2014.

——. "Hülya bu ya . . ." [This must be a dream . . .] (11 Şubat 1921). In *Ago Paşa'nın Hatıratı* [Ago Paşa's memoirs], 25–37. Istanbul: İnkılap, 2009.

——. *İlk Adım* [The first step]. Istanbul: İnkılap, 2009.

——. "İlk sefer" [The first journey]. In *İlk Adım* [The first step]. Istanbul: İnkılap, 2009.

——. "İttihatçı Diyor ki" [The Unionist says] (30 Kasım [November] 1919). In *Özalp, Refik Halid*, 60–62.

——. "The Joke." Translated by Walter Feldman. In *An Anthology of Turkish Literature*, edited by Kemal Silay, 303–8. Bloomington: University of Indiana Press, 1996.

——. "Kaleme Nasıl Çerağ Oldum?" [How did I become an apprentice in a bureau?]. In *Kirpinin Dedikleri* [The Porcupine's utterances], 110–16. Istanbul: İnkılap, 2009.

——. "Lisana Hürmet" [Veneration for language]. In *Tanıdıklarım* [People I have known], 100–104. Istanbul: Semih Lûtfi Kitabevi, 1941.

——. *Memleket Hikâyeleri* [Homeland stories]. Istanbul: İnkılap, 2009.

———. "Meşrutiyetperver Çinlilere Nasihat" [Advice to the Chinese constitutionalists]. In *Kirpinin Dedikleri* [The Porcupine's utterances]. Istanbul: İnkılap, 2009.

———. *Minelbab İlelmihrab: 1918 mütarekesi devrinde olan biten işlere ve gelip geçen insanlara dair bildiklerim* [Minelbab Ilelmihrab: What I know about the happenings and people in the 1918 Armistice period]. Istanbul: İnkılap ve Aka Kitabevleri, 1964; 2nd ed. Istanbul: İnkılap, 1992; 3rd ed. Istanbul: İnkılap, 2009.

———. "Son On Senelik Edebiyata Dair" [On literature of the past 10 years]. *Yeni Mecmua* 3 (ca. 1918).

———. *Sürgün* [Exile]. Istanbul: İnkılap, 1998.

———. "Sürgünde Yanıma Gelmek İsteyen Rum Kızı" [The Greek (Rum) girl who wanted to visit me in exile]. In *Bir Ömür Boyunca* [Across one lifetime]), 201–4. Istanbul: İnkılap, 2009.

———. *Tanıdıklarım* [People I have known]. Istanbul: Cihan Kütüphanesi, 1922; 2nd ed. Istanbul: Semih Lûtfi Kitabevi, 1941.

———. "Teşebbüs-ı Şahsi? Heyhat!" [Personal initiative? Alas!]. In *Kirpinin Dedikleri* [The Porcupine's utterances]. Istanbul: İnkılap, 2009.

———. "Üzüm ve İpek" [Grapes and silk], and "Kervanda Muaşaka" [Love in the caravan]. In *Ay Peşinde*, 36–42 and 42–48. Istanbul: Sabah Matbaası, 1922.

———. *Yer Altında Dünya Var* [There is a world underground]. Istanbul: Çağlayan, 1953; repr. Istanbul: İnkılap, 2009.

Karlıtekin, Selim, ed. *Sürgün'de Muhalefet: Namık Kemal'ın* Hürriyet *Gazetesi 1868–1870* [*Muhalefet* in exile: Namik Kemal's *Hürriyet* newspaper, 1868–1870]. (Istanbul: Vakıfbank Kültür Yayınları, 2019.

Kasaba, Reşat. *Cambridge History of Turkey*, Vol. 4, *Turkey in the Modern World*. Cambridge, UK: Cambridge University Press, 2008.

Kasaba, Reşat, and Sibel Bozdoğan, eds. *Rethinking Modernity and National Identity in Turkey*. Seattle: University of Washington Press, 1997, 2014.

Kayalı, Hasan. *Arabs and Young Turks: Ottomanism, Arabism, and Islamism in the Ottoman Empire, 1908–1918*. Berkeley: University of California Press, 1997.

Kemal, Ali. *Ömrüm* [My life]. Ankara: Hece, 2004.

Kemal, Yahya. *Siyasî ve Edebî Portreler* [Political and literary portraits]. Istanbul: Yapı Kredi Yayınları, 2006.

Kevorkian, Raymond. *The Armenian Genocide: A Complete History*. London: I. B. Tauris, 2011.

Kieser, Hans-Lukas. "From 'Patriotism' to Mass Murder: Dr. Mehmed Reshid (1873–1919)." In *A Question of Genocide: Armenians and Turks at the End of the Ottoman Empire*, ed. Ronald Grigor Suny, Fatma Müge Göçek, and Norman Naimark, 126–48. Oxford: Oxford University Press, 2011.

———. *Talaat Pasha: Architect of Genocide, Father of Modern Turkey*. Princeton, NJ: Princeton University Press, 2017.

Koçak, Cemil. *Karabekir'in Kavgası* [Karabekir's quarrel]. Istanbul: Timaş Yayınları, 2016.

————. *Tek Parti Döneminde Muhalif Sesler* [Voices of dissent in the single party period]. Istanbul: İletişim, 2011.

Kocatürk, Utkan. *Atatürk'ün Toplanmamış Telgrafları* [Atatürk's uncollected telegrams]. Istanbul: Edebiyat Yayınevi, 1971.

Koloğlu, Orhan. *Osmanlı'da Son Tartışmalar Mondros'tan Mudanya'ya* [The last Ottoman controversies from Mudros to Mudanya]. Istanbul: Doğan Kitap, 2008.

————. *Osmanlı'dan Günümüze Türkiye'de Basın* [The press in Turkey from the Ottomans to today]. Istanbul: İletişim, 1992.

Köker, Tolga. "The Establishment of Secularism in Turkey." *Middle East Law and Governance* 2, no. 1 (2010): 17–42.

Köroğlu, Erol. *Ottoman Propaganda and Turkish Identity: Literature in Turkey during World War I.* Library of Ottoman Studies 13. London: Tauris Academic Studies, 2007.

Kuneralp, Sinan. *Son Dönem Osmanlı Erkân ve Ricali, 1839–1922: Prosopografik Rehber* [Late Ottoman officialdom: Prosopographic guide]. Beylerbeyi, Istanbul: İsis Yayınları, 1999.

Kuntay, Mithat Cemal. *Üç İstanbul: Roman* [Three Istanbuls: A novel]. Istanbul: Sander Yayınları, 1976.

Kuran, Ahmet Bedevi. *İnkılap Tarihi ve "Jön Türkler"* [History of the revolution and the "Young Turks"]. Istanbul: Tan Matbaası, 1945.

Kurt, Ümit, and Taner Akçam. *Spirit of the Laws: The Plunder of Wealth in the Armenian Genocide.* New York: Berghahn Books, 2015.

Kuru, Alev Çakmakoğlu. *Sinop Hapishanesi* [Sinop prison]. Ankara: Atatürk Kültür Merkezi Başkanlığı Yayınları [Ataturk Cultural Center Presidency Publications], 2004: 3.

Kutay, Cemâl. *Yüzelliliklerin Faciası.* [The tragedy of the 150]. Istanbul: Tarih Kütüphanesi Yayınları, 1955.

Landau, Jacob M., and Metin Heper, eds. *Political Parties and Democracy in Turkey.* London: Routledge, 1991.

Lewis, Bernard. *The Emergence of Modern Turkey.* 3rd ed. Studies in Middle Eastern History. Oxford: Oxford University Press, 2002.

Lewis, Geoffrey. *The Turkish Language Reform: A Catastrophic Success.* Oxford: Oxford University Press, 1999.

MacMillan, Margaret. *Paris 1919: Six Months That Changed the World.* New York: Random House, 2002.

Manela, Erez. *The Wilsonian Moment: Self-Determination and the International Origins of Anticolonial Nationalism.* Oxford: Oxford University Press, 2007.

Mango, Andrew. *Atatürk.* London: John Murray, 1999.

————. *From the Sultan to Atatürk: Turkey.* Haus Histories. London: Haus Publishing, 2009.

Mardin, Şerif. *The Genesis of Young Ottoman Thought: A Study in the Modernization of Turkish Political Ideas.* Princeton, NJ: Princeton University Press, 1962.

————. "Opposition and control in Turkey." *Government and Opposition*, April 1, 1966, 375–88.

———. *Religion and Social Change in Modern Turkey: The Case of Bediüzzaman Sait Nursi*. Albany: State University of New York Press, 1989.

Mazıcı, Nurşen. *Belgelerle Atatürk Döneminde Muhalefet (1919–1926)*. [*Muhalefet* in the era of Atatürk, with documents]. Istanbul: Dilmen Yayınları, 1984.

Meeker, Michael E. *A Nation of Empire: The Ottoman Legacy of Turkish Modernity*. Berkeley: University of California Press, 2002.

Mevlanzâde, Rıfat. *Türkiye İnkılabının İç Yüzü* [The true face of Turkey's revolution]. Aleppo: Necib Matbaası, 1929.

Mills, Amy. *Streets of Memory: Landscape, Tolerance, and National Identity in Istanbul*. Athens: University of Georgia Press, 2010.

Nazif, Süleyman. "Dr. Reşid." *Hadisât*, 8 Şubat 1919. Reprinted in transliteration in *Dr. Mehmed Reşid Şahingiray Hayatı ve Hatıratı* [Dr. Mehmed Reşid Şahingiray's life and memoirs: The Union and Progress era and the Armenian issue], by Nejdet Bilgi, 167–71. İzmir: Kanyılmaz Matbaası, 1997.

Nur, Doktor Rıza. *Hürriyet ve İtilâf Nasıl Doğdu, Nasıl Öldü?* [How was Freedom and Accord born and how did it die?]. Istanbul: Akşam Matbaası, 1335 [1919].

O'Brien, Tia, and Nur Deriş, eds. *Sabiha Sertel: The Struggle for Modern Turkey; Justice, Activism, and a Revolutionary Female Journalist*. London: I. B. Tauris, 2019.

[Okyar], [Ali] Fethi Bey. *Muhaliflerin Esrarı* [The secret of the *Muhalifs*]. Istanbul: Matbaa'yı Âmedi, 1332 [1916].

Okyar, Fethi. *Üç Devirde bir Adam* [One man in three eras]. Istanbul: Tercüman Yayınları, 1980.

Özalp, N. Ahmet. *Refik Halid: Okları kırılmış Kirpi* [Refik Halid: The broken-quilled Porcupine]. Istanbul: Kapı Yayınları, 2011.

Özbek, Nadir. *Osmanlı İmparatorluğu'nda Sosyal Devlet: Siyaset, iktidar, ve meşrutiyet, 1876-1914* [Social government in the Ottoman Empire: Politics, power, and constitutionalism]. Istanbul: İletişim, 2002.

Özkırımlı, Attila. *Tevfik Fikret*. Istanbul: Cem, 1990.

Özoğlu, Hakan. *From Caliphate to Secular State : Power Struggle in the Early Turkish Republic*. Santa Barbara, CA: Praeger, 2011.

Özyürek, Esra. *Nostalgia for the Modern: State Secularism and Everyday Politics in Turkey*. Durham, NC: Duke University Press, 2002.

Pamuk, Şevket. *Monetary History of the Ottoman Empire*. Cambridge, UK: Cambridge University Press, 2000.

———. *Ottoman Empire and European Capitalism, 1820–1913: Trade, Investment, and Production*. Cambridge, UK: Cambridge University Press, 1987.

Parla, Taha. *The Social and Political Thought of Ziya Gökalp 1876–1924*. Leiden: Brill, 1985.

Parla, Taha, and Andrew Davison. *Corporatist Ideology in Kemalist Turkey: Progress or Order?* Syracuse, NY: Syracuse University Press, 2004.

Paşa, Şerif. *Şerif Paşa: Bir muhalifin hatıraları; İttihat ve Terakkiye muhalefet* [Şerif Paşa: The memoirs of a *muhalif: Muhalefet* against Union and Progress]. Istanbul: Nehir, 1990.

Paşa, Cemal. *Memories of a Turkish Statesman—1913–1919 by Djemal Pasha, Formerly Governor of Constantinople, Imperial Ottoman Naval Minister, and Commander of the Fourth Army in Sinai, Palestine, and Syria.* New York: George H. Doran, 1922.

Philliou, Christine. "When the Clock Strikes Twelve: The Inception of an Ottoman Past in Early Republican Turkey." *Comparative Studies in South Asia, Africa, and the Middle East* 31, no. 1 (2011): 172–82.

Philliou, Christine M. "The Armenian Genocide and the Politics of Knowledge." *PublicBooks* (May 2015).

Provence, Michael. *The Great Syrian Revolt and the Rise of Arab Nationalism.* Austin: University of Texas Press, 2005.

———. *The Last Ottoman Generation and the Making of the Modern Middle East.* Cambridge, UK: Cambridge University Press, 2017.

Reynolds, Michael A. *Shattering Empires: The Clash and Collapse of the Ottoman and Russian Empires, 1908–1918.* Cambridge, UK: Cambridge University Press, 2011.

Rustow, Dankwart. "The Army and the Founding of the Turkish Republic." In *Men of Order: Authoritarian Modernization under Atatürk and Reza Shah,* edited by Touraj Atabaki and Erik Jan Zürcher, 164–208. London: I. B. Tauris, 2004.

Safi, Polat. "The Ottoman Special Organization-Teşkilât-ı Mahsusa: An Inquiry into Its Operational and Administrative Characteristics." PhD thesis, Bilkent University, 2012.

Sami, Şemsettin. *Taaşşuk-ı Talat ve Fitnat* [The romance of Talat and Fitnat]. 3rd ed. Istanbul: Hiperlink, 2009. Originally published in 1872.

Şehbenderzâde, Ahmed Hilmi. *Muhalefetin İflası* [The bankruptcy of the *muhalefet*]. Istanbul [Konstantiniyye]: Hikmet Matba'a-yı İslamiyesi, 1331 [1915].

Sertel, Sabiha. *Roman Gibi: Anılar* [Like a novel: Memoirs]. Istanbul: Ant Yayınları, 1969.

Sertel, Zekeriya. *Hatırladıklarım* [My recollections]. Istanbul: Yaylacık Matbaası, 1968.

Shaw, Stanford J. *From Empire to Republic: The Turkish War of National Liberation, 1918–1923, a Documentary Study,* vols. I–IV. Ankara: Turkish History Foundation, 2000.

Shields, Sarah D. *Fezzes in the River: Identity Politics and European Diplomacy in the Middle East on the Eve of World War II.* Oxford: Oxford University Press, 2011.

Shissler, Ada Holland. *Between Two Empires: Ahmet Ağaoğlu and the New Turkey.* London: I.B. Tauris. 2003.

Şişman, Adnan. *Galatasaray Mekteb-i Sultanisi'nin Kuruluşu ve İlk Eğitim Yılları 1868–1871* [Establishment of the Galatasaray Imperial School and first education years]. Istanbul: Edebiyat Fakültesi Yayınevi, 1989.

Sohrabi, Nader. "Global Waves, Local Actors: What the Young Turks Knew About Other Revolutions and Why It Mattered." *Comparative Studies in Society and History* 44, no. 1 (January 2002): 45–79.

———. *Revolution and Constitutionalism in the Ottoman Empire and Iran, 1902–1910*. Cambridge, UK: Cambridge University Press, 2013.

Sömel, Selçuk Akşin. *The Modernization of Public Education in the Ottoman Empire, 1839–1908: Islamization, Autocracy, and Discipline*. Leiden: Brill, 2000.

Süngü, İhsan. "Galatasaray Lise'nin Kuruluşu" [The establishment of Galatasaray High School]. *Belleten* 7, no. 28 (1943): 315–47.

Suny, Ronald Grigor. *"They Can Live in the Desert but Nowhere Else": A History of the Armenian Genocide*. Princeton, NJ: Princeton University Press, 2015.

Tamari, Salim. *Year of the Locust: A Soldier's Diary and the Erasure of Palestine's Ottoman Past*. Berkeley: University of California Press, 2011.

Tanpınar, Ahmet Hamdi. *Beş Şehir* [Five cities]. Istanbul: Dergâh Yayınları, 2019.

———. *A Mind at Peace*. Translated by Erdağ Göknar. New York: Archipelago Books, 2008.

———. *XIX. Türk Edebiyatı Tarihi* [Nineteenth-century Turkish literary history]. Istanbul: Yapı Kredi, 2006. Originally published in 1949.

Tanrıkut, Asaf. *Türkiye Posta ve Telgraf ve Telefon Tarihi ve Teşkilât ve Mevzuatı* [Turkey Post, Telegraph and Telephone history, its organization and regulations]. Vol. II. Ankara: Efem Matbaacılık, 1968.

Tekin, Mehmet. *Hatay Basın Tarihi* [Hatay press history]. Antakya: Kültür Basımevi, 1985.

Thobie, Jacques. *Intérêts et impérialisme français dans l'Empire ottoman, 1895–1914*. [French interests and imperialism in the Ottoman Empire]. Paris: Sorbonne, 1977.

Thompson, Elizabeth F. *Colonial Citizens: Republican Rights, Paternal Privilege, and Gender in French Syria and Lebanon*. New York: Columbia University Press, 2000.

———. *Justice Interrupted: The Struggle for Constitutional Government in the Middle East*. Cambridge, MA: Harvard University Press, 2013.

(Tokgöz), Ahmet İhsan. *Matbuat Hatıralarım 1888–1923* [My memoirs in publishing]. Istanbul: İletişim, 1993.

Toprak, Zafer, and Bengisu Rona, eds. *Bir muhalif kimlik: Tevfik Fikret* [The identity of a *muhalif*: Tevfik Fikret]. Istanbul: İş Bankası Yayınları, 2007.

Tuna, Işıl. *Türkiye'de İktidar-Muhalefet İlişkileri 1946–1960* [Power-opposition relations in Turkey 1946–1960]. Istanbul: Libra Kitap, 2018.

Tunaya, Tarık Zafer. *İnsan Derisiyle Kaplı Anayasa* [The constitution covered with human skin]. Istanbul: Arba Yayınları, 1988.

———. *Türkiye'de Siyasal Partiler* [Political parties in Turkey], Vols. 1–3. Istanbul: Doğan Kardeş Yayınları, 1952; 2nd ed. Istanbul: Hürriyet Vakfı, 1984; 3rd ed. Istanbul: İletişim, 1998.

Tunçay, Mete. *Türkiye'de sol akımlar, 1908–1925* [Leftist movements in Turkey]. Istanbul: İletişim, 1967, 2009.

Turnaoğlu, Banu. *The Formation of Turkish Republicanism*. Princeton, NJ: Princeton University Press, 2017.

Uçman, Abdullah, ed. *Aziz Feylosofum: Refik Halid'den Rıza Tevfik'e Mektuplar* [My dear philosopher: Letters from Refik Halid to Rıza Tevfik]. Istanbul: Dergâh Yayınları, 2014.

———, ed. *Biraz de Ben Konuşayım, Rıza Tevfik* [Let me speak a little, Rıza Tevfik]. Istanbul: İletişim, 1993.

Uçman, Abdullah, and Handan İnci, eds. *Bir 150'likliğin Mektupları: Ali İlmi Fani'den Rıza Tevfik'e Mektuplar* [The letters of a member of the List of 150: Letters from Ali İlmi Fani to Rıza Tevfik]. Çağaloğlu, Istanbul: Kitabevi, 1998.

Ünal, Yenal. "Refik Halit Karay ve Millî Mücadele" [Refik Halid Karay and the national struggle]. *History Studies: International Journal of History* 5, no. (January 2013): 367–89.

Ünaydın, Rüşen Eşref. *Diyorlar ki* [They say that]. Ankara: M.E.B.; and Istanbul: Devlet Kitap Müdürlüğü, 1972.

Üngör, Uğur Ümit. *The Making of Modern Turkey: Nation and State in Eastern Anatolia, 1913–1950.* Oxford: Oxford University Press, 2011.

Üngör, Uğur Ümit, and Mehmet Polatel. *Confiscation and Destruction: The Young Turk Seizure of Armenian Property.* London, New York: Continuum, 2011.

Uysal, Rasih Selçuk, ed. *Cemil Gökçe'ye Ali Fuat Başgil'den, Münir Nurettin Selçuk'tan, Yusuf Ziya Ortaç'tan, Safiyet Ayla'dan, Refik Halit Karay'dan, Mesut Cemil (Tel)'den ve Başkalarından Mektuplar* [Letters to Cemil Gökçe from Alı Fuat Başgil . . . Refik Halit Karay . . . and others]. Istanbul: Post, 2017.

VanderLippe, John M. *The Politics of Turkish Democracy: İsmet İnönü and the Formation of the Multi-Party System, 1938–1950.* SUNY Series in the Social and Economic History of the Middle East. Albany: State University of New York Press, 2005.

White, Jenny. *Muslim Nationalism and the New Turks.* Princeton, NJ: Princeton University Press, 2013.

Yalman, Ahmet Emin. "*Muhalefetin* vaziyeti" [The situation of *muhalefet*]. *Vatan*, May 1923.

———. *Turkey in My Time.* Norman: University of Oklahoma Press, 1956.

———. *Turkey in the World War.* [Carnegie Endowment for International Peace, Division of Economics and History, Economic and Social History of the World War, Turkish Series]. New Haven, CT: Yale University Press, 1930.

(Yalman), Ahmed Emin. "The Development of Turkey as Measured by its Press." PhD diss., Columbia University, 1914.

Yilmaz, Hale. *Becoming Turkish: Nationalist Reforms and Cultural Negotiations in Early Republican Turkey, 1923–1945.* Syracuse, NY: Syracuse University Press, 2013.

Yosmaoğlu, İpek. "Chasing the Printed Word: Press Censorship in the Ottoman Empire, 1876–1913." *Turkish Studies Association Journal* 27 (2003): 15–49.

Zilfi, Madeline. *The Politics of Piety: Ottoman Ulema in the Post-Classical Age.* Minneapolis, MN: Bibliotheca Islamica, 1988.

Zürcher, Erik Jan. "The Ides of April: A Fundamentalist Uprising in Istanbul in 1909?" In *The Young Turk Legacy and Nation Building: From the Ottoman Empire to Atatürk's Turkey*, 73–83. London: I. B. Tauris, 2010.

———. *Political Opposition in the Early Turkish Republic: The Progressive Republican Party, 1924–1925*. Social, Economic and Political Studies of the Middle East, vol. 44. Leiden: E. J. Brill, 1991.

———. *The Unionist Factor: The Rôle of the Committee of Union and Progress in the Turkish National Movement, 1905–1926*. Leiden: E. J. Brill, 1984.

———. *The Young Turk Legacy and Nation Building: From the Ottoman Empire to Atatürk's Turkey*. Library of Modern Middle East Studies, vol. 87. London: I. B. Tauris, 2010.

INDEX

Page numbers in *italics* refer to illustrations.

46–47, 55; war crimes, 11, 101, 105. *See also* Raid on the Sublime Porte; *Tanin*
communism, 16, 186, 200, 249n9
Complete Works (Refık Halid), 177
Constitutional Revolution, 4, 5, 9, 29, 30, 38, 47, 210, 230n21; anniversary, 181, 198; euphoria following, 34, 194; eve of, 13, 42, 164, 237n15; first year after, 20, 229n10; Refık Halid's thought exercise on, 110–11, 178
"Correspondence with Mehmet Ç Bey" (Refık Halid), 113–14, 138, 178
Çoşar, Ömer Sami, 200
Çoşar (Ashworth), Selma Sami, 200
counterrevolution. *See* 31 March Incident
coup d'état: 1960, 187, 200, 201–3. *See also* Raid on the Sublime Porte
Crimean War, 20–21
Cumhuriyet, 151, 153, 172–73, 189

Decentralization and Individual Initiative Party, 43
Deli (play) (Refık Halid), 164–65, 177, 184–85, 210, 213; as *muhalefet*, 165
Deli (volume) (Refık Halid), 177, 184–85; "Ankara," 180–84
Democrat Party (DP), 187–88, 194; formation, 188, 191, 193, 195; Refık Halid and, 187, 198–99, 208; initial electoral victory, 187, 193, 194–95, 200–201; *muhalefet* and, 194–96, 199, 200; repression carried out by, 199, 201; successor of, 202. *See also* coup d'état: 1960
"Dervish Hasan's Conscience" (Refık Halid), 53–55
Doğru Yol, 245n52, 246n10; Refık Halid's open letter to İsmail Müştak, 244n40; Refık Halid's writings in, 154, 176–77
Duran (Sabri), Faik, 33, 34

Ebcioğlu, Hikmet Münir, 175–77, 223n3
Edebiyat-ı Cedide, 30
Edib (Adıvar), Halide, 3, 112, 178, 238n22; Friends of England Society, 98; memoir, 243n31, 245n56; PEN Club, 197; Turkey-Havas Reuters Agency, 237n11; voluntary exile, 136, 160, 163
Efendi, Abdurrahman Şeref, 27

Efendi, Agah, 38
Efendi, Ali Suavi, 25
Efendi, Behlül, 22
Efendi, Halacyan, 64
Ekrem, Recaizade, 30
Emin (Yalman), Ahmet, 163, 242n18; autobiography, 193, 236n9, 239n36, 249n9; pro-Americanism, 189–90, 249n9; *Tan*, 189–90, 248n3; *Vakit*, 236–37n10, 240n44; voluntary exile, 160
Erdoğan, Recep Tayyip, 205, 206
Esat, Ubeydullah, 33
Europe: Galatasaray's orientation, 24–26; Refık Halid in, 38–40, 157; Refık Halid's background and sensibility, 24–26, 28, 39–40, 45, 56, 154; influence in Ottoman Empire, 20–21, 25, 229n13; literary forms from, 30, 31, 45; quarter of Istanbul, 24, 26, 37; *Servet-i Fünun* and, 30, 31. *See also* British Mandate; France; French Mandate Syrian/Lebanon
exile. *See* Aleppo; Anatolia; Ankara; Beirut; Jounieh

Fani (Birgili), Ali İlmi, 161, 246n7, 247n25
"Farewell, Politics!" (Refık Halid), 124, 137, 178, 243n25
Fecr-i Âti, 30–34, 40, 45; title, 31, 226n39
Fehmi, Hasan, 52, 63
Ferit (Tek), Ahmet, 73, 139, 243n28; efforts to ban *Minelbab İlelmihrab*, 147; exile, 139, 231n7; List of 150, 139, 147; as minister of the interior, 73, 139, 147, 243n28; as *muhalif*/opposition, 73, 139
Fethi (Okyar), Ali, 163, 173, 189, 244n44, 246n15
Fikret, Tevfik, 30, 248n43
"First Journey" (Refık Halid), 39–40
France: influence in Ottoman Empire, 13, 20, 22, 24–26, 41; literary forms from, 29–30, 40. *See also* French Mandate Syria/Lebanon; Paris
Franco-Prussian War, 25
Freedom and Accord Party (Liberal Entente), 47, 48, 205, 231n1; formation, 45, 48, 66, 239n27; Refık Halid and, 14, 74, 98, 107, 142, 146; opposition to

Rasim, Ahmet, 30
Ratıp, Müfit, 29, 31
Recai, Mehmed, 25
"Regime That Kills Literature, The" (Refik Halid), 191
Republican People's Party (RPP), 9, 150, 155, 183, 186–88, 191–92; Atatürk and, 9, 155, 161, 163, 173, 185; coup (1960) and, 201–2; factions within, 16, 159, 164, 186, 190, 193, 243n29; formation, 142; hardline faction within, 193, 194, 196; *muhalefet* as opposition to, 190, 196, 199, 200–201, 202, 207; as opposition party, 200–201; opposition party from within (DP), 187, 191–94, 195, 196, 199; renaming, 242n21; second congress, 136, 155; as single-party regime, 163, 186–87
Republic of Turkey. *See* Turkish Republic
Reşid (Şahingiray), Mehmed, 83–86, 88, 118
Resimli Kitap, 33
Resmi Ceride, 137
Rıfat, Mevlanzâde, 39, 236n8, 243n31, 246n7, 247n25
Rıfkı (Atay), Falih, 147, 162 193, 197, 244n44; *Akşam* article, 146; in *Kendi Yazılar ile*, 175–76; *Yeni Mecmua*, 236n2
Rıza, Ahmed, 43, 47–48
Ruhsar, Nefise (Refik Halid's mother), 20, 22
Russia, 6, 22, 23, 41, 42, 114
Russo-Ottoman War, 21, 22, 25

Sabah, 98, 100, 127, 131, 176, 194, 239n25
Sabahaddin, Prince, 67, 72, 225n31, 232n10; Individual Initiative and Decentralization, 43, 48, 60; liberal coalition, 42, 43, 45, 48, 84
Sabis, Ali İhsan, 173
Sadık, Miralay, 66, 239n27
Sadık (Sadak), Necmettin, 142, 144, 146–47, 176, 193
Sahir, Celâl, 31, 87
"Şaka" (Refik Halid), 14, 75–77, 88
Salve, Louis de, 24–25
Samim, Ahmed, 31, 53–54, 55, 63, 237n15
"Sarı Bal" (Refik Halid), 88
satire: as dissent, 10, 44, 67, 206, 207, 209; Refik Halid and, 10, 14, 19, 30, 32, 40, 45, 90, 164–65, 179, 198, 247n29;

newspaper and journals, 45, 52, 127, 146, 193, 202, 229n12, 239n25, 247n30. *See* also *Kirpi* (Porcupine)
"Secrets of the New Year, The" (Refik Halid), 55–56, 230n20
Şehrah, 45, 53
Semavi, Sedat, 198
Serbesti, 39, 52
Sertel, Sabiha, 189–90, 191, 195, 248n3
Sertel, Zekeriya, 189–90, 191, 192
Servet-i Fünun, 30–33, 87, 228n4
Seyfettin, Ömer, 87–88
Şeyh Sait rebellion, 136, 150–51
Şinasi, Abdülhak, 29, 225n31
Sinop: Armenian genocide in, 76, 77, 79–80, 233n32; Refik Halid's deportation to, 14, 67, 69, 72, 139; Refik Halid's exile in, 45, 53, 72–74, 131, 139, 147, 152, 233n26, 235–36n67
social realism, 30, 72, 75, 90, 108, 179
Sohrabi, Nader, 43, 46–47, 229n10
Son Havadis, 33–34, 61, 226n46, 227n54, 227n60
Son Posta, 172–73
Sonuncu Kadeh (Refik Halid), 198, 250n15
"Story of Two Sons, The" (Refik Halid), 108–9
Sufism, 22, 113
"Suicide of a *Muhalif*, The" (Refik Halid), 120–21, 178
"Sulh" (Refik Halid), 96
Suphi, Mustafa, 71, 231n7
Suphi (Soysallıoğlu), İsmail, 31
Suphi (Tanriöver), Hamdullah, 31
Sürgün Halid (Refik Halid), 132–33, 179, 241–42n13, 250n15
Surname Law, 126, 158, 247n29
Syria/Lebanon. *See* French Mandate Syria/Lebanon

Tahtawi, 39
Tan, 179, 248n3, 250n15. See also *Tan* Incident
Tanin, 33, 52, 63, 64, 142, 151, 193, 226n35
Tan Incident, 188–92, 196
Tanıdıklarım (Refik Halid), 177, 239n25, 246n12; "Lisana Hürmet," 246n12; "A Perfect *Muhalif*," 121–22, 124

Founded in 1893,
UNIVERSITY OF CALIFORNIA PRESS
publishes bold, progressive books and journals
on topics in the arts, humanities, social sciences,
and natural sciences—with a focus on social
justice issues—that inspire thought and action
among readers worldwide.

The UC PRESS FOUNDATION
raises funds to uphold the press's vital role
as an independent, nonprofit publisher, and
receives philanthropic support from a wide
range of individuals and institutions—and from
committed readers like you. To learn more, visit
ucpress.edu/supportus.